SOE

M. R. D. Foot was an army officer
throughout the 1939–45 war, and was
awarded the French croix de guerre for
work with the SAS in Brittany. He taught
politics and history at Oxford, was for six
years professor of modern history at
Manchester, was the first editor of
Gladstone's diaries, and has written –
among other books – *SOE in France*
(the official history), *Resistance, MI9*
(with J. M. Langley) and *Six Faces of
Courage*. He is married, has two children,
and lives in London.

D1434249

Also by M. R. D. Foot

Men in Uniform
SOE in France
Resistance, MI9 (with J. M. Langley)
Six Faces of Courage

M. R. D. FOOT

SOE

An outline history of the
Special Operations Executive
1940–46

arrow books

A book can never tell us what we wish to know,
but only rouse in us the desire for knowledge

George Painter, *Marcel Proust*

A Mandarin Paperback

SOE

First published in Great Britain 1984
by the British Broadcasting Corporation
This edition published 1993
by Mandarin Paperbacks
an imprint of Reed Consumer Books Ltd
Michelin House, 81 Fulham Road, London SW3 6RB
and Auckland, Melbourne, Singapore and Toronto

Copyright © M.R.D. Foot 1984

A CIP catalogue record for this title
is available from the British Library

ISBN 0 7493 0378 6

Printed and bound in Great Britain
by Cox & Wyman Ltd, Reading, Berks

Contents

FINLAND

Helsinki

Leningrad

Tallinn

Riga

Kuybyshev

Moscow

1941 RK OF
OSTLAND

Kaunas

Smolensk

Vilna

Rastenburg

UNION OF SOVIET
SOCIALIST REPUBLICS

Bug

PRIPET

Warsaw

Brest Litovsk

Kiev

Kharkov

Stalingrad

Lublin

Cracow

GENERAL
GOVERNMENT
OF POLAND

Dnieper

1941 RK OF UKRAINE

Košice

HUNGARY

Dniester

TRANSNISTRIA

BESSARABIA

Odessa

Budapest

CRIMEA

ROMANIA

Ploesti

Sevastopol

Danube

Belgrade

Bucharest

Black Sea

SERBIA

BULGARIA

Sofia

ALBANIA
(Italy)

Tirana

Istanbul

Ankara

GREECE

TURKEY

Gorgopotamos

Athens

Izmir

SYRIA

PELOPONNESE

CRETE

LEBANON

Beirut

Damascus

miles

0   100   200   300   400   500

0   200   400   600   800

kilometres

⬤ Limit of axis control

── Boundaries of Germany in 1937

RK Reichskommissariat

⬛ Neutral countries

Author's Note

Historians, like sergeant-majors, like to arrange people and things in order, to assign everyone a particular job at a set time. SOE, like other bodies for waging war, was not so neatly organised in fact. It was on the contrary unusually complex, and its complexities have not been made any more easy to unravel by the dense fog of secrecy in which it lived. In that fog a few fragments of it have still to be hidden, and wisps of fog still keep getting in the way of the seeker after past truth.

The first half-dozen chapters of this book have to be devoted to explaining what SOE was, who ran it, who worked in it, and how they worked. Only by about page 246 will the reader get quite clear of technical detail and embark on an actual narrative. Readers must choose whether to skip ahead now, and cast back if they get puzzled, or bear with the author while he tries to make some rough places plain.

My own war career – of small importance to anyone but myself – lay outside SOE, but led me sometimes to rub shoulders with it in 1942–4, and taught me a little about strategy, tactics, logistics, intelligence, planning and secrecy. I have been shot at, have parachuted, have helped to plan raids, have taken part as observer in air operations and in a sea commando raid, have organised escapes, and have succeeded in hiding my military identity during German interrogations (aided by two strokes of luck: at an early stage, a souvenir-hunter cut off my SAS wings; and no one else present knew I spoke fair German).

I had hoped that this book would tie in with a television series on the same subject, but it did not prove possible to establish just what the programmes were going to cover before these pages had to go to press. This must therefore provide background for the viewer who wants to place them in their context in the history of the war.

This book was forty years in contemplation and two years in writing. Its main bulk was written while Brezhnev was still in power, before the Soviet monolith began to crumble. In order to complete it, I have had to trespass on the patience and plumb the knowledge of a great many people, to all of whom I am grateful. I must especially mention eight former members of SOE for bringing it alive for me; among the dead, Sir Colin Gubbins, Selwyn Jepson, Jack Beevor, and Victor Gerson; and among the living, Sir Peter Wilkinson, Tony Brooks, Pearl Cornioley (*née* Witherington), and Vera Atkins. I am also much indebted to Jane Carr, Melanie Crosse, Dominic Flessati, Jennifer Fry, Tony Kingsford, Naomi Klein, Gordon Lee, Philip Lord, Michael Sissons and Thomas F. Troy for support at various stages of production. My debt to my wife remains – as is common with authors – illimitable.

I need to make it clear that none of these people, nor anyone else, no government department, no university, is responsible for the pages below, which express my own view of the ascertainable facts, and mine alone.

London, 31 December 1989. M. R. D. Foot

List of Illustrations

Plate Section Three

List of Illustrations

I
What SOE was

SOE, the Special Operations Executive, was a small, tough British fighting service. It was formed in deadly secrecy in July 1940 to tackle one of the nastiest regimes even of this century, Hitler's German empire. It helped to bring down Hitler and Mussolini, fought also against their ally, imperial Japan, and was quietly wound up early in 1946 when its work was done.

It worked with the forces of resistance: classically, the resource of the weak against the strong. It was hardly founded before time. Though the British Empire expanded still further after the world war of 1914–18 than before it, and in the 1920s controlled a quarter of the world's land surface, that Great War had dealt the Empire a shattering blow: it had broken what was left of popular confidence in the wisdom of the high command. In it one in eight of the six million Britons who joined the armed forces were killed. Killings seemed to be extra heavy among the old ruling class; 'the lost generation' became a catch phrase. Most people got out of uniform as soon as they could when the war was over, and the Grand Fleet on which the nation's safety depended was broken up.

During and just after the war four other empires crumbled: the German, shrunken and transformed to a republic; the Austro-Hungarian and the Turkish, altogether dispersed; and the Russian, transformed after a brief liberal interval into a new kind of empire, the Soviet Union. The Soviet leaders breathed plenty of fire and slaughter, but no one in Whitehall took Trotsky's fulminations against empire seriously. Trotsky was driven out of the new state he had helped to create. Stalin, who ousted him from power, was seen by a few long-sighted men to be a long-term threat, but was known in the short run to be tangled up in the results of the peasant massacres he directed in 1930–1. Down to 1932, British defence policy was based on the secret assumption that there would be no major war for ten years.

In that year the chiefs of staff, aware of the Japanese threat, rescinded the 'ten-year rule' – but again in secret; several more years passed before it became at all widely known that the rule was cancelled. By then, a short-term threat to British security was in full view: Adolf Hitler. He became chancellor of the German republic on 30 January 1933, and at once set about turning it into the Third Reich, a new empire which was to last for a thousand years. His henchmen Goering and Himmler set up punishment camps for those who did not heartily agree with his national-socialist (Nazi) reforms. Most Germans were delighted with the new style, and were kept delighted by the masterful pageantry of another Nazi of genius, Goebbels.

Hitler, an Austrian art school drop-out, had a burning desire to be master, was highly skilled at politics and always ready to seize a chance. He had mesmeric gifts, and not an atom of good faith. It soon became clear to those who wanted to see – not many did – that he was out to build as strong a Germany as he could, by overrunning his weaker neighbours. He let his followers revive an old slogan, *Heute gehört uns Deutschland, und morgen die ganze Welt* – Germany is ours today, the whole world is ours tomorrow. In 1935 he tore up the clauses in the 1919 Treaty of Versailles that forbade Germany to have an air force or a large army. No one protested; indeed the pacific British signed a new treaty with him, which allowed him a fleet a third as large as the Royal Navy and equality with it in submarines. In 1936 he reoccupied with his new army the area along the Rhine which at Versailles had been declared a zone free of German troops: protests were only verbal. In March 1938 he annexed Austria, again without serious protest from abroad; indeed without a shot fired, save by some Jews who killed themselves sooner than submit to Nazi rule.

Hatred of the Jews amounted to mania with Hitler and with many of his followers. Jews in his Reich – one Jewish grandparent was enough to disqualify – were forbidden to hold posts in the professions, to own businesses, to marry gentiles, or to shop in gentile shops. Even Einstein, who was a Jew, had to leave the university of Berlin – once known as the First Guards Regiment of Learning – for America; even Freud was hounded from Vienna to exile in Hampstead because he was a Jew.

With the annexation of Austria to Germany (the Anschluss), the British government began to realise how acute the country's danger was. In the Foreign Office, it was remembered that Lord Northcliffe, the newspaper magnate, had had great successes in 1917–18 in corrupting the morale of the German army by propaganda. One of his chief helpers in that task, the Canadian Sir Campbell Stuart, had later been managing director of *The Times* and was thought an expert on communications. The FO invited him to set up and run, at its expense but not on its premises, a small branch to look into how propaganda systems worked, and to recommend what should be done. This branch was sometimes called CS, after its head, and sometimes EH after where it worked – Electra House, on the Embankment upstream of the Temple. (There are plenty more of these acronyms: secret service life teems with them. A list appears on pp. 367–70.) Stuart was no Goebbels, but he collected a few sensible journalists and broadcasters round him, and at least they started to think. To suit the Foreign Office's lasting nervousness about the press, there was no publicity; EH did not figure in the *Foreign Office List* for 1939 or 1940. But it was not particularly secret.

The secret or special intelligence service, SIS – now usually known as MI6 – was. Governments like to keep up with each other the pretence that no such bodies exist, though without one no strong regime can stand for long. A recent official history has now let on that SIS was created in 1909, as part of a secret service bureau which soon thereafter split up. From 1921 it was under Foreign Office control, though it also included sections from the navy, the army and the air force.[1]* Its job was to secure secrets from abroad. Founded in parallel with it, the security service (MI5) looked after preserving secrets at home, and came under the Home Office.

In late March 1938, just as Lord Halifax at the Foreign Office was setting up EH, Admiral 'Quex' Sinclair, the current C, as the head of SIS was known in Whitehall, borrowed an officer from the army, Major L. D. Grand, and told him to start a new section in the secret service. It was to be called section D. Grand's task was to look into the theory of secret offensives: how could enemies be attacked, otherwise than by the usual military means? While peace lasted, he was to *do* nothing; but he was to think over sabotage, labour unrest, inflation, anything else that could be done to weaken an enemy, and if he could he was to make outline plans for them. He was to consider who could do the work on the spot – communists, perhaps, or Jews? And he was to consider means of propaganda, to shift enemy opinion. No wonder Grand thought, when he put in his final report years later, 'Examining such an enormous task, one felt as if one had been told to move the Pyramids with a pin.'[2]

---

* The figures refer to the endnotes on pp. 371–87.

Lawrence Grand had some of the gifts needed for a successful secret service leader, including a striking personality. He was tall, handsome, well tailored, with a heavy dark moustache; wore a red carnation; smoked cigarettes, almost without cease, through an elegant black holder; had an equally elegant wit. He was brimful of ideas and energy, and he had a rare gift: he gave full trust to those under him, and backed them up without question against outsiders.[3] Unhappily he also had a gift for rubbing staid men up the wrong way.

Moreover, he had been given a task which overlapped with what two other bodies were doing. No one told Campbell Stuart about him, and no one told him about Campbell Stuart; they were left to duplicate each others' work on propaganda. Nor did anyone tell him for some weeks when, in the autumn of 1938, a new departure began on the general staff of the War Office. There was a tiny research section there, called simply GS (R) and consisting of a major and a typist. In 1936–8 it had held a major who invented the Army Education Corps. It went next to an officer in the Royal Engineers, J. C. F. Holland, who would have been promoted instead to active command as a lieutenant-colonel, if he had not been for the moment medically unfit. Jo Holland chose to research on irregular warfare: an unorthodox subject in the prewar army, but one that fascinated him, not least because he had been badly wounded in Ireland during the Troubles of 1919–20. He had earned a DFC in the Near East during the Great War, and had seen a little of T. E. Lawrence's irregular exploits against the Turks.

Holland collected reports on Boer tactics in the South African war of 1899–1902; on Lawrence and his partners; on guerilla activities in the Russian civil war of 1917–22, in the Spanish civil war, which raged from July 1936 to March 1939, and in the struggle between China and Japan, which had been acute since July 1937; on the smouldering Arab-Jewish conflict in Palestine, which a

British garrison was trying to contain; and of course on Ireland. He was a bald, burly, short-tempered, large-hearted man, another chain-smoker. He also had a mind wide open to new ideas – an unusual gift in a man just turned forty, which he shared with Grand who was a few months younger. They were both Royal Engineers, and had known each other since they had been cadets together at Woolwich. They were notable exceptions to Montgomery's dictum that 'all Sappers are mentally constipated'.[4]

Holland soon became an advocate of irregular operations of several kinds. He was enough his own master to extend his purview beyond the ambushes and skirmishes that were the normally accepted tasks of guerillas to sabotage and to problems of mobility for light infantry. He got plenty of support from Beaumont-Nesbitt, the deputy director of military intelligence, who came in turn under Pownall, director of both operations and intelligence at the War Office.

In the spring of 1939 Pownall's double directorate was broken up, and Beaumont-Nesbitt took over the intelligence half of it, taking Holland with him. GS (R) was renamed MI R. It continued to deal with operations, but in the minds of many regular soldiers MI R and its child, SOE, were tarred with the military intelligence brush. Few of them had read Aldous Huxley's novel *Point Counter Point*, in which Huxley teased the *Encyclopaedia Britannica* for distinguishing intelligence, human from intelligence, animal and intelligence, military. They had all been brought up to despise the bulletins – derisively called Comic Cuts – that were sent round the trenches during the previous Great War, full of a remote staff's guesses about an enemy whom the front-line troops knew only too well. Most soldiers then thought military intelligence was not to be taken too seriously. This was an unhappy mistake.

More important shifts in British policy than the reshaping of the War Office were made that spring. Hitler had secured by the Munich agreement of the previous autumn the first frontier change for Bohemia since the twelfth century: he had annexed to his Reich some frontier areas of Czechoslovakia, called loosely the Sudeten districts after a mountain range in one of them, which had never before been governed from Berlin. These were supposed to be his last demands for land in Europe. Yet on 15 March 1939 his armies overran Bohemia and Moravia, which were declared – no nonsense about elections – a protectorate of his Reich, and Slovakia became a nominally independent puppet state under a complaisant priest, Mgr Tiso. Within a week the Nazis also took over Memel in Lithuania.

With the barometer of world affairs thus set to 'stormy', the British high command was ready to take more notice both of MI R and of section D. The two bodies had been in touch since midwinter and had agreed on a rough division of labour: MI R would cover tasks that could be tackled by troops in uniform, while section D would look into undercover, unavowable work. Holland helped Grand prepare a major statement, which Grand put up to Lord Gort, the chief of the imperial general staff, on 20 March. Gort saw Halifax about it three days later, at a meeting in the Foreign Office to which Halifax brought Cadogan, his permanent under-secretary, and a senior man from MI6, as well as Grand. They agreed that Grand might now, if he took extreme care, move on from thought to action. He was authorised – unless the prime minister, Neville Chamberlain, objected, which he did not – to embark on sabotage and leaflet work in the Czech borderlands and Austria, and to put out leaflets and to prepare sabotage in any areas now obviously threatened by Germany in eastern and south-eastern Europe.

From this meeting on 23 March 1939 SOE was born; but after many more than the usual nine months of human gestation. It was eventually formed by combining section D, MI R, and EH: a combination approved by C, by the Foreign Office, and by the army high command. Yet, as with some human arranged matches, all did not go smoothly at first, for though Grand and Holland had long known each other, to know a man is not always to like him, and they got on badly.

As soon as Beaumont-Nesbitt heard from Gort about the meeting he sent Holland over to work alongside Grand in section D's new offices. These were at 2 Caxton Street, Westminster, on the corner of Broadway and just round the corner from MI6's then headquarters at 54 Broadway, which backed on to Queen Anne's Gate. They were the scene of several disputes, for Holland and Grand had quite different characters and approached their work in diverse ways. Holland thought Grand rash and careless of detail, while Grand thought Holland a stick-in-the-mud.

With the outbreak of war on 3 September Holland got out of Caxton Street and went back, with the handful of companions he had now gathered round him, to the main War Office building in Whitehall. One of these companions deserves early notice; he will figure over and over again in the pages that follow. He too had been at Woolwich, with Holland and Grand, a year their senior: (Sir) Colin Gubbins. He was a small, slight, wiry Highlander, who wore the toothbrush moustache that was then almost part of a Royal Artillery officer's uniform, yet hid behind formal neatness an original mind and a daring spirit. He was in many ways an unusual soldier, fluent in French and German, understanding Russian, fond of good living, widely read and widely travelled. He had been born in Japan in 1896 – his father, who was then in the consular service, had fluent Japanese – and had fought both in southern Ireland and in northern Russia in the aftermath of the previous world war. Just before the start of that war, he had successfully got out of Germany, disguising himself as a schoolboy when in fact he was on his way to join a field artillery battery.[5] He spent most of the war in the mud of France and Flanders and, like Holland, had been decorated for gallantry under fire.

The War Office used to be thought slothful by the army; Gubbins was anything but a sloth. In the late spring of 1939 he set out to complete a task Gort set to Holland on 13 April: to 'produce a guerilla "F[ield] S[ervice] R[egulations]"'. Every army officer was expected to have a well-thumbed copy of Field Service Regulations by him; in the then current edition, of 1935, clear and simple rules were laid down about what to do in any normal military fix. The whole point of guerillas was to start abnormal actions, to put the enemy in sudden fixes he had never thought about; there was something absurd in ordering anything so formal for them. Holland and Gubbins knew how to interpret the spirit of Gort's order.

They had both been ruminating on the subject ever since they had become friends as young majors in Dublin in 1919, where they had been struck by the success of Michael Collins's gunmen in plain clothes.[6] They now talked it over in detail, and Gubbins wrote two short, crisply-worded pamphlets, 'The Art of Guerilla Warfare' and 'Partisan Leaders' Handbook'. (Sir) Millis Jefferis, MI R's explosives and devices expert – another engineer, of whom more in Chapter 5 – added another, 'How to Use High Explosives', which turned out even more useful in wartime practice. By a long-standing rule no one has ever cared to alter, these pamphlets (which are crown copyright) have never been published in England; but during the war hundreds of thousands of copies were distributed free all over Europe and south-east Asia, both in their original form and in translations into sixteen different languages at least: Burmese, Chinese, Czech, Danish, Dutch, French, German, Greek, Italian, Malay,

Norwegian, Polish, Serbo-Croat, Slovak, Slovene and Thai.[7]

In these pamphlets Gubbins and Jefferis laid down in commonsensical terms the main principles of guerilla war, which are similar to those of war on a more formal scale. Gubbins stressed the need for surprise, for grouping a few armed men at the enemy's weak points, for swift and sudden attacks, for immediate retreat. The regular soldier's tenacity in holding ground spells doom for the guerilla, who must never tie himself to any single spot; must, on the contrary, begin every move by planning his line of retreat. If he is not mobile, he is nothing. He must also, even more than regulars must, be sure that he has plenty of exact intelligence about the ground over which he is to fight and the enemy he faces. Guerillas usually work near their own homes, so that they already know every lane, every path, every hollow; if far from home, they must make sure they have reliable guides. If enemy agents or informers present themselves and try to win the guerillas' confidence, no one must hesitate to kill them quickly.

For weapons, guerillas might have to rely on what they could steal. It was therefore important for at least some of them to know in minute detail about the small arms used by their own country's armed forces and by whichever axis power was in control. Gubbins reckoned that most guerilla combat would take place at very short range, and that the sub-machine-gun would be the most effective guerilla weapon. Al Capone was well known for terrorising his opponents in the Chicago underworld with the Thompson sub-machine-gun; Gubbins was happy to take a leaf out of a gangster's book to deal with the gangsters of Nazi Germany.*

* More of the results of this policy, not always happy, on pp. 97–101, 279-80.

Another point, on which the 'Partisan Leaders' Handbook' insisted, was part of the doctrine under which Gubbins, like the whole of the old officer class, had grown up: a point so obvious that it hardly seemed worth retelling until he remembered that not all of those who read him would have known it from childhood. It is the secret of sound leadership: never tell anyone to do anything you cannot (or dare not) do yourself. Hence the tendency of so many of the leading figures in the resistance struggle, whom SOE later brought forward, to lead from in front. As Orde Wingate once put it – he had been picked out for special work well before the war, by Wavell in Palestine – 'Never ask favours, but tell people if they care to help they can come along, that you yourself are going anyway.'[8] This is a sound method for leading men through perilous places.

Jefferis' demolition handbook was full of simple tips. It explained what a saboteur could attack with ease and profit – motor car or lorry or bus axles, railway-engine pistons, tramline or railway points, telephone junction boxes, electricity substations. He mentioned that, if you wanted to doctor a whole shed full of engines, you should take care to cripple the same part of each one (for instance, the right-hand piston); otherwise one could be mended quickly by cannibalising another. He described which kinds of bridges were, and which were not, readily breakable with small charges; where charges had to be placed; how their size was to be worked out; how they were to be laid, tamped – hidden, if need be – and fired. He pointed out the advantages of a stout hammer, not only for the sabotage of a glass factory: in those days many machines rested on cast-iron bases, which would crack if hit hard, thus rendering the machine unsafe to use.

All these simple and straightforward doctrines, worked out in MI R before SOE ever existed, formed the core of such training as SOE was ever able to give to active resistance movements 'in the field' – in countries overrun by the axis. Grand meanwhile, encouraged by the new C, Colonel (later Major-General Sir) Stewart Menzies, began to recruit, chiefly from among his friends in the City. Reinforcements were also posted to him from inside the secret service, notably M. R. Chidson. By July 1940 he claimed that his section had reached an officer strength of 140 (75 were actually counted on 4 August), but had only one serious triumph to show for it: the rescue by Chidson from Amsterdam of £1¼ million worth of industrial diamonds, whisked away from under the Germans' noses in May.[9]

One of Grand's weightiest business recruits, George Taylor, an Australian merchant of great enterprise and force of character, visited the Balkans and found a local agent, Julius Hanau – codenamed, of course, 'Caesar' – to prepare plans for attack on a prime sabotage target, the Danube gorge, called the Iron Gate, below Orsova on the Yugoslav-Romanian border. Hanau's efforts to be unobtrusive attracted too much local police attention to do any good. A further attempt on the same target by that enterprising buccaneer Merlin Minshall also miscarried. He seems to have been one of the originals of Ian Fleming's James Bond; certainly he shared Bond's susceptibility to blondes. He secured, through Fleming's good offices, a junior consular post in Romania and a score of naval ratings – ill-disguised as art students – whom he hoped to use to block the Danube channel at a point he had spotted when sailing down it before the war. The Germans outmanoeuvred him by stealing his stocks of stolen fuel, and he and his sailors were lucky to get away alive. His rumbustious account of his adventures provides eloquent evidence of how unready the British were for irregular war.[10]

Section D also included a technical subsection, which made two vital improvements in sabotage method: it helped invent plastic explosive, and it bettered German and Polish designs for time fuses – the Germans' captured in 1917, the Poles' a recent secret service gift. MI R's technical subsection, under Jefferis, worked mainly on small mines and anti-tank weapons. It conceived the riverborne mine that Churchill failed to persuade the French to launch into the Rhine until too late; it invented a hand-held sticky bomb, which the exceptionally brave could try to use against tanks; and it invented a short-range anti-tank mortar, called the Blacker bombard after its designer, L. V. S. Blacker, a strong-minded and inventive gunner from the Indian army (see p. 104–5), whose colourful past included infantry and flying corps action in France in 1915 and anti-bolshevik cavalry work, on yaks, in Turkestan in 1919.[11]

The two sections held jointly, mainly in the St Ermin's hotel, which lies between 2 Caxton Street and the Caxton Hall, a few discreet discussion courses for young officers and businessmen to whom it seemed sensible to teach some ideas about irregular and clandestine war. Several who later rose high in this field began their connection with it here.

Gubbins made two journeys abroad in the spring of 1939: one to reconnoitre the Danube valley; the other to visit Poland and the then independent Baltic states to its north-east, Lithuania, Estonia and Latvia. He made several useful friends in the intelligence community in Warsaw. Farther south, he took care to keep clear of Hanau. A week before the war began, he went to Poland again, as chief of staff to Carton de Wiart's military mission. With it he was able to watch the German army's first blitzkrieg from uncomfortably close quarters. De Wiart, Gubbins and his staff captain, (Sir) Peter Wilkinson, a discovery from St Ermin's, managed to get away into Romania and not to be interned.

Holland's section had been preparing to work into Romania through a sub-section called MI R(r). A mission several officers strong went there early in the war, while

Romania was still neutral, and prepared to attack its oilfields – the Tintea distribution plant in particular. One of them was Geoffrey Household, already author of one of the best thrillers ever written, *Rogue Male*.[12] He has given a crisp and revealing account of how their efforts came to nothing.[13] A regular engineer unit was standing by in Egypt to do the actual demolitions, at spots to be pointed out by the MI R mission, but the signal was not given in time. Word leaked out – in London, not in Bucharest – probably through an oil merchant rather than a diplomat. Two Romanian sentries were posted beside every intended target, and the mission dispersed.

Gubbins and Wilkinson were next sent to Paris, to work with the exiled Poles and Czechoslovaks. Section D had a small mission there also, commanded by L. A. L. Humphreys; it was involved in ineffective attempts to interfere with telephones in the Siegfried Line through a pair of crippled German refugees, and in equally ineffective talks with Grand's opposite number, Brochu, who was trying to set up a section to handle sabotage in a new department of the French staff, called the Fifth Bureau. From Paris Gubbins was withdrawn to England to deal with another of Holland's ideas.

This was the concept of what were at first called the independent companies – later famous as the commandos. Holland thought that the army needed, to act in front of it and on its flanks in fluid battles, small teams of dedicated soldiers: extra-brave, extra-enterprising men, who could raid spots vital for the enemy, and cause damage and dislocation quite out of proportion to their own small numbers.

Holland spent the winter of 1939–40 starting up various parts of the secret war and finding the right men to take them over – such as MI9, the escape service, which he entrusted to an old school acquaintance whom he had recalled from the Stock Exchange, Norman Crockatt. For the independent companies he chose Gubbins as commander, and Gubbins indeed – promoted acting brigadier – took five of them to Norway. From the disastrous campaign there in April–June 1940 the independent companies were among the few British units to emerge with any credit, and Gubbins was appointed to a well-deserved DSO for gallantry and leadership under fire. He also had a black mark scored against him by that always powerful body, the inner ring of officers close to the crown; for he dismissed on the spot for incompetence a battalion commander in the Guards. Guards commanding officers, like Rolls-Royce axles, do not break; Gubbins was never forgiven.

This did not stop Holland selecting him for another perilous enterprise. By midsummer 1940 the French had broken and surrendered; the British Empire was left to face Germany and Italy almost alone; a German invasion was expected. Holland had a device ready to help hamper an invasion: stay-behind parties, such as Gubbins had had no time to help the Poles organise in Poland. The mere fact that these parties had ever existed in England was kept secret, not least by the hundreds of men and women who had belonged to them (often under Home Guard cover) for many years. Only in 1968 was David Lampe able to put the core of their story into book form.[14] From his researches two points relevant to this book stand out. The early attempts to form stay-behind parties were made, by section D, so incompetently as to bear out all Holland's strictures on Grand (though it must not be forgotten that Grand had a great deal else on his mind, and spent his energies looking aggressively overseas instead of defensively at home). Secondly, the man who pulled these parties together, recruited the bulk of them, got the military high command to accept them as necessary, took care that nobody more junior who did not need to know about them had ever heard of them, gave them a strategy and inspired their early training, was Holland's nominee Colin Gubbins.

Gubbins was in demand also, though unavailable, to resume the running of the independent companies when they were renamed commandos and placed under a new staff authority, a director of combined operations – a post soon to be held by an old friend of Churchill's, Sir Roger Keyes, the leader of the raid on Zeebrugge. Holland, Grand, Godfrey (Director of Naval Intelligence), Keyes at the service working level, Churchill and several of his colleagues among ministers, all were busy thrashing around for some outlet for their offensive energies, but they were thrashing around separately. Section D and MI R were not merely independent, but frankly in competition with each other, and D's defeat over the business of the stay-behind parties rankled. It was high time for someone to straighten out the mess.

That master of co-ordination, the first formal secretary the cabinet had ever had, Lord Hankey, took charge of the problem. Churchill, forming his coalition government in May 1940, dropped Hankey from the War Cabinet. As Chancellor of the Duchy of Lancaster he had little to do, beyond finishing a major report on the secret services with which he had been entrusted before Christmas; as a former secretary, for many years, of the committee of imperial defence as well as of the cabinet, he knew the government machine inside out; he was excellent at keeping secrets, a good judge of men and had no party ties.[15]

As early as 25 May the chiefs of staff had foreseen that France might collapse, and that if she did 'the creation of widespread revolt in Germany's conquered territories would become a major British strategic objective. For this a special organisation would be needed, and in their view ought to be set up promptly.'[16] As he used to be their servant, and had lately been working with them daily, their opinion counted with Hankey. On Churchill's instructions, he acted as link between the War Cabinet, the chiefs of staff, and the various secret and semi-secret services. On the evening of 13 June 1940, when the collapse of France (indeed imminent) seemed only too likely, Hankey saw Grand and Holland together, and persuaded them both that raiding and subversion now had to be co-ordinated under a single minister.

In normal times months, perhaps years, of more or less amiable bickerings among officials would have gone into the creation of any new department; the wilder the new body's stated aims, the longer the debate. Nobody could call the summer of 1940 normal. The United Kingdom was really united, at that moment, in its desire to win the war: a fact that has been overlaid and overlooked with the passage of time. Not everybody, even among those still alive who shared it, recalls the kingdom's degree of unity, which is a good way removed from the electoral volatility and the acridity of debate at the present day. Extreme leftists and rightists are again ready to make trouble in the streets – as were the gangs from which the Nazis' original hold on Germany derived; slanging matches, more or less sincere, in the House of Commons are now normal. In 1940–4, after the dust-up of early May 1940 was over, this did not happen. Only tiny handfuls of fascists and communists had the least doubts about the rightness of waging the war, and they had the sense to keep their doubts to themselves.

One other small but weighty sub-class was prepared to cut up rough, if it had to, in the summer of 1940: not about whether it was right to fight – which all its members took for granted – but about details of how the fighting was to be done. This was the sub-class of senior professional politicians, by this time perceptible as a social group not quite like others. They knew that it was their task – to which most of them had appointed themselves – to take a share in guiding the nation's destinies. They had managed, having much else on their desks, to tie themselves in knots about the control of irregular warfare.

The knots were unravelled by mid-July. Halifax took the chair at the critical meeting, held in the Foreign Office on 1 July. Three other ministers were present, none of them in the War Cabinet: Hankey, Lord Lloyd, the Colonial Secretary, an old friend of T. E. Lawrence's, and Dr Hugh Dalton, the Minister of Economic Warfare. Cadogan was there, with Gladwyn Jebb, his private secretary, to take the minutes. So was C; so was the DMI (though there was no one from the Admiralty or the Air Ministry); so was (Sir) Desmond Morton, the Prime Minister's civil assistant who handled all Churchill's relations with most secret affairs. They went briefly over ground that was now familiar to most of them. Lloyd summed up the conclusion to which they all agreed: that what was needed was 'a Controller armed with almost dictatorial powers'.[17]

Dalton wrote to Halifax next day in an often-quoted but still requotable letter:

> We have got to organize movements in enemy-occupied territory comparable to the Sinn Fein movement in Ireland, to the Chinese Guerillas now operating against Japan, to the Spanish Irregulars who played a notable part in Wellington's campaign or – one might as well admit it – to the organizations which the nazis themselves have developed so remarkably in almost every country in the world. This 'democratic international' must use many different methods, including industrial and military sabotage, labour agitation and strikes, continuous propaganda, terrorist acts against traitors and German leaders, boycotts and riots.
>
> It is quite clear to me that an organization on this scale and of this character is not something which can be handled by the ordinary departmental machinery

18

of either the British Civil Service or the British military machine. What is needed is a new organization to co-ordinate, inspire, control and assist the nationals of the oppressed countries who must themselves be the direct participants. We need absolute secrecy, a certain fanatical enthusiasm, willingness to work with people of different nationalities, complete political reliability. Some of these qualities are certainly to be found in some military officers and, if such men are available, they should undoubtedly be used. But the organization should, in my view, be entirely independent of the War Office machine.[18]

This document became known to the high command of SOE, once it had been set up, and influenced a good deal of its early thinking about the problems of strategy that lay before it. A somewhat meaner chord needs also to be struck here; for there was a domestic political dimension to this struggle as well as a European one. Going back to the (never fully resolved) entanglement of the British secret services in the Zinoviev letter affair on which Labour myth-makers blamed their party's loss of the autumn general election of 1924, the Labour Party had various good reasons for being suspicious of MI5 and MI6. It was generally supposed by senior men in the party – many of whom knew nothing of Hankey's temporary role in charge of secret affairs – that, now Labour had joined Churchill's wartime coalition, one secret service at least would be put under a Labour minister. Yet there was no question, at least for the time being, of moving Halifax away from the Foreign Office, which was constitutionally responsible for MI6; and the Home Office, responsible for MI5 – a fact hardly known, save by privy councillors, till long after the war – was securely in the hands of a still higher Tory, Sir John Anderson, lately governor of Bengal. Anderson had been a target for terrorist attack in Dublin during the Troubles, and in

Bengal, where he twice narrowly escaped with his life; so he knew what he was doing. If a third secret service could be created, and run by a Labour man, the political difficulty could be quickly resolved.[19]

Halifax took the 1 July meeting's conclusions to Churchill, who had no doubt been forewarned by Morton. It can be guessed that Hankey informed the chiefs of staff – there was no need for anything so secret yet to be put on paper. Someone, again probably Hankey, must have squared the Treasury. Duff Cooper, the Minister of Information, whom in the general flurry no one had remembered to summon to the meeting, was mollified – for the time being – when Cadogan sent him the minutes and a note of apology next day.

A few days' hitch appeared to follow. Dalton thought that there might have been an intrigue by Brendan Bracken.[20] This in turn may have come to him in retrospect, after the quarrel with Bracken described in the next chapter. The delay, which was brief, may simply have been due to the intense pressure of business that currently weighed on Churchill. At any rate, on 16 July the Prime Minister sent for Dalton and invited him to take ministerial charge of the new body to control subversive warfare that the meeting of 1 July had proposed. Dalton had time on his hands at the Ministry of Economic Warfare, had not hitherto felt that he was pulling his full weight either in his party team or in the war effort, and did not hesitate to accept.

By a curious irony, the last details had already been handed over by Churchill to be settled by a personage whom Dalton particularly detested. The forging of a weapon intended to create the utmost difficulties for Hitler was undertaken by the man who is now commonly derided as having been too soft in his treatment of Hitler at Munich: Neville Chamberlain. Chamberlain had only resigned as Prime Minister on 10 May, when Churchill took over from him. His current post as Lord President of the Council, with a large salary and light duties, was meant to free him for tasks like this; he remained, moreover, a member of the government's innermost formal circle, the War Cabinet, and leader of much the largest element of its support in the Commons, a Conservative Party with a majority of some 250 over all the rest. There was no trace of a policy of appeasement in the paper he now drew up.

He circulated a draft on 13 July, and on the 19th signed what SOE always looked on as its founding charter. It was his last stroke for the nation: a few days later illness removed him from the active scene, and he died on 9 November. In his paper he laid down that, on the Prime Minister's authority, 'a new organization shall be established forthwith to co-ordinate all action, by way of subversion and sabotage, against the enemy overseas'. He christened the new body too: 'This organization will be known as the Special Operations Executive.' Dalton was to be its chairman; Sir Robert Vansittart, the government's chief diplomatic adviser – Cadogan's predecessor – was to advise him. SOE was empowered to extract such staff as it found necessary from other departments. All subversive plans, whether SOE's or others', were to be approved by its chairman; he in turn was to secure the agreement of the Foreign Secretary, and of other ministers if interested, to major plans of SOE's. The paper added: 'It will be important that the general plan for irregular offensive operations should be in step with the general strategic conduct of the war': Dalton therefore was to keep the chiefs of staff informed, while they in turn gave him a 'broad strategic picture'. The War Cabinet duly met and approved on 22 July, with a minor amendment.[21]

C concurred with the formation of SOE as an independent secret service, over which he was to have no formal control: he had no choice. At that moment he had more than enough on his mind. Indeed, so busy was he that he had no time to spare for the affairs of section D, and not till 4 September did he discover that, by a direct deal between Halifax and Dalton, Grand's section had been taken away from SIS control altogether. By another unhappy office error, no one had remembered to tell him. Quite apart from the sound technical point that SOE's agents (once placed) were likely to create conditions too disturbed for intelligence agents (when he had any) to work in with any ease, C now had a personal reason for feeling aggrieved at the mere fact that the new body existed.

His immediate worries were about decipher and spies. The Government Code and Cipher School (GC and CS), the decipherers at Bletchley Park, had succeeded in breaking – with fair regularity – the Enigma cipher machine messages sent by the German air force, and C by a deft political stroke had succeeded in arranging that it was through himself that their product – on which the nation's safety was about to depend – was to be handed out to the Prime Minister and to the tiny group of senior men who needed to know it.[22] On the other hand, the silence from all his prearranged stay-behind agents in north-west Europe had by now become deafening. Through a series of appalling indiscretions – by the service that long derided SOE as unprofessional – the Germans had in fact cleaned up the lot.[23]

SOE now existed. Dalton's first task was to find a strong swift man to run it. His original idea was to appoint Brigadier-General Sir Edward Spears, who had a month before returned from an important liaison mission across the Channel, bearing with him, in a good phrase of Churchill's, 'the honour of France' in the person of General de Gaulle.[24] Why Dalton dropped Spears is not known. It may be guessed that he was not anxious to have a character as strong as his own at his elbow. Moreover

Spears had a current seat in the Commons, as Conservative member for Carlisle. Dalton chose instead, in mid-August, Sir Frank Nelson, a 56-year-old former India merchant who had sat for seven years as a Conservative backbencher (1924–31) and had had 'recent experience of Secret Service work in the important post of Consul at Basle'.[25] That is, he was acceptable to C, and knew something about security and intelligence.

He and Dalton agreed at once that Grand must be dismissed, a hard necessity; they were strengthened in this view by Jebb, who had been placed by Halifax at Dalton's elbow and strongly disapproved of Grand.[26] Nelson took the symbol of CD. (Grand went back to the career of military engineering and died, a retired major-general, in 1975.) Holland left also. Nelson would have liked to keep him, but his health had been restored by his spell in Whitehall, and when an ordinary sapper lieutenant-colonel's command became vacant he thought that, as a regular soldier, he ought to take it. He had made his historic mark and could bow out. (He too died a retired major-general, in 1956.) The War Office's traditionary reluctance to do anything quickly held up till October, in the teeth of the ruling in the charter, the formal transfer of MI R's staff to SOE, although formalities did not hold back MI R's officers from getting on with the practical business of amalgamating with EH and section D.

Dalton, Jebb and Nelson – Jebb with the title of Chief Executive Officer (CEO) – divided SOE into three branches: SO1 for propaganda (Campbell Stuart too was shown the door), SO2 for active operations, and SO3 for planning. (Sir) Rex Leeper was brought in from the Foreign Office to take charge of SO1, a task for which Stuart was thought too old and too obstinate. Jebb and Nelson, aided by Robin Brook, concentrated on SO2 when they had any time to spare from Whitehall. Brigadier van Cutsem, wished on SOE by the War Office, headed SO3, and at once proceeded to strangle his subdepartment in festoons of paperwork.

How SOE was in fact organised will appear in more detail below. Unlike most government departments, it did not have any single large purpose-built office block to house its main headquarters staff: it was indeed an awkward body to get hold of. It never appeared in the London telephone directory. It started with twelve telephone lines, and grew in the end to have 200 for its central headquarters, but they were distributed over three exchanges, ABBey, AMBassador and WELbeck, and no address went with them. Letters from SOE, if they carried a letterhead at all – often they did not – carried either that of the Ministry of Economic Warfare, or one of three service cover descriptions – MO1 (SP) at the War Office, NID(Q) at the Admiralty, or AI10 at the Air Ministry; or that of the Inter-Services Research Bureau, one of SOE's cover titles (devised to account for the multiplicity of uniforms); or that of some quite bogus firm.

At first the inner core worked in 2 Caxton Street; this was far too small. SO2 was started up in three gloomy rooms in St Ermin's, next door; the whole of the hotel's top three floors were soon swallowed up, and were still too small. By a stroke of luck 64 Baker Street fell vacant: a large office building in south-east Marylebone, conveniently close to central London but neither in Whitehall nor in St James's. It already belonged to the government; the prison commissioners had just left it. The first flight of staff officers moved in on 31 October 1940; within a month it was full. Not till July 1941 did the Treasury give its indispensable formal approval for the change of occupier; this was not the sort of obstacle likely to delay SOE.

Around this headquarters building many of SOE's component parts set up sub-offices of their own, until by the winter of 1943–4 most of the western side of Baker Street, through to Gloucester Place, had been requisitioned by SOE under one or another of its cover names.

It included Marks and Spencer's new head office building, Michaelhouse, which held the cipher and signals branches; and spread northward across the Marylebone Road, close to Sherlock Holmes's mythical lodgings at 221B Baker Street (now the head office of the Abbey National Building Society). 1 Dorset Square, leased from Bertram Mills's circus by SOE's Gaullist country section (called RF), was thus hardly remote from the high command of SOE; it was also only a few minutes' walk from de Gaulle's secret service headquarters, which settled at the north-west corner of Duke and Wigmore Streets, just south of Manchester Square. This in turn was only a furlong, down a mews, from the flat in Orchard Court, Portman Square, often used by F, the independent French section. The Free French and several other groups of temporary exiles in London took to referring to SOE as 'Baker Street', just as many service staff officers found it easy to speak of MI6 as 'Broadway'.

Here then was the body, a fact of government. What was it for?

Chamberlain's charter had put down the outline: 'to co-ordinate all action, by way of subversion and sabotage, against the enemy overseas.' This was a great deal more easily said than done. MI R(r)'s mission into Romania had already failed; Minshall had had to skip; Humphreys had had to skip (in no very decent haste, by boat from western France); Hanau was on the run; nobody else was available at all except for twenty Frenchmen placed by Humphreys *en poste* in pairs in an arc from Rouen to Strasbourg, with a handful of sabotage stores, no base, no means of communication and no orders. (In the end, Humphreys was able to absorb some of them into escape lines.[27])

SOE in fact was starting from scratch, or very near it. In London it was guessed – it was only a guess – that axis rule would turn out highly unpopular. It was up to SOE to find out, fast, how to exploit that unpopularity to benefit the British cause. Nelson himself told Jebb that he saw 'no possibility of any quick results of a major type';[28] that did not make work any the less urgent. What SOE had to do was to bring nearer the victory that virtually everyone in the kingdom desired, but to bring it nearer by means other than those employed by the other fighting services. To do so, it had first of all to counteract that powerful flywheel, the Whitehall machine.

II

Quarrels
in Whitehall

One of the marvels and strengths of bureaucracy lies in the devotion that its servants each have for their own department. Some civil servants seem more jealous about their powers than about their wives; they hate the thought that somebody else might take over a task they regard as their own, or trespass on to territory once officially marked down as theirs. A fierce departmental pride was instilled into the Civil Service's wartime newcomers, just as a fierce regimental pride was being instilled into its recruits by the army. One side-effect of this pride was that much of the energy of SOE's high command was siphoned away from its proper work by quarrels in Whitehall, at their worst during SOE's first year. The most tiresome and time-consuming of these dealt with the control of propaganda.

This struggle involved several government offices and one large quasi-official body, the BBC. The Ministry of Information, hardly older than SOE, fought tenaciously to secure control of SO1; Duff Cooper, its minister, had the advantage over Dalton of a long-standing friendship with Churchill, at whose elbow he had toiled for rearmament in the thirties while Dalton's party opposed it. (Dalton's own stand on armaments differed from most of his fellow Labour members; Evan-Thomas, one of the heroes of Jutland, was his uncle, and he had himself fought in 1916–18.) When in July 1941 Duff Cooper left on a mission to the Far East, this brought no advantage to SOE. On the contrary: the new minister, Brendan Bracken, was an even closer friend of Churchill's, whose parliamentary private secretary and daily companion he had been all through the past busy year.

Bracken, like many new brooms, meant to sweep clean. He got on no better with Dalton than Duff Cooper had done, but did not let his combative spirit run away with him. He saw that the quarrel was doing nobody any good, and settled it promptly. In August 1941 a treaty was concluded – the phrase is hardly too formal for the fact – between the contending departments. SO1 was taken away from SOE, but not given to anybody else: it was turned into a new independent body, the Political Warfare Executive. The main contending departments, the FO, MEW, MOI and SOE, were each to be allowed some say in what the policies of PWE were to be; the Foreign Office was allowed overall control. In addition, the FO later regained the services of Rex Leeper (who had been running SO1) and put in a man it trusted to run the new set-up, (Sir) Robert Bruce Lockhart, who had made his name as the head of the first official British mission to Bolshevik Russia in 1918.[1] He has left a long and detailed diary,[2] and the work of his executive has been written up from the papers that have so far been released to the Public Record Office.[3]

A small, highly secret group in PWE, of which the core was formed by Sefton Delmer, Donald McLachlan (on loan from NID) and Ellic Howe, handled an affair that would have scandalised Sir John Reith, had he been allowed to know of it, and did appal Sir Stafford Cripps who tried without success to close it down. They dealt with subversive propaganda aimed at the German army and at U-boat crews, most of it by short-wave broadcasting, some of it by leaflet (Howe had an intimate knowledge of German printing techniques). To attract and retain an audience, they used a frankly scabrous tone, giving lewd accounts of the manners of the German high command and lubricious details about what was happening to absent servicemen's wives and girl-friends. This was fully in accord with SOE's doctrines, but after August 1941 SOE could offer no more than benign approval.[4]

In spite of the bitterness of the infighting at ministerial level between MEW and MOI, relations between the working staffs of PWE and SOE remained fairly smooth. SOE was able, through its wider experience and facilities, to provide transport for a number of PWE's agents into and even out of occupied Europe. Once these men got into the field, they were able to work in closely with any SOE agents they met there; they were not forbidden, as SIS's agents usually were, to have anything to do with SOE at all.

The point remains open for argument, though argument of an unhistorical kind (what Roosevelt would have called 'iffy'): would it have been more sensible to combine propaganda and military subversion under a single chief? This was Dalton's idea in the earliest days, and seems also to have been Churchill's and the War Cabinet's, at that hectic moment in July 1940 when SOE was set up. Not all the decisions taken at hectic moments are right. The first year of incessant bickering convinced most sensible men who had time to think about it (when time to think about anything in depth was desperately short) that the decision to combine the two, however desirable in pure political theory, was unworkable – at least caused inordinate and undesirable friction – in the Whitehall of the early 1940s. Hence the change.

Yet back in Whitehall large and small quarrels about SOE went on raging, more or less acridly, to the end. Nelson's great achievement – here following Grand – was to convince sensible heads of departments that SOE existed, was not to be shrugged off, had to be taken seriously, and was working against the common enemy, axis tyranny. While he did so, Nelson had also to insist that SOE was a secret service, so word did not spread far down the hierarchy. Lesser bureaucrats could not abide a body that was secret, powerful, and outside their control. Over and over again they made as much trouble as they could. For instance, somebody in the War Office branch run by the director of staff duties was trying to insist, as late as midwinter 1943–4, that no army officer in SOE was to be sent to work in France until, in each individual case, his director had been satisfied that the officer's mission would not imperil the security of the impending invasion of north-west Europe. Just possibly that obscurantist staff officer was wiser than he knew: SOE's work into France did turn out to contain one fearful risk to the security of 'Overlord' (see pp. 197–9), but hardly in a way he can have dreamed of at the time. Similar minor troubles were only too many.

From one familiar sort of worry, at least, SOE was free: money. The Treasury prided itself, then as before and since, on getting the best of each year's recruits for the Civil Service, and the best at war turned out to be big-minded. Petty points that might engage the energy and the venom of a dullard in a service or supply department did not trouble large minds at the Treasury, well-indoctrinated from the top. SOE got all the money it needed from secret funds, which were (as, by tradition, they remain) outside effective parliamentary control. As it developed, it began to find its own sources of income. Quite junior officers might discover that they held enormous sums (viewed in personal terms) in attaché-cases full of brand-new £5 notes; very little went astray (see p. 356).

One other important kind of Whitehall quarrel remained to plague SOE: inter-service jealousy. Nowadays, to a public most of which has never been in uniform, this seems startling; it is therefore worth emphasising that in wartime nothing is more normal or more usual, the whole world over.

Of SOE's secret rivals, PWE carried comparatively little clout and, as has just been seen, presented no severe challenge, at any rate at working level. With MI5 on the whole all went very well (see pp. 85–6, 197); with MI6, as has been hinted already, there were liable to be endless difficulties, and it was generally thought to carry a great deal of clout. At the summit it was in fact, and quite rightly, mistrusted early in the war; as it delivered more and more deciphered jewels from Bletchley, it later came to be regarded as above question. From the start, SOE was brought under the control of the chiefs of staff for purposes of major strategy; its relations with them will appear in the next chapter (see pp. 44–7).

With the ministries of supply and production SOE had comparatively little trouble, thanks to sound man-to-man discussions from the start. The worst difficulty came in the autumn of 1943 in a crisis over the supply of parachute silk, of which there was a world shortage; it was solved by an inter-service committee, on which SOE sat, without costing SOE a single lost parachute drop.

SOE's relations with the other armed services were not by any means always smooth. The Admiralty, secure in its prestige and in Churchill's friendship, insisted that no SOE operations by sea were ever to take place without prior clearance with the appropriate naval authority. One malevolent man in MI6, who had friends in the Admiralty, gave SOE a rough ride over cross-Channel naval work. That tangle was sorted out in the end (see p. 118–20); SOE thus acquired a small private navy, but still had to rely on the Royal Navy for the occasional use of submarines and for much logistic support. It never tried to acquire a private air force though, as will be seen, the air was an essential element in its life. The Air Ministry, like the Admiralty, insisted on controlling SOE's operations.

They all had to be cleared, either through the Ministry itself at home – a special branch, AI 2(c), was set up to do so – or through the relevant Air C-in-C's office for flights overseas. Some junior officers in SOE suspected that AI 2(c) was overprejudiced in favour of their rivals in MI6 or MI9; this was probably illusion. The special duties squadrons' operational record books show an overwhelming majority of flights for SOE – and not only because one or two of the flights they carried out for MI6 were too secret to be put down on paper at all.[5]

With some branches of the War Office SOE had a lot of trouble. For elementary purposes of cover, most people in SOE held some sort of army rank; and a few comparatively junior War Office civil servants, with plenty of ivory between their ears, maintained that army rank implied War Office control. Some of them were never undeceived. With the war establishment branch, in particular, SOE had to maintain a perpetual conflict: this was one of the most tiresome crosses its administrators had to bear.

Still more tiresome, and a good deal heavier, was one direct burden of inter-service competition: with RAF Bomber Command. Sir Arthur Harris, who became its wartime head, outlived nearly all his senior opposite numbers in SOE, and until his death in April 1984 from time to time reminded an attentive public that his force was in action almost nightly against the enemy. So was SOE's. All through this book will run another leading theme alongside secrecy and daring: the rivalry between clandestine attacks and air bombing. Several examples will appear of SOE's superiority to Bomber Command in attacking pin-point targets in occupied territory. The brute fact remains that in the main enemy homelands, Germany and Japan, SOE could not operate effectively at all – the locals were too unfriendly and the police too strong. In Germany Bomber Command could, at a cost in its own dead of about four times SOE's total strength;[6] and at a cost in German dead never accurately reckoned, but about ten times larger still. Bomber Command was far more a subject for press photographs than SOE: its airfields took up a sizeable slice of the farming Midlands; its aircraft could be heard most nights in eastern England on their way to and from their targets; it was a familiar, visible part of the nation's way of life at war. It figured often in newspapers and bulletins, it gave everyone the feeling that Britain was hitting back at Germany. It had Churchill's backing, for strategic and political reasons; SOE's secrecy was here an extra handicap.

III
Control

SOE was a secret service, not an ordinary one. The cabinet minute that formed it laid down that it would be 'very undesirable' for questions about it to be asked, let alone answered, in the House of Commons. Parliament was to have no say in how it was run, what it did or did not do. Money for it – and it was clear from the start that it was not likely to be cheap – was to come from the secret vote, into which, by longstanding convention, the Commons do not inquire, and which the Lords by statute cannot touch because it forms part of a money bill. It fell therefore to ministers to control SOE – but to which minister?

In retrospect, it looks as if SOE might have done better had it come directly under the Ministry of Defence, as do some of its modern successors in the Special Air Service. Yet it might also have done worse, for the wartime Ministry of Defence was hardly more than notional. Its minister was also prime minister. Though no day passed in all the war on which Churchill did not think about defence, he also had a great deal else on his mind, ranging from food rationing through grand strategy, party politics, weapon design, relations with the Royal Family and the conduct of foreign policy, to whether one of his daughters ought to divorce. His tiny personal staff, headed by Ismay and Jacob, also had far more than enough to handle already, without taking charge of a secret department as well. Churchill, with his strong and buoyant schoolboy streak that so much endeared him to his countrymen, enjoyed dabbling now and again in secret service business, but knew too little about its technical aspects to do so often or safely.

The Ministry of Defence, then, was ruled out on grounds of pressure of time and of business. No one was going to entrust the nascent body to the Foreign Office; had that been done, SIS would quietly have strangled the newcomer in the cradle. None of the three service departments would do, if only because of rivalry with the other two. The solution was found, or fudged, by a kind of compromise common in politics. The job went to a man who let it be known that he wanted it, though not quite in the way he wanted. It was handed to Dalton, Minister of Economic Warfare, who had expected to run the still unnamed service as Attlee's deputy. The orderly-minded Attlee had no taste for SOE's often eccentric plots and ploys; Dalton was left on his own. He did not belong to the War Cabinet. The outer ring of ministers of cabinet rank, in which he revolved, had not much say in making strategy.

It needs to be said that though SOE came formally under Dalton's ministry, it was not in any sense run by it. To most of the ministry's ordinary employees even SOE's existence was unknown. Members of SOE could tell their friends they worked for MEW; that was only cover. The ministry was sited in Berkeley Square House, a new brown building filling much of the eastern side of the square; but only in the minister's own room and in one of the private secretaries' rooms was any SOE work done there at all. Dalton's successor, Lord Selborne, once said that SOE took up four-fifths of his working time and attention; MEW, keeping abreast with papers moving round the outer circle, Parliament and his family farm filled the rest.

Hugh Dalton was a doctrinaire economist, one of the Labour Party's leading intellectuals. He was over six feet tall, with a big bald head, a loud voice, and a thrusting manner: a manner that was all to SOE's advantage when it came to demanding that other departments take note of it. Dalton was a forceful rather than a lovable man. Even on his own side in politics he was not regarded with much affection, and in the ranks of the Conservative establishment he was frankly hated: he was called a traitor to his class. Churchill had to struggle to be civil to him.[1] As a child he had been brought up at Windsor, where his father, a canon, was so much a favourite of Queen Victoria's that he was made tutor to the dukes of Albany and York – York was the future George V. Little Hugh revolted. Court life had no charms for him; Eton did not make him a conformist; at King's, Cambridge, he befriended Rupert Brooke and became a Fabian socialist. During the 1914–18 war he served in France and Italy, in the army service corps and in heavy artillery; he taught at the London School of Economics; and had been (on and off) a Labour MP since 1924. This was not a career to enthuse right-wingers.

Dalton had three personal assistants whom he used, much as a French minister would use his personal staff, to investigate current problems in any part of SOE. This was a practice that the Civil Service abominated; it provides an early instance of SOE's freedom from the normal tramlines of correct official manners. Two of these three, Hugh Gaitskell and Christopher (now Lord) Mayhew, had later careers in left-of-centre politics; the third, (Sir) Robin Brook – who did not join till April 1941 – moved on from SOE to high distinction as a banker. Gaitskell's official biographer believes that Gaitskell had no concern with SO2, but at once contradicts himself by saying that he organised SO3,[2] which was intimately concerned with

SO2's business, and soon swallowed up by it. Gaitskell had been born into the Anglo-Indian community, and knew what ought to leave no traces on paper.

These three energetic and intelligent young men brought Dalton plenty of news, but did not at that stage seek much impact on policy. More influence was exerted at Dalton's elbow by a rising diplomat, Gladwyn Jebb (now Lord Gladwyn). Jebb had been Dalton's private secretary when he was under-secretary at the Foreign Office in the Labour ministry of 1929–31, and they had got on well then. Much more recently, Jebb had held – indeed he came to Dalton from – the post of private secretary to Cadogan, the Foreign Office's permanent head. As such, he too had learned to keep his mouth shut, and he had often acted as Cadogan's link with MI6; some secret personalities and something of the nature of secret work were therefore known to him. As an early exercise in rumour-mongering, SO1 put about London the story that Jebb had been planted in SOE by Halifax to keep an eye on the wild Dalton; this, again, was only cover. Jebb threw himself into SOE's work with energy, and was a useful guide to his new minister in steering round some of the pitfalls of wartime Whitehall.

Between them, Dalton, Jebb and Nelson established the fact of SOE in Whitehall, but had no time to do more before they were all moved out of it. As Chapter 10 will show, nowhere in its first eighteen months had SOE been able to exert an important influence on the war except in the USA and in Abyssinia. Churchill's often repeated original order to Dalton – 'And now, set Europe ablaze!' – had not yet been carried out: the twigs of early resistance were still too damp outside Poland, which SOE could hardly reach, to do more than smoulder.

In February 1942, as part of a general post among ministers, Dalton was kicked upstairs from the Ministry of Economic Warfare to the apparently wider, but far less secret, realm of the Board of Trade. The new minister, who was already in the House of Lords, was to be Lord Selborne. The parliamentary under-secretary at MEW, (Sir) Dingle Foot, remained in the Commons, fending off occasional questions about what on earth was going on in Baker Street with the bland reply that he had never been there. No one by now bothered any more about Labour's claim to run one of the secret services; everyone was too busy getting on with the war, which was at about its blackest point for Great Britain. Singapore had just fallen. Though the Russians were no longer allied with the Germans but fighting them, it was uncertain whether their front would hold; and though the Americans too had entered the war, they were for the moment weak as water.

'Top' Selborne was certainly born, as the saying goes, with a silver spoon in his mouth: his grandfather, the great Lord Salisbury, was prime minister; his other grandfather, the first Earl of Selborne, was a retired lord chancellor. After his grandfather's death he took the title, as eldest son of the second earl, of Lord Wolmer; he moved up to the House of Lords, in his father's barony of Selborne, in 1940. He took charge of SOE a few days before his father's death brought him the earldom. As Lord Wolmer he had been through University College, Oxford, where he took a third in history, and entered Parliament. He was a junior minister in 1916–18, helping his brother-in-law Lord Robert Cecil run blockade, and a back-bench Tory MP for most of the twenties and thirties, not rising above assistant postmaster-general in 1924–9. He was one of the few MPs who supported Churchill's line in debate on the India Bill in 1934–5 – that India was as yet quite unfit for self-government – and he became known as the embodiment of the old Tory conscience in the Commons.

He had a sound practical gift for business, which led him among other tasks to the chairmanship of the Cement Makers' Federation in 1934 (though he never held a cement share in his life). When Churchill formed his wartime coalition, Wolmer went to direct cement production inside the Ministry of Works. Those concrete pillboxes which strangers still stumble on now and again at hedgerow corners, with a good field of fire over the English countryside, were built of cement made on his orders during the invasion scare of 1940–1. He was a small, slight, stooping man, a great deal less insignificant than he looked. Those who thought his appearance indicated a weak character were swiftly undeceived. To the delight of his senior staff, he proved a great deal firmer than Dalton in his dealings with other ministers, and kept SOE's end up far more effectively in Whitehall.

He, like Bracken, made a clean sweep on arrival. He noticed at once what Dalton, who saw CD too often, had failed to observe: that Nelson had burnt himself out and would have to retire. (A quiet staff job was later found for him in America.) Hambro, Nelson's deputy, had already proved his energy and his worth to SOE, and in April 1942 Selborne made him CD on the delightful ground that a man who could run the Great Western Railway could run anything.

Sir Charles Hambro was a merchant banker and in every sense a man of distinction: as captain of the Eton XI he had taken seven Winchester wickets for six runs;[3] he had won a Military Cross with the Coldstream Guards in France before he came of age; he had been a director of the Bank of England when he was thirty and general manager (he was currently chairman) of the Great Western; and he was noticed by Dalton – at six foot three, Hambro was a couple of inches the taller – in MEW. Dalton recruited him early into SOE, where he had already done such stalwart work in Scandinavia (his father's family was of Danish origin) that he had been knighted (see pp. 123–4).

Jebb and Dalton had long been friends; Jebb and

Nelson had worked closely together; Selborne, a Wyke-hamist, did not care to retain the Etonian Jebb as supervisor to Hambro, whose fag Jebb had been at school. The new minister preferred businessmen to diplomats; Jebb was returned to the Foreign Office.[4] There he narrowly escaped a posting to South America, at that time a backwater, and rose in the end to the pinnacle of the Paris embassy.

Selborne and Hambro met daily at noon in the minister's office, when both were in London, sometimes only for a few minutes, sometimes for a prolonged discussion. This enabled Selborne to keep himself informed of what SOE was up to, and Hambro to draw on Selborne's political strength – which was considerable – when SOE needed it. They co-operated closely until, within eighteen months, they took opposite sides on a major question of policy. Neither would change his mind.

They fell out on two points, one fundamental, one personal. Should SOE retain its independence of all other authorities, as Hambro wished, or should it be brought under direct military control where the needs of battle seemed to demand it? As Hambro well knew, there had been a series of awkwardnesses with Wavell in Egypt (see pp. 254–63); SOE's attempts to operate at all in southeast Asia had been severely crippled in the winter of 1941–2 by military bans; and when GHQ Cairo and Allied Force Headquarters (AFHQ) Algiers both sought to claim a deciding military voice in what SOE did within their spheres of command, Hambro thought the sensible course was to resist. Selborne overruled him; the more willingly, because of their personal clash. Selborne wanted to be an executive chairman, one who could – when he thought it necessary – pry into the precise details of what was being done. Hambro preferred to keep him at arm's length, as overseer of SOE's strategy rather than one of the guides to its tactics. Several times already, in pursuit of his policy, Hambro had kept back details of current operations from Selborne, on one excuse or another: that a vital message had arrived corrupt in cipher and had had to be repeated always made a plausible tale. He did this once too often. At a critical moment, he kept in his own pocket an important signal from Cairo about affairs in Yugoslavia, and did not mention it to Selborne. Selborne was summoned that very evening to a meeting of ministers on that very subject; some of them, including Churchill, were much better informed than he was. He found himself worsted in argument, felt he had been humiliated, and on discovering Hambro's action said simply, 'Charles, you'll have to go'. Hambro, like Nelson, went to America, ostensibly as head of the British raw materials mission in Washington, but in fact as cover for a more onerous task: supervising the flow of nuclear secrets between England and the United States.

The next, and as it turned out the last, CD was Gubbins. As a regular soldier he appreciated the need for unity of command, and gladly agreed with Selborne that SOE near a battlefield must make itself the servant of the battlefield general instead of holding out for the lone hand on which Hambro had insisted. His promotion to be SOE's executive head came at an awkward moment for him personally, for his first marriage had just broken down. He was unable to tell his wife what he was doing, and the combination of secrecy and frequent unexplained, unexplainable absences was too much for her. His personal anguish was not lessened when his elder son was killed in action with an SOE party at Anzio in February 1944,[5] though this deepened his fellow-feeling with Selborne, whose eldest son had been killed with the Hampshires on active service a year before. The loss made both of them plunge deeper into the best anodyne – work. They continued the habit of a daily meeting between SO, the minister, and CD, the executive head.

Gubbins had in abundance the gift of leadership that the great dictators have made unfashionable, but that nations must produce in critical times, or perish. Even through the veil of anonymity in which heads of secret services are supposed to be shrouded, Gubbins managed to exercise it: men and women gladly worked under him, trusted his judgement and went where he told them.

Much the same had been true of Hambro and indeed of Nelson. None of these three was much impressed by that dull serviceman's shibboleth, rank. Nelson, on becoming CD, was made a pilot officer (later he became an air commodore, the air force equivalent of a brigadier), but seldom wore uniform. Hambro, as his deputy, held the rank of squadron-leader, nominally three steps in rank above him. As a pilot officer, the lowest commissioned rank in all the armed forces, Nelson issued orders to a rear-admiral, the head of SOE's naval section, and Hambro commanded a full general; both nominal seniors readily obeyed. When Gubbins was secured for SOE by Dalton in November 1940, against tough competition from Keyes and others, he held the rank of brigadier, which he kept. Initially, he was SOE's director of operations and training, with the symbol M.[6] Selborne had him promoted major-general at Christmas 1942, when he became Hambro's deputy, and early in 1944 tried to get him raised to lieutenant-general. This proposal was turned down on the grounds that, though Gubbins's fitness for it was undisputed, and the work-load deserved it, such a promotion would upset Menzies, who was already a knighted major-general and certain not to rise higher (see also p. 355).

Gubbins brought back into SOE, as his chief of staff when he became CD, a younger regular soldier who had worked with him in the nascent operations department in the winter of 1940–1 – R. H. Barry. Barry came fresh from the staff college in 1940 with the light infantry's briskness of touch, an old Wykehamist's devotion to duty, the staff college's punctilious accuracy, and a Mephistophelean laugh.[7] His quality can be judged from two posts he held in succession after the war: chief British military representative with NATO, and joint master of the Hampshire Hunt. Gubbins and Barry made a formidable team. They led in a style that contradicted the impression that some of the rest of the armed forces who had heard of SOE had allowed themselves to form: that it was a slack and lackadaisical body in which shysters could get away with anything. In the winter of 1943–4, for instance, an army subaltern turned up, in grubby uniform and without bothering to salute, at an interview to find out whether he was fit to be trained for the 'Jedburgh' teams (see pp. 172–3); and was astounded to be bawled out and packed off back to his unit by the battle-hardened Yeo-Thomas.[8] But this chapter is concerned with the high command rather than with individual agents, and to the highest command we must return.

Though Churchill played a major part in creating SOE, he only kept one fragment of it at all closely under his eye – Jefferis' devices team, carried forward from MI R (see pp. 92–3). He was always liable to make sudden irruptions into SOE's, as into SIS's, work but neither Dalton nor Selborne had trouble in keeping his incursions from doing harm; sometimes they did real good (see p. 317). He trusted Selborne at least to run SOE properly. Just possibly, once or twice, he may have seen individual agents on their way into the field, and misbriefed them to suit a deception plan of which only he and Colonel Bevan (who headed the deception service) held the key. If he did, he may not have been aware that this was a faulty deception tactic, but must have known that it was grossly improper conduct towards the secret service that he landed with the results. On the whole, however, SOE could be delighted to have him as its best friend in high quarters.

The crown, by tradition, is interested in secret service. Queen Victoria, towards the end of her reign, prided herself on being better informed than her ministers through her network of family connections on a mainly monarchical Continent. George VI had fewer crowned heads in his family than his great-grandmother, and restricted his direct interest in SOE to the loan of one of the royal gamekeepers, who helped with fieldcraft training; to keeping in touch with a brother-in-law and some officers of the Royal household, who served in MI R in 1940; to a visit to the two home RAF special duties squadrons, one of them commanded by his own pilot, 'Mouse' Fielden; and to a single visit to SOE's 'toyshop', the display offices of the devices section, housed suitably enough in the natural history museum at South Kensington. He also received, from Fielden, after an RAF pick-up operation of the type run for SOE, a couple of bottles of 1941 Burgundy, one of which he served to Churchill at one of their regular Tuesday luncheons *à deux*. Churchill asked sharply how the King had got hold of it, and was much put out to be told that kings have their secrets, for he supposed that George VI was reviving the family's private continental networks. The King was only pulling his leg.[9]

If the War Cabinet, as such, sought to exercise any direct control over SOE, the fact has not yet been allowed to surface among the delicately graded cabinet papers in the PRO.

The chiefs of staff, on the other hand, were much concerned with SOE, as with the rest of the war effort. Now and again CD would be summoned to their committee to discuss with them the part that SOE could play in impending operations. As a security measure, C did not sit with the chiefs of staff; Lord Louis Mountbatten did, for a time, and successive CDs were a trifle jealous of him for doing so, and of Laycock, who followed him at Combined Operations in 1943 when Mountbatten went off to the supreme command in south-east Asia. It was seldom much use arguing with the princely sailor, who did what and went where he liked; SOE had to live with his affable superiority. Both he and Laycock co-operated closely with SOE. SOE, for example, provided and fused the mass of high explosive hidden in *Campbeltown*'s bows, which blew up the dry dock at St Nazaire at noon on the day after the great raid. (The shower of decorations after that raid did not include its most heroic figures, a pair of commando subalterns who were being interrogated in *Campbeltown*'s wardroom, who kept to themselves the knowledge that she was about to explode, and died with her.) SOE provided the limpet mines for the 'Cockleshell hero' raid on blockade runners at Bordeaux.[10] SOE was ready to consult COHQ, and COHQ was ready to consult SOE, about a dozen details of raiding techniques at any moment. SOE kept a liaison major and his secretary at COHQ – the one who went to Dieppe in August 1942 did not return. COHQ had nobody at SOE's headquarters, as was only to be expected.

The chiefs of staff's directives to SOE are set out in their chronological places below (e.g. pp. 250–1). For more detailed liaison, Gubbins and Barry eventually worked out a drill with Ismay, who combined being Churchill's military private secretary with secretarial work for the chiefs of staff and the War Cabinet. At least once a week he would see Gubbins or Barry or both, show them any documents from the joint intelligence or planning staffs that he judged they needed to see, and thus meet the original charter provision about keeping SOE in the broad strategic picture. He also took this opportunity to lend a folder – not to be taken out of his room, nor to have notes taken from it – that contained any ultra-secret messages deciphered at Bletchley of which he knew, and thought SOE's staff ought to have knowledge. Menzies had known about the possibilities of breaking the Germans' Enigma cipher machine traffic since before the war. He was present, ill-disguised as an Oxford professor of mathematics, a subject of which he knew little, at the critical meeting near Warsaw in the summer of 1939, when the Poles handed over two of the fifteen Enigma machines they then possessed, one to the British and one to the French secret service. By a deft political stroke, Menzies had already ensured that it was his own department – MI6 – that was to pass out to everyone else what Bletchley discovered. It did not suit his book to tell SOE any more than he had to, and to deal with them through the clear prism of Ismay suited him better than having to deal direct.

From SOE's point of view, this was not much of a bargain. Yet the very few senior people in SOE who were privy to the ultra-secret work that Bletchley was doing had respect enough for secrecy, in principle, not to want to pry. Besides, they had common sense enough to realise that, whenever they could, the German security authorities would use teleprinters, which the British could not intercept; this was, for example, the uniform practice of the Sicherheitsdienst offices, a main Gestapo headquarters, in Paris.[11] And though Bletchley quite early broke, and regularly read, the Abwehr's Enigma key, it did not manage to break the main Gestapo key at all.[12]

Sir Alan Brooke (later Lord Alanbrooke), chief of the Imperial General Staff from November 1941, soon thereafter became chairman of the chiefs of staff committee. Brooke had known and liked Gubbins, a fellow gunner, before the war. His first reaction when he discovered that Gubbins had gone into secret work was regret, on technical grounds, that the regiment had lost the services of a promising officer. Later he came to appreciate what Gubbins was trying to do with SOE, and took in the part that subversion could play in grand strategy. The fact that neither Gubbins's name nor Stewart Menzies' appears in Brooke's published diaries,[13] from which so many war histories have been built, does not mean that Brooke did not often see and think about them both (usually he saw them separately). He made sure that SOE always got a fair hearing from the chiefs of staff, when its business reached that august body.

The Colonial, India and Dominions Offices very occasionally had to do business with SOE. This never raised any serious trouble.

One other external body had, at the start, a supervisory interest in SOE, and remained intimately concerned with most of what SOE did: the Foreign Office. Its influence was at first both strong and inhibitive. SOE had trouble enough getting itself into action at all; this was compounded over and over again by the doctrine of 'no bangs without Foreign Office consent'. Many British ministers abroad – this was before the war's diplomatic inflation had turned most of them into ambassadors with embassies – did not see why their legations should be cluttered up with arms and explosives, essentially undiplomatic instruments, in the charge of some notional assistant military or press attaché, often a person of abrupt manners and no perceptible breeding. The office staff in Whitehall was not embarrassed in quite the same way, but was slow to come to terms with something that was at once new, thrusting and unconventional. Relations with the governments-in-exile in London, all of them prickly, were difficult enough without the extra complications that SOE brought. Relations with General de Gaulle, who was always idiosyncratic, and was not recognised by the British as head of a government until after he had set himself up in liberated France, were seldom smooth, and SOE made them a good deal rougher than – in the Foreign Office's view – they need have been.

Gradually SOE moved away from the FO's tutelage, though it could never ignore the place altogether. Neither Halifax nor Eden loved it; Gubbins never forgot how Eden once kept him standing at attention for several minutes in his Downing Street office, while the Foreign Secretary – velvet-slippered feet on his desk – read a novel. Cadogan showed sympathy and understanding, but took care to keep SOE quiet in such delicate areas as Spain, and to muffle it as best he could in unoccupied France. He was a combative spirit, and he was a profound patriot, yet a through-and-through civilian, never quite in tune with SOE's offensive aims. He had a formal meeting once a fortnight with CD and in times of crisis (which were frequent) after Jebb had left saw CD or his political assistant, Harry Sporborg, almost every day. He was as good as anyone else at keeping secrets off paper; neither Hambro nor Gubbins nor Sporborg figure in his published diaries at all.

Some of his juniors seemed, to the more junior SOE staff who encountered them, positively to revel in putting obstacles in SOE's way. Yet as time passed and SOE gained experience, it gained stature as well. Even the Foreign Office ceased to plague it, and its high command did not fail to remember that what they did could affect foreign policy for many years to come.

It is time to turn to the intricate, but not quite insoluble, problem of SOE's own command structure: how it was articulated to pass down orders and pass back reports.

All British subjects in SOE took for granted that they were under orders, subordinated to the cabinet and the crown. As it was a coalition cabinet of unusually wide range, only extremists were liable to feel entirely out of sympathy with the political high command, and not many extremists were in SOE.

The minister now and again appeared at SOE's schools, and at a few demonstrations of special equipment or exercises. Dalton, through his emissaries, also tried from time to time to exert some direct influence on policy, and could be heard grumbling about reactionary underlings from the City; most of his grumbles were LSE froth. Selborne, though he would show up to conduct the King and Queen around the toyshop, normally left direct contact with SOE's staff to CD, but was liable now and

SOE in the allied chain of command March 1944

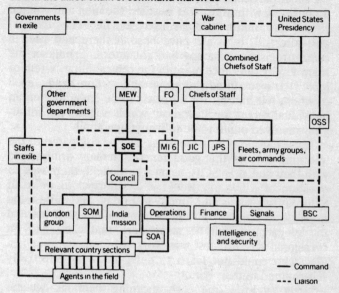

again to demand to be briefed in detail. As a security precaution, CD hardly ever saw agents himself.

Common sense laid down the need to divide SOE's staff roughly into two halves, those providing facilities, and those in actual charge of operations. The various sections of the organisation were also grouped, either by area or by function, under senior men. This led to an interesting development. By a sound early arrangement of Nelson's, either he or Jebb or both (if both were present, Jebb took the chair) had a meeting in Baker Street at nine o'clock every morning, to which they summoned those who had important business on hand, however senior or junior in such staff hierarchy as there was. There was no settled office system, nor any central registry. This must have been something of a nuisance at the time, particularly for other departments which had to do business with SOE. Yet it suited the men and women on the spot, and helped them to feel safer. How dangerous, after all, it would have been if there had been a central registry and a spy had got into it. (Think of the harm Philby did, once loose in the central filing system of MI6.[14]) It also suited the group and section heads, each of whom felt himself (or herself*) to be embarked on an individual secret journey about which nobody not intimately involved ought to be told anything at all.

These early morning meetings may be compared to the 'morning prayers' that good generals in many armies hold with their staffs. In SOE, as on a battlefield, there was no question of a five-day week: it was normal to work all Saturday as well as all Monday to Friday, and quite usual to work on Sunday as well. Sensible senior staff learned to delegate enough to make sure that they had an occasional day off, lest overwork drove them frantic; a few, who could not learn to delegate, were effectively self-chained to their oars.[15]

Little by little, the early morning meetings became formalised, to consist only of CD and his principal heads of department and advisers. By the end of 1941 they had crystallised into a Council. Council met as a routine every Wednesday, and much more often at times of tension. When in London CD always attended, and after Jebb's departure always took the chair. His position was much that of a prime minister in cabinet, *primus inter pares*, first among equals. Fortunately, there is a vivid pen-picture of Council drawn just after the war by a perceptive observer who had delved deep in SOE's papers and talked to several Council members.

Members of Council represented a great variety of experience: out of sixteen there were five regular

---

* About a quarter of SOE's total strength were women (see pp. 74–7 below), but hardly any of them held this kind of responsibility.

soldiers (one of them a signaller), two airmen (one 'wingless'), a sailor, a professional civil servant, a Foreign Office man, a solicitor, an accountant, and [four] business men of various types . . . All alike believed passionately in the purpose and possibilities of SOE; the fact that they had heavy administrative duties did not prevent them from speculating and debating on the nature and power of 'subversion'. There was no agreed and analysed 'staff college' doctrine: but there was none the less an immensely strong 'public opinion' within the organization which expressed itself forcibly on Council level and was felt much lower down. The administration of SOE had many failings which can be defended only by explaining the stress under which the organization grew: but much had been put right by the summer of 1944, and there was a spirit of excitement and personal concern which atoned for much. The distribution of duties was sometimes obscure or overlapping; but the entire staff was looking for duties, not seeking to evade them. This was not an unmixed blessing, but it meant that things somehow got done, fairly speedily and fairly correctly, though not with perfect economy. Luckily the staff as a whole were relatively young even at the top, at least by Whitehall standards, and many of those physically fit for it had intervals of operational experience: if security prevented them from going to the field [as it invariably did], at least they took part in training and in many cases visited missions and stations overseas. This had two advantages: the organization was in spirit pretty close to the fighting line, and it suffered less than many departments from sheer physical collapse under the strain of overwork. Few of the 'old SOE hands' were absent from duty through sickness for any long period during the war.[16]

The details of SOE's organisation were in a state of permanent flux: this is not the place to attempt any analysis in detail. The broad division between operations and facilities has been noticed already. Nelson dealt at first through two deputies: George Taylor from section D for operations, and Colonel F. T. Davies from MI R for facilities. Tommy Davies, like Taylor, was a businessman – he came from Courtaulds and brought several other senior Courtaulds men with him. He shared Taylor's ruthlessness and his efficiency.

As soon as a legal problem cropped up, the Courtaulds men thought of their firm's City solicitors, Slaughter and May, most of whose partners, including Harry Sporborg, found their way into SOE before long. (Hence Walter Fletcher's cruel crack about SOE's early lack of success: 'Seems to be all may and no slaughter'.[17]) Usually those who entered SOE were given army rank, of one sort or another; those who came in, as a few did, from the navy and several from the air force as a rule kept the rank and uniform in which they arrived. The majority of SOE's staff and agents were in the army before they joined SOE. This gave the body something of a military flavour, and 'War Office' was quite often used instead of 'MEW' as a cover description of their employers.

Just as there was no central registry, there was no permanent secretary: no single individual in charge of all the staff and of the smooth running of the whole body. One senior civil servant was brought in – late: M. P. Murray from the Air Ministry, who was not appointed till November 1943. With the title of D/CD, he undertook to deputise for CD on all matters of administration. His arrival was hardly before time, and he buckled down to the attempt to reduce to order the often chaotic arrangements of the country sections.

Taylor, following an obviously useful system of MI R's, had set up separate sections, each to look after an individual country. France was so awkwardly placed politically that it involved no fewer than six,[18] but one was normal. These country sections were 'the organizational bricks on which SOE's staff pyramid rested'.[19] Several of them were in regional groupings: the Americas, Scandinavia, north-west Europe, south-west Europe, south-east Europe and south-east Asia. The boundaries within the European groupings were not hard and fast. SOE's system remained flexible, even fluid. Sections could be switched about from one senior controller to another as the needs of war and personality dictated. Gubbins, for example, as M, ran training – which, sensibly enough, was grouped with operations rather than with other facilities. He also ran a section called MO, for operational dispatch, of which the first head was Barry (MO was later transformed into AL, air liaison).[20] In course of the earliest efforts to get agents into Europe, MO hived off what became RF, the Gaullist country section working into France, a name that echoed, by a delicate compliment, that République Française which de Gaulle felt he personified. Gubbins also had under his eye, because he knew the Poles and the Poles liked him (indeed it had been at a dinner party given by some exiled Poles that Gubbins had first met, and deeply impressed, Dalton who sat next to him[21]), a section called EU/P, which dealt with the Polish settlements in Europe outside Poland, most of them in France. EU/P long continued to come direct under Gubbins, even after RF had been put together with DF, the western European escape section, and F, the independent French section, under a group called D/R which also directed work into the Low Countries. EU/P kept itself distinct from F and RF sections all through the war – how like the Poles – even when, after the landings in Normandy, F, RF, DF and the 'Jedburgh' teams were all thrown together under one vast (and in my experience at least exceedingly incompetent) headquarters in London called the Etat-major des Forces Françaises de l'Intérieur (EMFFI).

SOE's passion for combative secrecy was not confined to London, though that was where it got most in the way. It spread also to Cairo, where a sprawling British headquarters – misleadingly called GHQ Middle East, for Cairo to a geographer is in the Near East – has been unkindly compared to the second brain that a diplodocus kept near the base of its spine to manage its back legs. During the world war of 1914–18, a secret branch of GHQ Cairo called MO4 had done its best to support the Arab revolt against the Turks. MO4's title was taken over by section D, perhaps in the hope that some of the glamour of T. E. Lawrence's name would rub off on them. MI R, also anxious to have a finger in the Levantine pie, set up a secret office in Cairo, and called it G(R).

MO4 and G(R) were each jealous of their own independence as well as of each other. In spite of the integration of their parent bodies in London in the autumn of 1940, and the existence of a single Cairo desk in Baker Street – manned for four years by the Wykehamist J. S. A. Pearson – the two little headquarters sections in Cairo managed to maintain their separate identities until they were forcibly amalgamated by Lord Glenconner in autumn 1942. Sweet-Escott has testified to the rancour of wartime Cairene life:

> Nobody who did not experience it can possibly imagine the atmosphere of jealousy, suspicion and intrigue which embittered the relations between the various secret and semi-secret departments in Cairo during the summer of 1941, or for that matter for the next two years . . . It was not quite Hobbes's war of every man against every man. But certainly every secret organization seemed to be set against every other secret organization.[22]

As Wavell put it to Slim in the autumn of 1941, 'SOE think they have taken over G(R), and G(R) think they have taken over SOE, so I suppose everybody is happy'.[23] Momentarily they may have been, but bickerings soon broke out again.

Glenconner – Margot Asquith's nephew – was the sixth man chosen to run SOE Cairo in just over two years. Three of his predecessors had been sacked, another never passed Dalton's preliminary scrutiny, and one – a newly promoted brigadier – was shot down on his way across the Bay of Biscay, and spent the rest of the war in a prisoner-of-war camp as a major. One of the first things Glenconner did on reaching Cairo was to pen, or at least sign, a violent memorandum opposing the appointment of Paul Vellacott – Master of Peterhouse, Cambridge – to take charge of PWE's affairs in the Levant. Vellacott found a copy in his in-tray when he arrived a few days later.[24] He was able to get Glenconner to see reason – this was evidently a rare event in Cairo; but it was not until March 1943 that SOE relinquished its hold on a broadcasting station in Jerusalem to PWE.

Other regional headquarters were a good deal less fraught; largely no doubt for reasons of climate. One, codenamed 'Massingham', which opened at Guyotville, just west of Algiers, in November 1942 to run operations into Iberia (if need be), southern France – through a section called AMF – mainland Italy and the western Mediterranean islands, was right on the sea, not right on the desert. Its first commander was J. W. Munn of the training section, soon replaced by (Sir) Douglas Dodds-Parker, an early recruit to MI R from the Sudan political service, who had been backstop in Khartoum to the SOE party invading Abyssinia (Ethiopia) (see p. 253). In the autumn of 1943, after Italy had changed sides, this head-quarters sent an advance headquarters called 'Maryland' forward to Monopoli near Bari, on the Adriatic. Cairo also sent an advance HQ into Italy, which settled at Bari to work into Yugoslavia and Albania.

In October 1943, simultaneously, there was yet another

purge at SOE Cairo. Glenconner too was dismissed, or retired ill; his chief of staff, the pushful Brigadier Keble – of whom more on pp. 333–4 – was so unpopular locally that he was locally dismissed as well. The military high command insisted on a soldier to replace Glenconner, and secured the chief of staff of Southern Command in England, a previous deputy to the DMI called Stawell. A sapper, he was promoted major-general and took up his new post on 20 November 1943; for cover purposes, he was called head of Force 133. (The Abyssinian party had been Force 101.)

It was soon clear to him that he needed to get forward into Italy, both to shorten the range he had to cover to get at occupied Europe, and to bring him closer to the allied commander-in-chief Mediterranean, whose AFHQ settled eventually at the palace of Caserta outside Naples. Stawell had trouble getting away, because Paget, the new commander-in-chief, Middle East, did not want to give up any say in what SOE was doing in Greece, Bulgaria and Romania to his superior, Maitland Wilson, at Caserta; moreover – a merely technical point, but a vital one – Stawell's wireless HQ had to remain in Egypt (see p. 155).

Eventually, in spring 1944, Stawell set up his headquarters – called SOM (special operations Mediterranean). Under SOM came Force 266 to work into Yugoslavia and Albania, and Force 139 for Poland and Czechoslovakia. Liaison between it and AFHQ was provided by Dodds-Parker and by another recruit from Slaughter and May, Jack Beevor, who had been SOE's man in Lisbon and then Hambro's planning assistant. Beevor commented in retrospect that 'it is to be hoped in the interest of posterity that no similar set-up will ever again recur', as the problems of remote control were horrifically complicated. SOM's actual base was at Bari; distance from Caserta did not make it too remote from the local commander-in-chief, who usually had a good deal else on his mind. Stawell too moved away – he had fallen ill by Christmas 1944 – and was followed by Colonel Franck, who had been SOE's chief liaison man in Washington.

In the Far East, two businessmen, Valentine Killery of Imperial Chemical Industries and Colin Mackenzie of J. and P. Coats' spinning combine, headed two successive missions. Killery's Oriental Mission was to have operated from Singapore but was swiftly overwhelmed by the tide of war. Mackenzie's India Mission had its headquarters at Meerut – forty miles north-east of Delhi – till December 1944, when Mountbatten persuaded him to move alongside the supreme headquarters at Kandy in Ceylon. Mackenzie, who had lost a leg at Passchendaele, was not upset by small disasters. He was expected at first to operate into Afghanistan and Tibet, and possibly Persia, Russia and China; his attention in fact was focused south-eastward rather than north-westward. His mission, originally called GS I(k) – part of the intelligence staff at GHQ India, for cover – eventually (from March 1944) took the name of Force 136, and operated as far as it could reach over the colossal distances of south-eastern Asia (see pp. 350–3).

In the western hemisphere, all SOE's affairs were controlled from New York by Sir William Stephenson, a Canadian steel millionaire who had been a successful fighter pilot during the Great War and happened to be a personal friend of Churchill's. Churchill gave him – this distinction was unique – control over all MI5's and MI6's, as well as SOE's and PWE's, business in North America. Stephenson was known as 'Little Bill', to distinguish him from 'Wild' or 'Big Bill' Donovan, the New York lawyer who successively was Coordinator of Information and head of SOE's American opposite number, OSS, set up in June 1942. Stephenson's invaluable work was solely concerned with what happened west of the Atlantic.[25] Franck and other liaison officers in Washington came under his orders. He taught OSS a great deal. That body dealt with intelligence as well as subversion, and Donovan's own comment was that 'Bill Stephenson taught us all we ever knew about foreign intelligence'.[26] So some of such glory as OSS gained reflects on Little as well as on Big Bill. Little Bill's reputation has not been well served by a host of sensationalist articles and a book that suggest he did a great deal more that lay quite outside his domain.

Gubbins tried for a few months, even after he had become Hambro's deputy, to keep a detailed eye both on the training schools in England and on operations into north-west Europe. In the spring of 1943 he was able to hand the latter over to an old friend, a fellow gunner who had served with him in Ireland and had later been an instructor at the staff college: Brigadier E. E. Mockler-Ferryman (AD/E). 'The Moke' had been Eisenhower's chief of intelligence for the 'Torch' landings in north-west Africa, and thereafter. When Eisenhower sacked an American corps commander after the setback in the Kasserine Pass, he felt he ought to sack a British general too, to preserve the Anglo-American balance he thought so important. He could most easily spare Mockler-Ferryman, who indeed appeared to be partly to blame for the defeat. Not till after he and Eisenhower were both dead did an official history make clear that the fault had lain not with the brigadier but with inadequate signals organisation, a familiar military snag.[27] When 'The Moke' returned to London, club gossip had it that he was in disgrace and had gone back to helping to run the Boy Scouts, a prewar part-time hobby of his. In fact Gubbins snapped him up at once for SOE, where he proved a valuable member of Council. SOE sometimes enjoyed appearing disreputable.

A little more can be said about those parts of the infrastructure of SOE that were scattered around the United Kingdom, most of them in the south-eastern quarter of it if not actually in the capital. There were separate sections in and near London for coding, signalling, signals research, weapon research, supply, clothing, forgery, finance, dispatch, disposal and so on. Boyle from the Air Ministry ran a directorate of intelligence and security that succeeded to SO3 (which was formally disbanded in January 1941) when that abortive division had stifled itself entirely in paper. He used the symbol AD/B. He was a great asset to SOE. Under the cover that he was just dear old Archie Boyle, he hid a keen and suspicious mind, honed by twenty years' experience of air intelligence.

Nothing sinister attaches to the disposal section. It was an elementary security device, also under Boyle's wing. Its tasks were two. It had to devise cover stories for trusted men and women who had done their stint in SOE and were going to leave it to press on with some other part of the war – stories that they could tell their friends and families with an air of entire conviction, simple stories that nobody was going to bother to check, but that, if checked all the same, would stand up. It had also a less intellectual task: it maintained a country house, nicknamed 'the cooler', in the remote Scottish highlands. Retiring agents could be kept out of sight there until no security dangers would attach to their going back to service life outside SOE. It was in the cooler that a bewildered RAF fighter pilot found himself in the following absurd circumstances. One Saturday night he got engaged at an evening party at the Savoy to a girl he found delightful, and arranged for an engagement party to be held there a week later. Next Monday morning he was shot down during a fighter sweep over northern France, landing in the grounds of a château. He was hidden by the gardener, introduced to the owner who happened to keep a safe house for SOE, and found himself flown back to England on Wednesday night by a light Lysander aircraft, which landed in the park. After his engagement party, SOE insisted that he spend six months in the highlands; his girl stood by him, and unlike many SOE characters they did live happily after.[28]

As a character in a postwar short story of Household's puts it, 'Inefficiency is a much more potent factor in war than logic'.[29] Hardly any of SOE's staff, except Gubbins, Mockler-Ferryman, Boyle and Barry, were graduates of any staff college, and their staff manners sometimes looked frightful to those who had been properly taught,[30] but they were more than competent. They were looking for duties rather than shirking them. SOE was no place for someone who wanted to *embusquer* himself (or herself) quietly till the noise was over.

The ideal country section head knew intimately the territory into which the section was to work, spoke its language fluently, was well versed in its history and customs and had influential friends there. Ideally, again, his staff would all know the language, history, geography and social customs well. Practically, it was much harder to find more than one or two people in each section who were fully qualified for their task. F section was lucky indeed to contain both Thomas Cadett, *The Times*'s (later the BBC's) man in Paris, and Nicholas Bodington, who had represented Reuter's news agency there. Bodington spoke French so well that he could pass for a Parisian without a tremor, and had a brilliant and versatile mind as well as high courage, offset by some character defects, including an apparently insatiable desire for money. This standard was rather above par for a second-in-command of a country section (the post he held in F in 1942–3) and helped him on three missions into enemy-held territory. Heads of country sections were not supposed to go so far forward, though de Chastelain – quite as well qualified as Bodington, and with a much steadier character – parachuted into Romania where he had the misfortune to spend almost all his time in jail.

A section as large as F or RF, each of which sent over

400 agents into the field, might well have a sizeable staff, of thirty or forty people – including conducting officers, who went around on the training courses with the agents; signals experts; and the necessary office staff of typists and tea-makers, without whom no English office could then stand. The price for size was not always efficiency: the Germans were able to hoodwink F section in a big way in the winter of 1943–4, because Buckmaster, its head, was too busy to give meticulous attention to every one of the flood of telegrams that were reaching him from numerous agents. Smaller sections usually did better. But small size was no adequate protection for the Dutch. N section encountered a memorable catastrophe (see pp. 177–85). Schiller's proverb is in point: *Mit der Dummheit kämpfen Götter selbst vergebens*, Against stupidity the gods themselves fight in vain.

Country section staffs, particularly their heads, bore a heavy load of responsibility. This worked upwards towards their superiors, downwards towards their agents, and outwards into the country they studied. Their judgement would as a rule be deferred to by their seniors, who were both too remote and too busy to wish – or to need – to involve themselves in detail. A sound country section head could exercise a noticeable influence on the way a guerilla campaign developed, or indeed on whether it got a chance to develop at all. Everyone, from the king and the prime minister down to the humblest sub-sub-agent, was perpetually obsessed with the problem of reprisals, as they might be wreaked by an axis secret police force against the innocent abroad. Country section staffs perhaps felt this burden more heavy on them than did anybody else.

Agents sometimes carried with them into the field – as occupied territory was known – warm memories of the staff who had just briefed them, but not always. In F section, which was large, agents were normally given – just before departure – something made of gold: for women, a powder compact; for men, heavy cufflinks or a fountain pen. This bore no compromising hallmarks,[31] and served a double purpose. It would be easily pawnable if its bearer ran short of cash and dared show false identity papers to the pawnbroker; and it would be a reminder of how much one was cherished by the staff at home. On the other hand, one F agent recalled later that when it came to this point in his briefing, the staff officer conducting it said that with such a proletarian cover these would never do, and slipped the agent's pair of cufflinks into his own pocket.[32]

Heads of country sections, and those senior to them in SOE, were forbidden by a sound security rule – which was hardly ever broken – to risk themselves in the field. It was thought probable that the enemy secret police – the Gestapo, OVRA, or Kempeitai, three formidable bodies – could extract from any prisoner anything that prisoner knew, an unacceptable risk. It was a risk that de Gaulle none the less allowed Dewavrin ('Passy'), the head of his secret services, to take. He parachuted twice into France, evaded capture, and came safely back (see p. 315), proofs alike of his own courage and, the British thought, of French carelessness about sound security.

More junior staff officers could, and quite often did, go into hostile territory and almost all of them returned. Yeo-Thomas and de Chastelain were the most important ones captured. Both were brave enough to keep silent. Marko Hudson and his party had the odder experience on his last mission of being imprisoned, in fierce discomfort, and interrogated by the Russian NKVD: they also emerged, angry and verminous but intact (see pp. 227–8). It was an enormous advantage to a section to have someone in it who had actually met some of the perils against which the agents were pitted. Not every section could manage this; none could at first. And just as country sections had to be left alone by the high command to do their best, agents too – as in fiction – were very much out on their own.

How much control an SOE organiser had in the field over his companions in his own network, and how much control the group of them could exercise on the society around them, varied enormously, both with time and with place. Closeness of touch could vary enormously also, from intimacy in every sense to frank dislike. Later chapters will give some examples from a remarkably diverse series.

Agents in the field, organisers especially, bore an even heavier responsibility than did their section heads. Once they emerged from the dense clandestine cloak in which at first they normally had to wrap themselves, they were looked on by all who even guessed at their political origins as the spokesmen on the spot for the British government in particular and for the allied cause in general. Agents responded to this, as to other challenges, as their training and character inclined them: each ran his or her own show.

But who, after all, were they?

IV
Recruiting and training

As SOE was secret, no one could recruit for it directly by
advertising. However, it had been given power by the
cabinet decision that created it to demand officers and
men from all three of the more formal armed services, or
from elsewhere. Useful recruits came its way from the
routine inquiries the services put out from time to time to
discover who among them spoke foreign languages well.
The more usual, safest and fastest way of finding recruits
was to bring in those who were known already to the
original staff. This was how both section D and MI R
began to grow, and the habit remained.

Even this system was not perfectly secure: the cases of
Donald Maclean and Kim Philby, well-educated sons of
well-known men, yet traitors to the Crown, remain fresh
in memory. Recruiting on the old-boy network could have
its disadvantages. SOE threw up an odd example in the
Near East of how this too could lead the well-intentioned
astray. Terence Airey was an ambitious regular soldier,
whose regiment – the Durham Light Infantry – had
released him (as a major) for service with the Egyptian
army before the war. He was early recruited into G(R) in
Cairo, and rose to brigadier. One day in his office he was
brought a cup of tea by an NCO whom he recognised as
the cleverest boy who had ever been (after his time) at his

school – Gresham's at Holt in Norfolk, largely maintained by one of the great City livery companies, the Fishmongers. He soon had the NCO promoted major, to assist operations into the Balkans. A routine reference to MI5 – on which the local security staff, more alert than the brigadier, insisted – produced the routine reply that nothing was recorded against him. A chance incendiary bomb at Wormwood Scrubs had burnt the file which recorded the ex-NCO's affiliations; this was how the brilliant and devious James Klugmann, secretary of the Cambridge University Communist Party in the mid-1930s, acquired a post from which he could exert leverage.

Sceptics can point out that no connection between Klugmann and the Comintern has been proved. None was needed: any Bolshevik as bright as Klugmann knew where his party duty lay. Basil Davidson, not unsympathetic to him, has recorded how the elastic timetables of Cairo made room for Klugmann often to hold forth to an interested group, mostly of Canadian ex-miners, about the Marxist view of the war.[1] After the war Klugmann joined the central committee of the Communist Party of Great Britain. He was trusted enough to write, or rather to start, the party's official history – discontinued after the second volume had reached the General Strike of 1926.[2] Fate led him to regret his wartime activity: he had to write a book denouncing Tito, after Tito fell out with Klugmann's master, Stalin.[3] Presumably like all other recruits into SOE he had been handed a form to sign, which said that he was neither a communist nor a fascist, but as a good communist he knew his duty to tell a lie. This, after all, was exactly the sort of conduct that SOE demanded from its members farther forward, under the axis enemy's eye. The fact that the form existed, and was of inadequate use in securing loyal recruits, is an interesting instance of the fix free men are always in as they try to combat tyrannies.

When in 1966 half a page of the first published official

history of SOE was taken up by details of which schools and universities the staff officers most concerned with its subject had attended,[4] a few young reviewers protested that this was a needless fragment of old-world snobbery. The author still defends it as necessary to explain – at least to the staff's contemporaries, if posterity does not care to understand – who they were. For England in the late 1930s and early 1940s was run, almost entirely, by an educated governing class drawn from headmasters' conference public schools. Among these schools there was a pecking order, endlessly contested in detail but well known in outline to everybody concerned; to know which school a man had been at was to know something about his probable competence and character. As another published official history has recently put it, 'That the early staff lists of SOE abound with names of graduates of the public schools and older universities did not reflect a conspiracy on the part of the old-boy network, nor did it necessarily mean that those selected were not as well qualified as others. It was an inescapable fact of life.'[5]

Nor did the fact that many of SOE's senior staff officers came from, and returned to, posts of influence in the City of London mean that SOE was in any sense the tool of big business, finance capital, or any other economic interest, sinister or benign. They all of them took for granted the rule of English common law, that those on government service pay no attention at all to private business interest. They would certainly use their own prewar acquaintances to help provide SOE with weapons and materials, but they had no eye to fostering any particular firm's profits. To claim that SOE was run to support the City is a propaganda slogan with no historical backing; as the rest of this book will make clear.

There was a separate objection, not voiced at the time, to the City element in SOE's staff. It was not altogether fortunate for SOE, as a body that was meant to do a lot

of industrial sabotage, that so few of its directing personalities had ever actually made anything themselves, unless
with a toy Meccano set or in a school carpentry shop, or
performed any mechanical task more intricate than changing the punctured wheel of a motor car. Almost all of
them who were not regular officers came from banking,
merchanting, insurance, stockbroking, shipbroking, the
law, teaching or journalism, that is, from service industries rather than from manufacture. Luckily Rheam, the
head of sabotage training – of whom more shortly (pp.
90–1) – came from the iron and steel industry, and his
strong practical sense made up for much.

One of the faults most often urged against SOE is that
it was amateurish. The cry was first raised in MI6, where
the permanent staff thought themselves professionals; an
odd cry to be raised by those who had, all unknowing,
provided the Sicherheitsdienst with a secret wireless transmitter and a cipher in the belief that they were dealing
with a dissident German general; or by those whose
headquarters at The Hague for work into north-western
Europe had been under constant scrutiny by the Germans
for four years before the war; or by those who were to
appoint a devoted agent of Stalin's to be head of their
anti-Russian section. There was this much truth in the
charge all the same: SOE was mounted in a tremendous
hurry, and had no time to acquire a professional patina.
The modern Russian secret police like to have ten years
at least to train a spy.[6] SOE did well to have ten months
to train an agent and might not always get ten weeks. The
urgencies of wartime are easy to forget in an era of
nominal peace. Sometimes they condemned SOE to send
into action men and women whom it might have been
more sensible to train for longer or not to send at all.
When this was done it was because there was some
desperate need. SOE's staff were quite as aware as
anyone else, after 22 June 1941, that the great bulk of the
German armed forces was locked in combat with the

Russians, and that the only proper, decent line of conduct open to the British was to lighten the load on Russia as best they could. Hence many scrambled, perhaps amateurish, ploys.

Another objection urged against SOE was that its staff were too gentlemanly for the tasks they had to perform, too concerned with decent conduct to get on with skulduggery, too decorous and public-schoolish to organise strikes or to sympathise with the proletariat of Europe, and too imperialist to appeal to the peasantry of Asia. As far back as 8 May 1940, while Chamberlain was still prime minister, Commander Bower, the Tory back-bench MP for Cleveland, had spoken up during the Norway debate against the dangers of over-gentlemanly conduct:

> When you are fighting for your life against a ruthless opponent you cannot be governed by Queensberry rules. This Government would rather lose the war under Queensberry rules than do anything unbecoming to an absolutely perfect gentleman. That kind of thing will not do.[7]

SOE was quite sure that it would not do. Council never forgot the slogan Churchill launched early for SOE, that it was under its MEW cover to be 'the ministry of ungentlemanly warfare'.

The clearest sign that SOE's managers were not over-gentlemanly or inclined too far to conservatism lies in the extraordinarily wide social and political spread of the agents they found to work with them in the field. 'SOE was ready to work with any man or institution, Roman Catholic or masonic, Trotskyist or liberal, syndicalist or capitalist, rationalist or chauvinist, radical or conservative, stalinist or anarchist, gentile or Jew, that would help it beat the Nazis down.'[8] Who were these agents in occupied lands? Strictly speaking – and survivors all take care, on this point, to speak strictly – it is not correct to call them spies. The slip is only too often made, and can be found in authorities as austere as the *Dictionary of National Biography*;[9] here at least it can be avoided. They were secret agents: agents, through SOE, of the allied – rather than the British – high command, working (so far as they could see where they were going at all) to secure the grand end of allied strategy, that is, the complete overthrow of axis power.

The Germans' usual name for them was terrorist; and though not myself in SOE – I spent some months with one of its rivals, SAS – I may be allowed to slip in a fragment from my own past. Pursuing an apparent villain in the Sicherheitsdienst, I got close to him and was captured; to hear the phrase used at my interrogation, '*Das ist ganz einfach, wenn er Terrorist ist, ist er sofort erschossen*' ('That is quite simple, if he is a terrorist he is shot at once'). Mercifully for me, the villain was not my interrogator; I was able to go on pretending that I spoke no German and to turn the conversation with a white lie.

SOE's agents did not as a rule think of themselves as terrorists, though a few men and women of exuberant character and courage were capable of using terror as a weapon of clandestine war. Most of these came from a social stratum SOE neither neglected nor despised, indeed sometimes found most useful: the criminal class. SOE's forgery section would have got nowhere at all without help, secured through police and prison records, from some recently released professionals. As it was, it was able on one occasion to 'produce, between a Friday and a Monday morning, a virtually indistinguishable copy of a document part printed and part written, first manufacturing and water-marking the paper to do it on and cutting the type to do it with'; and on another, to provide several of its circuits in France with forged ration books of a new style, for issue on the same day as the Vichy government's official change.[10] Agents in many countries found that their London-forged identity documents excited not the least suspicion. This last was not, as it should have been, universally the case. A pair of agents, dining at separate tables at the same hotel in France and purporting hardly to know each other, were flummoxed when asked to explain by a Vichy policeman why their identity cards, made out in separate *départements*, were both written in the same handwriting.[11] London was not always quick to pick up local changes of rule about the kinds of papers that had to be carried, and Cairo's tiny forgery section seems to have been more concerned with keeping ahead of MI6's tiny rival branch than with the hard facts in which it ought to have dealt. SOE's lock-picking course, again, depended for its success on a retired burglar. Another burglar, still in full practice, did so well as an agent that he was awarded a well-earned DSO, for services not specified in the citation. (One wonders whether George VI, who decorated him, was told.) Another agent, quite as successful, owned a large chain of brothels.

These examples may be enough to show that SOE's leaders had taken in Bobby Bower's point about the Queensberry rules, and were not going to walk too delicately. Yet it would be absurd to think that more than a handful of agents or supporting staff were real criminals. Hamlet was quite right: 'Use every man after his desert, and who should scape whipping?'[12]

Political orthodoxy was no more required than social. SOE in Yugoslavia, Greece and Albania worked with tiny but efficient communist minorities; a few of SOE's agents in France got on well with the vigorous local communist resistance after Russia changed sides on 22 June 1941; in Italy, SOE and the PCI could work together once Mussolini had fallen; in Malaya, such effort as SOE could exert partly hinged on the Malayan Communist Party (MCP), which was bitterly anti-imperialist and consisted almost exclusively of Chinese. More of all this when politics are studied more closely (p. 207). Plainly, then, SOE, even under Selborne, was not merely a buttress for a vanishing empire.

How to recruit in the field – always primarily a matter of chance – was one of the things on which agents were advised in SOE's schools. But how were they themselves chosen?

Most of what is known of SOE's recruiting techniques comes from one of the most skilled craftsmen in this field, Selwyn Jepson, the author, who was able in old age to recall some of his triumphs and disasters of over forty years ago. As the recruiting officer for F, the independent French section, he conducted hundreds of interviews.

He would know something, probably not much, about each candidate before the interview began. He took care to see them, one at a time, in an absolutely bare, bleak room – usually in the Northumberland Hotel, a few yards behind the War Office, which had been requisitioned. Two folding chairs, a naked light bulb and a blackout screen composed all the furniture. He made a point of never keeping anyone waiting. Sometimes he wore civvies, sometimes plain army battledress, sometimes the service uniform of a major in the Buffs (which he was), now and again the uniform of a captain, RN – to which he was not entitled, but the Admiralty never knew. He did not as a rule give his name, not even a false one, and he kept his clean-shaven face as masklike as he could.

After a sentence or two in English, he would switch to French, in which he was perfectly at home; for he presumed everyone who was brought to him to have an unusually good command of the language (rather a rare attribute among the English). Naturally enough, he could inquire how his visitor came to speak French so well, and what parts of France he or she knew – and was known in – best. If the French proved so inadequate that there was no hope of passing, in France, as French, he would politely close the meeting. Otherwise he persevered.

Soon he would start to probe two points – motive and character. It was important to find out whether the candidate held normal views about the abominable nature of Nazism and the iniquity of axis occupation of France, or whether hatred of Nazism was abnormally, pathologically strong; or whether there was some strong but hidden personal motive behind the desire for a change of work – an impossible mother, perhaps, or an unsatisfactory private life, or mere recklessness. Jepson had lived enough in the worlds of the theatre and cinema to have become knowledgeable about how people behave.

Once he had cleared up the problem of motive, there was one character trait in particular that he found he had to watch out for, and avoid: impulsiveness. Prudence, after courage, was probably an agent's most useful quality. Brisk, decisive types, inclined to make up their minds promptly, were all very well in fast traffic or a destroyer action, but were not what was needed in the secret war. There, the need was for reflective men and women, people who could look several moves ahead. Cautious inquiry by Jepson gave him an idea which sort of person he had before him.

If the candidate looked promising to him, he would probably wind up the interview after forty or fifty minutes, and arrange another meeting in a few days' time. During these few days he would run a check with MI5, to make sure there was no reason to doubt the prospective agent's loyalty. In the second interview, he would be more explicit about what he had in mind. First he would hint, and then directly state, that it might be possible for his visitor to get closer to the enemy than work as an interpreter would involve – actually to be sent to France to work in some subversive capacity. At this point he would try to get the candidate to go away and sleep on the idea. 'I'd like to think about this,' he would say, 'we'd both like to think about it. I don't want you to make up your mind too easily; it's a difficult decision to make; it's a life-and-death decision for both of us. I have to decide whether I can risk your life and you have to decide whether you're willing to risk it.' Even if the visitor now pressed to be taken on, Jepson normally insisted on more time to think. At this point he had to put on his sternest face, and remind his hearer that their interview had been secret: this was something that it was quite out of the question to discuss with anyone else, even with a wife or child, a parent or husband. Every prospective agent had to make up his or her mind, alone, to volunteer – or not.

Before dismissing his visitor, Jepson made no secret about the risks. He made it clear that the chances of survival, once sent to France, were thought to be about evens. In fact it was discovered after the war that of some 470 agents F section sent into the field, 118 failed to return: one vanished, all the rest were killed. So the chances of death had been one in four, not one in two. This was quite bad enough, but not unendurable by the normal standards of world war. The British engineer brigade that went ashore at the bottom of the tide at first light on Normandy D-Day to remove mines from the beach obstacles (to make it safe for landing craft to follow them in) lost three in four, killed and wounded (seventy-five per cent casualties), on that single morning of 6 June 1944. Bomber Command of the RAF expected thirty missions by its aircrew to complete a tour of duty; its average rate of loss per operation was four per cent – that is, after twenty-five missions a crew could, statistically, expect to be dead. Some crews nevertheless survived two tours of thirty missions; a few survived three. Everybody in SOE remembered what the fathers of my own generation never let any of us forget, that the expectation of life of a British infantry subaltern on the western front in France in 1917 had been three weeks.

At the third meeting with Jepson, the visitor – who had by now become a prospective agent – would finally decide to take the plunge, or finally withdraw. Hardly anyone was offered another bite at this cherry.

Jepson took a great deal of trouble over these interviews, weighed up agents' characters with care, and probed as deeply as he could into their capacities for various clandestine tasks. This enabled him to give to the section some idea of what the agent might be called on to do, if later probings during training bore out his initial judgement. That judgement was indeed initial, but he found that he hardly ever had to alter the impression he had formed within the first few minutes of meeting each of his visitors, whether this one was likely to do well or do badly, to be no good at all or to be outstanding. Other good judges of personality have felt much the same.[13]

From June 1943 SOE adopted a new recruiting system based on War Office and Air Ministry experience in acquiring officers well after the first rush of volunteers had passed, and had absorbed most of the best people. The process of initial interview tête-à-tête was scrapped. Instead, candidates went before a students' assessment board composed largely of psychologists, with whom they stayed for several days while their characters and capacities were thoroughly probed. By this time plenty of data had been accumulated, which could be laid before the board's members, about the sort of work that SOE was capable (or incapable) of doing and the qualities that a successful agent was going to need. After the board, candidates were either sent on to paramilitary training or politely returned to the places whence they had come. This was a more scientific and perhaps a safer system, but it was a less individual one; and there was less chance in it for men of eccentricity and panache to find their way into a body original enough to get the best out of them.

Both private interviewers, such as Jepson, and the official board were prepared to treat women on a perfect equality with men. This was usual in SOE. The organisation was far in advance of the recent fashion; for clandestine purposes, there were several tasks that women would perform a good deal better than men. F section sent thirty-nine to France, thirteen of whom did not return.[14] The statistical sample is too narrow for any broad conclusion to be drawn from it about whether women were more exposed to danger than men. By no means all of F section's women agents had that ordinary, unassuming air which is so precious an asset for a clandestine; several had the stunning good looks and vibrant personality that turn men's heads in the street. This helped to make them noticed; it was counterbalanced, in the section's view, by making it more easy for them to appear to belong to that leisured class, the comings and goings of which only the surliest policeman is ever going to disturb. It was a mistake to forget how surly some of Hitler's or even Pétain's policemen could be.

Some of these young women did indeed come from the leisured class of prewar England. They belonged to one of the least known of the women's services, a somewhat socially exclusive one, the First Aid Nursing Yeomanry (FANY) or Women's Transport Corps. Gubbins happened to know their commandant ('not what you know, but whom you know' is after all Society's motto); and from this happy accident SOE derived a great deal of benefit, so much so that over half of FANY's total strength was devoted to its work. It did some useful work chauffeuring generals for the army, quite outside the secret world, and a great deal more for SOE.[15] One of the most awkward spells for agents in SOE might be the days – weeks – months spent waiting, after training was over, for the right moment to arrive to move into action. The move might be held up by a thousand accidents of politics, weather or war. The wait was usually spent in a holding station, a secluded country house staffed and run by FANYs, who made the stay there as delectable as they could.

A large number of FANYs, girls in their late teens

when recruited, with quick brains and quiet tongues, performed an essential service for SOE. They manned the base wireless stations on which most SOE working circuits depended, at first in England and Egypt, later in Algiers and Bari, later still in Calcutta, Colombo and Kunming (see p. 169). Some operated the actual sets, some coped with coding and decoding: tricky, finicky, pernickety work that called for the taking of infinite pains, work on which many lives depended; unglamorous, undecorated work without which everyone else's efforts in SOE would have been in vain.

The FANYs relaxed their social standards enough to let in the fiery Violette Szabo, *née* Bushell ('Louise'), the half-French daughter of a Brixton motor-car dealer, who was reputed to be the best shot in SOE and was certainly among its outstanding characters, as her posthumous GC testifies. She was one of the few FANYs who were allowed to move out of housekeeping, transporting, clerical or signals tasks into actual warfare. Most of her companions who did likewise were, as she was, commissioned as junior officers before they left, if not in FANY then in the Women's Auxiliary Air Force (WAAF). Similarly, five of the eleven Frenchwomen sent in by air by RF section belonged to the Corps Auxiliaire Féminin. (One of them, the nineteen-year-old Josiane Gros, arrived by parachute to find her own mother – who had gone in two months earlier by light aircraft – in charge of receiving her.) This was done to give them a better chance, if captured, of passing themselves off as prisoners of war. There was a lot of debate in Baker Street about whether it was legal to use women on warlike operations at all. Gubbins led, with success, the party that contended that against the Nazis no holds ought to be barred. A final appeal had to be made to Churchill, with whom Jepson happened to have been in touch years before over some articles in a journal. This connection smoothed the way to success.

Most of these women worked in the field as couriers –

that is, as messengers and liaison officers; some, as wireless operators. Some of them provided invaluable support for their organisers (more than one of whom married his courier); all of them were courageous. One of them, after a year's arduous courier work, became an organiser herself, and ended up with a private army over 2000 strong under her command. This was the incomparable Pearl Witherington, later Madame Cornioley. She was codenamed 'Marie'. So, earlier, was Virginia Hall of the Baltimore *Sun* (later Mrs Guillot), who worked under her own real identity – in spite of the handicap of an artificial foot – in Lyons. She was in charge of a big liaison network till she got out over the Pyrenees late in 1942 just in front of the Gestapo.* She had herself taught morse privately, and then persuaded F section to send her back to France in 1944 by motor boat to Brittany, to run a small combatant network round Nevers.

What was an American doing in SOE? MI5 and MI6 had a rule – had always had a rule – that their members must have been born subjects of the Crown, and they only broke it when they had to. SOE was expected to conform to this rule, though it repeatedly found it had to break it. Some of the very best of its staff and agents had dual nationality – Anglo-French, Anglo-Polish, and so on. Many volunteers came from foreign, even from enemy countries: these SOE was happy to take on, once it was sure they were reliable. They included several Americans, several score Spaniards, Germans and Austrians, and several hundred Italians and Frenchmen. Their social range reached from a head of state – the regent of Siam – through an Indian princess (born in the Kremlin), several exiled Russian grandees, a prince and a duke of Napoleonic creation and some still more splendid French and

---

* One anecdote from that journey bears repeating. Before it began, she signalled to London that she hoped Cuthbert would not be troublesome. London replied, 'If Cuthbert troublesome eliminate him'; having forgotten that Cuthbert was the codename for her brass foot.

Belgian families, through the whole range of the upper and lower European and east Asiatic bourgeoisie, to railwaymen, telephonists, clerks, labourers, peasants, prostitutes and coolies.

Exactly who did and who did not belong to SOE are questions so intricate and difficult that no attempt will be made to answer them here. One French example may illustrate the complexities. The three de Vomécourt brothers, Lorrainer barons who had been at school in England, played a leading part in getting F section set up at all. Pierre de Vomécourt led the first, widespread F circuit, 'Autogiro', and spent the second half of the war at Colditz. His brother Philippe led 'Ventriloquist' with enormous éclat; both clearly belonged to SOE. Did also their elder brother Jean, who had a close understanding with them, had done a great deal of sabotage, but never came to England – as they did – during the war, and was murdered in Sachsenhausen within sound of the Russian guns?[16]

Similarly, the exact size of SOE has never been revealed; probably it has never been worked out. It seems to have reached its greatest strength in the summer of 1944, and then to have contained just under 10,000 men and about 3200 women.[17] Some 5000 of this total – nearly all of them men – were agents, either on operations already or waiting to go. The rest were staff – for planning, intelligence, operations, supply, research, security, signals, transport and administration. The tooth-tail ratio was high. Some of the staff had earlier been agents; and some, in the closing stages of a campaign, pressed forward on to the edge of occupied territory in little expeditions that were – were sometimes meant to be – almost as much holiday as warfare.

There was nothing holiday-like about the start of any normal SOE mission, but the horrors of life in axis-held lands could be overdone. In Europe, SOE's money often gave access to the comforts of the black market. Remote

Burmese villages could go on living, just inside the margin of subsistence, as they had done for centuries, with no more likelihood of seeing a Japanese than an Englishman. So could remote French ones, out of the Germans' way; Harry Rée, once he had settled in northern Franche-Comté, felt that he was surrounded by friends and back on holiday again, save when work took him into towns and danger.[18]

The characteristic that SOE's agents had in common, besides their courage, was that they were liable to be drawn from any class at all in the community in which they lived. The best of them were like the strong, silent men of romantic fiction: calm, clear-headed men and women, who knew that Nazism was abominable, and were ready to use disreputable methods – if clean ones would not do – to make sure that it was crushed. They dislike having what they did 'twisted by knaves to make a trap for fools'; but seldom say anything about it.

SOE's training system can be compared to a set of sieves, each one with a closer mesh than the one before. Recruiting and training intermeshed; one of the objects of the training system was to sieve out the unsuitables before they could wreak havoc abroad.

Those thought likely to become agents were sent first of all to a two- or three-week course in a country house. Old-style country-house living became all but impossible during the first eighteen months of the war, when the servants on whom it then depended – there were over a million domestic servants in England in 1939 – either volunteered, or were called up, or were directed into more warlike work. It was therefore a positive advantage to the owners of great houses to put their furniture into store, move into a smaller house or an hotel, and have a government department take over roof repairs and look out for dry rot. Many had no idea then, some never discovered, exactly for what purpose their house had been requisitioned.

The initial course was in physical fitness, with plenty of cross-country runs and other exercise, elementary map reading, and some training with pistols and sub-machine-guns. Word was let seep out to the villages that this was some sort of commando training; they were left to wonder for themselves why women might be taking part in it. There was always a well-stocked bar; it was important to find out early how soberly would-be agents could behave after a few – or a great many – drinks. There are several accounts in print of the best-known of these schools, run by F section at Wanborough Manor, south-west of Guildford. Roger de Wesselow, its commandant, retained his Coldstream Guards' panache, and showed how warmly he agreed with Gubbins's homily about leading from in front by never failing to take part – aged over sixty – in the early morning run along the Hog's Back (see pp. 11).[19] Wanborough Manor was only one among a dozen such schools in England, each kept up for a different national group.

Those who passed out from this starting stage – by no means all did – then went to Scotland for a much more intensive three or four weeks of frankly paramilitary training. Gubbins found the site, not far from his own Hebridean home. SOE took over a group of big houses in beautiful, deserted country in Arisaig, on the western coast of Inverness-shire. The Admiralty was persuaded to declare the whole neighbourhood a prohibited area; this screened off from inquisitive tourists what the Arisaig schools were up to. Peter Kemp found that 'the shores of Lochailort and the Sound of Arisaig reveal a wild, bleak beauty of scoured grey rock and cold blue water, of light green bracken and shadowed pine, that is strangely moving in its stark simplicity and grandeur'.[20] But he was there in the summer on an MI R course, before ever SOE was founded. Like so much else in these islands the character of the neighbourhood changed with the weather. Pieter Dourlein, a Dutch agent, was there some sixteen months after Kemp, and found 'a wretched barren countryside, thinly populated; rain fell from a heavy sky that never cleared completely . . . a most depressing place'.[21]

Small arms training here included German and Italian as well as British and American pistols, rifles, machine-guns and sub-machine-guns. The Anglo-Czech Bren light machine-gun was not hard to master – Kemp, with a guardsman to instruct him, learned all about it in a couple of hours in Birdcage Walk, and found it much less elaborate than the Hotchkiss and Fiat weapons he had used in Spain.[22] In Arisaig students learned about all three, and the British Vickers, and the MG 34 and 42 (the Spandau) and Schmeisser MG 38, the standard German light and sub-machine-guns, and the tommy-gun. The Sten (see pp. 98–101) was also much in evidence, as it was likely to be supplied in bulk to the SOE. Rifles, British and foreign, and the American carbine were not left out either. Students were expected to know how to strip, reassemble, load, fire and maintain all the weapons they handled. Stripping and loading had to be practised in total darkness as well as by day; and firing both in the calm of a small range and, more practically, shooting at snap targets at the end of an obstacle course.

SOE had the good fortune to get hold of two officers from the Shanghai police, Sykes and Fairbairn, who taught in Arisaig. They dropped the old-fashioned, upright duellists' stance for pistol shooting – the right arm first bent up, then levelled at the target – in favour of a knees-bent stance and a two-handed grip on the pistol, which is aimed by instinct from waist level instead of by eye along its barrel. The new style is now familiar in several armies: SOE introduced it. They taught their pupils to fire two shots quickly at each target, not to rely on one – what, again, several armies now call 'double tap'. They taught them also how to be quick on the draw, whether from a hip or a shoulder holster, a pocket or a handbag.

One of them, Fairbairn, invented also a still more important contribution: the art of silent killing, the extreme version of what less secret bodies called unarmed combat. Fairbairn's methods were conflated from ju-jitsu, karate and what he had learned in hard practice on the Shanghai waterfront. The marvellous impact they had on agents can be judged from the report by George Langelaan of F section. Fairbairn, he said (without naming him),

> gave us more and more self-confidence which gradually grew into a sense of physical power and superiority that few men ever acquire. By the time we finished our training, I would have willingly enough tackled any man, whatever his strength, size or ability. He taught us to face the possibility of a fight without the slightest tremor of apprehension, a state of mind which very few professional boxers ever enjoy and which so often means more than half the battle. Strange as this may seem, it is understandable when a man knows for certain that he can hurt, maul, injure, or even kill with the greatest of ease, and that during every split second of a fight he has not one but a dozen different openings, different possibilities, to choose from. One fear has, since then, however, haunted me: that of getting entangled in a sudden row and of seriously injuring, or even killing, another man before even realising what is happening.[23]

One contrary opinion needs to be put in: Bernard Fergusson forbade the teaching of silent killing methods to his Chindit column, on the ground that, so far, 'we've only fought decently in the British Army'.[24] Though the Chindits had, in Wingate, an ex-SOE commander (he had

1. Where it all began

2. 64 Baker Street today, second to sixth floors. The ground floor is a car showroom

3. *Above* 1 Dorset Square.   4. *Below Evening Standard*, 2 August 1939

5. Winston Churchill with tommy-gun, August 1940.   6. *Right* Millis Jefferis

7. Lawrence Grand   8. Jo Holland

9. L to R: Dalton, Ingr(?), Gubbins, Jebb

10. Duff Cooper, July 1941

11. Eden and de Gaulle, November 1941

12. Lord Selborne as MEW

13. Sir Charles Hambro

14. C

15. Churchill and Macmillan, 1943

16. CD

17. External resistance: de Gaulle talks to his men

18. External resistance: Wilhelmina talks to her people

helped reconquer Abyssinia), they rightly fell outside
SOE's control.

Langelaan, who had worked for the *New York Times*,
was, like Virginia Hall, one of the Americans who had
joined the British war effort before his country came into
the war. A great many more Americans were taught by
Fairbairn, for he went across from Arisaig to SOE's
training school in Canada on the shores of Lake Ontario
near Oshawa, not far east of Toronto. This school – where
the syllabus was similar to Arisaig's – was popular with
Americans in the Office of Strategic Services, SOE's (and
MI6's) American opposite number; not least because
attendance there brought a medal for service outside the
United States, of which the frontier was almost twenty
miles away as the gull flies.

Fairbairn was such a success with the Americans that
he was borrowed by OSS for much of the second half of
the war.[25] The spirit he left behind him and Sykes
continued to represent in Arisaig was passed on to everyone else who passed through there. All those who moved
on from Arisaig into SOE did so with plenty of trust in
their own capacities.

Both at the preliminary country-house course, and in
Arisaig, students were accompanied by conducting officers from their own country section, who could speak
their language, tried to make friends with them, and had
ears wide open to listen to their problems. The ideal
conducting officer was a returned agent: not, of course,
the sort of person who could at first be found at all,
though F section had another of its habitual strokes of
luck when it engaged Bernard Hanauer who had been an
inmate of Dachau concentration camp, and had had the
good fortune to be let out before the war ever began. The
commandant of each school consulted the conducting
officer, as well as the instructors, before he reported on
each candidate's merits. Country sections were by no
means bound to accept the training section's assessments,

and the schools did now and again make mistakes: they failed, for instance, to spot the gift for leadership of Francis Cammaerts ('Roger'), who was destined to inspire thousands of resisters in south-eastern France, and recommended against the acceptance of some other later famous agents. Yet by and large they did well, as well as time allowed.

Just as it was up to the staff to say that they thought prospective agents unpromising, it was up to the students to make it clear if their hearts began to fail them. Nobody needed to be accused of being a coward through deciding, on reflection, that an undercover life was not for him or her.

Only gradually did it dawn on most of the students quite what was in the wind. On her second day in Arisaig – having passed four weeks already on a country-house course – one girl asked another, 'What *are* we being trained for? I answered an advertisement for a bilingual secretary.'[26] The Arisaig group of schools – called Group A – was pretty explicit: the syllabus went on from small arms and silent killing training to practice in demolitions using live explosive, and in railway sabotage, for the London, Midland and Scottish railway was persuaded to part with some spare track, engines and rolling stock. There was also a lot of intensive map reading and cross-country work, foreshadowing the current SAS tenacity tests, and some basic infantry tactical training – how to combine fire and movement, how to lay a simple ambush, how to storm a house. The more energetic and high-spirited of the students on the Scottish courses found time also to experiment in salmon-poaching with grenades or plastic explosive, or to try raiding each others' messes for drink – which was not quite so plentiful here as it had been in the south.

Others might find the pace too hot for them. Sometimes as many as a third of the students on an Arisaig course might be told at the end of it, gently but finally, that they had not the stamina – or were otherwise unqualified – for the task that had been foreseen for them, and had better go away. They might have to spend some time in the cooler at Inverlair before they returned to more ordinary wartime life.

Those who had stayed the course then moved on to Group B, a set of schools – again in country houses – round Beaulieu in the New Forest. The teaching staff lived in Beaulieu Manor (now famous as the site of the Montagu motor museum), beside what was left of the abbey; students were parcelled out, by country sections, in neighbouring great houses, which the staff went out to visit. Here all the pretence of commando training was dropped (except for what the villagers were told). The aim was made clear: students were being got ready to go into occupied territory to raise hell for the enemy.

Part of the Group B teaching was defensive. It explained what the axis police services were, how they worked, and how they meshed in with whatever particular police system interested the country section involved. Only in Poland was there no trace at all of co-operation between some sort of indigenous authority and the German occupier (a fact of which the Poles remain justly proud). In other occupied countries there was some sort of quisling regime – named after the Norwegian Nazi who was too extreme even for the Nazis. In every such regime the minister of the interior worked as closely as he could with the occupying police; the minister of the interior at Vichy had no fewer than fifteen separate police forces to help him to do so, all armed, and some of them dangerous. The milice were always hostile, but some ordinary gendarmes went out of their way to be helpful, and many were prepared to look the other way when allied agents passed by. This meant a lot of extra work for possible agents, who had to mug up titles and uniforms.

They were also, with help from Scotland Yard and MI5, given advice on how to deal with the snap police controls that are a regular feature of tyrannies. Returned agents were often used at this point to describe, in as matter-of-fact a way as they could, what it was like to have one's papers gone through. One needed to be brisk, polite and dull; above all, to take care not to volunteer a syllable more about oneself than was strictly necessary. Agents could come unstuck on painfully simple points. If asked, for instance, why they had not drawn their tobacco ration for the past fortnight, they might get away with answering pat that they had been laid low with influenza, but if they havered or looked flustered they would be in for trouble.

Without warning, students would be woken up in the middle of the night, and marched off for interrogation by men in Gestapo or Abwehr uniform. Sooner or later – usually sooner – they recognised these men as members of the Beaulieu staff, and some then tried to laugh the whole occasion off. It was in fact worth taking seriously. Not all the resources of a vicious police were employed – there was no physical torture at all; but practice in being cross-questioned turned out by no means useless to several Beaulieu students, who could be grateful to these first interrogators for giving them enough sang-froid to survive actual contact with an axis policeman with a cover story still intact. For example, one remembered vividly months later Beaulieu's warning that the Germans would be likely to alternate polite and brutal handling. He was stopped in the hills behind Marseilles by a snap road control, about July 1944. His forged papers, proving him to be a forester, were passed at a glance on inspection in a nearby barn. As he was leaving, a stentorian bellow summoned him back, and a sergeant-major tore his identity card from his hand – held it in front of a corporal with a cry (in German), '*That's* what an identity card is, you bloody fool' – and handed it back. The agent found that his worst problem was to make himself stroll away, as if unconcerned; the impulse to break into a run was all but fatal.

His problem brings out Beaulieu's main task, and major

difficulty: agents had to be taught how to play a part, how to act their cover. To be one person in reality, and quite another in appearance – to *live* one's cover – was unusually hard, but vitally important: survival hinged on it. There was a great deal more to this than knowing what to do with one's fork after finishing a plate of food; though minute points of behaviour such as this all had to be taken on board also, as they had been taught to Kim by Lurgan Sahib.[27] It was a matter of becoming a new character, and knowing in advance how – in one's new character – one was going to behave in particular social settings. The overwhelming object was to do nothing that was going to draw attention to oneself. The talkative had to learn to be quiet; even the quiet had to be reminded to phrase their every sentence so that they would never offer a stranger more than he (or she) needed to know, in reply to any inquiry, however apparently random.

The cockiness that a lot of students had taken away from Arisaig was thus overlaid at Beaulieu with a thicker layer of diffidence, of readiness not to push themselves forward, that has made quite a lot of former SOE agents appear rather indifferent company in peacetime; it helped to make them formidable in war.

Two of the Group B instructors were notably good at their work. One of them, the poet Paul Dehn, came from the film industry, and combined a vivid imagination with a rollicking sense of humour. He spent most of the war there, and was warmly remembered. The other was only there in 1941; the staff understood that he was marking time, waiting for an appointment for him to fall vacant in SIS; as was indeed the case. Yvon Morandat, a young Christian trade unionist who carried out several important missions for de Gaulle in France, remembered that this man had given him an extra vivid impression, in the autumn of 1941, of what it was going to be like to live in enemy-occupied territory while retaining allegiance else-where. His name was Kim Philby.

One other defensive point needed to be covered before agents left for the field; if it could not be handled at Group B, it could be inquired into while they were staying in safe flats in the west end of London, in the intervals between technical training courses. Did they talk in their sleep, and if so in what language? There was a devastating blonde codenamed 'Fifi' who made it her business to find out, until 1943, when SOE was able to borrow a trick from Crockatt's MI19 and had the bedrooms in the Beaulieu houses wired for sound. After that, 'Fifi' was only called in if a student was bright enough to find and silence the microphone.

Once the defensive part of the Beaulieu training had been absorbed, students could be taken back to one of the leitmotifs of Arisaig training: aggression. 'Incessantly during these courses agents had it dinned into them that their task was aggressive, that they must make aggression part of their characters, eat with it, sleep with it, live with it, absorb it into themselves entirely.'[28] They did not have to engage in the 'hate sessions' forecast by Orwell in *Nineteen Eighty-Four* and encountered in cold fact by Leonhard in training for the Russian secret police;[29] but they learned to hate tyranny most thoroughly.

They also had some routine intelligence training on axis forces' order of battle, in message writing, in the basic elements of how to compile and condense reports, and in elementary coding – nothing more elaborate at this stage than Playfair. Advice was given on how to think about recruiting in occupied territory; and in some cases, in conjunction with PWE, agents were given courses in propaganda methods. Such news as there was about the state of whatever country the agents might be going to was shared by the staff. It is important to remember that extremely little was known, as a rule, in England at the time. The English Channel was not only wide enough to deter the Wehrmacht from invasion; remarkably little real news crossed it either.

Some training was also given at Beaulieu in the elements of what initiates call tradecraft: how to drop a prearranged password into a desultory chat in a bar; how to hand over a written note unobtrusively in public; how to spot if one was being followed in the street; and how to shed a follower (make sure there is no taxi in sight, then jump on a bus or tram as it moves off, or enter a metro carriage and then leave it as its doors begin to close).

This culminated, as a sort of passing-out test, in an exercise that lasted several days. Students were sent off in small groups of two or three, with a set task, such as stealing a machine-gun from a barracks, or placing explosives on the points at a busy railway junction, or stealing a chief constable's car. On the way, they had to collect a previously unknown companion at a set rendezvous. They were warned that the local police, wherever they were going, had been alerted, and had been given rough descriptions of them. This provided plenty of scope for the energetic and ingenious, and brought even the idlest face to face with some practical problems of tactics and disguise. SOE's pocket was deep enough to cover the expense. In case they were arrested, students were provided with a cover story. As a last resort, if their cover story broke down, they were given a telephone number to remember, to which appeal could be made: touch with this would reveal to the police that they were handling some sort of unspecified secret training (to which the previous warning would have referred). SOE's arm was long enough to make sure that none of them were actually prosecuted; anything they stole was returned intact; and the explosives they laid were provided with dummy detonators.

More technical courses might be needed after agents had passed out from Beaulieu. Parachuting was taught at STS 33 from a merchant's house at Altrincham near Manchester, with drops into the grounds of Tatton Park from Whitley aircraft stationed at Ringway, now Manchester's civil airport. Those who needed it took a course in clandestine printing; or in lock- and safe-breaking; or in clandestine wireless techniques. The wireless school was at Thame Park, east of Oxford, and wireless operators were given a thorough grounding there, both in theory and in practice; advanced coding and ciphering techniques were taught here too. In retrospect SOE thought it a pity that all its organisers had not been put through Thame Park, as the shortage of trained operators was one of the biggest brakes on its expansion; in the early stages, many organising types refused to go in for the extreme attention to detail that Thame Park involved.

There were also two important stations in Hertfordshire, IX for research and XVII for training, which dealt with sabotage techniques. XVII at Brickendonbury Manor, between Hertford and Hoddesdon, was run by George Rheam, a large man with a large mind, the inventor of many industrial sabotage techniques and an instructor of genius. He had that rare combination, accurate hands and a highly imaginative brain. Those who did exactly what he told them never had cause to regret it. Brigitte Bardot's film *Babette Goes to War* took him off as a figure of fun; the Germans thought him anything but funny.

He was a tall man with steady grey eyes; his pupils tended to think him dour. He was not much given to suffering fools gladly, and knew rather better than most of them the rigidities of the systems they were trying to conquer. His friends knew that behind his stiffish manner lay a keen sense of humour, as well as intense sympathy for the exiles from the European continent with whom he often worked. Of these, he once said in retrospect, he thought on the whole the Norwegians impressed him the most, for bravery, for readiness to run risks, and for steadiness in facing the dangers of sabotage. He was an exacting teacher, with the gift to foresee the sorts of problem his pupils were likely to encounter on the ground, and has been called 'the founder of modern industrial sabotage'.[30] Anyone trained by him could look at a factory with quite new eyes, spot the few essential machines in it, and understand how to stop them with a few well-placed ounces of explosive; to stop them, moreover, in such a way that some of them could not be restarted promptly by removing undamaged parts from comparable machines nearby.

Rheam's methods were taught not only by him and his staff at Brickendonbury, but by pupils of his at the school on Lake Ontario, and in various other SOE schools abroad. Munn stayed long enough at Algiers to make sure that 'Massingham', SOE's base just west of it, had an adequate sabotage school that taught Rheam's doctrines, as well as a parachute school run by the admirable Wooler. Gubbins had brought Wooler into SOE from the independent companies – before the war he sold motor cars in Canada – and he had been chief instructor at Altrincham for eighteen months, varying the monotony of teaching and testing by going on sorties over Europe to dispatch his former pupils. There were facilities outside Algiers also for duplicating Beaulieu's work on a small scale, as there were in Italy (from 1944) and (from 1941) in Egypt, where there was a parachute school at Kabrit, north of Suez. Rheam's lessons were not forgotten in Palestine either, where SOE's links with the Jewish Agency produced some recruits of real distinction on Mount Carmel, and parachuting was taught near Nazareth. Near Singapore the Oriental Mission would have set up several schools had it had time and local backing; Mackenzie took responsibility for several in India and Ceylon; there were others round Brisbane.

The equipment of an SOE school was not quite like that of the ordinary town or village school; just as the life of an SOE agent was not quite the same as life as it is usually lived.

V

Devices and methods

Most of the special equipment designed for SOE has long ceased to be secret, but not all the aura of secrecy in which it was born has yet quite been dispersed. The feeling prevalent in many newspaper and television offices – on the free side of the Iron and Bamboo Curtains – that no secret can be worth keeping forty minutes, let alone forty years, is unsound. There are sometimes good reasons for reticence. For an obvious example, would it raise or lower the quality of British life if the lecturers' notes from SOE's lock-breaking school were published? Most but not all of the beans have already been spilled; it would be foolish to inquire what has been left out. The first verses of Psalm 39 – prefaced by Bickham Sweet-Escott to his long-delayed survey of his life in SOE, *Baker Street Irregular* – are in point.*

There were two focal points round which the invention of devices for SOE clustered. One derived from MI R, the other from section D. Jefferis' subsection, MI Rc, took over 35 Portland Place – a few doors from the BBC's main building – in the spring of 1940. Churchill described

---

* I said, I will take heed to my ways that I offend not with my tongue: I will keep my mouth as it were with a bridle, while the ungodly is in my sight.

him on 24 August as 'a singularly capable and forceful man' and gave him his full backing.[1] When bombed out of Portland Place in the early autumn, the section cast up – accompanied by the head barman from the Langham – at The Firs, Whitchurch, a large stockbroker's Tudor mansion a few miles north of Aylesbury. There Jefferis spent most of the war, making inventions at an average rate of about one a week, trying them out in the adjoining paddocks and ponds, and passing on those that worked properly either to SOE or to the rest of the armed forces. His deputy, R. S. Macrae, an engineering journalist turned soldier, did his best to provide a steady administrative keel for the sprightly craft of Jefferis' mind. They had another political patron of real weight, Professor Lindemann (later Lord Cherwell), the Prime Minister's constant companion. It was Cherwell who preserved them from being swallowed up by the ever-gaping maw of the ordnance board inspectorate, whose members believed that no work on explosives ought to be done except under their wing and in accordance with their rigid safety rules. Cherwell protected them also against empire-builders in SOE, who would have acquired The Firs readily enough. Eventually the station acquired the title of MD 1, and the appearance of a section within the wartime – otherwise all but notional – Ministry of Defence: technically outside SOE, yet constantly consulting and co-operating with it, and deriving directly from Holland's original impulse.[2] One of Macrae's deputies, 'Nobby' Clarke, alternated between The Firs and Rheam's Station XVII in Hertfordshire, thus maintaining a lasting link.

The other focus was still more secret, and awaits reliable treatment in print: Station IX at The Frythe, Welwyn Garden City. Before the war, The Frythe had been a small private hotel. Section D, warier than MI R, had requisitioned it at the start of the war, and used it as a headquarters for the winter of 1939–40; some subsections of D were still there when SOE was set up. From

August 1940 The Frythe was used for wireless research; after D. M. Newitt was made SOE's director of scientific research on 9 June 1941, he also moved to Station IX the research laboratory at Station XII, which dealt in weaponry. Newitt, who had got his first job at the age of sixteen in a Nobel explosives factory in Scotland, was among other things a chemical engineer of standing: he was made a fellow of the Royal Society in 1942.[3] He turned Station XII over purely to production. This was located at Aston House, near Stevenage.

Station XII derived from a small experimental devices section with the clumsy official title of Signals Development Branch Depot No. 4, War Department, which Grand had set up at the end of 1938. By the end of September 1939 this unit was at Bletchley and known as Station X; two months later it was crowded out by the decipherers, moved to Aston House, and renumbered as Station XII. Eventually, in May 1941, it acquired an official war establishment and a new cover name – Experimental Station 6 (War Department), or ES6 (WD). Soon thereafter Newitt took its development side away from it; it remained important to SOE, because of the weapons and equipment it produced from Station IX's designs.

At Welwyn, as at The Firs, there was a steady run of invention and testing but Welwyn went in even more for devious devices. There was rivalry, obviously enough, between the two bodies of designers; there was a good deal of friendly interchange of ideas as well. Station IX, for example, persevered in designs for a time-operated detonator that could be embedded in a primer, which in turn was set into an explosive charge. This was an obvious need for a saboteur, who would prefer to have his bomb go up after he had left the factory where he had planted it rather than have it explode in his presence. This detonator, called a time pencil, was indeed pencil-thin, just over six inches long. The user chose the time delay desired, which could vary from ten minutes to a month (a colour code showed which was which); and had to remember, at the critical moment, to press a ridge on the pencil. This was surprisingly easy to forget; unless it was done, nothing would happen at all, and the enemy police would find the unexploded bomb the next day. Pressing the ridge released acid, which ate through a piece of wire of set thickness; the wire held a spring back from a detonator. When the spring was finally released, the detonator exploded and up went the bomb.

The device, pioneered by the Germans in 1915–16[4] and improved by the Poles, was perfected at Station IX. Over twelve million time pencils were produced during the war.[5] The Firs preferred what the army came to know as the L delay, an object of the same shape fused by the pulling out of a safety clip on which the time for which it was to work was written (in English). The L delay, acid-free, worked not on a chemical but on a mechanical principle: the fact that lead stretches. A delicate calculation worked out, for each batch of lead used, precisely how much it would stretch till it broke, and, again, released a spring-loaded pin to set off a detonator and so a bomb.

Both kinds of time fuse depended on temperature; the colder the weather, the longer they took to work. L delays were set to perform at 65°F (18°C), and saboteurs were provided with conversion tables to show how much tropical heat would advance, or arctic cold delay their action. At freezing point the pencil fuse took double its marked time to work. At The Firs they claimed that in extreme cold their rivals' fuses would not work at all, while theirs would.

No evidence for this has been produced, unless cold was the reason for fuse failure when an attempt in March 1943 by some of Hitler's entourage to kill him – using SOE's material, but without benefit of SOE's advice – failed to work. The would-be assassin, von Tresckow, used a home-made bomb composed of two of SOE's portable clams (see pp. 109–10) stuck together by their own magnets, fused with a half-hour time pencil, and disguised as a bottle of Cointreau slipped into Hitler's aircraft as a present for one of his staff. It took some nerve to recover the package ('Sorry, old boy, there's been a bit of a mix-up') and to unravel the faulty fuse.[6]

Now SOE – had von Tresckow but known – had a tool designed to do this particular job: a sixteen-inch rubber tube, flexible because it was filled with plastic explosive, armed at one end with a barometric fuse. It could be slipped unobtrusively under a pilot's seat, after turning a little screw on the end of the fuse, half a turn to make it go off at 5000 or a full turn for 10,000 feet. The natural fall in air pressure would do the rest, once the aircraft had taken off. The only catch in this system was that nobody ever seems to have had an opportunity of using it. Or if they did, the fact has remained unreported, unless by Ronald Seth.[7]

Some of these devices had a touch of Heath Robinson about them; others were plain and effective. Fairbairn, the silent killing instructor, invented one of the plainest and most deadly: the fighting or commando knife, with a double-edged steel blade, honed razor-sharp. Results were often messy.

A miniature version of it – only three inches (76mm) long – was available in a thin leather sheath. This could be sewn on the reverse of a coat lapel, and provided a last-ditch chance of getting out of a scrape. If suddenly summoned to produce one's papers, one could reach for the breast pocket – and riposte with a slash to the jugular. Results, again, were likely to be messy. Like so many of these ingenious, almost toylike, agents' tools, this was something for which a theoretical case could easily be made out; but was anyone ever vicious enough to use it?

Much the same query – was it ever of any real use? – can be raised about a less lethal but more diabolical weapon, itching powder. This was supposed to be scattered by agents into the underclothing of the enemy's armed forces – not a completely impossible task: static units would be likely to use local laundries, and it ought not to have been beyond the wit of anyone trained at Beaulieu to talk round a local washerwoman. The powder, once lodged in coarse cloth, was far from easy to remove, and the itch was highly disagreeable. Was it any worse than the attentions of the body louse, endemic on continental battlefields and especially vicious (in Peter Kemp's experience at least[8]) in Poland, through which most of the German army passed?

Only one definite instance of itching powder in action has so far gone on record. Some sub-agents of 'Tinker', Ben Cowburn's efficient F section circuit round Troyes, claimed in 1943 that they treated some shirts intended for U-boat crews with it. It came to be thought in Troyes that at least one U-boat had surrendered because its crew thought themselves incurably ill with dermatitis.[9] This is the sort of story resisters like to tell each other to keep their spirits up; there is no other evidence that it was true.

The most urgent need was for a reliable cheap submachine-gun. The tommy-gun, excellent man-stopper though it was, belonged to an American patent holder. The dollar shortage therefore impeded supply. Moreover it was heavy to carry, big to conceal, and too delicate in its mechanism for much rough use. There is a famous photograph of Churchill holding one with a certain relish; it first appeared in the *Daily Mirror* in August 1940, and it suited Goebbels' book to publish it in a propaganda leaflet that depicted Churchill as a gangster. It was exactly that element of toughness in the old man that so much endeared him to Goebbels' opponents.[10] Yet Churchill was the least clandestine of men: something less obtrusive was needed.

The problem was not one that either Jefferis' or Newitt's teams were able to solve before the Royal Ordnance factory at Enfield provided an answer to it in June 1941. The same factory had taken over British production of the Czech light machine-gun developed at Brno, called the Bren (cp. illustration no. 25). The latest weapon, devised there by two engineers called R. V. Shepherd and H. J. Turpin, was called – from their surnames' initials and its place of origin – the Sten. About three and a half million Stens were turned out before the end of the war; of these SOE distributed over a million to potential guerillas of various kinds. It is now obsolescent, but in its day gave new heart to many hundreds of thousands of oppressed people who saw it as a tool for throwing off a tyranny.

It arrived in three pieces – barrel, body and butt – with simple instructions (in several languages) about how to fasten them together and to add the indispensable fourth piece, the magazine. Three or four magazines, ready loaded, were usually supplied with each gun. The magazine stuck out at right angles to the barrel, to the left; incautious or untrained recruits used it as a grip, the simplest way to provoke a misfire. It must be said early that the Sten was subject to misfire a good deal. Its calibre was 9mm (.35 inches), exactly the same as the Schmeisser MP 38. This was not an accident; the ammunition was interchangeable. It could be fired either by single shots, or in bursts. Single shots were likely to miss because the barrel was so short – only 7½ inches (under 200 mm). Bursts ran through a single magazine in a moment, for the rate of fire was high by 1941's standards: 550 rounds a minute. The magazine, though built to hold 32 rounds, normally only held 28 – to avoid more misfires, because two rounds jammed together in the breech. The magazine took time to load; but keeping it loaded weakened the spring. The bolt worked on a strong spring, and it was easy when trying to clear this common stoppage to have a couple of finger-tips sliced off.

The commonest Stens – mark II and mark III, about two million and one million of which were issued respectively – had either a T-shaped metal butt, or one made of a thin iron pipe bent round into a butt-shape. The mark V had a wooden butt and two pistol grips, one just behind the trigger and one beneath the foresight; using these two grips, and the crouching Sykes-Fairbairn pistol stance, the firer did not need a butt at all. This comparatively luxurious version, available from the summer of 1944, was issued to airborne troops – SAS had some, and so did the fated First Airborne Division at Arnhem; it was uncommon in SOE's supply drops.

Someone in the War Office, obsessed by those tales of hand-to-hand combat on Gallipoli, then still in living memory, insisted that the Sten be modified to carry a bayonet. The army's heavy standard rifle bayonet, 22 inches (560mm) long, was nearly as long as the mark II Sten at 28½ inches (720mm), and would have hopelessly overbalanced it; but the new model spike bayonet, at 10 inches (254mm), was lighter and less cumbersome. It could fit on the mark V Sten. A few were parachuted, with that mark of Sten, to resisters, but there was a much better weapon than the bayonet available when the tactical need for cold steel arose in resistance: Fairbairn's fighting knife.

For very short-range work in the hands of untrained guerillas laying ambushes in jungle or in country lanes, the Sten was deadly. At ranges of more than a few feet, it would not do. Otto Skorzeny – David Stirling's opposite number in the German armed forces, the man who rescued Mussolini – thought well of a Sten mark II that he was shown, but never had to use it. He particularly admired its robustness; neither water nor mud did it much harm (though sand did, till the Australians devised a sandproof Sten).[11]

The overwhelming advantage of the Sten was that it was cheap. Its designers took care to make it robust and simple. It cost only thirty shillings (£1.50). In an age when the Treasury was by far the most influential government department, the Sten's cheapness did SOE's standing no harm. Unfortunately slapdash labourers in small firms did not pause to think that they were no longer making toys, but were building fighting tools, weapons on which their fellow men and women might suddenly, in some desperate hitch, depend for their lives. Sten-makers did not even always make sure that the short and lightly rifled barrels of these guns were free of burrs of metal. Unless the receiving agent took care – as good ones did – to check for this before issuing them, the first shot fired through such a defective barrel would burst the gun and maim or kill whoever held it.

There was one other snag about the Sten, which could make it positively dangerous for anyone trying to use it in secret: it was liable to go off by accident when jolted. This made it an awkward load, the cause of many wounds, and the ruin of some attacks. Perhaps this fault was at the bottom of a well-known incident in Paris on the afternoon of 26 August 1944, the day after the city had been liberated.

General de Gaulle marched in triumph down the Champs Elysées from the Arc de Triomphe at the head (in Dansette's words) of 'a crowd flowing between two crowds';[12] and was driven on – in the very car in which Pétain had been acclaimed in Paris in April – from the Rue de Rivoli to the square outside Notre Dame. As he left his car, a shot – by no means the first of the afternoon – rang out. Several armed men in the mob round him, supposing a sniper on a rooftop, fired upwards at random. All the civilians flung themselves to the ground. De Gaulle himself remained upright and impassive. He had been in real bombardments – his unit had left him for dead on the battlefield of Verdun in 1916 – and was not going to duck for small arms fire. He strode off into the cathedral, where the thanksgiving service was punctuated by more random shots. The incident has never been explained. It may most easily have been due to somebody's Sten juddering off.

Station IX produced a gun suitable for quiet urban killings, called the Welrod. Its calibre was 7.65mm (.32 inches). It was a single-shot weapon, with an excellent silencer built into it; it measured 300mm long (11.75 inches), with an outside diameter of 32mm (1¼ inches), with a detachable butt, 110mm (4¼ inches) long. The two pieces of it could be carried out of sight on loops inside one's trousers (then almost always worn loose), and would elude a casual search. The user would need a few seconds' privacy to assemble the weapon, and reloading was slow. The Welpen, or .22-inch pistol disguised as a fountain pen, was developed by Station IX but not put into production. For those who did not insist on a silencer, there were plenty of pistols and revolvers to be had. Lavish details of all the marks parachuted into France can be found in Pierre Lorain's admirable book.[13]

The short model Lee-Enfield was the standard infantry arm of the British Expeditionary Force in France and Flanders in 1914–18. The Lee-Enfield remained in the early 1940s – and is to this day, though obsolete – a first-class killing machine. In the hands of an expert it can bring down a man at two kilometres. Its rate of fire was so high that the Germans who first encountered the BEF in August 1914 thought there were twenty machine-guns per battalion, not two. The War Office was already dissatisfied with the calibre – .303 inches (7.7mm) – in 1912,[14] but was unable to settle on an alternative till 1957.[15] Even if one of the rare German airmen shot down within the Dunkirk perimeter in late May 1940 was able to say to the Tommies who guarded him with Lee-Enfields, 'Good Lord, are you still using those?', resisters to whom these rifles were dropped later felt they had a thoroughly professional weapon in their hands; and were quite right.

Rifles were admirable weapons for middle- and long-range work. They were too clumsy – even with bayonets fixed, even with the crushing power of their strong butts – for the mêlée of the ambush laid for a motor vehicle, for which Gubbins had correctly predicted the sub-machine-gun as the right tool. Unlike the hideable Sten, or the hidden Welrod, rifles were unlikely to get through a search unnoticed; obviously, these were weapons for the time after resisters had declared themselves, had come out into open revolt, rather than for the preliminary, underground struggle.

To assist them in the open warfare stage, resisters in touch with SOE could usually get hold of the Bren light machine-gun, justly described by Lorain as 'one of the best automatic rifles in the world'.[16] It fired the same rimmed cartridge as the Lee-Enfield rifle. It had a rate of automatic fire of 500 rounds a minute. Marksmen reckoned it was dead accurate up to 800 yards (750m). Its safety catch, like the Lee-Enfield's, was reliable.

Those who could get it preferred the American M-1 Winchester carbine, .30 inches (7.62mm) calibre. With a 30-inch (762mm) barrel, it was accurate up to 300 yards; it only weighed a quarter as much as the Bren. It only fired single shots, but could fire them rapidly; it had two sizes of magazine, one with fifteen rounds and one with thirty. The weapon had been developed steadily since 1866,[17] and combined the lessons of several generations of American sportsmen and warriors. It was simple, elegant and tough. SOE distributed a few; it was far more commonly passed out by the rival OSS. Every member of a 'Jedburgh' team had one, as well as a Colt revolver.

OSS also distributed the Americans' rival to the Sten, the M-3 sub-machine-gun. It was not as cheap as the Sten, but had a rough-and-ready air – it looked rather like an electric drill painted olive drab. It was an automatic – it could not fire single shots. It had a .45-inch barrel, and so had great stopping power, but could also be fitted with a 9mm barrel, if enemy ammunition was more readily to be had than American. SOE was occasionally able to provide it.

Offensively-minded agents and resisters had an alternative line of supply available, if they had the nerve and the opportunity: theft, or even purchase, from the enemy. Italy's change of sides in September 1943 produced some notable hauls of arms, especially in Yugoslavia. Old battlefields of eastern and western Europe could be scoured, by those who had the time, the enterprise and the transport. In all the occupied countries, moreover, there were likely to be arms dumps, in which the weapon and ammunition reserves of the defeated national army had been stored before the local war had begun. Not all of them would have been cleaned out by the occupier; the Poles at least knew how to exploit them.

Yet the Poles, as a matter of history, were best placed to do so: for them at least occupation was nothing new. The ancient kingdom that as late as 1648 had stretched from the Baltic almost to the Black Sea had vanished in the three partitions of the late eighteenth century, re-emerged as a republic in 1918, and sunk once more at the fourth partition of September 1939. Poles knew what to tell the children, what not to tell the enemy; they knew too that if Poland could survive at all, it would only be by their own efforts, for no one else reliable was there to help. But this is not the moment to move away from arms supply to international affairs.

Small arms, more or less damaged, were likely to be plentiful in the wake of passing and defeated armies; hence Arisaig's training in how to use the types of pistol, rifle, carbine, sub-machine-gun most likely to be met wherever it was intended an agent should go. The German 9mm Lüger pistol, sharing ammunition with the MP 38 and the Sten, was an important prize, usually snapped up by the first finder.

Another sort of weapon common enough in battlefield debris, and useful to guerillas for an ambush, was the hand grenade. SOE provided plenty of Mills bombs – called No. 36 Grenades in the army ordnance vocabulary: powerful little weapons, noisy and fatal at once.[18] The Italian army had a smaller, still noisier, not quite so dangerous egg-shaped grenade; the German, a bigger one with a long wooden handle – called the potato-masher by Tommies. With its handle, it could be thrown thirty yards; but so could the Mills, without one, by anyone any good at cricket.

One sort of portable artillery SOE did now and again provide from army stocks: two-inch or three-inch mortars. It needed plenty of practice to handle them with any expertise, and there was seldom chance (or ammunition) to provide much, if any, practice in the field; so they were not a great deal of use. Indeed, F section lost a promising organiser called Sarrette ('Gondolier') when a mishandled mortar bomb killed him in 1944 at what was meant to be a training demonstration at a maquis in the Nièvre.

SAS once managed to parachute in a six-pounder anti-tank gun and knocked out a German armoured car with it,[19] but such weapons were thought too sophisticated for SOE's following. A few Boyes anti-tank rifles were dispatched; good-looking weapons[20] but not much use – their solid shot bounced off tanks. The Firs produced a much uglier, and vastly more efficient, anti-tank device, the PIAT (projector, infantry, anti-tank). This was a much improved Blacker Bombard: instead of firing a bomb, it fired a small rocket, weighing 2½lb (just over 1kg), with a hollow charge in its head. At 34lb 5oz (15½kg) it was heavy, but not too heavy to be fired by one prone man from his shoulder; it was a metre long. It was effective up to about fifty yards. The hollow charge, though small, had great penetrating power, and a light tank hit by a PIAT rocket was not likely to move again.[21] Several very brave men won Victoria Crosses using PIATs in formal warfare;[22] and SOE distributed a large number of these weapons, for example sending over 1200 of them to France.

The American bazooka did the same job more efficiently and looked a lot more elegant; it was also, though a foot longer, a great deal lighter (it weighed 13lb 3oz, 6kg).[23] It took two men to work it, one to hold it over his shoulder and sight it, while the other inserted the rocket (3lb 5oz, 1.36kg) into the tube and kept well clear of the backblast. The PIAT was available from the late summer of 1943, the bazooka from the end of 1942. SOE was able to get hold of a few bazookas, and did some execution with them against Germans retreating into Germany in the autumn of 1944; but they were primarily American weapons.

The British provided one other close-combat weapon, which could dispose of an armoured car and might not be useless against a tank or a pillbox: a descendant of Blacker's sticky bomb, designed at The Firs, called the gammon grenade (No. 82).[24] A bakelite top held its fusing mechanism; below that hung a black cloth skirt, to be hand-filled with a kilogram (2¼lb) of plastic explosive – of which more shortly – in which the extra venomous could insert nails, tacks, or bits of broken flint. The act of throwing it armed an extra-sensitive fuse, which made it burst as soon as it hit anything. Dropped from an upper window, or thrown from the top of a bank, it could inflict terrific damage.

SOE does not seem to have used Jefferis' original invention, which attracted Churchill's attention to him very early in the war: the floating mine, meant for use against barge traffic on the Rhine. Jefferis did not then know of section D's work on time pencils. He designed a detonator that would explode on contact with fresh water, and fused it with the only objects he could find that could be relied on to dissolve in fresh water at a constant rate – some children's sweets called aniseed balls, spheres a centimetre across. He impounded the entire stock from the sole manufacturer. But we must turn to more serious business.

Over and over again, groups of resisters in contact with SOE appealed for heavier weapons than light machine-guns, PIATs, bazookas, light mortars; SOE resolutely refused to provide them. For this policy, deeply resented on the ground at the time, there were sound reasons, and SOE stuck to it. As has been indicated before, guerillas who did not keep on the move lost their *raison d'être*, might just as well not be there; their task was to harass the enemy, not to pin him down by set bombardments. The best way to create a national redoubt, where the pre-occupation regime could set itself up again, was to drive the enemy out altogether, rather than to liberate a too-easily-isolated corner of the national territory. A sternly practical logistic reason lay at the bottom of SOE's ban on artillery supply: it would be quite impossible to provide ammunition in any reasonable quantity.

At the opposite end of the tactical scale from artillery barrages came something that SOE was quite good at: arranging to hamper the movement of vehicles. One of the simple tricks agents learned in Arisaig was how best to waylay a motorcyclist by putting a stout wire across a road. They learned also the soldiers' adage that obstacles are of little use unless they are covered by fire; all sorts of problems could arise with an ill-fastened wire and a too alert motorcyclist. If the trap worked well, it ought to be possible to get the man's uniform, pistol, dispatches and tyres.

To stop or at least to hinder motor cars SOE produced a scaled-down version of a medieval device that had proved an effective stopper of horsed cavalry: the caltrop, a bunch of four sharp metal prongs – three form a tripod stand and the fourth points upward and punctures tyres. SOE's caltrops had two- or three-inch steel prongs and worked well.

A sub-station of Welwyn's, moved into the basement of the natural history museum in South Kensington, went a good way beyond the caltrop. It had a secret showroom in the museum, but from June 1942 did most of its work as Station XV at a former road-house, the Thatched Barn on the Barnet bypass, just north of London. There they worked up an invention by the wayward genius of section D's man in Alexandria, an explosive turd: imitation horse, cow, camel or donkey droppings with an explosive filling fired by a pressure switch. It was supposed that axis truck and car drivers would enjoy driving over piles of mess in their roads, and would blow up their tyres at least, if not themselves. The Firs provided the pressure switch; SOE did the rest. This was probably another of those over-ingenious toys that kept its devisers out of mischief, but did little else useful for the war effort.

Much the same can be said of the explosive rat, which came from the same stable. An authentic black rat's body was stuffed with plastic explosive, and fitted with a fuse that would (after a brief time delay) explode it after the rat had been shovelled into the boiler of a ship or a factory. A life of J. Elder Wills, who had entered SOE from the film world, claims that nine Belgian factory boilers were thus put out of action, before an aircraft crashed with four score loaded but unexploded rats inside it and the game was up: not a tale that commands much credence.[25] According to the history of SOE's camouflage section, after the Germans found the unexploded rats 'the trouble caused to them was a much greater success than if the rats had actually been used': a major and prolonged security scare wasted a great deal of enemy effort.

But what was plastic explosive? It seems to have been developed in the Royal Arsenal at Woolwich just before the war; thence two experts joined Section D's technical subsection to see how it could be applied to sabotage. Newitt wrote in 1942 that it

> consists of cyclonite mixed with a plasticising medium; it is considered to be one of the safest explosives and will not detonate if struck by a rifle bullet or when subject to the ordinary shocks of transit; it requires a detonator well embedded in the mass of the explosive. It is particularly useful to us as in addition to its insensitivity, it is plastic and can be moulded into shape like dough.[26]

It could safely be eaten, though it can hardly have been either tasty or nutritious; one enterprising agent, stuck high up in the Pyrenean foothills, warmed himself over a fire of it.[27] The best types were odourless and looked and felt much like butter. Other types smelt of almonds. Peter Hoffmann discovered from German records that one type, C, was made of '88.3% hexogen and the rest axle grease and other additives to prevent crystallisation and hardening'.[28] It was more powerful than other explosives then known, and did not need to be tamped unless it was required to explode in a particular direction. For a saboteur's purposes, it was ideal.

If plastic was unavailable, Nobel 808 could be used (if that was handled for long, one got a terrible headache); or ammonal; or dynamite; or gelignite. None of these were anything like as safe to handle or to carry about as plastic was.

In any mining community, explosives, detonators, and men who know well how to use both, can be found. It should not be impossible to secure enough to put a mine out of action, or to break up roads, or to destroy bridges, or to damage railway points (always a sensitive spot, just the sort Rheam taught his pupils to watch out for). The price might well include disposing of a small guard round the shed where the explosives were kept. The miners in the Polish community around Lille did not fall in with this general pattern, probably because, being Polish exiles, they were intensely suspicious of foreigners. The de Vomécourts did better among the miners of the Aveyron: a coal-mine at Decazeville was subject to a constant run of attacks, which only once closed it entirely – for a fortnight – but often cut its production irritatingly. Such maddening use of the pinprick was a frequent SOE tactic. It seldom surfaces in history books; pinpricks are after all minor, they are not mortal wounds. The tactic was nevertheless a useful one against an enemy short of temper and humour.

Jefferis' invaluable handbook explained to anybody who could get hold of it how plastic, or any other available explosive, could best be applied to the enemy's confusion. The Firs produced a large number of pressure switches – including one that worked when pressure was released: ideal for the making of booby-traps – and the army could supply more or less unlimited amounts of Bickford fuse, detonators and primers. Plastic could be cut as easily as butter, as well as moulded; specially shaped charges could therefore be made up to tackle any particular object on the spot.

Two kinds of pre-shaped charge were supplied: the limpet and the clam. Both originated in Jefferis' fertile brain. The limpet consisted of half a dozen powerful magnets fastened round a kilogram of plastic and fused by a waterproof time device. Three or four limpets placed on the hull of a ship below the waterline, whether inboard or outboard, would sink her, as some devoted Australians proved in Singapore roads in 1943 (see pp. 91–2, 126–7, 353–4).[29] SOE's limpets had been used already by some of Mountbatten's canoeists in the Gironde. The limpet was impossible to conceal as anything else – it was about the size of a steel helmet, too big to hide in a search; but it was worth having. The clam could at a pinch be popped into the covers of a book: it measured less than six inches by four by two; it too worked with a time pencil.[30] With a single clam, a saboteur could bend a railway line or crack a cylinder block or break an axle: a useful little tool (see illustration no. 58). Sabotage had in fact moved forward a good way from T. E. Lawrence's 'tulip' techniques, which had played havoc with the Hejaz railway in 1917.[31]

Station IX did not only do destructive work; sometimes it designed vehicles, instead of the means of destroying them. An early, useful product was the Welbike, a collapsible mini-motor bicycle capable of being dropped from the air for the use of resisters in the field. This was a good, tough, sturdy machine, but it had one disadvantage: wherever it was used, it did not look local. It was therefore all right for moving around remote areas where there were no inquisitive axis policemen; but in towns it would not do. It was an ancestor of the moped.

A subsidiary problem, also solved by Station IX, was the supply for resistance of used bicycle tyres of continental make. New tyres were conspicuous, the last thing (except dead) that any agent wished to be; Dunlop or other non-local makes of tyre were conspicuous also; rubber was in horribly short supply, particularly after the fall of Malaya in the winter of 1941–2. That Station IX turned this corner at all is a sign of SOE's flexibility and readiness to rise to a challenge. Station IX also invented a motor attachment for swimmers, with the ungainly name of the Welbum; like the Welpen, it never reached the wartime production line.

From MI R's original connection with the proposal that British volunteers should take part in the Russo-Finnish war of 1939–40 – a proposal almost fatal to Britain's survival, as it nearly landed her in war with Germany and Russia at once[32] – there survived a permanent interest in winter warfare, which was useful to the Norwegian section. This led in turn to the earliest version of what is now called the snowmobile – then called a weasel – a tracked vehicle of which the engine would start in very low temperatures, and which was able to manoeuvre over ice and snow. Mountbatten took a keen interest in this, as he hoped that his commandos might be able to use the results.

Mountbatten and the Admiralty were both also keenly interested in another of Station IX's inventions, the Welman or one-man submersible. This was not the same as the Admiralty's X-craft, nor the Sleeping Beauty – officially called the Motor Submersible Canoe, developed in 1943 for the Special Boat Section to lay limpet mines unobtrusively. The Welman was a tiny submarine, nineteen feet (6.2m) long, steered by a joystick, powered by a 2½ hp electric motor, which carried a large bomb – 255kg of explosive – at its forward end.[33] It had an endurance of ten hours at 2½ knots, and could submerge – if it had to – to fifty fathoms deep. Mountbatten narrowly escaped drowning when testing one in the waters of the Welsh Harp in north-west London; he had to jettison the heavy keel, which kept the craft fairly steady while submerged, and arrived late and soaked for a meeting at Chequers.[34]

Unhappily, like so many of SOE's inventions, this one does not seem ever to have been of much use. After years of correspondence between SOE, the Admiralty, and combined operations headquarters, the decision was reluctantly arrived at that there was no opportunity after all to use the Welman in French waters; it was not risked in Germany; it was not (it appears) used in the Mediterranean or the Far East. One or two attempts were made to use it in Norwegian waters, but it does not appear that it ever actually sank anything.

A few other devices deserve mention, one employed against anything that used thick oil, the others against anything that would burn. Most emerged under Newitt's wing. The first was abrasive grease, which in fact consisted of very finely ground carborundum, a polishing agent; it looked at a glance – even at a glance at a dipstick – like heavy motor oil. SOE could supply it in any quantity, disguised if need be – Wills's camouflage department enjoyed this sort of thing – in brands of oil can or drum or dispenser suitable to the area where it was to be used. Abrasive grease had for SOE an interesting quality: it quickly caused the parts that it was supposed to lubricate to seize up. Liberal use of abrasive grease on the axles of German rail tank-transporters, carried out in early June 1944 by a couple of French teenage sisters acting on an Englishman's orders, had a perceptible impact on the rate of panzer reinforcement against the Normandy bridge-head (see pp. 323–4). There is hardly a neater example of SOE's use of the lever principle in war.

Other devices were incendiary. A thermite-filled firepot was not confined to SOE: it became an ordinary army engineers' store, available when – as only too often happened in the first half of the war, and sometimes in the second half as well – large quantities of stores, such as blankets or clothing or haversacks, had to be destroyed lest they be overrun by the enemy. A competent agent who could set a firepot going in a Wehrmacht clothing store was doing a useful job for SOE; but could never explain it away at a control. Nor could he (or she) account innocently for the possession of SOE's own one-kilogram (2¼lb) thermite bomb. This, as Jefferis' pamphlet put it,

> burns quickly, generating intense local heat and fierce flames. It will penetrate mild steel plate 3.1mm thick.
>
> Its main uses are:
> (i) For igniting petrol and other inflammable oils in closed containers, e.g. army petrol cans in stacks.
> (ii) For attacking difficult non-inflammable targets of compressed material, in conjunction with incendiaries.
> (iii) For demolition work, e.g., for attacking tele-communication cable, electric motors, etc.[35]

Newitt's chemical ingenuity extended further: he devised an 'incendiary block', a brick-shaped object that not only generated heat, but emitted oxygen, so that a fire, once started in a confined space – such as a jam-packed warehouse – could be refuelled at source till it grew strong and took hold properly. Lorain even claims for it the gift of 'setting parcels in packing cases on fire through their lids'.[36]

Last came the pocket incendiary, hardly as large as a pocket diary; only a thorough search would discover it. There was a slot on one side of it, covered by a small wooden rod coloured to fit the time pencil key.* All the agent had to do was to remove the rod, and slide the edge of a coin along the slot. This activated the timer. When time ran out, the object burned fiercely for nearly a minute: quite long enough to set a petrol tank, or the inside of a vehicle, bar, barn or bedroom on fire.[37]

---

* Red for 30 minutes, white for 2 hours, green for 6 hours, yellow for 12 hours and blue for 24 hours.

VI
Communications

In modern war, before as well as after the making of the atom bomb, communications remain critical. Caesar, Belisarius, Gustavus Adolphus, Marlborough, even Wellington and Napoleon could oversee their battles by eye, and ride themselves – or send mounted messengers – to untie or retie knots on the spot. Railways, telegraph, telephone, gunnery, wireless and powered flight wrought a complete change: battlefields stretched far beyond a single commander's sight. Nelson could count every ship in the French and Spanish line as he sailed towards Cape Trafalgar and his death; all that Jellicoe ever saw of his enemy on Jutland Bank were three or four grey smudges on a dim horizon. SOE had to conform to the new shape of war: its chiefs could only affect the course of history from afar. The ways by which agents could be sent into action, and the ways in which orders and supplies could be passed to them once they were in the field, were critical: they above all shaped the kinds of work that SOE could and could not do. As the unlovely Georges Delfanne, one of the Gestapo's main local props in Paris, put it: 'My object was always to break up the liaisons, even more than arresting the chaps – what could they do without communications?'[1]

Every means of travel and of message-sending was

beset with troubles. Occupied Europe was not quite inaccessible by land for those who had cast-iron cover as neutral citizens and some excellent reason for wanting to travel into it: the first of SOE's women agents to visit France, for example, Madame Victor Gerson, went there in May 1941 by tedious train journey from Portugal under her maiden name of Giliana Balmaceda, carrying her own authentic Chilean passport, for the purpose of pursuing her profession of actress. She spent three weeks ostensibly hunting for a part, actually collecting a mass of indispensable intelligence for SOE, and came out by train with as little trouble as she had gone in. Later in the war, also from Lisbon, SOE Cairo was about to launch into Europe (without consulting London) a Bulgarian businessman – known to history only by his cover name of Vilmar – who was to have shot Hitler, but talked too much.[2]

The trouble about this method of approach was that it involved passing through the enemy's routine frontier control posts, and was therefore unsuitable for the movement of really secret agents, of forces of any size moving together, or of any warlike stores larger than a hidden knife or pistol. (This, remember, was before the invention of the metal-detecting security frames now familiar to air travellers.) An alternative was available: a clandestine crossing of the Pyrenees, or a mountain pass between Norway and Sweden, or whatever other frontier into axis Europe happened to be accessible. This could be safely arranged, usually with the help of a local smuggler who would require a cash fee but – if paid – was quite secure. However, the actual crossing of the frontier was not likely to be easy. One Irish Guards officer, compelled to walk through the Pyrenees, described his journey as 'Hell on earth'.[3] Numerous agents found that their guides' purpose was less firm than their own. One, who could not find a guide at all, managed his own transit through Andorra at the price of several hours' walking in knee-deep snow. Another, still at the probationary stage – he had earlier tried without success to talk himself into SOE when he met the half-legendary 'Xavier' in the course of an escape through the foothills of the Alps – found himself abandoned by the guide, effectively in charge of a mixed group of frightened men and women, most of them civilians: he had the good sense to take them back to Perpignan and start all over again.[4] One hero, Harry Peulevé, succeeded in crossing the Pyrenees on crutches; he had broken both his legs parachuting into France, had been patched up by a local doctor – without anaesthetic, lest he talk under its influence[5] – and had the good fortune to be in the charge of one of SOE's own hired guides, who in this special case did not insist on the cracking pace that was so often ruinous to passengers who were out of training.

Peulevé's case shows up another of the obstacles land travel presented to SOE: the dangers of delay while crossing nominally neutral ground that was in fact unfriendly. He was one of many thousands who were held for months by Franco's regime in the noisome dump of Miranda de Ebro, south of Bilbao. There were other grisly camps in which those who could give no sound account of themselves to a local policeman might get pinned, for weeks or even for years, in Bulgaria and Romania and even, as Arthur Koestler – not in SOE – and several of SOE's agents found to their cost, in France.[6]

In Asia there were two further obstacles, between them often conclusive, to introducing agents by land: severe terrain, and the brute fact that most Asiatics and Europeans look utterly unlike each other. A half-Indian princess whose mother was American had a short, tragic career in one of SOE's circuits in Paris – although private treachery, rather than her striking appearance, proved her undoing (see pp. 191–4). Spencer Chapman and a few friends were able to circulate on the roads of Malaya, with limited ease, by bicycle; only after dark could they move with much hope of safety.

In Asia as in Europe, a lasting trouble for those who sought to move on illicit business overland lay in the controls on movement that formed a routine part of the system of axis tyranny; complicated further by the inquisitiveness of policemen, who were – as so many remain – ready to stop any stranger and start asking questions. Routine police procedures had to be studied carefully by SOE. As will be shown in the next chapter (p. 174), Scotland Yard and MI5 gave helpful advice; more came from refugees, and more again from returned agents once traffic with occupied countries had been opened up.

Even if all these troubles could be overcome, a further handicap affected movement by land: it was usually slow. In western and central Europe, while trains still ran comparatively undisturbed by air or terrorist attack, they could be used – normally in acute discomfort, little understood by those who have never had to undergo it. Another of SOE's women agents, new to France, disgraced herself on first being told to make a long journey in a hurry by exclaiming, 'But my dear, I shan't have time to book a sleeper': she learned, fast, to get on without a sleeper or even a seat. By the winter of 1943–4 train journeys were subject to prolonged delays and disruptions, as well as frequent police searches. In south-east Europe, as in south-east Asia, there were few trains and life was altogether more leisurely (cp. pp. 336–7). The lucky could move on horseback, muleback, donkeyback; most had to walk. There were buses in some country areas now and then, all as subject to search and control as trains (cp. p. 339).

There were troubles also about traffic with continental Europe, or with south-east Asia, by sea; and not only because the coasts were guarded. Sentries along the Dutch and Belgian coasts stood almost impenetrably thick; so they did also around Calais, where the Germans confidently expected the British to try to land. Thick

117

guards did not absolutely deny access: SIS once managed to put a man ashore on the Dutch coast, near a casino, in full evening dress and reeking of brandy (poured over him just as he left his dinghy); he succeeded in hiccuping his way past the sentries, in a style SOE envied. For SOE, another incomparable character, Andrew Croft – polar explorer and aide-de-camp to a maharajah by turns in peace, Gubbins's IO in Norway, assistant military attaché in Stockholm and head of a Corsican boating party called 'Balaclava' by turns in war – once managed to put a party of agents ashore on the inner side of Genoa quay: a feat that called for rare nerve and skill combined.

The technique of getting in and out of dinghies and skiffs silently was among the skills taught in Arisaig. The problem of getting within dinghy range of the shore was a naval, rather than a clandestine one; SOE included several naval officers ready to tackle it, and some army and air force ones as well. Peter Harratt, one of the leading experts, had been a hussar officer; horsed cavalry training turned out no bar to maritime ability. The navy always remembered with anguish its two cardinal errors, in 1915 and 1918 – the Anzac troops had been put ashore on the wrong cove at Gallipoli, and a blockship meant for Ostend had been beached a mile clear of the harbour mouth; so all naval authorities insisted that no attempt at a landing be made unless there was some clearly visible object on shore to provide a guiding mark. Freedom from offshore rocks, offshore minefields and onshore batteries went without saying.

The navy could never spare, and SOE could never afford, a warship as large as a destroyer or even a corvette to get dinghy parties close enough to the shore. The choice lay between fishing smacks, which were slow but might pass as local, and any available sort of small fast motor craft. Croft preferred motor torpedo boats (MTBs) when he could get them. Holdsworth and Brooks Richards, setting up the first of SOE's small private navies on the Helford river in Cornwall at the end of 1940, hoped to use what would seem like local fishing smacks on the coast of Brittany. Unluckily for them, so did SIS, and their man in charge of cross-Channel traffic, Captain F. A. Slocum, RN,[7] managed to countervail most of SOE's efforts of this kind. He had a sound point: SIS needed to use the Breton coasts for the movement of agents, most of them provided by de Gaulle's supporters, in and out of France; and SIS's protégé, MI9, hoped to use these coasts also to rescue escaped prisoners of war and airmen who had evaded capture after being shot down. Their aims ran counter to SOE's. SOE wanted to promote military disruption and civil unrest in areas where SIS and MI9 wanted as much peace and quiet as they could get, with a minimum of interference from police busybodies. Sound though Slocum's point was, he urged it with far more ingenuity than tact: relations between SOE and SIS, seldom altogether smooth, seem to have been at about their most vicious on this marine front in the first half of the war.

In the spring of 1943 the Admiralty decided to create a deputy director, Operations Division (Irregular) – DDOD(I) – to work under the director of operations. 'In home waters clandestine operations are controlled by the Admiralty,' their lordships stated bluntly in a most secret letter;[8] and the new DDOD(I) turned out to be Slocum. However, his successor at Broadway had the good sense to move his flotilla of fishing boats at Falmouth a few miles down the coast to the Helford river, where they were amalgamated with SOE's. This turned out a startling success. According to Bevil Warington-Smyth, SOE's one-legged base commander who had taken over from Holdsworth,

> It enabled everyone to get to know each other, and it came as a source of great surprise to more than one Officer (and to some of the more intelligent Ratings)

to discover that – contrary to what they had been educated to believe – the principal enemy was Hitler and not their opposite number in the sister organization. Nothing but good came of this amalgamation at the same Base, and the personnel of the two Organizations at Helford worked thereafter in the closest co-operation, with the discomfiture of the Hun as their sole objective.[9]

The trouble about fishing boats, even if their appearance would pass muster, was that they were slow: 6 or 7 knots was their usual speed. Most of them could carry several tons of stores, a continual staff worry in Baker Street, but hardly any of the hopes the sections working into France placed in sea transport as a means of arming resisters were realised. Until September 1944, when France was almost liberated and it was too late to matter, only a ton or two of stores had reached Brittany by sea.[10]

Even if stores could not be shifted, could agents? Much work was being done at the time, outside SOE, on the problems of landing troops by sea on a hostile coast. This was normally done by means that were too public for SOE to be interested in them, though there was an SOE presence in several big commando raids (in the person of one or more of X section's agents, a born German speaker, available to confuse the enemy or for instant interrogation of prisoners).[11] One technical landing problem affected SOE as well as quite differently composed and more formal invasion forces: beach exits. There was not much point in putting an agent ashore on a pile of rocks backed by an impassable mountain, or on a mud-flat backed by an impassable marsh. Luckily there was plenty of intelligence to be had on this sort of point, collated by the Inter-Services Topographical Department at Oxford, one of Admiral Godfrey's most brilliant strokes.[12] SOE was one of the many bodies that was grateful to it for the speed and courtesy with which it disgorged its excellent information.

Yet SOE needed to get beyond topography on to politics, to be sure that particular landing places would be safe; this had to be looked into on the spot, by somebody who had local cover dense enough to cope with a stern rule in occupied western Europe (and indeed sometimes in southern wartime England): no residence in, or even entry to, the coastal zone without a police permit. SOE's most successful enterprise in Brittany turned on local reconnaissance by Peter Deman ('Paul'), then known in SOE as Irving Dent (he changed his real first name from Erwin to Peter in memory of Peter Harratt, with whom he had done two months' intensive training in small boat work on the Dart). He was a young agent of DF, the escape section: a Viennese Jew, trilingual in English, French and German, who had fought in the French army in 1940, escaped from a German prison camp, got out of France by joining the Foreign Legion, and reached England after deserting; so he had had some useful experiences already. 'Paul' had a base in Rennes from the autumn of 1943 and adequate cover – with permits – as an insurance agent with a weak heart. By a method more in place in a fairy story than a world war, he made a friend in St Cast, west of St Malo: he produced an ancient Irish ring, which belonged to the absent owner of a villa where he called on the maid. (The owner, Cecily Lefort, was already in SOE and destined not to return from Ravensbrück.) Near St Cast, 'Paul' found and used a secluded beach, unaware that the English had been using it for the same purposes in the 1790s.[13] Nature sometimes imitates art: the path from the beach up to the safe-house, where agents were hidden before and after landings, is thick with scarlet pimpernels. There 'Paul' was able to handle several parties carried across the western Channel by fast craft SOE had at last extracted from the navy (28-knot MTBs or 21-knot motor gunboats with three diesel engines, improvements on the 15-knot RAF seaplane tender launch with which Holdsworth and his crews had been operating into Brittany two winters before, to try and sustain an unlucky Gaullist *réseau* (network of resisters) called 'Overcloud').

'Paul' also had a beach farther west, near Morlaix, which Harratt thought the best of all and used six times. It lay within forty feet of an occupied German pillbox. This seemed barely credible to me, and I conjectured '[400?]' when quoting the report officially; years later, I was able to meet Deman's beach lieutenant, Aristide Sicot – by this time translated from a teenage student/ fisherman to director of a technical training school. He confirmed that it had indeed been within forty feet: 'We knew the sergeant; he didn't want to go to Russia, and took care not to look'[14] (see p. 124–5). One of those he would have seen, had he cared to look, was François Mitterand.

In Norwegian waters there was far less trouble about the use of fishing boats than in French. This was partly because SIS was not as interested in Scandinavia as in France; most of its excellent coast-watchers in Norway were already in place and did not need relief. Moreover, a great many Norwegian fishermen had escaped, with their boats, when the Germans overran their country (April–June 1940), so there were plenty of authentic craft and plenty of men with detailed local knowledge. There was a political difference, too: Norwegians knew that their loyalties lay with their exiled king and government in London, not with Quisling and Reichskommissar Terboven in Oslo; so nine in ten of the hundreds of Norwegian ships that were on voyage in the spring of 1940 made for allied ports instead of returning to Norway as Oslo ordered. The French were in much more of a muddle: only one French merchant ship in twenty failed to obey the Vichy government's order to return to a French port. It was a standing exasperation to de Gaulle that so few other people recognised quickly that he incorporated in his own person and movement the best hopes for eternal France.

Primarily with fishing boats, SOE began a system of sea links with Norway so reliable and so efficient that it came to be nicknamed 'The Shetland Bus' from its base near Lerwick; David Howarth, in a book of that title, has described its activities in detail.[15] A man I knew, a Norwegian naval officer in exile since 1940, regarded it as so reliable that he used it now and again to go home to visit his wife on leave, and never overstayed (she bore him a son in 1943). In 1940–3 these boats moved nearly 150 tons of stores into Norway, as well as 84 agents, and brought 26 agents and 109 refugees out; but at a cost of eight boats and 50 men lost, mainly through stress of weather. The generosity of Admiral Nimitz of the US navy then produced three 110-foot submarine chasers, bristling with anti-aircraft artillery. In the two seasons of 1943–4 and 1944–5 (the short nights made sea operations highly inadvisable towards midsummer), these new boats shifted another 150 tons of warlike stores into Norway, with 135 agents, and brought 46 agents and 243 refugees away. None of them was lost.[16] All these boats were crewed by Norwegian volunteers; SOE looked after their base, and secured for them food, ammunition, fuel, charts and other necessities. Their work was planned jointly by SOE's Norwegian section and the Norwegian military authorities.

Affairs in Sweden were much trickier, because Sweden remained neutral all through the war, and in the early years was (as many of her service staff remained) frankly pro-German. Sweden was not the only power whose policy varied to fit in with the tilting balance of apparent military success. Much stress was laid officially, above all in the early stages, on Sweden's neutral status. Many British and Norwegian ships were interned in the ports of south-west Sweden; from among them, an SOE organiser – George Binney – managed to recruit volunteer crews, and to set up a mass escape by sea, operation 'Rubble'. Five cargo ships took part in this, sailing out into the Skagerrak at nightfall on 23 January 1941 and next day meeting a British naval escort adequate to scare off some attacks by the Luftwaffe. A million pounds' worth of special steels and ball bearings, vital for the British armaments industry, were carried; the only casualty was a Swede who died of wounds received from a German seaplane. Binney was knighted ('There must be some mistake,' the minister in Stockholm said: 'I recommended you for a CBE').[17]

Ten more ships took part in operation 'Performance' in April 1942, much less a success; two got through, with over a quarter of the cargo between them, six were sunk, and the others turned back into Swedish waters. Several ships had opened fire on the Luftwaffe, and there were some highly disagreeable rows with the Swedes, who wanted to know where they had got their weapons from. A series of motor gunboat operations, code-named 'Bridford', looked after the rest of the steel and ball-bearing smuggling till the war was over; and were able to do a little for Denmark on the side in an operation called 'Moonshine'.

Danish resistance, notoriously, was somewhat slow off the mark; once it had got going, SOE found that supplies to it were almost as easily organised by sea as by air. An eleventh of the 700 tons sent into Denmark went by sea. Fast small craft using east coast bases, on the 'Bridford' model, were employed, with none of the jealousies that had upset the Helford river parties in the early days: for SIS disinterested itself in Denmark, from which SOE secured intelligence as well as sabotage. Fortunately for history, a participant in the boat parties to the Danish coast in the last two years of the war has written a lively book, based originally on his own experiences. John Oram Thomas, its author, bears out Ralph Barker's indications that some of the Swedes were prepared not merely to turn a blind eye like the sergeant near Morlaix but actually to co-operate in what SOE was doing.[18] 'Rubble' would never have got away without close German pursuit if a Swedish security officer, Ivar Blücker, had not thoughtfully cut some telephone lines. 'Moonshine', the landing of fifty tons of arms for the Danes at Lysekil on the Swedish coast north of Gothenburg, only worked because a party of Swedish policemen accompanied the arms on a rail journey southward, and made sure nobody interfered with them until they were quietly shipped across to Denmark.[19] Hambro, who had supervised all this activity, was summoned to give an account of 'Rubble' to George VI, always interested in the navy in which he had himself been in action at Jutland, and mentioned Blücker's invaluable help; as, for security reasons, he could not be put in for a decoration, could he possibly have a pair of cufflinks with the royal monogram? The king slipped off the pair he was wearing and said: 'If Captain Blücker wouldn't mind a second-hand pair, you'd better take these.'[20]

SOE did little in Africa outside Abyssinia, Madagascar, 'Massingham', and the loan of wireless sets and operators to the Long Range Desert Group and SBS. One of its more astounding coups, with an old-fashioned buccaneering flavour about it, was brought off in the second half of 1941 at Fernando Po, the Spanish island east of the mouth of the Niger. Its commander was Gus March-Phillipps, a gunner major of unusual force of personality who cherished the belief that 'the spirit of Drake and Raleigh, of Robert the Bruce and of Oliver Cromwell is the spirit that will save England today and give her a name that the world will once again look up to' (these phrases come in a letter from his companion Geoffrey Appleyard, a Cambridge athlete[21]). They took a small team of friends out to West Africa from Poole in a requisitioned Brixham trawler, the *Maid Honor*. Gubbins saw them off. They got hold of a couple of tugs, sailed into Fernando Po harbour while most of the crews of the vessels they meant to seize were at a party ashore, and cut out a 7600-ton Italian liner and two smaller ships. Next morning they met – not by accident – a British cruiser, which regularised the capture.[22] *Maid Honor*'s crew sailed her back to Dorset, where they formed the nucleus of 62 Commando, the Small Scale Raiding Force, operating across the Channel in attempts to annoy the enemy and (unknown to themselves) to assist various processes of deception.[23]

In the western Mediterranean also SOE was able to embark on some small-boat operations. A pair of twenty-ton feluccas – basically, sailing craft (one of them was also powered with the engine from an old SOE motor car) – worked out of Gibraltar on to the adjoining coasts, as far afield as the French Riviera. They were crewed by Poles described by General Sikorski to Gubbins as 'too rough even for the Polish navy'; though, Gubbins added at once when recounting this, 'they never gave *me* any trouble'.[24] Their commanders were two young Polish lieutenants called Buchowski and Krajewski, enormously brave and resourceful sailors; Buchowski came to an embarrassingly sudden end in London afterwards. The round trip between Gibraltar and the Riviera might last as long as a fortnight; would be conducted under several flags; and was often intensely uncomfortable. Bodington, the second-in-command of F section, had to share a felucca with thirty-three companions in August 1942, and Henri Frenay, a leading French resister, claimed to have shared his with eighty-nine: worth it all the same, to get out of German-occupied Europe.[25]

A Levant fishing patrol, working in parallel with MI9's caique parties and the freebooters of the Special Boat Service, was busy in the Aegean;[26] 'Balaclava' in Corsica has been mentioned already. In the Far East, some use could be made of captured Japanese motor fishing craft to get canoeing parties somewhere near their targets.[27] Unfortunately, efforts to equip them seem to have been in the hands of one of the least competent of SOE's sections, N (distinguish it sharply from the Netherlands section in western Europe, also called N, and also not always noted for efficiency). This Far Eastern paranaval body seems to have carried to excess SOE's frequent desire to be different and to do things its own way.[28]

The huge distances of Asia sometimes compelled SOE's boating parties to use one other naval means of getting near their goal, which had been used in the Bay of Biscay – once – as early as the spring of 1941, and became a regular feature of traffic with the French Riviera and across the Indian Ocean: submarines.

The cases for and against the submarine were nicely balanced. Though not quite silent, it left no tell-tale tracks on the water when submerged: even when surfaced, a submarine lay (its conning-tower apart) almost flush with the water, and was all but imperceptible to wartime radar. So a submarine should be able to get, quite undetected, close to an enemy shore; whence or whither a party could travel in a very light craft. Trained men could disembark from it into a canoe or inflatable dinghy. The folbot, a light canoe developed for SBS, was portable up a submarine's conning-tower hatch, though often damaged in the process.[29] So long as there was no sudden fog, simple signals with a shaded torch or with a luminous ball held in the fist could establish contact with the beach – if anyone was waiting on it – and make it possible for a light craft coming from the beach to find the submarine. It might even be possible to use the S-phone, of which more later (p. 149–50).

On the other hand, though submarines had not yet advanced to their modern eminence as capital ships – a category then filled by battleships and battle cruisers – they were serious ships of war, and the Admiralty had not so many of them that they could lightly be risked. None of them were fitted to carry passengers, so any SOE parties had to be small, and were sure to be uncomfortable. Several days' almost complete immobility did nothing for the training or the morale of energetic outdoor types; they had only too much time to think over the dangers and uncertainties of their impending mission, and to recall the questions they ought to have insisted on having answered at their briefing. Moreover, it hardly ever happened that the SOE task came top of the submarine commander's list of priorities. A couple of instances can show how this affected work.

Captain (later General) Bergé, the first man SOE ever put into France – on operation 'Savanna' in mid-March 1941 – was rescued at the last minute by Geoffrey Appleyard from a Vendéan beach on the night of 4/5 April. Time was running out; Appleyard took two passengers back to HMS *Tigris* with him, putting three men in a frail little canoe designed to hold two (and leaving another agent, Joel Letac, *plaqué* on the shore – the canoe that was to have rescued him was swept away by a chance wave on launching). They got to *Tigris* just as she was closing her conning-tower to dive and depart. After this narrow squeak, Bergé found he had ten immobile days to spend while *Tigris* finished a routine patrol in the Bay of Biscay. He spent the time composing a report on why his mission to disrupt the Luftwaffe's pathfinder force near Vannes had failed.[30] And the commander of the submarine sent from Fremantle to make touch with Ivan Lyon's fated 'Rimau' party, which had sailed thence on 11 September 1944, 'considered that his first priority was to hunt and attack enemy shipping so long as his torpedoes lasted'; he did not reach the rendezvous with 'Rimau' in useful time, and all that party were killed – some in action, some later.[31] There was, moreover, 'always a fearful risk that accident, indiscretion, or treachery might betray a prearranged rendezvous to the enemy; in that case a powerful warship and its crew might be lost in an attempt to bring out a single and not necessarily a valuable agent'.[32]

The mixture of discomfort, elation, boredom and fright that SOE's submarine passengers encountered is best set out in a book by a Frenchman, one of another trio of well-born brothers who were active in resistance: Emmanuel d'Astier de la Vigerie.[33] At a common friend's house in Antibes, he happened early in 1942 to run into an F section liaison officer, Peter Churchill, who took him out to a submarine immediately. This precipitated some fearful staff rows, because (a) the navy had had no warning and (b) d'Astier wanted to work with RF section, not with F, and did indeed – after an RF mission to France – become de Gaulle's minister of the interior. This impromptu incident was typical of SOE's manners, which naturally enough the Royal Navy found trying. Cruickshank's reflections on the incompetence of the India Mission's paranaval section, referred to just now, would be echoed by many survivors among the sailors with whom SOE tried to work.

It was by submarine that General Giraud was extracted from France – neither by SOE nor by MI9, but in comic-opera conditions by MI6 – to fail to take charge of the 'Torch' landings in north-west Africa on 7/8 November 1942.[34] 'Torch' had been prepared by a visit, again by submarine, to Algeria by an American general, Mark Clark; this famous indiscretion was decided on by Eisenhower, and confirmed at a meeting of the British War Cabinet on a Sunday afternoon at which Mountbatten, Pound (the First Sea Lord) and Brooke were also present. Churchill, 'as enthusiastic', in Clark's words, 'as a boy with a new electric train', entered into the minutest details. SOE in retrospect was delighted not to have been involved.[35] With the help of another d'Astier brother, Henri, Clark was able to meet a junior French general and to get away undetected; his journey, though gallant, had no useful impact on the success of the landings it might easily have imperilled. North-west Africa then lay in any case outside SOE's main range of activities, in the sphere of OSS.

Two other sets of submarine operations deserve notice. When on 27 November 1942, sixteen days after their operation 'Attila' had quietly taken over Vichy France, the Germans entered the port area of Toulon, the bulk of the French warships there scuttled themselves. The submarine *Casabianca* – named after a famous Corsican fighting family – escaped to north Africa, and under its formidable captain, L'Herminier, made frequent journeys between Algeria, the Riviera and Corsica. This was the sole channel by which de Gaulle could communicate with France without having to use British or American intermediaries: a point of some political weight.

As there seemed to be no other means of getting agents into the Japanese-occupied areas of the Andamans, Malaya and Sumatra, submarines were used several times by the India Mission in early attempts to get operational parties ashore. Cruickshank has summarised in a few pages, and Ian Trenowden has described in a short book, the tribulations that attended these efforts, and the poor results there were to show when they were done.[36] Much more might have been achieved, had the war lasted longer.

Another element remained: the air. SOE had to take to the air for lack of opportunities by sea: it might even be said that the naval obstacles placed in its way in the early stages drove it from the sea into the sky. Slocum's historic importance is that his obstinacy compelled SOE to seek other ways than naval ones of crossing the Channel; by doing so he created a myriad of chances – quite against his will – for SOE and the RAF to make friends.

SOE never had its own air force to match its various private navies. It depended, to a degree that alarmed its high command, on the services of the RAF and, towards the end of the war, the USAAF; these services were not always available. Indeed, near the start it looked for a moment as if they were going to be refused. On the very first occasion when SOE asked the RAF's help to put a party into Europe for a specific task of killing – 'Savanna', Bergé's assault on the Luftwaffe's pathfinding pilots – the chief of the air staff protested. Portal wrote to Jebb, in a secret and personal letter of 1 February 1941:

> I think that the dropping of men dressed in civilian clothes for the purpose of attempting to kill members of the opposing forces is not an operation with which the Royal Air Force should be associated. I think you will agree that there is a vast difference, in ethics, between the time-honoured operation of the dropping of a spy from the air and this entirely new scheme for dropping what one can only call assassins.[37]

Jebb was able, with some trouble, to talk round Portal and Harris, then his assistant; they were prepared to help SOE a little, but not much. Portal often took the line with Sporborg, as the latter remembered it in 1945: 'Your work is a gamble which may give us a valuable dividend or may produce nothing. It is anybody's guess. My bombing offensive is not a gamble. Its dividend is certain; it is a gilt-edged investment. I cannot divert aircraft from a certainty to a gamble which may be a gold-mine or may be completely worthless.'[38] Harris as commander-in-chief, Bomber Command, acted as a permanent brake on SOE's military effort in western Europe, lest his own attempts to lay the area waste be too much hindered.

Three sorts of air effort could be applied to SOE's purposes: stores could be parachuted; agents could be parachuted; and light aircraft could land, deposit agents and mail, and take off again with return traffic.

Parachuting from cliff-tops was not unknown in medieval China or indeed in ancient Greece. In the twentieth century it was reintroduced, to benefit airmen in distress; and the Russians, still then in a revolutionary rather than a conservative mood, showed in some army manoeuvres in 1930 (of which Gubbins was later shown a film by their London embassy) that soldiers could be dropped by parachute to disturb an army's command network. Wavell, already interested in this problem, saw a further parachute show on a much larger scale at the Russian manoeuvres in 1936.[39] At the start of the next world war, parachuting could be foreseen as a probable way of getting troops into action; the Germans gave some demonstrations of this in Norway and the Low Countries the next spring.

The British developed parachuting rather slowly. Only late in 1940 was Gubbins's contemporary, 'Boy' Browning, appointed to assemble the first British airborne troops, whom he rapidly turned into a *corps d'élite*. For secret purposes, two elderly Whitley bombers were available from September 1940, in a new unit called 419 Flight RAF, in East Anglia. A third Whitley was added on 9 October, and a fourth in February 1941 when the flight moved to Charles II's playground, Newmarket racecourse. But only one of them was equipped to drop containers of arms as well as men; and that one crashed on landing, killing some of its crew and wounding all the Polish agents on board, when it returned from an unsuccessful sortie over France on 10/11 April 1941.[40] On 25 August 1941 the flight was expanded to become 138 Squadron, with ten Whitleys and three four-engined Halifaxes; and in March 1942 it settled at Tempsford in Bedfordshire, its home for the next three years. This airfield, though heavily camouflaged, was somewhat public – it was sandwiched between the main railway line to Edinburgh and the Great North Road; but the Germans never seem to have spotted it. 138 Squadron shared it with 161 Squadron, which specialised in pick-ups rather than in parachuting; they were the only two squadrons in

England almost entirely devoted to special operations. Almost, but not quite entirely: for they might be called on to aid such special efforts by Bomber Command, under which they came for some purposes, as the thousand-bomber raid on Cologne in May 1942.

Harris took care that Lancasters, his best four-engined bombers, were never available for special duties. 138 Squadron grew eventually to a strength of fifteen Halifaxes in November 1942 and twenty in May 1943; in May 1944 they were exchanged for twenty-two Stirlings, slightly larger in their load capacity but lower in their ceiling and even less popular with Bomber Command crews on operations over Germany. Whitleys were phased out of operations overland in November 1942, though Coastal Command was still using them for mine-laying in the late summer of 1944. 161 Squadron began with five Whitleys and two Wellingtons in February 1942, exchanged the Whitleys for Halifaxes that November, and lost them in May 1944 when it went over entirely to pick-ups and to an odd series of operations, not for SOE, called 'Ascension'.[41]

Containers, familiar objects to anybody actually in the business of resistance at the time, deserve a few words' description. They were metal cylinders called C type, just over a foot in diameter and 5' 9" long (35 × 175cm), with four carrying handles; they opened along their long axis.[42] When full, they might weigh anything up to a tenth of a ton (100kg), a four-man load. When empty, they made admirable man-sized targets at which recruits could practise, in remote areas where the enemy would not hear the shots. SOE's orders, on the contrary, were that they were to be promptly hidden or destroyed; better destroyed, because a mine detector might be used by the enemy when searching for them. An ingenious Pole proposed the H type, which was the same overall size, but consisted of five metal drums, each with a carrying handle, fastened one above the other by a pair of long metal rods, which held the endpieces also – one to deaden the shock of landing, the other with the container's end of the static line that plucked open the parachute as the container fell, and was then broken by the object's weight. C types hardly ever broke up on impact, whereas H types quite often did.[43]

In containers, arms and explosives were dropped. On a few rare occasions, explosives would burst on hitting the ground, no doubt because the detonators had not been packed carefully enough. Sometimes those waiting on the ground supposed that bombs, left behind by accident in the bomb racks from a previous raid, had been dropped instead: a source of some mistrust.[44] Wireless sets needed to be packed specially, in kapok packages or specially lined wicker panniers. Containers could be loaded into an aircraft's bomb bay and released by the bomb aimer as if they were bombs; a Whitley could hold twelve, a Halifax fifteen and a Stirling eighteen. (When the Americans joined in, it was found that a B-17 Flying Fortress could only hold twelve; a B-24 Liberator could manage eighteen.) Packages and panniers were stacked inside the aircraft's fuselage – the Stirling's was particularly roomy – and manhandled out into space by an airman, the dispatcher, through a hole a metre across cut specially in the floor.

Through this hole agents dropped also. At parachute school – at Altrincham, Kabrit, or wherever – agents were drilled to do this in a fragment of fuselage from a crashed aircraft, until it became quite automatic. Just as in Wellington's army soldiers learned, by drill, to form square and stand steady when men on horses waving swords galloped down on them, so in Gubbins's army agents learned, by drill, an even less natural process: an awkward seated sideways shuffle, on hands and bottom; a swivel, to put one's legs into the hole; and then, when a red light turned to green, and the dispatcher swept his arm down and cried 'Go!', a gentle push forward and a spring to attention. If one pushed too hard, one banged (or broke) one's nose on the opposite side of the hole. If one did not spring to attention, one's body might get entangled in the cords of the parachute as it was plucked open by the static line. If the dispatcher had forgotten to connect up the static line, one was about to die: this did happen once or twice. One still less fortunate agent was hooked up hurriedly in the dark through a piece of webbing on his own jacket; his parachute did not open, he was towed behind the Halifax. The combined efforts of everyone on board could not exert force enough against the slipstream of four engines to get him back in; and the mountain cold killed him.[45]

From two other types of aircraft, a parachutist's exit was not quite so awkward. From an Albemarle light bomber, five men could jump at once through an oblong hole. SAS used this; SOE thought it was all right for trained troops, but would not do for agents, less amenable to strict discipline. SOE did, when it could, use the Douglas Dakota C-47 (DC3) transport, an American aircraft of which by 1944 there were several squadrons in 38 Group of RAF transport command. From the Dakota the parachutist taking care, as always, that his static line was properly hooked up – simply leaped out of the side of the aircraft through a door, up to which he could run, if he liked, to give himself momentum.

With parachuting, as with everything else in SOE, nothing was quite fixed except anti-Nazism. By a stroke of bad luck, a new and (it was believed) reliable form of parachute packing was tried out in action in December 1941. It had performed well in trials, but it killed Dr Bruhn, a leading figure on his way into Denmark. Tony Brooks, parachuting into France in July 1942, was also equipped with a new variant: it landed him horizontal. By a stroke of his habitual luck, it did so in the only tree on the dropping zone, and he got away with a bruised leg instead of a broken spine.

Tree landings are notoriously tricky, and a fruitful source of parachutists' anecdotes;[46] none of them odder than the tale of Denis Rake's landing in the Auvergne in the summer of 1944. It has been said that by the time he had got out of his harness, he could hear German being spoken all round the tree he was in; and that he hid, stock-still, in the midsummer branches till his enemies had gone. This tale would be more easy to believe if we had not got Rake's word for it that he never jumped by parachute at all – he found it too frightening – and went to France by felucca for his first mission and by a Lysander light aircraft for his second.[47]

Agents only jump from Lysanders in fiction. Parachuting had this at least to be said for it, it was prompt. As Glen put it ruefully, 'When years later I was on the board of BEA I used to compare nostalgically the so-called "slight technical delays" of scheduled airlines with the promptness of travel into occupied Europe'.[48]

A few stores did not need either containers or packaging: uniforms (usually British battledress), blankets, even boots strung together, could be bundled straight out of an aircraft onto the ground if the party at the receiving end were alert enough to avoid getting hit by a falling parcel. There is an odd tale, of Crimean incompetence, of a drop into Yugoslavia that consisted wholly of boots for the left foot, balanced by a drop of boots for the right foot only into northern Albania: a grisly quartermaster's joke, played by a prankster who had given no thought to the horrors of life in the mountains to which the drops were sent. One troubled group of guerillas in France is supposed to have received, when short of ammunition, a package full of lampshades.

Parachute and container packing became minor war industries. In the earliest stages, parachute failure rates were reckoned at about five in a thousand, a rate still current in the Far East in 1944–5. By 1944 in Europe the failure rate was said to have been reduced to little over one in a hundred thousand: reasonable odds on which to stake one's life, and a confident figure to give to someone about to make his first jump. At STS 33 at Altrincham, students were taken over to Ringway to watch teams of intent young women folding silk in a hangar bearing along both sides, in letters a yard high, the slogan REMEMBER A MAN'S LIFE DEPENDS ON EVERY PARACHUTE YOU PACK.*

Container and parachute packing for 'Massingham' at Algiers seems to have been a lot less careful than elsewhere, supposedly for lack of adequate skilled labour. Francis Cammaerts, who was one of SOE's leading agents in Provence, claimed that he lost as much as a fifth of the stores sent to him because of faulty parachutes or containers that burst open in the air or on impact. In April 1944 he sent a furious message: 'At last delivery parachutes failed to open as usual containers fell on house and crushed the back of mother of one of reception committee this bloody carelessness absolutely inexcusable you might as well drop bombs stop relatives didn't even complain but my god I do':[49] a justified outburst, but it did no good.

Packing in England was developed towards a fine art, and there were good local packers later in south Italy too. It was said that an English-packed container would be so cunningly filled that once it had been unloaded no one in the field could manage to get back into it everything that had come out of it. Gaps between warlike stores might be filled up with clothing (spare socks are always useful), or tobacco, or such goodies as coffee, almost unobtainable even on the continental black market; or, near invasion time, with armbands in the local national colours, to provide guerillas with the 'visible distinguishing mark' on which the 1907 Hague convention insisted for combatants. The Germans and Japanese had ceased to bother much

---

* I saw it.

about the Hague convention; the armbands may have saved a few lives all the same.

Those who received tobacco by parachute needed to think where they were going to smoke it, and might well hesitate to smoke Virginia brands under Gestapo or OVRA noses. One agent, aware of this, particularly requested that on his second mission to France he might be supplied with Gauloises. He paid several visits to Wills's South Kensington offices to assure himself that the packaging of his cigarettes was absolutely up-to-the-minute in every detail of paper, colour, tax stamp and typeface. He landed rather heavily, felt he had earned a cigarette, reached in his pocket, and lit one: only to find he was smoking Player's Navy Cut.

He, being a suspicious man, had dropped 'blind', by himself; so every starting party of agents had to do; but once SOE had got any sort of organisation going, it was more usual to drop to a reception committee. To belong to one of these committees was itself an act of resistance, if only a small one, because it meant breaking curfew. Extra-ingenious members got hold of gamekeepers' or doctors' permits to be out late, in case they were stopped by a chance control on the way to the dropping zone. The number of men to attend would hinge on the amount of carrying to be done before daylight, and the kind of transport – anything from donkeys through farm carts to lorries – available to move the stores away; and on where and how they were to be hidden. As has been said,

Countrymen are good at hiding things from townsmen, and their natural gifts of this kind were sharpened during the war by contacts with policemen and black marketeers. Every conceivable sort of hiding-place was used; arms were buried, hung in trees, put behind piles of logs or backs of ovens or rows of empty casks, put into false cask or wardrobe bottoms, into milk churns, into bracken, into ponds, into plough, into dung.[50]

German and Japanese anti-aircraft defences did not have much success in interfering with the special duties squadrons' flights, except in the Netherlands, partly because most flights were made at a level too low for wartime radar to track, partly through some elementary – but surprisingly efficient – deception. Special duties aircraft carried, as well as their clandestine load, bundles of PWE's leaflets: the most enduring bond that remained between the old SO1 and SO2 with which SOE had begun. After their drop was done, or on the way to it, the aircraft would scatter the leaflets over the nearest undefended town. This explained why a low-flying aircraft had been in the neighbourhood, and distracted the local police, who went round trying to collect all the leaflets before anyone read them. Cruickshank even found a dropping zone in Burma which lay two miles from a Japanese outpost and was used repeatedly for five months before the enemy became aware of the fact.[51]

Ingenious systems were worked out for using the BBC's overseas broadcasts as forewarnings that a drop was coming to a particular ground. One was set up by the Poles. It was similar to the system by which Czech deserters had identified themselves when going over to the Russians in 1914: by whistling a particular tune.[52] Particular tunes, played at 1.45 p.m. after the news broadcast to Poland, meant drops to particular groups. One absurdity must not be left unchronicled: SOE's Polish section insisted vehemently to the BBC that they *must* play a popular jig, 'Poor old Matthew's dead and gone', at the end of a long obituary broadcast on Cardinal Hinsley.[53]

F section's first wireless operator in France, Georges Bégué, started up a variant in the autumn of 1941. After the news bulletins in French, personal messages were sometimes broadcast; on Bégué's system, these became a daily event. Mixed in with genuine fragments of family reporting and inquiries came coded messages, which gradually grew odder and odder: such as *Aesculape n'aime pas le mouton*. From this stream of apparent gibberish, an agent could pick out the one phrase that meant an impending drop to him or her, and could set out to mobilise transport and labour for the night to come. The resonant tone and impenetrable sense of these arcane sentences was wonderfully picked up by Jean Cocteau – who spent the war being himself in Paris – in the opening minutes of his film *Orphée*.

Only too easily it could happen that curfew was broken for no useful purpose, because the aircraft never turned up. There were many reasons for this, such as fog over English airfields (Tempsford was specially liable to fog) when the Continent's weather was fine; defects in the aircraft; or difficulties in finding the way. At a time when most of Harris's bomber crews did not know what country, let alone what county, they were flying over, special duties aircraft made a point of finding not only a particular county, but a particular field in it. Fifty-five per cent of the first year's flights for SOE from England failed to end in a drop, either because the crew could not find the DZ, or because some hitch prevented the reception committee from getting to it. By 1944 two-thirds (but only two-thirds) of SOE's dropping sorties from England succeeded, for the same sorts of reason.

Politically-minded resisters, and many postwar authors, have been a little too inclined to think of parachute drops as if they were like the Lord's scattering of manna in Sinai for the people of Israel, or (on a less exalted plane) like rain-storms: simply events that happened from the sky. An enormous amount of hard, detailed work, both physical and mental, had to go into packing containers and getting them onto the right aircraft, labelled so that the aircrew would know what to do with them; while the navigator had to spend hours working out every minutest detail of his route, with possible variations; and before either of these tasks could be begun, let alone completed, the agent had to choose the ground, the RAF had to approve it, a code letter to be flashed from the ground had to be fixed, and the agent had to get hold of a torch to flash it with, and three other torches for his friends to hold. An upside-down L was the usual pattern for the torches, with the crossbar at the upwind end, and the ground commander at the outer end of the crossbar. In wild country, bonfires could be used instead of torches; but left scars.

When a sortie did succeed, it had a moral impact on the neighbourhood that amply repaid the trouble that had gone into arranging it. The fact that aircrew had come all the way from England to their own village meant, for villagers, that they could feel themselves sharing in a grand allied effort; this was worth a very great deal.

Moving agents in and out, though at first glance more risky, was in fact more easy than moving stores: mobile, intelligent adults are less hard to hide than container-loads of ammunition and explosives. At a pinch, a solitary agent who could collect three sticks, three working bicycle lamps, some string and a hand torch could manage to receive an aircraft himself, run round to collect the sticks and lamps after it had landed beside him, and take off in it; leaving no trace on the ground beyond tyre marks in the grass and three small holes.

Three kinds of aircraft were available for this work, the Westland Lysander, the Lockheed Hudson and the Douglas Dakota. The Lysander was a small sturdy high-wing monoplane, modified for secret purposes by the removal of guns and bomb racks and the addition of a ladder on the port side, leading to the second cockpit. The pilot sat alone in the small front cockpit. Behind him there was a stout bulkhead, and behind that the second or passengers' cockpit, which had room for two in comfort (sitting side by side, facing aft), three at a pinch, or in a crisis four.

Voltaire's quip about God has been applied to the

Lysander: had it not existed, it would have had to be invented. Westland had designed it for army co-operation, for which it was all but useless; for secret purposes it was all but ideal. It could land and take off in three or four hundred yards of flat grass or clover. It cruised at 165 mph (264 kph); its top speed was only 210 (336), slow even for those days. 161 Squadron's version of it was unarmed, except that the pilot carried a pistol. Such helicopters as then existed were too slow and much too noisy; the Lysander stepped in for them, and did well.

The drill was simple: lights like a capital gamma, Γ, with the agent at the bottom (light A) and his helper, if he had one, at the corner (light B), the wind blowing from B to A. The pilot landed as near A as he could, with that light on his left, taxied up to B, turned around within the crossbar, taxied back to A, turned around again; stopped; let his passengers land and embark; and took off. The whole business should be over in two or three minutes; in five or six, if one agent was doing all the ground work (including collecting sticks) by himself. Three Lysanders landed on the same field in Touraine, not far from Saumur, on 12/13 September 1943; put eight men into France and collected eight to take out; and were all airborne again in nine minutes flat.[54]

Rigid orders were given to the agents in charge on the ground, all of whom had taken a preliminary course with 161 Squadron in England:

> You are in charge of a military operation. Whatever the rank or importance of your passengers they must be under your orders.
>
> There must be no family parties on the field. If the pilot sees a crowd he may not land. Ensure that at the moment of landing you and your passengers and NOBODY ELSE are on the left of Light A, and your assistant on the left of Light B. Anybody anywhere else, especially anybody approaching the

aircraft from the right, is liable to be shot by the pilot.[55]

Exactly the same drill was used, and the same rules applied, with the other aircraft usually used from England, the Hudson, a twin-engined American light bomber. This carried a couple of fixed forward-firing machine-guns, and the RAF added to it a Boulton Paul power turret near the tail, which held two more; this gave it some chance of self-defence if intercepted, which it hardly ever was. The King had now and then used a Hudson before the war to fly round the British Isles; his own aircraft, and Fielden, his personal pilot, formed the nucleus of 161 Squadron. When the squadron formed, it had seven Lysanders as well, raised to ten in January 1944, when it also got four more Hudsons, and to thirteen next May, when the Hudson total rose to six.[56]

The Hudson needed an open space twice as large as a Lysander for landings and take-offs: a long half-mile at least (say 850m), and agents were told to look for a thousand yards (nearly a kilometre). It could fly faster (240 mph, 360 kph), and could carry far more passengers – ten were no trouble, thirteen on a single flight are on record.[57] Disused grass airfields were quite often used for it.[58]

As it was bigger than a Lysander – it had a 60-foot (18.29m) instead of a 42-foot (12.71m) wingspan – and, with its two engines, noisier, it was more conspicuous, but it had other advantages besides carrying capacity. One was range. A Lysander, even with an extra petrol tank, could hardly cover more than 700 miles (1120km); that is, from the advance base the squadron habitually used at Tangmere near Selsey Bill, it could just about reach Lyons. A Hudson's range was 200 miles (320km) longer; it could therefore reach farther into occupied Europe.[59] Moreover, in a Hudson the pilot did not have to navigate himself. Lysander pilots had to find their own way; careful map reading, before they left and in the air, was indispensable for them, and without it they would be lucky to return at all, as well as most unlikely to reach their goals. The Hudson pilot could leave all that to his navigator, who had to read his maps just as carefully, but did not have to look after the business of flying the aircraft as well.

By a stroke of luck, the notes written for his fellow pilots by Hugh Verity, who commanded the Lysander flight of 161 Squadron in 1943 – and went to France, and came back, twenty-nine times that year – have survived and are in print. In them he explains in precise detail how he and his companions did their job. He began: 'By far the greatest amount of work you do to carry out a successful pick-up happens before you leave the ground.' He went on to describe which maps to use and how to use them; what to take and what to leave behind; how to relate map to ground from the air; exactly what to do on arrival at the target; and how to navigate equally carefully on the way back. 'Finally, remember that Lysander and Hudson operations are perfectly normal forms of war transport and don't let anyone think they are a sort of trick-cycling spectacle.'[60]

Verity's achievement in safe multiple secret landings and take-offs, astounding as it was, did not remain a record for long. Peter Arkell made thirty-five successful Lysander sorties through the Burmese mountains, much trickier flying country than France, between October 1944 and August 1945.[61] He flew in 357 Squadron, under (Sir) Lewis Hodges, a former flight commander in 161 Squadron. 358 was the other special duties squadron allocated to the Far East; three more, 618, 240 and 160, were added in the closing stages of the war. All of them had to cope with the Asiatic difficulty that was not much appreciated by senior staff in London who had never ventured east of Suez: Asia, like Oceania, is very large.

But before looking at the Far East, we must glance at

the Near. Dakotas, sturdy aircraft used a few times into France in August and September 1944, were extensively used into Italy and the Balkans, both for drops and for pick-ups. The 7th and 51st American Transport Squadrons operated under 334 Wing, RAF (an unusual but not an inefficient system) from Brindisi into Yugoslavia and Albania, in the spring of 1944; and were replaced in April that year by the 60th Troop Carrier Group, of four Dakota squadrons, doing the same work. By this time the Balkans were so honeycombed by SOE and OSS missions that the ludicrously named Balkan Air Terminal Service (BATS) had thirty-six different landing strips for them to use.[62] They were backed by 624 Squadron RAF, with one flight of Halifaxes and one of long-range American Liberators, moved forward from Derna on the Libyan coast, and a Polish unit, 1386 Flight, with Halifaxes. This of course was well on in the war. Then as before, aircraft range was a vital limiting factor for SOE.

While Russia and Germany were on friendly terms with each other, from August 1939 to June 1941, there was no prospect that RAF aircraft on secret missions could land on Russian territory to refuel; this meant that eastern Poland and Finland were out of SOE's range, and western Poland could only be reached in a fourteen-hour flight in a Whitley. Even after the Russians changed sides, they stonily maintained the rule that no foreign aircraft on clandestine business would be allowed to land on Soviet soil. They relaxed it once only, during the Warsaw rising, for some American bomber units untrained in this sort of work, who dropped from much too high; never for the British.

A Whitley's range, greater than a Wellington's, was about 850 miles (1360km). At that extreme range the load was hardly an economical one, as six or seven tons of fuel would have to be carried for a single ton's load of stores or agents. A Halifax could reach out about a hundred miles (160km) farther: 624 Squadron's pilots found they

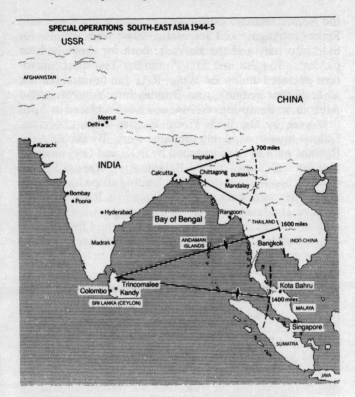

SPECIAL OPERATIONS SOUTH-EAST ASIA 1944-5

could just get to Warsaw from the heel of Italy, but had no more than a few minutes in which to find – or not to find – their dropping zones before they had to turn for the long haul back, or face the prospect of ditching in the Adriatic; if indeed a Luftwaffe or Red Air Force fighter had not picked them off already. Men might be recovered from a ditching; their machines would certainly be lost.

Similar troubles affected the pilots of very long-range American aircraft in Asia: Catalina flying boats, or Liberators. (It took a long time to modify the Liberator's far

too visible exhausts before it was safe to fly at night.[63])
Super-fortresses, like Lancasters, were never available for
SOE. To get to the coast of Malaya by Catalina from
Ceylon, put agents ashore in a dinghy, and return might
take eighteen hours or more; a few Liberator sorties,
from eastern Bengal down towards Singapore, lasted for
more than twenty-four (see map opposite).

Moreover, difficult as it often was to find a DZ in the
comparatively open country of western or southern
Europe, hunting for a smoke or torch signal in the jungles
of south-east Asia was often a nightmare. Normally pilots
required a moon more than half full, in a sky more than
half clear of cloud, before they would contemplate going
on a night operation for SOE at all: conditions not by any
means sure to be got in the sky, however bright the
forecaster. Yet though weather forecasts could not be
relied on, the moon's phases could. Hence, in a memorable phrase of Robin Brook's, in SOE 'for at least two
years the moon was as much of a goddess as she ever was
in a near eastern religion':[64] the air force absolutely
insisted on her presence. On the other hand, the navy
absolutely insisted on her absence: risking one of HM
submarines, or even an MTB, for the sake of the apparent
ragamuffins whom SOE wished to transport was bad
enough, but would be unacceptable if heightened by a
moon. It was not therefore difficult for SOE's enemies to
suggest that in the organisation's ways of going about its
work there was something lunatic. SOE could not help
this; but was never quite able to shake off the implications
of craziness.

Pilots on clandestine drops did not always have to rely
entirely on map reading and dead reckoning, though a
Lysander with its one-man crew could never manage
navigational aids supplied for the rest of Bomber Command, such as Gee and H2S. Two special devices were to

be had for Hudsons, one codenamed 'Eureka/Rebecca', the other called the S-phone.

'Eureka!' – ancient Greek for 'I have found it!' – was what Archimedes called from his bath when he discovered his hydrostatic principle. The name was given to a radar device invented by the Telecommunications Research Establishment (TRE) and available from late 1942 to work from a fixed point on the ground to a travelling set, codenamed 'Rebecca', which could be carried either in a ship or in an aircraft. Lysanders were too small to carry the straight 25-foot aerial that 'Rebecca' required; Hudsons and MTBs were not. 'Eureka' had a slim, 5-foot metal mast, put up on a metal tripod 7 feet high, connected up to a closed box below it. The agent working it had nothing to do but set it up, switch it on and off, and from time to time renew its batteries (it needed 8 watts of power). The whole thing packed away into a just-manageable case – it weighed nearly a hundredweight – measuring about $30'' \times 15'' \times 10''$ ($76 \times 38 \times 25$cm). When – but only when – 'Rebecca' called it (in a prearranged code) on 214 megacycles, a set-up 'Eureka' responded at 219 megacycles. A dial in the aircraft or ship carrying 'Rebecca' showed how far away and in what direction the 'Eureka' beacon was.

This was almost too good to be true. TRE was proud of its invention; the RAF was delighted with it; SOE's staff thought it fine; airborne forces used it often and with great success. SOE's agents were far more dubious. Once the box was opened at a control, there was no possibility at all of explaining it away. One strong man could carry it, but not for long. It was so secret that nobody was ready with explanations to agents of what it was for, or how much it would be to their advantage to use it. Sometimes headquarters urged, sometimes ordered, agents to receive and deploy 'Eurekas'. A few obeyed; most looked the other way. 'The few who did set up their Eurekas were delighted with the results; old mine shafts, deep river beds, old quarries hold the rest.'[65] The Germans knew all about the 'Eureka' by the spring of 1943:[66] but had no counter to it.

The S-phone was of more immediate profit to the agent, a lot less bulky at the ground end, and more warmly received. This was SOE's own invention; the signals staff were as proud of it as TRE was of 'Eureka'. It was a variant on the portable radio-telephone which soldiers and civilians alike had developed before the war; it used very little power – its output was as low as 0.1 to 0.2 watts; it was an early experiment in the miniaturising of wirelesses that has since become commonplace. It was a small transceiver (transmitter and receiver combined), which an agent could wear strapped to his chest; it contained four or five valves, according to the model; and with it one could talk, over a short range, and if one took care to keep oneself pointed towards the other set, as clearly and as easily to a set carried in an aircraft or a ship as one could on a well-run domestic telephone. It could talk to an aircraft at 10,000 feet at about forty miles, and one at 500 feet at about six miles. From ground level, it could hardly be intercepted at all. Its user could stand on a beach and lean forward to make it audible by sea. By a nice clandestine touch, the mouthpiece was so designed that nothing could be heard by anyone standing beside the speaker. The whole apparatus, with carrying belt, batteries, aerial and all, only weighed some 15lb (6.75kg).[67]

The great advantage of the S-phone was that conversations on it were clear enough for friends to recognise each others' voices: it therefore provided a cast-iron genuine method by which home base could probe the security of a circuit about which doubts had been expressed, from any quarter. Not the least mysterious feature of the entanglement with the Abwehr and the Sicherheitsdienst into which the Netherlands section (N) of SOE in north-west Europe fell, is that no use was made of the S-phone to try to talk to any of the agents on the ground, though several sets were sent to Holland. Certainly, German anti-aircraft defences were thick along the Dutch coastline and between Amsterdam and Eindhoven; and the country did lie athwart the RAF's main route to Germany, therefore attracting some of the best German night-fighter defences. RAF losses in drops to the Netherlands were unusually heavy. No one realised till too late that they were heavy not wholly because of the strength of the defences but also because of the weakness of SOE's arrangements on the ground; which a single daring S-phone sortie might conceivably have unravelled.

SOE made one other use of the air: for the indispensable links between base and circuits in the field by wireless telegraphy. Every circuit of any size included a wireless operator; almost every parachute drop was preceded by wireless arrangements for it; without wireless, circuits were out of touch with arms supply, ammunition supply, in some desolate areas food supply as well. The ideal circuit organiser was his own wireless operator; this was not often the case. The more usual grouping to run a circuit consisted of an organiser – usually, but not always, a task for a man; a courier – often, but not always, a woman; a wireless operator, who might be a man or a woman as chance and friendship under training arranged; and a sabotage instructor who was always a man. Men and women at Beaulieu were encouraged to look out there for those with whom they felt they could, and those with whom they felt they could not, work closely together in the field.

In towns, sensible organisers and wireless operators took care not to see too much of each other; for the wireless operator was always the circuit's weakest point. The Germans, like the British, kept a constant watch on every wireless wavelength, and it took only twenty or thirty minutes for a team of their armed direction-finders to get within a few yards of an operator who was fool enough to remain on the air so long.[68] Relays of thirty clerks with cathode-ray tubes in the Gestapo's head-quarters in the Avenue Foch in Paris, for example, kept up a continuous watch on every conceivable frequency. When a new set opened up, it was bound to show up on a tube; the frequency could be read off at once. In a couple of minutes, alerted by telephone, direction-finders at Brest, Augsburg and Nuremberg were starting to take cross-bearings; within a quarter of an hour, detector vans would be closing in on the triangle a few miles across that the cross-bearings had indicated. Some of SOE's early organisers in France and Belgium insisted on sending messages so verbose that their operators had to remain at their morse keys for hours at a time; and, inevitably, they were caught.

It did not take long for Gubbins, as head of operations, to spot what was wrong, or for the signals training school at Thame Park to start to impress on operators – as Beaulieu explained to organisers – that mortal danger lay in trying to send long messages by wireless. If long messages had to be sent at all, they could go by courier – which might take several weeks – or by Lysander. The Poles operated almost routine courier services out of Poland southwards into neutral Turkey and westwards to Gibraltar – three or five weeks at least would be needed for these journeys; nearer England, agents preferred to find a Lysander, or not to send long messages at all.

By the winter of 1943–4 – hardly before time – there was an order: no wireless telegraphy (W/T) transmission was to last longer than five minutes. This, if agents stuck to it, made life difficult for the enemy; but not impossible, unless the agent moved often and kept varying the frequency he used. If by the time they got to the triangle of error picked out by the massive fixed stations the set had fallen silent, detector cars and vans that had missed an original broadcast on a new wavelength might hang about for days or even weeks, waiting till the set came on the air again; and might then be able to pounce quickly. Not all the operators – or all the staff in SOE – were bright enough to take in the degree of danger involved, obvious though it can look to anybody in retrospect now that we know what the Germans' detailed arrangements were. As late as mid-January 1944 Yolande Beekman, the Swiss operator of the unforgettable Gustave Bieler ('Guy'), a Canadian of great shrewdness and steadiness of character,[69] was committed to sending to London from the same attic in St Quentin, at the same hour, on the same three days of every week: this was fatal both to her and to 'Guy', who happened to be with her when the direction-finders finally closed in to arrest her. Neither came back.

An agent's life was always composed of weighing one risk against another: Bieler and Beekman presumably thought that it was safer to stay with a reliable French family, secure from prying eyes, than to run the risks of constant movement through enemy controls; and got it wrong. It was more usual for an operator to protect herself – or himself – with a team of watchful friends, than to rely on a fully friendly landlord and landlady.

It was particularly bad luck for Yolande Beekman that the timetabling of calls between home station and overseas was improved shortly after she left for the field (by Lysander) in September 1943. Up till then operators had each taken a schedule – called a sked for short – of precise times at which to call home station, or to stand by to receive traffic from it. These might, as in her case, be narrowly limited and repetitive. It was an advance to vary the schedules so that operators called up at irregular hours; it was still more of an advance to arrange for them to switch frequencies at short intervals. A further advance towards operational safety was made in 1944. It was then arranged that all home station's traffic – or at least all its routine traffic – went out by night, so that operators could listen to it quietly in their bedrooms, and do all their deciphering behind locked doors. For a few minutes, at irregular times, each day, the operator had the chance to send traffic to home station. Ideally there was also a frequency on permanent standby, which could be used in emergency by any circuit that was in an immediate crisis: this was something of a counsel of perfection. The complaint from operators in the field that they could not raise home station was almost as frequent as the complaint, sent through some neighbouring operator or by courier, that they could not get their sets to work at all, because they had not survived the shock of being parachuted. This last complaint got less frequent as the war went on and the quality both of sets and of parachute packaging improved.

Wideawake operators soon became aware of the signs of Gestapo interest in themselves: closed unmarked light vans, moving slowly – these carried detector equipment; and, when the hunt got closer still, fat men in raincoats, walking slowly, who seemed often to consult their wristwatches. In fact they wore on their wrists small portable detector dials wired up to sets strapped to their waists – hence the apparent fatness. Well-organised operators had a protection team to warn them if either of these kinds of enemy approached, or if anything else alarming happened. These teams were usually armed, if only with Stens, and prepared if need be to try to shoot their way out of trouble. It was much more prudent to slip away unobtrusively, abandoning that hour's schedule and, if worst came to worst, the set (wiped clean of fingerprints): bad luck for the family in whose house the set was found by the enemy. They would certainly be arrested, probably deported to Germany, possibly shot straight away.

Sets were not, till 1944, small enough to be slipped into the pocket: at first, far from it. Indeed, when SOE was founded short-wave wireless transmission was still wrapped in a cloud of mystique at senior staff levels. No radio hams moved in such circles (except the Earl of Suffolk, and he was soon killed in action), and it was taken for granted by all concerned that when C said it was an esoteric business, best left to those who knew about it, he was right. It was therefore left to SIS to provide SOE with any secret transmitters it could spare, and with its ciphers, and to handle any traffic that arrived from the field.

Here was another sphere in which inter-secret service rivalries could and did flourish. Old SOE hands used to debate, long afterwards, whether SIS had been more obstructive in its delays over producing forged documents – before SOE got its own forgery section, which duplicated a lot of SIS's work[70] – or in the troubles it made about wireless; and decided that on the whole wireless had been worse. Not surprisingly, SIS always gave first priority to its own projects and its own friends; SOE got exasperated at being treated as the runt of the litter.[71]

One wireless mystery caused a lot of confusion then, and still sometimes trips up the inexpert: a phenomenon called skip. All sensible technicians agreed that clandestine messages would have to pass by morse code in W/T on short-wave sets: short-wave means a frequency between 1.5 and 30 megacycles a second (mc/s). Anything sent out at these frequencies skips – bounces back off the ionosphere on to the earth, and then bounces up again, and back once more, repeatedly: creating zones of silence and zones of good reception that may alternate all around the globe – and may vary according to time of day, season of the year, or prevalence of sunspots.[72] Geology can affect W/T also: from some kinds of soil or subsoil transmission is much more effective than from others. Operators under training for SOE learned about this at Thame Park, and did their best to site their sets accordingly in the field. It was not an easy subject to understand in any detail, and sometimes positively caused confusion: once at least, at an alarmingly high level.

In the spring of 1944, after Stawell had replaced Glenconner in the Mediterranean, the army authorities were anxious to send forward all the Cairene SOE wireless and cipher staffs to join him in Italy as soon as possible. The point was referred right up to the chiefs of staff committee. Gubbins was not in London; Sporborg had to present SOE's case to the chiefs, and found that Brooke, their chairman, was pressing him hard to conform to the army's wishes. Sporborg was no wireless expert, but had been carefully briefed by Nicholls, SOE's director of signals, about skip and about the unbearable technical intricacies of re-equipping all of SOE's wireless operators in the Balkans – there were about forty of them by this time – with new crystals (to work on new wavelengths), and in some cases with new sets (to suit different and shorter ranges), all at the same moment. Cunningham, the First Sea Lord, who in Sporborg's experience as a rule dozed amiably while SOE's affairs were in debate, listened attentively and took the point. 'CIGS,' he said to Brooke, 'the young man is quite right, you must leave the wireless base in Cairo'; so it was settled.[73]

By this time of course SOE was fully in charge of its own wirelesses; but it had had to begin with whatever SIS dispensed from its wireless headquarters at Station X, Bletchley Park – a spot ultimately to become famous as the home of the Government Code and Cipher School (GC and CS) and so the source of ultra-secret decipher: not SOE's business.[74]

Agents were not best pleased at SIS's first offering, a plywood box that weighed some 45 lb (20kg), already looked old-fashioned and contained a Mark XV two-valve transmitter fitted with a morse key, and its power pack, a 6-volt car battery. A similar box held the Mark XV three-valve receiver. The transmitter could develop 20 watts, and be tuned to any frequency between 3.5 and 16 mc/s. Though cumbrous, to put it mildly, it was adequate for the passing of morse traffic over any range; one of these sets survived the whole occupation in Paris, and is now to be seen in the army museum there. SIS next developed a smaller and much more manageable device, called the paraset: a cadmium steel box measuring 8½″ × 5½″ × 4½″ (220 × 140 × 111mm), a transceiver. By itself it only weighed about 3½ lb (1.6kg); its power pack, also with a 6-volt battery, was nearly twice as heavy. Its single transmitting valve could use any frequency between 3 and 7.6 mc/s; its power output was 5 watts.

Both these transmitters were tuned with slices of quartz, cut to a precise wavelength: these all-precious objects, called crystals, which determined frequency, were about the size of a postage stamp. Each was mounted in a little rectangular bakelite box, with a pair of prongs to plug it into the set.[75]

The Poles meanwhile, working quietly in an electronic instrument factory at Letchworth, were outdistancing SIS in transmitter design. Lorain claims that 'the advanced technology of their devices pushed all other existing devices down to the status of museum pieces'.[76] Among some ten sets they developed in 1941–4, he illustrates two, the BP3 and the AP4; each a little larger than SIS's paraset, each covering 2–8 mc/s, and each much tougher and more efficient.[77] But these were designed by the Poles for their own purposes. They used them for their own exiled government's communications with Poland, and were prepared to provide them for EU/P parties in France; at first, when asked for more, they protested that there were none. Gubbins was friendly enough with Sikorski, their prime minister, and with Colonel Gano, whom he once described as the brightest intelligence officer he had ever met,[78] to coax a few out of them; but SOE needed more than a few.

The solution was not hard to find. Sweet-Escott, as a businessman, thought it uneconomic;[79] Gubbins and Ozanne, Nicholls' predecessor as head of signals, fighting men who understood the needs of war, knew what had to be done. SOE designed and built its own sets. From 1 June 1942, its wireless organisation was entirely separated from SIS's; so was its coding and ciphering. 'Passy', the head of de Gaulle's secret services, no mean judge, remarked in close retrospect that SOE's wireless services were both more comprehensive and more competent than SIS's.[80]

C thereby lost his strongest grip on SOE. Up till then, he could – if he cared – read all SOE's signals traffic, and know exactly what successes and failures came his rivals' way. Thereafter he was much less well informed. GC and CS was far too busy trying to unravel the Germans' cipher traffic, on solving which the fate of the nation hung, to have time to spare for the comparatively trivial task of deciphering SOE's.

It is only fair to SIS to remark at once that, while they had been running SOE's signals traffic, there had never been any unavoidable delays in passing messages on, nor had they been mutilated at all in transit. At first they went from Bletchley to Baker Street by dispatch rider, which added a further hour or two to the gap between the sending of a message and its receipt; before long teleprinters were used, almost instantaneous and adequately secure.

SOE set up two home stations, between Bletchley and Thame – at Grendon Underwood and Poundon, on the Oxfordshire-Buckinghamshire border. They lay in flat farmland, and were suitably placed both to receive and to transmit. Lorain publishes a diagram of the great festoon of aerials in which Poundon was eventually shrouded in the summer of 1944.[81] As with so much in the English (contrast the Italian) countryside, when the villagers around discovered they would not be told what went on there, they ceased to ask. The stations normally transmitted on 250 watts, but had a 15kW transmitter in reserve if any operator reported severe difficulties in reception.

Nicholls had had a long past in the Royal Corps of

Signals, which he had joined during the 1914–18 war; he had been appointed MBE as far back as 1921, for services not publicly specified – in fact to do with his work in the Y service, the army's interception branch. So he already knew something about the problems of clandestine wireless traffic; and, like Sir Frank Nelson, he was acceptable to C: an important drop of oil on the point of friction between SIS and SOE that SOE's departure to make its own sets occasioned.

Nicholls had working under him a small, efficient body of designers; the S-phone is testimony enough to their competence. Some of them were technicians, some physicists, some radio hams; all knew their business, and had sympathy with the people who were going to carry the sets they designed into danger. Their original preference was for a set that could be carried in an ordinary attaché-case – an object that should not collect a second glance in the streets of a large European town, though it would look far out of place in a Burmese or Malayan jungle. They had the A Mark II* in action by October 1942 (preceded by the A Mark I in August): three metal boxes, each 11″ × 4″ × 3″ (264 × 96 × 67mm), packed side by side in their case with a little room at the end for operator's oddments; sending at 5 watts on 3–9 mc/s, and weighing about 20lb (9kg).[82]

Its successor, known as the B2 (technically, the 3 Mark II), was even more popular with operators, was considerably more powerful at an output of 30 watts, and did its job well. Like the A Mark II*, it used American valves called Loctal, sturdy and compact; it only needed two of them. It could transmit between 3 and 16 mc/s; it could also receive. None of SOE's sets suffered from a tiresome disadvantage of the paraset, which when switched to receive would upset any other wireless set in use for a hundred yards around: a severe brake on action in built-up areas where civilians were still allowed their own receiving sets (in some occupied areas these were forbidden). The B2 filled its little suitcase entirely, and weighed 32lb (14½kg).[83] It had an ingenious built-in device meant to foil a common interceptors' trick. When the search for a clandestine set had been narrowed down to a particular suburb, Gestapo agents might switch off the electric current at the main, block by block, while the set was on the air, and then close in on whichever block fell silent. With the B2, all one had to do when the power failed was to throw a single switch, and thus go over immediately to the 6-volt battery it contained; this was supposed hardly to cause a tremor in the transmission, and to leave the operator comparatively safe.

A defect in the B2 was its recognisability. A woman whose flat lay near Marylebone station got to know several SOE operators in training by sight because she would see them on Saturday mornings trotting past her window, all clutching identical little attaché-cases as well as some other piece of luggage, getting used to the feel of their sets as part of their personality. Luckily she knew how to keep her mouth shut. A more dangerous and absurd incident shows how recognisable it was to the enemy. The story has been told before, but bears retelling, as an example of the extra strong nerves and extra quickness of grasp anybody might need to get through a clandestine crisis. This is the case of

'Felix', a Jew of Alsatian-Polish origins was assistant [to the] wireless operator to the young 'Alphonse', a British agent in southern France. He, 'Alphonse', and 'Emanuel' the wireless operator [a quiet Canadian] all got out of the same train at Toulouse; 'Felix', carrying the transmitter in its readily recognisable suitcase, went up to the barrier first. Two French policemen were conducting a cursory check on identity papers. Behind them, two uniformed SS men were sending everyone with a case or big package to the *consigne*, where more SS men were making a methodical luggage search. 'Felix' took in the scene; ignored the French police; held his suitcase high; and called in authoritative German, 'Get me a car at once, I have a captured set.' He was driven away in a German-requisitioned car; had it pull up in a back street; killed the driver, and reported to 'Alphonse' with the set for orders.[84]

SOE's signals section next went on to design the A Mark III set, much smaller and lighter than the B2; on the verge of the miniature, but the transistor had yet to be invented (see p. 149). The A Mark III weighed some 5½lb (2.4kg); with all its accessories – in a tiny suitcase – 9lb (4kg). It measured 8½″ × 7½″ × 3¼″ (216 × 191 × 82mm), in its case 13″ × 9″ × 4″ (330 × 228 × 102mm). The catch about it was short range: it could not reliably reach more than 500 miles with its 5-watt output.[85] For longer ranges the B2, six times as powerful, was needed.

Late in the war, SOE did produce a transmitter that could fit in to a large pocket: called 51/1. It had three miniature valves, weighed only a pound and a quarter (567gm) even with its battery, and measured 5¾″ × 4½″ × 1½″ (146 × 114 × 38mm). In spite of its small size – hardly larger than a fat volume in the *World's Classics* – this set could send admirably clear messages over ranges up to 600 miles.[86] The Poles were rumoured to have a transmitter, no less efficient, twice as small – not much larger than a packet of cigarettes; no details of this are known to the present writer.

SOE treated a great many B2s to survive tropical conditions, and sent them out to the Far East in the winter of 1944–5 (the set had become available in 1943). Unluckily, suspicious signals officers in SOE's far-flung supply depots in India, who had had no personal experience of the design department at work and did not trust it, readjusted them, sometimes with distressing results. Concealment remained a problem; but then, the set was a good deal more easy to hide away under a pile of leaves than was the still more conspicuous operator.

One aspect of operator training gave everybody confidence and has been commented on constantly by later writers. As they learned morse (if they did not know it already – many did, having come in from the Boy Scouts or from one of the service signals units) wireless operators came to tap it out in their own individual style; and they were encouraged to believe that this style, once fully developed, was as instantly recognisable as a handwriting. Before they passed out from Thame Park (or wherever else farther afield, such as Guyotville, they received their W/T training) they left behind them a record of their sending styles. Many of them got to know in return the sending styles of particular girls at home station. Anyone who has had much to do with listening to morse will know that some operators' idiosyncrasies are instantly spottable on the air.

Unfortunately, just as handwritings can be forged, so can morse styles. For once I have to disagree with the invaluable Pierre Lorain, who goes so far as to state that 'each time there was a change in operator, it was immediately detected'.[87] Unhappily, the evidence does not bear this out. In the Netherlands, the Abwehr and the Sicherheitsdienst – co-operating for once – were able to simulate the touch of a morse key of more than a dozen of N section's operators, to the confusion of that section's efforts to organise Dutch armed resistance. In France, several other operators were also imitated with entire success: including one unhappy Canadian who was arrested before ever he had had a chance to work his set at all. He was put into solitary confinement in Fresnes prison, close to Orly on the south side of Paris. He was bored beyond tears. A sympathetic warder gave him a morse key to play with, to give him something to fiddle with to while away the time; and a German signals corporal sitting in the next cell was thus able to discover his precise sending style, which was imitated to the Germans' profit for several months to come (see p. 189).

On the other hand, every single wireless operator the Germans sent to England during the war was played back to them with success by MI5, by a few operators in the Royal Corps of Signals; so not all the credit lies with one side. What these three examples make only too clear is that 'fingerprinting' an agent's sending style was no sure way of detecting that he had not been captured. SOE's own security section did not rely too much on fingerprinting; it insisted on the presence also in messages of some sort of security check. This, again, has become well known and has been much commented on, not always by those who have understood the subject properly.

There are two kinds of security check in a text: routine and random. SOE long insisted on routine ones: a particular error inserted at a particular point was the most usual (tenth and twentieth letter of every message misplaced by three places in the alphabet, for example). It was soon known to the Germans that these routine checks existed, so agents took two of them: one to confess to the Germans (the bluff check), the other to be kept back from the enemy, but always inserted in messages to friends (the true check). A staff officer (never yet publicly identified) in F section sent to a newly parachuted wireless operator, who had been arrested on the landing ground because of earlier F section errors and had left his true check out of his first message sent under duress, a rap over the knuckles for forgetting it so soon: a monumental error and one several times repeated[88] (cp. p. 194).

The random check was much more efficient, but called for a little subtlety. It had to be prearranged by word of mouth before the agent left. To an obvious message, such as 'Shall we send whisky', to which the reply was obvious ('Whisky welcome'), the agent – if free – was to send instead some wholly inapposite remark such as 'Love to Deirdre'. Even this system would not work with an agent who had determined to change sides altogether and support the axis powers wholeheartedly: none altogether did.

Security checks, like provision of sets, had in principle to be arranged from the allied side; but one vital innovation was made in the field. This was the development of the high-speed transmitter, which has now (if we can believe the newspapers) become commonplace. It was invented by a Danish wireless engineer, L. D. A. Hansen, in 1944; it improved the speed of sending about seven times, a lifesaver quite literally for those who were able to use it.[89] This developed too late for SOE to be able to make use of it elsewhere.

One point in wireless tactics remained fixed: no one in the field could use a set to anyone but home station. Even if agents were close together and in urgent need of getting in touch with each other, unless they could manage touch direct by courier, they had to go through base. This seemingly cumbrous system was the only safe one. Everyone in SOE's high command agreed that, once agents started broadcasting to each other direct, they would multiply the Gestapo's, or the OVRA's, or the Kempeitai's, chance of catching them: the risks were unthinkable.

A single exception was thought up all the same, but never came to anything. A mirage of a secret army in southern France, a quarter of a million strong and under trained regular officers, dazzled F section in the autumn of 1942. This purely notional body – as it turned out to be – was named 'Carte' after its prophet, the painter André Girard (father of Danielle Delorme). He was a marvellously persuasive talker, and talked Bodington – second-in-command of F, who visited him at Antibes by felucca – into the notion that so large a force would have to have internal wireless sets to make its work more easy. F section indeed sent thirty at least of them into the Riviera by sea; they were put on one side, turned up later 'already almost useless with damp and neglect', and were never used.[90]

One of the difficulties that would have attended the provision of wireless sets for field use would have been cipher security; and this chapter must end with a few words on what SOE's code and cipher systems were.

SOE's ciphers were devised by Leo Marks, then in his twenties, son of the famous bookseller at 84 Charing Cross Road. He was already widely read, and had an ingenious mind that was prepared to turn in any direction at a moment's notice. Night duty officers in Baker Street found him ready to defend or attack any philosophical position, at any hour; after the war, he became well known in the entertainment industry. He took infinite trouble to get to know each of the agents with whom he dealt, and to make quite sure that each agent had fully grasped the particular cipher method he or she was to use. This inner knowledge was often a help to SOE, for only too often messages would arrive garbled: either because the operator was too cold, or too hot, or too hurried, or too frightened, to transmit quite accurately, or because atmospherics, or enemy jamming, or both, had interfered with reception. Marks, having devised the cipher, having morse code at his fingertips, and knowing the agent, could often unravel tangles that seemed to the inexpert quite impossible to resolve. This was much safer than asking the operator to repeat his or her message and thus expose the set further to the risks of enemy direction-finding.

At Beaulieu agents were taught the Playfair code, invented by Sir Charles Wheatstone, one of the devisers of the telegraph. Wheatstone proposed a single word as the Playfair key; SOE went one move farther, and used any memorable line of verse. Let us take an easy example:

'Who killed Cock Robin?' It is written out in lines of five letters, omitting any letters used already; the rest of the alphabet then fills the 5×5 letter square. I and J count as one.

W	H	O	K	IJ
L	E	D	C	R
B	N	A	F	G
M	P	Q	S	T
U	V	X	Y	Z

The message to be sent – let us suppose another easy one, 'Robert taken' – is divided into bigrams, groups of two letters; any dud being used to fill up a blank space: RO BE RT TA KE NY. Each of these bigrams is encoded by taking the two opposite corners of the rectangle it forms in the word square; thus RO becomes DI or DJ. If both letters of the bigram are in the same line, the next letter to the right of each is used; if both are in the same column, the next letter below. RT thus become GZ. The simple message, simply encoded, becomes DI NL GZ QG HC FV. The wireless operator can confuse things slightly more, by putting the bigrams in groups of five letters: DINLG ZQGHC FV, and filling up the gap at the end with three more null letters. This is by no means an impenetrable code, as Lord Peter Wimsey showed in a Dorothy Sayers novel;[91] though it takes a clever intelligence officer with a particular cast of mind to unravel a Playfair quickly. It might provide some degree of tactical security for a circuit.

Another comparatively simple coding system, known oddly enough as a barn code, was useless by wireless but useful for couriers to carry, or even to send through the post: it was also known as the 'innocent letter'. Prisoners of war made a lot of use of it, both for smuggling in tools to help them escape and for smuggling out fragments of intelligence from enemy territory. In this code, after a prearranged simple signal (such as underlining the date at the head of the letter), particular words could be picked out of the text; any specially sensitive phrase could be spelled out, using the first letters of preselected words. It took a lot of time, patience and paper to compose a really innocent-looking barn-code letter; it suited prisoners of war, who had only too much time on their hands, much better than secret agents, who sometimes had only too little. Alternative systems are explained by Lorain and by Foot and Langley.[92]

For clandestine wireless purposes, Playfair was banned as too dangerous from 1942, and from 1941 agents were already being trained in the more intricate, but still not impenetrable, ciphering system called double transposition. For this the agent had to remember two random numbers, each some six or seven figures long; Thame Park insisted very firmly that they must never be written down, but agents who did not trust their memories preferred writing them down to forgetting them. The plain text was written out under the first random number; then transcribed, reading each column of letters vertically downwards, in the numerical order of each column; then, so enciphered, written down under the second random number, and again read off by numerical order of columns (3 before 4 and so on). Again, an illustration may help. Let us take 487295 and 3258497 as the random numbers, and 'Robert taken Friday' as the message. First, the message is written out under the first number (below left). The columns are then read off in numerical order: EEA RTR TF BKD OAI RNY. This text is then written out under the second number (below right):

4	8	7	2	9	5		3	2	5	8	4	9	7
R	O	B	E	R	T		E	E	A	R	T	R	T
T	A	K	E	N	F		F	B	K	D	O	A	I
R	I	D	A	Y			R	N	Y				

Again the columns are read off in numerical order: EBN EFR TO AKY TI RD RA, and the result is put in groups of five letters: EBNEF RTOAK YTIRD RA. This text is ready for transmission. At the receiving end, the text is written out in vertical columns, by numerical order of column again, under the second key, read off horizontally, and put under the first key in vertical columns; the message then ought to be readable horizontally at a glance.

In actual practice, such a message would also include a serial number and the operator's codename, and the date (if not also a time of origin): all of them useful points of entry for enemy decipherers trying to break down the code. (Some of SOE's sections, moreover, made their operators' tasks clumsier, and might make things more easy for the enemy, by saddling the operators with long codenames that would take time and trouble to encipher. One F set for example was called – as F used garments for some operators' codenames – 'Mackintosh blue', which took up fourteen letters; something briefer might have been more safe.)

This sounds complicated; indeed it was. It took much more time than Playfair; and still further complications could be added to it by combining it with a book code. Book codes were favourites at the time with the Russian intelligence services; Radó of the 'Red Three' and Trepper of the 'Red Orchestra' are both supposed to have used them. To work a book code, agent and home station had to have two absolutely identic copies of the same book; the opening of each message would show what page and line were being used to guide the transposition of what followed. This was all right for someone who had Radó's excellent cover as a man who made maps for newspapers; for a wireless operator on the run in the hills of the Auvergne or the mountains of Montenegro it was not quite so easy. Lorain, as before, makes most of the complications clear.[93]

In 1943 SOE moved over to the more intricate Delastelle system, which went back to the 5 × 5 letter square used for Playfair, but made it less readily solvable by putting numbers along the upper and the left-hand sides of the square, and reading off co-ordinates (as from a gridded map) instead of using letters at the corners of rectangles.[94] This was getting close to the system upon which SOE settled in the autumn of 1943 for its agents, the system that the world's secret services all now seem to use: one-time pad. Agent and home station held the only two copies of pads of random figures or letters; as each one was used, it was burnt.[95] For mainline traffic between its bases, SOE had been using this for two years already.

This was fine and secure but there were still one or two catches in it. At first the maps were printed on silk; this turned out to be hard to burn, a distinct awkwardness for an operator whose protection team told him the enemy were closing in and he had better disappear. Readily inflammable nitrate-coated paper was then used instead; that was bulky. An operator remembers having to set off into the Carinthian mountains with half his rucksack full of unused one-time pads: heavy to carry and impossible to explain away. But then, in a perfectly organised circuit, the enemy were never going to discover the operator's whereabouts, and the fact that there was no chance of any of his messages ever being read by the wrong side was a counterbalance to no end of minor inconveniences.

'Jedburghs', SAS and interallied missions into north-west Europe benefited from a spin-off from SOE's cipher difficulties: from the necessity of making every message as short as possible. SOE produced a piece of silk about twenty inches (50cm) square, printed with some five hundred phrases often used in messages, such as 'safe house available at' or 'drop containers of Bren ammunition'; against each phrase was a four-letter code, BOBO RARA ZUZU or whatever. This was an enormous saver of time and trouble; the code group would be re-enciphered by the wireless operator, so it was quite secure. The Germans undoubtedly knew about this, for they must have captured several of these apparent silk handkerchiefs and understood their use; they were of no real use to their deciphering teams, who wrestled with the impenetrable secrets of the one-time pad.

Very much more elaborate codes were used between SOE's various home stations when they needed to communicate with each other. They had vast trailers, quite unthinkable for clandestines, in which cipher machines could prepare texts with keys hundreds of thousands of letters or figures long. With these Grendon and Poundon could talk, not only to sub-stations at Bicester and Dunbar, installed during the periods of heaviest traffic, but to New York, Cairo, Algiers, Bari, Meerut, Kandy, Brisbane and Kunming, in perfect security.

Axis secret police forces spent a good deal of effort in trying to decrypt SOE's, among other allied services', communications by secret wireless, without much useful result. A lot of their effort was siphoned off, uselessly, into the problem of trying to make sense of the personal message codes (see pp. 198–9); until the moment when an unwary prisoner gave away what two of the codes meant. This grave mistake would have imperilled the whole 'Neptune' landing in Normandy on 5/6 June 1944, on which the fate of the western front depended, had the Germans been more competently organised for making war and prepared to listen to what their secret intelligence staff told them. Such a howler needs discussion in a wider context of security.

VII
Security and penetration

George Washington said in 1777, in a well-known letter discussing the problems of military intelligence, that 'upon Secrecy Success depends in most enterprises of the kind, and for want of it, they are generally defeated, however well-planned or promising of favourable issue'.[1] SOE took this very much to heart. An old secret-service proverb lays down that 'Three can keep a secret, if two of them are dead': hence the loneliness in which many of SOE's leaders, in and out of enemy hands, had to live. The necessary passion for secrecy was now and again carried to absurd lengths: most notably by a London staff officer who received from America, in a message marked 'most secret and personal', the proposed division of labour between SOE and OSS, worked out by Donovan and Taylor in Washington. He kept it to himself. An important emissary of OSS happened to be in London at that time, and on his own initiative started talks on the same point, which reached a conclusion more favourable to the British. When he cabled his results to Washington, OSS believed it had been doublecrossed by SOE: an impression never wholly removed, to which the split in the Anglo-American alliance can perhaps be dated back. As Sweet-Escott put it wryly, 'I was never quite clear whether they suspected our integrity or doubted our competence. Whichever it was it did not help us.'[2]

This is only an extreme example of a general point: that SOE's cloak of secrecy, admittedly indispensable, was often as much of a handicap to it as an advantage. It was indeed a considerable nuisance to those on the inside that they had to go through so many contortions when dealing with the outside world. A minor but telling exasperation arose from a habit some staff officers in SOE developed – using several surnames at once. It was not unknown for those who had to consult Baker Street from other head-quarters to find themselves appearing to speak to two differently-named persons, who shared not only the same telephone extension but precisely the same voice: what Lord Metroland would have called bad tabulation.*

Those who belonged to SOE were expected to tell even their own closest relations that they worked for the relevant service ministry, or for MEW. The fact that they were in a secret service had to remain a secret. Outside the office – in the streets of London, in the pubs round Beaulieu or any other training school – members of SOE staff did not know each other, and were ordered to cut each other dead. One of Holdsworth's junior companions, working small boats from Helford over to Brittany – under a cover that they were doing signals training, which accounted for the forest of masts that the S-phone and so on required – was told by his wife that it was time he went and did something dangerous, like other boys.[3] In the field, the same rule about cutting one's acquaintances dead applied; though it was much more often broken, by agents who were lonely and longed to talk to somebody without reserve. It might also reasonably be broken by an agent whose wireless operator had been arrested, so that he had to have another circuit's help to get in touch with

---

* This happened to me and to several of my colleagues on the intelligence staff at combined operations headquarters.

home base at all; in that case, it was up to him (or her) to take extra care to make sure that the old acquaintance he recognised was not being shadowed by (or worse still had not gone over to) the wrong side.

The rule about not knowing one's fellows in public, as applied in Great Britain, was held a necessary security measure, in the belief that there might be enemy agents on watch near SOE headquarters; though in fact, it is now known, there were none. SOE in its turn did from time to time watch enemy secret service headquarters, closely enough for an operation called 'Ratweek' to be mounted in western and northern Europe in February 1944, with some success, against leading men in the Gestapo.[4] The same codename was used later in the same year for a major assault by partisans, the RAF and the USAAF against German communications in Yugoslavia.[5] This now reads oddly, but there was nothing odd about it at the time. Codenames were allotted in blocks, by an inter-service committee in Whitehall, to formations that needed them, and were supposed to be used at random: those who chose them (occasionally I did so myself) glanced down the list and picked whichever seemed suitable for the job. Once used, and finished with, a codename could be reallocated: hence the odd reappearance during the Falklands troubles in 1982 of codenames elderly service-men had known in entirely different climes.

Whole blocks of codenames of a particular type were used by different country sections of SOE for their agents and circuits: N (Netherlands) used vegetables, F (inde-pendent French) used English occupations, 'Jedburghs' (stiffening parties in 1944) used forenames, and so on. The categories were seldom kept quite distinct. F also used a few names of trees, and its first circuit – 'Autogiro' – was *hors concours*, in every sense in a category of its own. 'Jedburghs' occasionally used spices or drugs or plants instead of forenames (so did other allied missions into France in 1944, such as 'Aloès' in the Vendée or

'Verveine' in the Morvan). 'Jedburghs' had a few other codenames, such as 'Minaret' in the Gard, quite out of their usual run. This was sound security practice: the whole point of a codename ought to be that it gives nothing away.

Giving nothing away lies at the root of security. This applied quite as much in the field as it did under training or at SOE's – or any other – great secret headquarters. A really first-class agent – there were not many of them – took endless trouble about it. Before making any move, he would ask himself (or she would ask herself) whom it would expose; and till the closing stages of the local war, would make it a rule never to expose anybody.

One precaution, at least, a sensible underground leader could take: never to let anyone who worked with him (or her, again) know where, or under what covername, the agent lived. For SOE's work in towns, this usually guaranteed safety. In the country, it was a sound – if not always an easy – rule to make a point of moving house very often indeed, never staying more than a night or two in the same bed or bivouac. In the wilder terrains in which they worked, beds did not often come SOE officers' way; excellent sleeping-bags might serve instead. One at least had the mortification of having his sleeping-bag stolen, almost from under his nose, by a member of his host's household in Albania; the rigidities of Albanian etiquette prevented him from complaining.[6] One extra-cautious agent did not tell Baker Street his real address on operations, either – just in case; and is still alive to say so.[7]

To sum up, in an excellent phrase of one of SOE's men in Stamboul, 'Caution axiomatic, but over-caution results in nothing done'.[8] Those who bothered incessantly about security survived, but few of them had much beyond survival to their credit. To strike and then to survive was the real test.

* * *

A routine part of agents' training consisted of course in listening to lectures and advice from policemen and members of MI5 – some of them seconded to SOE, most of whose security seniors came from this sound source – on what to do when questioned, as many agents were sure to be, as a matter of tyrannous routine, in axis-occupied Europe or Asia. They were warned of the routine police questions: who are you? where are you? where are you going? why? how much money are you carrying? and so on – and advised to keep answers to them pat in their heads, all the time. Part of what being a secret agent means lies in this incessant readiness to play one's part, and explain with perfect naturalness why one is in so unnatural a spot as enemy-held country. Part of it lies too in talking in a dull manner, as has been mentioned earlier (p. 87).

It was vital also to be prepared to answer quite naturally and quite readily – without pausing to wonder what on earth the answer might be – when asked slightly odder questions, such as, where were you demobilised? how many uncles have you got? what was your wife's maiden name? If the string of questions got at all long, it was at once clear to the agent that the police thought that they had got hold of somebody interesting; so it was doubly necessary to be brief, dull, to the point, and – so far as any of the answers might be checkable – accurate. SOE's forgery section knew that an inquisitive policeman might hold a suspect, and ring up the birthplace on the suspect's identity card first of all, to check the details: hence the suspiciously large number of F, RF and DF agents born (if at all elderly) in St Pierre de Martinique, destroyed by volcanic eruption in 1902, or (if born before 1917) in Péronne where the *mairie* had been burned out during the battle of the Somme. Hence also Sweet-Escott's lasting suspicion of anyone who said that he had been born in Vilna.[9]

In England, quite a lot of outsiders who became aware

of edges of the veil of secrecy in which SOE was wrapped tried to pry beneath it: never with disastrous results for SOE, and not often to their own advantage either. Some were simply too stupid to take in the benefits that might come to their own country from having a secret service of which every detail was not laid before them in person. Some guessed what SOE might be doing, believed that they could help, and were unwilling to accept the judgement of those who knew SOE's task better than they did, that they were not adequately, or not in any way, suited for it. Some were nature's troublemakers, shrillies who wanted something to be shrill about and thought they had stumbled on some sort of scandal. Some, well-intentioned but under-informed, believed they had come across an abuse that ought to be exposed in Parliament or in the press. A few questions about ISRB found their way onto the order paper of the House of Commons; they were fielded deftly enough by Dingle Foot.

None of the axis powers succeeded in planting an agent at any SOE headquarters or training schools (so far, it must be added, as is known, but this does amount to a virtual certainty). 'No twelve apostles without a Judas,' says the proverb. It was noticed at the trials at Nuremberg that the Nazi leaders supposed that one among themselves must have been a traitor; how otherwise account for the defeat of invincible Germany? Similarly, some of SOE's enemies have supposed that there must have been a traitor in Baker Street, but have never been able to produce one. A short proof that there was none may be found in the conversation of two French agents of the Sicherheitsdienst, interrogated in Fresnes early in 1945. They were asked whether the SD had in fact got an agent in SOE's headquarters in London, and replied that they had often heard Götz, the head of the SD's wireless section in Paris, complain to his assistant, Placke, that 'we must try and get somebody over there' and regret that they had failed to do so.[10] Neither the Italians nor the Japanese appear to have done any better. Had the Italians done so, Ciano, Mussolini's son-in-law and foreign minister, would have known and would have boasted about it in his diaries; he did not. The Japanese had no real chance, on simple grounds of recognisability. They had had plenty of agents, quite senior army officers disguised as waiters and taxi-drivers, scattered round south-east Asia before their war began, collecting intelligence, but none of them got even an insight into SOE.

Nor did SOE commit SIS's gaffe, and parachute a fully paid-up member of the British Union of Fascists into occupied territory, where he did his best to betray his companions – who court-martialled him and sentenced him to death (what else were they to do?).[11] There was one disagreeable incident in a large SOE circuit, already much plagued by enemy penetration, when a photograph of Hitler was found in the belongings of an agent newly arrived from base, whom nobody liked; he was unobtrusively disposed of, and posted 'missing, believed killed'.

However, there is no getting away from the fact that the Germans did manage three important break-ins to SOE operations through what they called *Funkspiele*, wireless games. A secret-service officer's ideal coup is to plant an agent of his own deep in the bosom of an opponent's service: as Harry Dexter White was, it is clear, in the United States Treasury, or Kim Philby was in the secret intelligence service, by the Russians. The Germans were not as good at this as the Russians; they had to fall back on the lesser, but sometimes quite adequate, ploy of running enemy circuits through captured codes, captured sets, and prisoners who changed sides.

That prisoners were not meant to change sides goes without saying. MI9 joined MI5 in providing lectures at SOE's training schools to explain the duty of a prisoner of war: to tell his captors nothing but his name, his rank and his service number. This doctrine was dinned into all the allied armed forces, but with limited effect. Captivity affects different people in different ways. Some accept the MI9 doctrine, and realise that for them the war is *not* over, despite what their captors have told them; that they can go on playing a useful minor part in it by distracting enemy troops onto the business of guarding themselves, at least, and that they may be able to do a little more, by affecting enemy morale or even by collecting and passing out intelligence. Others give in; a few of them give in so far that they change sides. SOE tried to recruit people who appeared perfectly normal, and to avoid neurotics; the entirely abnormal fact of being a secret agent did make its mark on many of their recruits, and in some cases twisted their characters in ways such recruiters as Jepson had not foreseen. Interrogating Germans often found that it paid them to suggest to some agent whom they thought they had caught that he was small fry; his vanity touched, he would – or might – reply that on the contrary he had been extremely important, and go on to explain how. A few prisoners were far too talkative, with unfortunate results.

Much the worst of the three cases was the Dutch one. Well known though it is, it deserves summary.[12] A diplomat and three army majors headed N section in London: Laming, till the autumn of 1941; Blunt, till February 1943; Bingham, till early in 1944; and Dobson. 'Blunt' was a cover name; he had no connection at all with Anthony Blunt of MI5, the art historian. His real name was Blizard; but as he is called Blunt in the contemporary accounts, Blunt he can remain. N section insisted on looking after all the more technical aspects of sending agents to Holland – clothes, forged papers, wireless, transport; on politics and tactics it co-operated, closely enough, with the Dutch government-in-exile. On the exiled Dutch side, intelligence operations came to be run by the Bureau Inlichtingen (information office) under Major Dr J. M. Somer, and subversion by the Bureau Voorbereiding Terugkeer (office for preparing the return – of the queen) under M. R. de Bruyne – who should be distinguished from his namesake, H. B. A. de Bruyne, 'Bo-Peep' of MI9. De Bruyne often got on badly with Somer and the other leading Dutch intelligence officer, F. van 't Sant. (SOE and SIS were not alone in being rivals.) Their then quite unknown opponents on the continent were H. J. Giskes, a major in the Abwehr, and J. Schreieder, his opposite number in the Sicherheitsdienst.

What N section got done under Laming remains almost unknown. Bad troubles began under Blunt, and got no better under Bingham. The Germans' success turned on three hinges: decipher, interception, and double agency. A Dutch intelligence agent, operating for the Dutch and MI6, called Zomer (distinguish him too, of course, from Dr Somer), was arrested in the late summer of 1941 with a large pile of back messages, from which the Germans' cipher expert – Sergeant E. May – was able to work out MI6's cipher system. On 13 February 1942 two more MI6 agents, Ter Laak and van der Reyden, were arrested; van der Reyden was so angry and so dislocated at getting caught that he said a great deal more than he might have done when May interrogated him, and May's grip on MI6's cipher system became even firmer. At this time, it will be recalled, SOE had not yet got its own cipher section; it depended entirely on MI6 for ciphers as for sets.

With the help of a double agent, the Germans next closed in on an SOE group. They could never have had the successes they did in Holland without the aid of these informers – Dutchmen who pretended to be resisters, but in fact worked with the occupiers: what the Germans called *V-Männer, Vertrauensmänner*, those who could be trusted. These fellows could not; all over Europe they were the bane of honest men and women. Even in Norway there were some; even in Poland they were not absolutely

19. 'Passy' just after the war

20. Jean Moulin

21. Links: packing C-type containers, Italy 1945. 3-inch mortar aslant in foreground

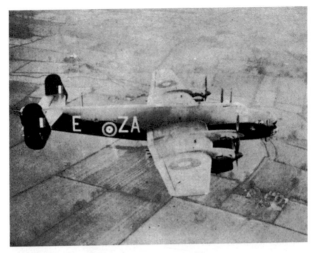

22. Links: a Halifax bomber

23. Links: a daylight Lysander pick-up south of Turin, April 1945: all rules ignored

24. Links: removing stores from a French reception

25. Bren light machine-gun: studio portrait

26. Links: an A Mark III transceiver.

27. *Below* Encipherment in the Double Transposition Code

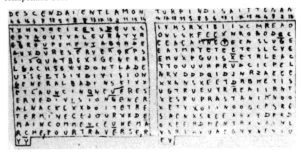

28. A free French wireless operator contacts London.   29. *Below* An SOE One-Time Pad code (on silk)

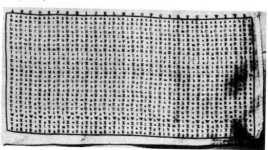

НОВО ВРЕМЕ

Нове мере против бандитизма

30. A Belgrade newspaper offers 100,000 gold Reichsmarks for Tito or Mihailović, 21 July 1943

31. Tito in the mountains

32. Mihailović

33. Marko Hudson

34. Mihailović (hand to chin), Bill Bailey (behind him, wings on breast) and a četnik group

35. A late rail cut, south of Mâcon, France, 30 August 1944. Note plastic, cordtex, Lee-Enfield rifle

36. 'Today we have naming of parts': a maquis instructor holds a Mark II Sten. Its magazine lies on the table, with Ruby, Colt and Le Français pistols and Colt and Bulldog revolvers

unknown, though rare; in France they pullulated; in Holland there were more than enough.

The SOE group was led by Thys Taconis, a fully-trained saboteur, and his wireless operator, H. M. G. Lauwers. They had been parachuted in on 6/7 November 1941; dressed, by a ludicrous gaffe in the clothing section, in absolutely matching clothes – the same raincoats, shirts, socks, shoes, ties, briefcases; one tall thin man, and one short, rather tubby man. As if their clothes were not danger signal enough, there was a howler on each of their identity cards. These included the royal arms of the Netherlands, with two lions as supporters; their lions, instead of facing each other across the shield, both faced the same way. When – at the last minute, in the briefing-shed at Newmarket – Taconis and Lauwers noticed this, they protested. Their conducting officer assured them nobody was going to bother about details like that. This was, to put it mildly, gross over-confidence; though in fairness to him it was not through this crass error, but through others, that they came unstuck.

They settled down to work: Lauwers in The Hague, Taconis at Arnhem. A man called Ridderhof made himself useful to Taconis; he ran a small road-haulage firm, and could provide lorries to take stores away from drops. Now Ridderhof was a *V-Mann*; he told Giskes what was going on in Taconis's circuit, and was used in return to feed bogus intelligence into it. Lauwers' set was in a downtown flat at The Hague, which belonged to a family called Teller. On 6 March 1942 he was at the start of a transmission to England when Teller told him that there were four black cars near by. He left Mrs Teller to get his set out of the window, and strolled away down the street – having made only one slip. He had got in his pocket the ciphered texts of the three messages he had been about to send.

One of the cars drove up to him, and he was arrested. His set was found stuck in a washing line beneath the

Tellers' window. The Germans, to his astonishment, deciphered one of his telegrams under his nose: no wonder, because they found in it bogus data about the German warship *Prinz Eugen*, fed in by Ridderhof, which gave them clues enough to which code Lauwers was using. Lauwers, with a decent show of reluctance, agreed to send the messages after all, on his own set, confident that SOE in London would spot that he put in a faulty security check, as he did. SOE in London took no notice; indeed, shortly thereafter they instructed him to receive another agent, who was duly parachuted in. That agent, Baatsen ('Watercress'), arrested on arrival on 27 March, was furious, and talked only too much; and so the cumulative process went on, as other agents arrived, till by the autumn Giskes and Schreieder knew not only the names and appearances of every officer in N section, and of every instructor at all the schools their captured SOE agents had attended, but which brands of cigarette or pipe tobacco each of them preferred, which one was married and which a bachelor, which one had a moustache and which was clean-shaven: newcomers, overwhelmed by the body of knowledge the Germans had already assembled, each brought his own pebble or two to add to the cairn.

This was, from the German point of view, a model operation. The two majors who had started it up, Giskes and Schreieder, were allowed to carry on with it, reporting daily through Canaris and Himmler to Hitler: by teleprint, unluckily for SOE, so that there were no Bletchley intercepts to warn them how much things had gone wrong. Lauwers continued to work his set, and continued to leave his security checks out; he tried also to warn home base by inserting, as often as he could, CAU and GHT among the jumbled letters with which (as a normal anti-decoding precaution) every message began and ended. Unluckily for him and all his friends, those who deciphered the messages skipped these jumbled fragments, so that their eyes were not caught by these warnings; and when the deciphered texts appeared on Blunt's and Bingham's desks in Baker Street, they had been shorn of the signals apparatus of jumbled letters, filtered out on the way by the signals staff as something with which the operational staff would not need to bother. They were each marked 'BLUFF CHECK ABSENT, TRUE CHECK ABSENT', a point N section chose to ignore.

Before long the Germans wanted to have more sets than Lauwers' one to carry the traffic. When they started up a new one, with one of their own operators, they mentioned that a Dutch wireless expert had been recruited as an assistant operator, as the English-trained one had sprained his wrist. London replied to a message that had no security checks in it at all, 'Instruct new operator in use of security checks': how monumentally stupid can a staff officer be? In the end Giskes used fourteen sets. London never noticed that most of them were sending from near his office at Driebergen, east of Utrecht and close to Doorn, where the last Kaiser had just died in 1941. Nor did London take in that nearly all the DZs – plenty of stores and agents were dropped in during the winter of 1942–3 – were in the Veluwe, the patch of open countryside south-east of the Zuider Zee but north of the great rivers, while London was ordering the bulk of operations to be conducted south of the rivers: a difficult transport problem across guarded bridges, which ought to have occurred to N section's only too unimaginative staff.

De Jong prints a complete list of the Dutch agents sent over by the allies who fell into German hands as a result of what Schreieder called the *Englandspiel*, the match against England: fifty-one from SOE, nine from MI6, and one from MI9 – the only woman in the party: Beatrix Terwindt, a KLM air hostess who displayed all the self-possession of her trade when handcuffed by her reception committee and grilled for information. As she had not been through many of the SOE training schools, and knew few officers in N Section, she was less disconcerted than most of the rest of the prisoners, and put up a brave show of ignorance, under four days' almost continuous interrogation. She survived Ravensbrück and Mauthausen: she died aged 76 in 1987.[13]

Almost all of her fellow captives were, in the end, shot; though Lauwers (who is today still living) was spared, and five escaped from Haaren concentration camp, north-east of Tilburg, where they were all kept for a time. Two of these escapers managed to get out of occupied territory altogether into neutral Switzerland, where they arrived just in time to save SOE from a further disaster. These were 'Cabbage' and 'Chive', Sergeant Dourlein – who seems to have taken the initiative – and Lieutenant Ubbink, who managed a good escape from Haaren on a Sunday night (29/30 August 1943). They sent a message to London at once, but it was intercepted by another *V-Mann*, van der Waals, and never got through. They got into Belgium in early November, and went on by train through Paris to Belfort; thence, on 22 November, into the Dutch legation at Berne. Berne warned London immediately. They reached Switzerland in time to alert SOE before another major operation was set up through the existing, contaminated channels.

The initiative for this had come from the Dutch in exile: Dr Gerbrandy, the prime minister, himself went to call on Selborne to explain what needed to be done. The Dutch had learned, through channels clear of German interference, that a new style of identity card was soon to be brought in by the occupation authorities in the Reichskommissariat. It was going to be more difficult to forge; its arrival would present all sorts of troubles to the scores of thousands of *onderduikers*, Dutch citizens who hid from the Germans. Stocks were about to be printed by the great firm of Enschede at Haarlem. Could SOE please destroy them before they were issued, and so nip trouble in the bud? Lord Selborne offered to do what he could, but the message from Berne raised doubts. Enschede got on with the job while SOE debated the security problem; the *onderduikers* had, as usual, to fend for themselves.

While Dourlein and Ubbink were on their slow way through Spain by a land escape line, SOE got an ingenious telegram from Giskes – ostensibly of course from one of their own sets – which explained that the travellers had gone over to the Gestapo. So when they reached London they were shut up in Brixton prison, till after the Normandy beach-head had been secured. Eventually the Dutch authorities relented and decorated them.

The *Englandspiel* was by then over. Giskes, who called it by another codename – 'North Pole' – had blown the gaff on All Fools' Day 1944. By then it was clear to him that Dourlein and Ubbink had got out of his control and that SOE was no longer pouring in men and munitions with the same insouciance or plenty. He sent the following in clear:

TO MESSRS BLUNT, BINGHAM, AND SUC-CESSORS LTD STOP YOU ARE TRYING TO MAKE BUSINESS IN THE NETHERLANDS WITHOUT OUR ASSISTANCE STOP WE THINK THIS RATHER UNFAIR IN VIEW OUR LONG AND SUCCESSFUL COOPERATION AS YOUR SOLE AGENT STOP BUT NEVER MIND WHENEVER YOU WILL COME TO PAY A VISIT TO THE CONTINENT YOU MAY BE ASSURED THAT YOU WILL BE RECEIVED WITH SAME CARE AND RESULT AS ALL THOSE YOU SENT US BEFORE STOP SO LONG[14]

N section's disaster was SOE's major catastrophe, and it would be folly to describe it as anything else; it has become a textbook illustration, the world over, in how not to conduct clandestine work. But Giskes' signal did not end the story. SOE, which had already sent some agents independently into Holland to try to probe what on earth was going on, next showed that it was capable of learning from its mistakes.

Bingham (who came into SOE from the consular service) was posted away, hardly before time; he went out to Australia. Dobson took over N section, and a newcomer to SOE, but not to secret-service work, took over control of T and N sections together: that is, of SOE's work into the Low Countries (hence his symbol: LC). LC was a 44-year-old naval lieutenant-commander called Philip Johns, who from an apprenticeship in Belgium had been promoted to be SIS's man in Lisbon in 1941–2, and had then worked under 'Little Bill' Stephenson in America. The Dutch in London had been understandably upset about the *Englandspiel* fiasco, and several middle-rank staff officers were disinclined to work with SOE at all. Yet they had to use SOE's facilities, and the RAF or more rarely the navy, to reach their fellow countrymen; and they were ordered back into contact with Baker Street by a personage too highly placed for them to disregard: Prince Bernhard of the Netherlands, Queen Wilhelmina's son-in-law.

Spurred on by Bernhard and by Johns, the Dutch in exile brought off a remarkable achievement through SOE. Starting in the late spring of 1944 they sent twenty-five two-man sabotage parties into the Netherlands, few of whom were detected by the German security police, who had shown such professional skills in the conduct of the *Englandspiel*. Meticulous care was taken about security checks, clothing, coding – the previous weak points; and Johns made sure that Blunt's other cardinal error, that of sending many agents through a single channel, was not repeated. Each party had a wireless, one-time pads, plastic and delay fuses; arms for some 20,000 men were safely parachuted in.[15] That there was never much chance for these saboteurs to deploy into action resulted from the course that the land fighting on the Continent took; the technical feat is still worth remark.

The impact of the *Englandspiel* did not end with its discovery by the Dutch and British. That disaster, following on the troubles of 1939–40 at Venlo and The Hague, had soured the high commands of SOE and SIS alike against such potential weight as Dutch resistance might still be able to exert. Neither Prince Bernhard, a young man of German extraction – whose brother was in Wehrmacht uniform, being persecuted in a labour battalion on the eastern front – nor Johns, a newcomer to SOE from its rival, was senior enough to counter this mistrust: which was among the causes of failure at Arnhem.

On 17 September 1944 Montgomery launched 'Market Garden', the partly airborne attempt to advance across the great rivers of south Holland onto the right bank of the Rhine. The British First Airborne Division, aimed at the farthest bridge – Browning's 'bridge too far' – at Arnhem, was ordered to ignore local offers of help. One such offer could have helped save it from one of its worst troubles, bad communications, but was hardly used.

It was bad luck for the division that the German formations closest to Arnhem at the time, 9 and 10 SS Panzer Divisions, were made up of battle-hardened cadres who had just finished a run of exercises in warding off airborne attack. It was bad management by the Royal Corps of Signals and by the British and American signals supply staffs that equipped 'Market', the overland advance by XXX Corps, with only two wireless sets for air-ground liaison (both of which had broken down by the end of the first day) and 'Garden', the airborne component, with none; while almost all the short-range sets on which units of First Airborne Division relied to talk to each other failed. They may possibly have failed on account of the sandy subsoil, not foreseen; in any case, they failed. A few SOE agents dropped with the airborne

division; only one of their sets worked. The local telephone service was in excellent order, subject to hardly
any German watch, and available: but, because the British had been warned off contacts with the Dutch, hardly
used.[16]

Only after the remnants of the division had been
withdrawn – after nine days (it had been expected to hold
for two) – did Airey Neave of MI9 spot that there was
still a telephone link that worked between captured
Nijmegen and the power station at Ede, west of Arnhem.
He used it to help organise the rescues.[17]

Bad as the *Englandspiel* was for SOE, it did not stand
quite alone. MI5's achievement in running a complete set
of agents back with success (see p. 197) was not copied by
any of the axis powers. The Italians did well against
agents sent in from Switzerland in 1942, but not thereafter. (Nothing about this has appeared in English.) One
of the few serious attempts by the Japanese in this field
broke down early; the Germans did have two coups
outside the Netherlands, both worth attention.

The Japanese case is worth a brief word first. Captain
(later General Tan Sri) Ibrahim bin Ismail ('Oatmeal')
and three Malay other ranks landed from a Catalina
flying-boat on an island on the east coast, off Kota Bahru;
they were at once betrayed by informers and arrested.
They had with them a W/T set ('Violin') of which the
operator had not only got the ciphers with him, but had
jotted down on them (in case he forgot) the security
checks. These were proper, random ones: to the question
'Have you met Miriam?' the reply 'Yes, I've met Miriam'
meant 'I am under enemy control'; if the mission was
safe, it was to answer 'Two Scotsmen left here two days
ago'. One resource remained, and Ibrahim managed to
use it: he brazenly told the Japanese that, as a measure of
security, the operator had written the checks down the
wrong way round, and that 'Yes, I've met Miriam' meant

that all was well. They believed him. For the rest of the war, 'Violin' exchanged messages with Peter Fleming, who ran deception for Mountbatten; Ibrahim was put in for a Japanese decoration for helping them, as well as a British one for not having done so; and nobody got hurt.[18]

The Germans had a moderately successful wireless game in Belgium, from which they secured a large proportion – Giskes thought almost a third – of the stores SOE sent in,[19] and several agents; no details about this have yet been made public by anyone. Henri Bernard's excellent short history of Belgian resistance does not mention these troubles; his training in security during the war – he did two missions into Belgium and held a leading intelligence post in London in between – outweighed his training as a professor of history.[20]

Of the other German wireless game successes, in France, a good deal has been said. They began with a failure; then they did better. F section's youngest agent, one of the most successful, was Tony Brooks (mentioned already for his defective parachute), who had just turned twenty when sent to France to set up a sabotage circuit on the main-line railways. For cover, he worked in a garage at Montauban, north of Toulouse. Thither he was sent a wireless operator, a cheerful south Londoner called Marcus Bloom ('Bishop') who spoke with no regard for grammar and did not look French in the least. None of the rest of the garage staff suspected that their unobtrusive new mechanic was not as French as themselves; till in August 1942 a pipe-smoking figure in a pork-pie hat strode in, walked up to him – recognising him from a photograph – and held out his hand with a welcoming cry of 'Ow are yer, mate?'

Brooks took much more notice of Beaulieu's rules than Bloom did, and passed the newcomer on as promptly as he could to his nearest F section neighbour, Maurice Pertschuk ('Eugene') at Toulouse. He had, not long afterwards, to seek them out; he found them in a black-market restaurant, chattering away in English amid the debris of an excellent meal. He for one was not surprised to hear, a few weeks later, that both Pertschuk and Bloom had been arrested.

Bloom was caught with his set, and they managed to break his code. This they did with no help from him; beyond admitting to one of his captors, on the night of his arrest, that for the first time since his arrival in France he 'felt safe', he said nothing at all of interest to them.[21] His splendid spirit in captivity, matched with equal courage and discretion on Pertschuk's part, foiled a German attempt to take F section in. Both were executed later in Buchenwald.

The Sicherheitsdienst sent down its wireless expert from Paris: Dr Jozef Götz, a junior officer in his early thirties and a highly intelligent man. He was a schoolmaster by profession, bilingual in French and German and with excellent Spanish as well, who had been brought into the SD from the *geheime Feldpolizei* (field security police). This was his first attempt at running a set back without being spotted; he failed. One reason for his failure was Bloom's and Pertschuk's silence. Another was that he was run on a tight rein from Berlin: he had to submit every word of every message he proposed to send to England to Kopkow in the RSHA before he dispatched it, and Kopkow in turn often had to consult senior personages in Himmler's headquarters before he teleprinted back consent. Again, it was bad luck for SOE that the Germans used the teleprinter; much of MI5's success in playing back every used German set in England stemmed from the fact that there was then no teleprinter connection between Lisbon and Berlin, so that a lot of the Germans' consultations with each other passed in an Abwehr Enigma code that GC and CS could read.[22]

In the summer of 1943 Götz did a good deal better, thanks to indiscretions by F section wireless operators and a gaffe in Baker Street. On the night of 15/16 June that year a pair of Canadians, Pickersgill, the organiser, and Macalister, the wireless operator, dropped south of Orléans to an F section reception. They were held up in the country for a couple of days, part of which one of them spent in writing out, from memory, his operation instruction, which he had read and handed back to his briefing officer before he left Tempsford. He put what he had written in his pocket. Macalister meanwhile had jotted down his security checks on the back of a code pad, in case he forgot them. They set off by car to take a train to Paris, on their way to set up a circuit in Lorraine. By mere accident, on the way to the station they were stopped at a road control by a Waffen-SS unit practising controls. The Canadians spoke excellent French (one of them used to teach it) but one had a marked accent and had no time to deploy F section's ingenious cover story. A glance at the contents of their pockets revealed the operation instruction; a glance in the boot of the car revealed their weapons and Macalister's set.

The only thing the Germans did not know was his sending style; that too he revealed, unconsciously, while held in Fresnes (cp. p. 161–2). 'Archdeacon', their circuit in Lorraine, ran for nine months: it received drops of arms, money, and on one disastrous occasion early in March 1944 men, the 'Liontamer' party of four and 'Bargee' – Adolphe Rabinovitch, who had survived being wireless operator for Peter Churchill and was off on a mission of his own – and another Canadian, called Sabourin. Rabinovitch and Sabourin heard their reception committee talking to each other in German, and opened fire on them; but were at once shot down themselves, and killed in bad camps later. 'Liontamer' came quietly; that did not save their lives, either.

Götz, who was in no way responsible for these deaths – they were handled by a quite different branch of the SD – was on the whole relieved when he settled down to use

Macalister's set; it was so much more straightforward than the effort he had to make at almost the same time to play back the set of Gilbert Norman ('Archambaud'). Norman had been wireless operator to Francis Suttill ('Prosper'), the head of a huge and far-ranging circuit that centred on Paris. Its members had formed an unfortunate friendship and a fatal habit. The friendship was with Henri Déricourt ('Gilbert' – often confused with Gilbert Norman, sometimes confused with others of the several 'Gilberts' then active in resistance). Déricourt was a trick pilot by profession – Bodington had befriended him when he worked in a circus before the war – and organised SOE's Lysander and Hudson trips between the Loire valley and Tangmere. He also worked hand-in-glove with the SD in Paris, not often for personal profit, but often to the confusion of his fellow agents in F section. Tipped off by him, the Germans watched most of the arrivals and departures; the fatal habit helped here. For the inner circle of 'Prosper' – Suttill, Norman, Andrée Borrel their splendid courier, and Armel Guerne, the poet, who (though never trained in England) had joined the circuit as Suttill's second-in-command – used to meet almost every day at a black-market restaurant near the Arc de Triomphe for a midday meal and almost every evening at a café near the Sacré Coeur for cards; they did not always remember to talk French; and they forgot how many Paris waiters were in the Gestapo's pay.

All those four were arrested on 23–24 June 1943; and one of them, almost certainly Norman, quite certainly not Andrée Borrel, soon began to talk. Norman was one of those who succumbed to the insinuation that he had had a minor job, and would not have much to let on to the enemy. He let on an enormous amount; but he kept quiet about his security checks. When Götz got a German signals corporal to play the set back, he did not quite convince Baker Street. For a moment, Buckmaster's juniors thought that as the set was still transmitting, and

Norman was not the sort of man who (they believed) would think of changing sides, he must be all right; but he did not answer such plain questions London put him as 'Where is Prosper?', and before long the penny dropped.

The only trouble Götz had about using Macalister's set was that, to preserve plausibility, it had to be worked from Lorraine, where his assistant, Placke, who spoke fair French, ran the circuit with a fair amount of success. As a well-placed source in Baker Street put it twenty years later, 'We had reason to believe in that circuit as an existing circuit because it did in fact exist.'[23] What Götz really longed for, well though this 'Archdeacon' ploy was working, was a set in Paris through which he could try to feed disinformation to the British, as Giskes had tried to do from Holland. Giskes had not had much success, partly because what he sent was of slight interest, partly because under C's influence most of the secret intelligence community in England looked askance at SOE as a source.

Chance put a set in the smart west end of Paris into Götz's grasp. Noor Inayat Khan ('Madeleine'), Tipu Sultan's descendant through her father and Mary Baker Eddy's cousin through her mother (she was known as Nora Baker when in training), combined strength with sweetness in her character. Before the war, she used to read her own children's stories on Radio Paris; during it, she qualified as an air force wireless operator before her excellent (but not perfectly French) French brought her into SOE. She went to France by Lysander on 16/17 June 1943 – a bad moment to arrive: the night before the 'Archdeacon' party's arrest and the week before the 'Prosper' team were pulled in. She nevertheless managed to settle in Paris and to open up transmissions to and from England, unaware that she was being listened to carefully by the enemy, who had not yet pinpointed her but had no trouble in receiving her loud and clear. She provided wireless touch between Paris and London for those in SOE who needed it, till she tripped over an unforeseen personal difficulty. Someone who knew what she was doing – she was not particularly discreet – and was jealous at not being allowed to join in, delated her to the Germans; and one evening when she came back to her flat near the Porte Dauphine there was a Gestapo man waiting inside it, who after a sharp struggle handcuffed her. Her betrayer was paid 100,000 francs (£500), a tenth of what the Germans would have paid for the capture of a British officer, having failed to ask for enough.

A search of her flat revealed how right the training section had been to remark that she was 'not overburdened with brains'. In the drawer of her bedside table she kept a school notebook in which she had written down, on facing pages, the precise texts in cipher and in clear of every message she had exchanged with home station. This she had presumably done because an inept sentence in her operation order (and in that of several other wireless operators) had told her: 'We should like to point out here that you must be extremely careful with the filing of your messages.'[24] She supposed that this overrode the warnings she had repeatedly been given that she should destroy her back traffic the moment it was done with. (She had not done a regular Thame Park course because she was already a fully trained wireless operator before ever she entered SOE.)

The first Gestapo officer with whom she was confronted in the Avenue Foch, who was in uniform, got nothing out of her at all – not a word: 'She glared at me,' he recollected years later, 'as if she was a caged tiger, but she wouldn't speak.' He unhandcuffed her; she demanded a bath; and within minutes was outside the attic bathroom window, perched on a narrow gutter and trying to get away. She was promptly brought inside again; and then fell for one of the oldest tricks in the interrogators' trade. A polite, friendly interpreter in plain clothes was nice to her; and to him, being a well-brought-up girl, she was prepared to gossip. She gave nothing whatever away at her formal interrogations; this did not matter. There was no need to torture her. As the Germans had all her back traffic, from which they could read off her formal security checks, they had little trouble in playing her set back in the morse style with which they were well acquainted. When Baker Street, rather dubious about her messages' tone, tried a few random security checks – which no one had remembered to pre-arrange – in the shape of questions about her family and childhood, the answers to them were readily enough secured through the Alsatian interpreter, who took care never to wear uniform in her presence and told her (and her biographer[25]) that he was Swiss.

This went on for months; for months indeed after she had been taken away to Germany, and chained in solitary in a cell at Pforzheim. This was a convenience to Kieffer, the head of the SD section that had held her; he came from Karlsruhe near by, and used the excuse that he had gone to interrogate her (whom he never saw again) to provide himself with frequent weekends at his own home. She was arrested about 12 October 1943; her set was still on the air in February 1944. On 28/29 February SOE sent a crack F section team to a reception arranged through it on the great plain east of Chartres: France Antelme, who had distinguished himself in Madagascar, with Lionel Lee as his wireless operator and Madeleine Damerment – who had been brought up in a convent school, and was all the more combative for that – as his courier. He had been one of 'Prosper's' intimates in Paris in the previous summer, and the Germans knew exactly who he was. Even they were awed by the tremendous outburst of temper he displayed on being handcuffed by his reception committee. None of the three new captives said anything at all; none returned. Nor did Noor Inayat.

F section had arranged verbally with Lee that he would

send a particular anodyne message on arrival; he did not. They therefore knew that he had been taken; and took little notice of a message sent both by Noor Inayat's set ('Nurse') and by his, that Antelme had cracked his skull against the edge of a container on landing and was dying of meningitis. In brute fact he was murdered later in the concentration camp of Gross Rosen.

The disaster with Antelme's party brought on much more careful inquiries in London than had been made before. The signals section, for instance, was blithely sending Lee's traffic on his 'Daks' set through to F section, all marked 'special check present', until invited to take a closer look, when they noticed that the special check was in fact absent.[26] The country section at last got suspicious of 'Butler', François Garel's circuit, into which the Germans had broken through a routine police telephone-tap in September 1943. Everyone was warned at Beaulieu never to use the telephone at all, unless in a carefully prearranged and watertight code; Beaulieu forgot that in the field agents, however carefully trained, would be working with sub-agents who had never heard of this elementary clandestine need, and would make appointments on the telephone as they always had done. Marcel Rousset, Garel's operator, did his best. He had occasionally sent messages for Bieler as well as for Garel; for Bieler in English, for Garel in French. He told the Germans the opposite was the case. London's only reaction was to inquire why he had changed language. He also, after the necessary forty-eight hours' silence, admitted what his security checks were, but deliberately misdescribed how they were to be used; London did not notice. To other operators, dropped to messages apparently from Rousset, who had in fact gone smack into the enemy's hands, London sent reproaches for having forgotten all about their security checks in their very first messages: not having taken in that that was precisely what security checks were for.[27] Stupidity by the London staff was not

194

confined to N section, but at least analysis of 'Butler' traffic, and of sets started off through 'Butler' receptions, did in the end lead London to understand that all was far from well.

About 'Archdeacon' also doubts began to seep into F staff's minds. Random questions were asked of the operator so out of the ordinary that Pickersgill was brought back from the concentration camp in Germany to which he had already been consigned, to try to help the Germans answer them. He had other ideas. He was befriended in the Avenue Foch by his colleague John Starr, who was hanging about there – apparently on decent terms with the guards – and assured all the captured F agents he met that they had better talk, because the Germans understood F section inside out already. Starr's real aim seems to have been to make himself so trusted by the Germans that they would relax their guard and he would be able to slip away altogether, get onto a DF escape line, and bring some important intelligence home. He, Noor Inayat Khan and Faye, of the 'Alliance' intelligence circuit ('Noah's Ark'), did indeed once all get out of 84–6 Avenue Foch onto the roof, but were recaptured in an adjoining building during an air raid. Pickersgill had more combative ideas. When the Germans had got slightly used to his presence, and were at ease in his company – even offered him a drink – he picked up a bottle, broke it on a table edge, killed the men on either side of him with the broken end of it, and jumped out of the window. He landed intact, from the second floor, but the sentry on the door happened to be alert, and brought him down at once: he was packed off back to Germany for the last time.

Starr was called on by the Germans to go and talk to Gerry Morel of F section when Morel announced he was going to visit Lorraine with an S-phone (one had been sent to 'Archdeacon' already). Starr went along as far as the ground, but then remained silent; Morel perceived the SD man's voice he heard instead as unmistakably

German; and 'Archdeacon' was at last wound up, after nine months' running entirely in German hands.

For a few weeks – it was by now April 1944 – F section went on making drops to circuits which it now understood to be German-controlled, in a rather amateur attempt at deception: a tactic so tricky that it is always best left to experts. F was trying to draw the enemy's attention away from areas in which some experienced agents were being established along the right bank of the Loire, in the belief that they would be of serious use when 'Overlord', the impending invasion of the Continent, began.

On Normandy D-Day, 6 June 1944, after prolonged consultations beforehand with the highest command in Berlin, the SD in Paris sent F section a message on 'Butler's' set in clear: their equivalent to Giskes' All Fools' Day message to N section. They sent their thanks for 'large deliveries arms and ammunition' – one night they had had twenty-seven drops out of the thirty the *messages personnels* had announced for that night, and collected arms for a brigade. They claimed to be grateful too for 'good tips concerning your intentions and plans'. Buckmaster, the head of F, replied, light-heartedly enough, 'Sorry to see your patience is exhausted and your nerves not so good as ours . . . give us ground near Berlin for reception organiser and W/T operator but be sure you do not clash with our Russian friends.'[28] His reply reached Paris at about the same moment as a change-of-mind order from Hitler himself not to send the SD's piece after all; Göring having persuaded his Führer that it would be better to keep silent a bit longer, and find out whether the Normandy landings were the real thing or a feint to draw attention away from the coast south of Boulogne, where German general staff doctrine laid down the allies were all but certain to make their main effort. This provides a suitable note of muddle on which to draw this discussion of wireless games towards an end.

F section will seem at first glance to have done as badly

as N section; this was not really so. They were badly taken in over a few circuits, and lost a number of heroic figures unnecessarily; but they were not entirely bewitched, as N section had been. Not only did F section staff, like poor Romeo, do all for the best; they did all that could reasonably be expected of them, given the fixes of time and temper they were in, given who they and their agents were and whom they were up against. There was too much, far too much, going on at once for every circuit to get the minute care that it deserved, and that much smaller country sections were able to devote to every single message. It was bad luck for Buckmaster that he might have anything up to a hundred and fifty important messages to handle a day; so that, unluckily for F's ultimate reputation, a few circuits went badly wrong. On the other hand, a great many circuits went thoroughly right; as will be shown before long (pp. 317–27).

When, as sometimes happened, SOE was in doubt over a circuit's security, MI5 could be called in to help. Senter, the head of security, would collect a pile of the relevant telegrams and go round to see T. A. Robertson, the head of MI5's section B1a. This section was busy simulating the agents the Abwehr fondly thought it had placed in Britain: with what entire success it did so has been lucidly described by Robertson's deputy, (Sir) J. C. Masterman.[29] If Robertson and Senter were unable to make up their minds on the spot, Robertson usually referred Senter's bundle to one of his own case officers who was not at that moment too busy; and a case officer, fully experienced in German secret service method and vocabulary, was often able to give a definite opinion.

F section made another mistake on the security front, which might have led to a far worse catastrophe than any wireless game, had the Germans organised themselves efficiently enough for war. F no more took in than N did the extent to which agents, once unmanned by the shock of being handcuffed by an enemy reception committee, might pour out to the enemy the inmost secrets confided to them before they left England. Among these inmost secrets, where F was concerned, was a system of code messages that would tell the field first roughly, and then precisely, when the 'Overlord' invasion was going to take place. These were more of the *messages personnels* put out after the 7.15 and 9.15 evening news bulletins of the BBC in French; they were co-ordinated direct between the BBC and the country section, thus bypassing both the intelligent Marks and the suspicious security section. They consisted, for each circuit – and F had, or thought it had, over forty organised fighting circuits on Normandy D-Day – in a pair of phrases, usually two consecutive lines from a poem, each devoted to a particular kind of target. When for instance the racing driver Robert Benoist heard '*C'était le sergent qui fumait sa pipe en pleine campagne*', he was to alert his railway sabotage teams, because the invasion was imminent; when in turn he heard '*Il avait mal au coeur mais il continuait tout de même*', he was to send them into action that night, which would be the actual night of invasion. He was only sent to France (on a second mission) with two sets of messages, one for railway and one for telephone targets; larger circuits might also have pairs of messages to cover attacks on roads, headquarters, petrol dumps, or electricity stations. (Benoist in hard fact was captured soon after D-Day, and did not survive.)

So the number of messages involved was quite large; and confusion has been added to a subject that was never in the first place simple, by the frequent statement that only one pair of messages was involved. This was a couplet from Verlaine, slightly misquoted in each line:

Les sanglots lourds des violons d'automne
Bercent mon coeur d'une langueur monotone.

(Verlaine had written *sanglots longs* and *Blessent mon coeur*; either a typist's error or BBC insistence that the revised version was more easy to hear impelled the change.) These messages were meant to alert, and then to activate, Philippe de Vomécourt's 'Ventriloquist' rail-cutting teams between Vierzon and Orléans: an important line to damage at the start of 'Overlord'. Originally they had been allotted to 'Butler', Garel's dead circuit in the Sarthe; quite possibly they had been passed to Rousset's W/T set while it was being worked by the Germans. They were not a general call to resistance to come out and fight, the sense often now attributed to them.

F section held a general post among its BBC messages in the late spring of 1944, after it had realised that several of its circuits had been run, for far too long, by the enemy. But the quantity of messages that so large a section needed was itself large; nobody had the time or the emotional energy to sit down and work out an entirely new set; they simply rearranged the use of the ones that they already held.

The end result was that Götz, who never spared himself at work – he reckoned he worked a fourteen-hour day, seven days a week – heard as he listened to the *messages personnels* on the evening of 5 June 1944 no fewer than fifteen which he recognised as D-Day messages for circuits that he had been running: that is, 'Neptune' – not a codeword he knew, but the assault phase of 'Overlord' – was going to take place that night. He at once informed his superiors in the Avenue Foch, and sent a most immediate teleprint to Berlin; all the German army commands in France were alerted. The proverb about the boy who cried 'Wolf!' is in point: they had been warned too often. Fifteenth Army, holding the coast round Calais and Boulogne, did send a warning to its troops that invasion might be imminent; Seventh Army, which held the threatened area in the Baie de la Seine, did not.

* * *

Considering how leaky SOE's own agents could be, in spite of all that they had been taught at Beaulieu about the need to keep their mouths shut when in enemy hands, it is not surprising that captured sub- and sub-sub-agents often said a great deal more than they might have done, and helped the enemy's security forces in their task of unravelling what SOE was up to. There was another permanent factor on the secret battlefield, a weapon SOE's men and women were all warned would be used against them, but one which struck them hard now and again: the double agent. Wherever axis police forces suspected there might be clandestine activity directed against themselves, they did their best to feed their own people into it as friends; so that, having got to the core of whatever trouble was brewing, they could move in quietly and wind the whole business up before any actual harm was done. Earlier in this chapter, the part played in N section's undoing by Ridderhof and van der Waals was as remarkable as the part played by ineptitude (it was only ineptitude, though many people at the time suspected treachery) in Baker Street. All over occupied Europe and south-east Asia, there were citizens who were not quite sure on which side their political bread was buttered; thousands of them took the risks that attended working with the occupiers' secret police, instead of working against them. Only in Poland were such people rare.

When they were discovered, SOE's advice was – had always been, right from the start – that they were to be disposed of straight away, no shriving time allowed. No one in an SOE circuit was likely to be in a state to take and keep prisoners. Such barbarous habits as knee-capping left their victims able to move and talk: not what SOE's security demanded.

Guerilla is not like ordinary war; where it rages, prisoners are seldom taken. As a rule, once SOE's activities passed out of the clandestine stage into that of active warfare, there was nothing to be done with those who tried to surrender but to kill them. Few indeed were the guerilla parties who had food to spare, or men to spare to mount guard, or any available prison; or who were ready to run the risk that people who had seen their faces from close to might report on them to the enemy secret police. Notoriously, some French miliciens who were taken prisoner by maquisards on the Glières plateau in March 1944, and rescued by the Germans, went round the local villages afterwards and pointed out to their Gestapo companions the men who had saved their lives: conduct only to be expected of Gestapo narks.

A few luckily-placed chieftains could make exceptions. The crew of a captured German field gun, for which the captors had no ammunition, are said to have made assiduous mess waiters in a corner of eastern France in the closing stages of the fighting there, late in August 1944.[30] Several weeks earlier, also in France, an eighteen-year-old recruit to one of Cammaerts' best maquis was appalled by the spectacle, on the day he joined it, of the shooting (on the order of a visiting French bigwig) of four Germans whom the maquis had made prisoners out of sentimentality, and used as potato-peelers and washers-up. These four men were in effect shot in reprisal for the SS massacre at Oradour, which reconciled the young witness to their fate and held him steady in his new task.[31]

The massacre at Oradour, perhaps in revenge for the abduction (never accounted for) of a popular SS major – like the massacres at Lidice and Ležáky, in revenge for the killing of Heydrich – were extreme instances of normal SS behaviour: reminders of the kind of society the war was being fought to suppress. Oradour and Lidice (not, oddly enough, Ležáky, whose inhabitants were not gently handled either) have become synonyms for outrage in the west. The west might remember more often than it does that, though the atrocity of Oradour was unique in France, much worse was done, much more often, in Russia. The cadres of the SS division that disgraced itself at Oradour had just arrived from the eastern front, where such brutality was commonplace.[32]

It is time to consider those whom Buckmaster called, a few pages back, 'our Russian friends'; for relations with them presented quite another kind of danger to British security, then appreciated by very few in SOE. One of these few was Gubbins, who had seen Lenin's revolution in action in north Russia – he was on the Archangel expedition before he went to Dublin – and cherished for the rest of his life a mixture of contempt and distaste for Bolsheviks, based on direct experience. Another was Eddie Boxshall, the Romanian expert under Pearson in SOE's Balkan section in London; he had spent December 1917, as a very young man, in Moscow, waiting for a train to Vladivostok, and had found the experience revolting.

Guy Burgess had talked his way into section D, to work on propaganda. One of Gubbins's first actions on joining SOE was to ensure that Burgess left it, and he refused to allow him back: not for political reasons, but because he knew that Burgess was a heavy drinker and a homosexual, and looked a dissolute rake. The man was therefore a visible security risk. Jebb concurred. How Burgess later got himself accepted by the Foreign Office is another story.[33]

His friend Philby was in SOE for a year, in the training section, as was mentioned above. His cover was far denser than Burgess's; his father was a famous man, a cousin of B. L. Montgomery who was best man at his wedding;[34] far to the right, and his schooling had been impeccable. He drank heavily at the time; so did many others, and on a major's pay, tax free, he could afford it. (No one in SOE paid British income tax.[35]) As Yvon Morandat testified (p. 87), he was extremely good at his job; his colleagues at Beaulieu found him reserved but likeable, and were sorry to see him go. Presumably he reported to his Russian masters what he knew about SOE, which was quite a lot; it would certainly have included Dalton's and Nelson's identities and those of several other senior personalities, such as Gubbins, and some firm news of the areas in which SOE was preparing to operate. He was in no other way a liability to SOE. On the contrary, for the year he was in it, he was an asset.

There was one other known Soviet sympathiser in SOE in England. In April 1943 MI5 discovered that this man was in touch with Douglas Springhall, the national organiser of the Communist Party of Great Britain, and was starting to explain to him what he knew about SOE (which was a good deal less than Philby did). Springhall was arrested, and sentenced to seven years for quite another matter: receiving secrets from a woman in the Air Ministry. His acquaintance in SOE, Ormond Uren, a captain in the Highland Light Infantry who was a junior staff officer in SOE's Hungarian section, was a recent convert to communism, and was also sent down for seven years, four of which he served. (He recalled long afterwards that he spent his last free evening at the theatre, seeing *Arsenic and Old Lace*, seated one row behind Anthony Eden.) As he remarked in a wry restrospect, if he had been at Cambridge instead of Edinburgh university he might have had much more to tell the Russians, and might have got away with it.[36] As it was, he can have told them little if anything they did not already know, before he was caught. His case was heard *in camera*; its result was reported in the newspapers at the time, without reference to SOE or to MI5, and then forgotten till a recent mole-hunt revived it.

There were no known moles in SOE's headquarters in Algiers, Brisbane, Kandy, Kunming, Meerut or New York. (Whatever Charles Ellis, supposed by some to have been a mole, was doing in New York, he was not working for SOE.) In Cairo and Bari this was not so. There were two at least: James Klugmann, whose promotion by Terence Airey has been noticed already (pp. 64–5) – he came to high rank in Cairo's section in charge of operations into the Balkans – and John Eyre, the intelligence officer of the Albanian section in Bari. Kemp said of Eyre that 'like Klugman[n] and so many other Communists he had great sincerity combined with charm';[37] both Eyre and Klugmann, like so many other staff officers in SOE, also worked tremendously hard. So did Philby in MI6. What harm, at that moment, was any of them doing to the allied war effort against the axis?

'Our gallant Soviet ally', that phrase, reiterated from countless platforms and in countless broadcasts in 1942–3, was a great deal more than a phrase. It was only this solidly tyrannous lifebelt that kept the grand alliance of free peoples afloat through those two terrible years. Stalin's and Beria's iniquities have now become journalists' commonplaces, and were iniquitous indeed; yet hindsight, though sometimes it clarifies, can also distort. Had it not been for Stalin and Beria and their iron grip on the Soviet empire, no British reader of this book aged under forty would (in all probability) have been born at all, because his or her father would have been deported to work in a Nazi labour camp in eastern Europe, with no chance to beget a child. Without Russian help Great Britain would have lost the war against Nazi Germany.

The Russian empire was even more closed against foreigners then than now, and little reliable news came out of it. A whole generation of western Europeans was systematically misled about what had been going on there since 1917. Newspaper readers – in a pre-televisual age – were inclined either to despise the regime too much, or to admire it too much, out of plain ignorance. Young left-wing romantics of the 1930s were swept out of their depth by waves of enthusiasm for the Soviet experiment. They knew little or nothing of it beyond what Soviet propaganda told them: nothing of the famine and massacres that went with collectivisation of the land, nothing of the army purge, nothing of the *Yezhovshchina* except the puzzling fact of the show trials, nothing of the secret police and its labour camps. They read the salient clauses of the Stalin constitution of 1936, and believed they were true; living in free societies, they could not understand the ways in which a dictator's highly centralised party can seep into every cranny of a nominally liberal society and corrupt it. (A great many of today's commentators are just as blind.) Some were caught in the ratchet-like teeth of the Communist Party machine, which never let them go; some died early in Spain, believing they fought for freedom; some died later, in Siberia and disillusion; a few survived. Of these a few, such as John Eyre, were in SOE.

Of SOE's official co-operation with various communist organisations there will be more to say in the next chapter (see pp. 209–10). This one ends with an evocation of one of SOE's most engaging characters – of whom I write in part from personal knowledge, because we were in the same house at school and the same college at Oxford as exact contemporaries – who, like Ormond Uren, in his early twenties found himself captivated by communism as the obvious answer to all the world's problems. This was Frank Thompson, son of two Wesleyan missionaries – his father was Edward Thompson, historian of India, who like himself was a poet; his mother was American. He moved into SOE from Phantom, the headquarters signals unit,[38] after the invasion of Sicily in July 1943; and being among other things good at languages, was picked in Cairo for operations into the Balkans. He had ten thumbs, a razor-sharp brain and a large heart.

He was parachuted, in uniform, into southern Yugoslavia on 27/28 January 1944 to join Major Mostyn Davies's mission, which was arming the local partisans. Davies was soon thereafter killed. Thompson set off into Bulgaria, apparently on his own initiative, and marched on Sofia with a couple of hundred companions who called themselves the Second Sofia Brigade. Numbers and food dwindled; on 31 May Thompson and his English wireless operator were captured by Bulgar police. After a show trial, Thompson was shot. He now has a railway station named after him, and became a minor national hero under a despotic regime he would have abhorred.[39]

VIII
Politics

War and politics cannot clearly be separated from one another. SOE was a tool for making war, often a sharp tool, sometimes a faulty one; it could not help getting entangled in politics as well. It was intensely political: it could do nothing that did not impinge on current and postwar politics alike. It affected the ease, or the difficulty, with which the peoples of axis-occupied countries lived with their occupiers – this might unsettle the daily lives of tens of millions. It exercised a constant impact on the standing of staff officers and ministers in the small but vital sphere of the regimes in exile from axis tyranny, and helped to set the bounds for postwar politics in much of Europe and part of Asia.

British domestic politics it hardly affected. As we have seen (pp. 18–21), Dalton was put in to head it in the belief that the Labour Party was entitled to have charge of one secret service; but its stance in home politics was necessarily neutral, quite unconcerned with party. For at the moment of its foundation the War Cabinet laid down that parliamentary questions about it 'would be very undesirable';[1] Parliament played no part in the conduct or the criticism of its work. Chamberlain, who drafted its charter, was an elderly imperialist, son of a greater; Dalton, its first political head, was a strong socialist;

Selborne, its second, even more of an imperialist than Chamberlain, came from the opposite – anti-Munich – wing of the same Conservative Party. None of these three let home politics affect SOE's work, though Dalton could now and again be heard grumbling about his reactionary subordinates from the City, and Selborne did not always see eye to eye with earnest young leftists.

One future lord chancellor, then Quintin Hogg, served in MI R, but soon left to join his regiment in the desert. Several personalities in postwar parliaments came from SOE: Julian Amery, (Sir) Douglas Dodds-Parker, (Sir) Walter Fletcher, Sir Neil Marten, Sir Fitzroy Maclean, Neil (Billy) Maclean, and C. M. Woodhouse were – like Hogg – Conservative MPs, while (Sir) Frank Soskice (later Lord Stow Hill) went straight from SOE's security section to the post of solicitor-general in the great Labour government of 1945–50, in which Dalton held for over two years the leading post of chancellor of the exchequer. Indeed, since the war only the Labour cabinets of 1974–9 have not had one minister at least from MI R, SOE, or PWE; and they included, in the present writer's namesake, the son of a member of the security executive and the brother of MEW's under-secretary. SOE's postwar influence has been much greater abroad than at home.

All through its short life SOE stuck to one primordial political rule: it was anti-Nazi. Therefore it opposed the Nazis' friends and allies, fascist Italy and imperialist Japan. The Foreign Office's prewar concept that Italy could be coaxed away from alliance with Germany had no shred of support in SOE, which was not founded till Mussolini had already hurried to join what seemed to be the winning side; and by the time Killery was trying to set up the Oriental Mission, Japan's menace to south-east Asia was real enough to be seen.

A corollary to this doctrine of opposing the Nazis' friends is sometimes overlooked: in the early days, while the Nazi–Soviet pact operated (23/24 August 1939 to 21/

22 June 1941), SOE and its predecessors were anti-Russian, or at least anti-Soviet. As SOE's headquarters was under constant, and many of its country houses under intermittent, threat in the winter of 1940–1 from a Luftwaffe largely powered by Soviet petrol and using Soviet ores to case its bombs, this was no unreasonable line to follow.

Agile as a seasoned Marxist hard-liner, SOE reversed its line overnight, on 22/23 June 1941, to conform with the Prime Minister's memorable evening broadcast: anyone the Nazis attacked was SOE's friend as well as Churchill's. There were never any SOE missions into occupied Soviet home territory behind the German lines; all the partisans there were supposed to be under strict party control from Moscow. Most were; there were also several large Jewish partisan groups, and – as in previous great wars – various gangs of outlaws. A small SOE staff mission was sent to Moscow; rather an odd choice was later made for its head, George Hill. His previous visit to Russia had been as back-up man for the mysterious and colourful 'Sidney Reilly', the agent for whom it has often been claimed that he almost toppled Lenin's shaky original regime altogether.[2] Hill seems to have been quietly nobbled by the NKVD; he gave them, and they gave him, no trouble. They gave him no advice either; no fragment of the experiences of the party-dominated partisan groups was ever passed officially to SOE. SOE provided some data about explosive devices, but got nothing in return at all except complaints when a few agents entrusted to SOE by the NKVD for parachuting into western Europe were delayed, quite unavoidably, by the accidents of western European weather and aircraft availability.

Outside the Soviet Union itself, SOE got somewhat more response from the communists with whom it tried to get in touch. While Eden, the Foreign Secretary, was all but infatuated – in a recent biographer's phrase[3] – with the excellence of Anglo-Soviet friendship, SOE can be excused for having co-operated closely with communist elements in occupied territory: notably in Greece, Yugoslavia, Burma and Malaya. The communists, after all, had thought of this sort of thing before. Soviet foreign policy has always been hallmarked by the clandestine origins of the Soviet regime; so have the more repressive aspects of its policy at home. Stalin himself had lived clandestinely: he had robbed banks; he had been arrested, interrogated and released; he had run an underground newspaper and fought in a civil war. He therefore, like Hitler, was fully aware of the perils and possibilities of the secret life. His Comintern branches abroad already contained forgery and killing groups; one of the reasons why the communists came to the fore in so many resistance struggles was the technical but important one that they had the services of first-class forgery teams, something that an amateur local organisation could not secure except by a wild stroke of luck.[4] Communists on party duty could stroll through road or train identity controls that would make some members even of SOE pause, and would make more amateur resisters want to dodge out of the controllers' way – if they could.

Relations with the Americans were a good deal more smooth than with the Russians. The language barrier was much less severe; the foundation of common historical outlook, based on the common law, turned out stronger than the antipathies left over from the War of Independence of 1776–83. Well before the Americans came into the war in December 1941, the British secret services – MI5 and MI6 as well as SOE – had gone out of their way to be helpful and friendly to them. 'Wild Bill' Donovan, whom the British believed (perhaps wrongly) to carry special influence with Roosevelt, was warmly received by Menzies on his important visit to London in the summer of 1940, and was taken by Gubbins round some of SOE's training schools in 1941.

The Americans were aware of SOE's existence, therefore; and ready to copy a number of its methods, besides sending many of their agents to its Canadian training school (see p. 83). A rough division of spheres of influence was worked out, not without difficulty (see p. 170); OSS, founded in June 1942, was to run all clandestine operations in north-west Africa and on the eastern coast of Asia, while SOE (as well as SIS) could be left in the lead elsewhere. OSS combined both SOE's and SIS's tasks under its single head; though its SO and SI branches kept themselves at arm's length from each other.

Through a plethora of vice-consuls (who were well known to the Gestapo), OSS did some useful softening up of the French colonial territories in north-west Africa – all dutifully subordinate to Vichy France, itself a German satellite – before the 'Torch' landings of 7/8 November 1942 established Eisenhower's armies in Morocco and Algeria at an awkward political price. Pétain's deputy, Admiral Darlan, happened to be in Algiers at the time; he talked his way out of momentary arrest by some teenage resisters, and agreed with Eisenhower that he would order the local civil servants to obey Eisenhower's orders. The appearance of collaboration with someone so close to Pétain appalled liberals and left-wingers in America and Great Britain (though Stalin approved it), and deeply shocked resisters in France. All the nascent French resistance movements came to a temporary standstill, while they waited to see what was going on in north Africa.

They did not have to wait long. A young French royalist, who was an officer in SOE's training section just outside Algiers, shot Darlan dead on Christmas Eve with an SOE pistol, though SOE's head of mission insisted that this was an act of private enterprise, not an SOE operation.[5] The young man, who had been tipped off that he would be court-martialled, sentenced to death, and reprieved, was shot two dawns later; all the resistance movements in France heaved sighs of relief at Darlan's death and restarted work.

Certainly the killing of Darlan was not OSS's work, for OSS followed what the local commander wanted and Eisenhower got on well enough with Darlan. Indeed, after Darlan's death he had ordered the local OSS and SOE commanders – Eddy and Dodds-Parker – to co-operate as closely as his own linked hands, which he held before them as he spoke; Donovan and Gubbins happened both to be present and to hear the general's exhortation. Donovan nevertheless drew Dodds-Parker on one side afterwards, and explained that it was politically indispensable for OSS to be able now and again to operate on its own; so Dodds-Parker must not mind if Eddy now and again did something quite independent, which Donovan could report to President Roosevelt as a piece of OSS initiative.[6]

The two secret services, British and American, in fact co-operated without serious difficulty in north Africa and southern France. In Italy and the Balkans things did not go quite so smoothly. OSS was more reluctant than SOE to back Tito's partisans against Mihailovic's royalist Četniks in Yugoslavia, and OSS's missions in Greece were much readier than SOE's to approve ELAS as a democratic army – partly because it was opposed to a King George, as the original American revolutionaries of the War of Independence had been. American trust in Stalin as a democrat and suspicion of Churchill as an imperialist continued to colour OSS's attitudes, particularly in Siam where OSS and SOE seemed to be more at war with each other than with the Japanese.

In north-west Europe, however, they managed to integrate themselves; partly because David Bruce, the head of SO in Europe, got on well with Mockler-Ferryman, partly because everybody involved could see that they had a common interest in defeating Hitler before they fell out among themselves. Few Americans could manage perfect French, fewer even than the English, so not many Americans were sent to France or Belgium before D-Day on 6 June 1944; but thereafter ninety-three 'Jedburgh' teams, each consisting in principle of an American, an Englishman and a Frenchman, parachuted into France and fought with excellent cohesion. Moreover, there was plenty of exchange of ideas between OSS and SOE about weapons and equipment. The Americans were richer than the British and could, and did, spend more on fitting out their teams; on the other hand, the British had had longer experience and were prepared to share it. By and large, their rivalries were no worse than those between different regiments in the same brigade, or different ships in the same squadron; relations were probably less arid at the secret service level than they were between the highest commanders on the western front, once that front had been opened.

In its dealings with OSS, SOE was not hampered quite as much by secrecy as it was in its dealings with the minute secret services of the various governments-in-exile in London, Cairo and elsewhere. All of these felt themselves bound by tradition to revere MI6, or rather the British Secret Service: '*L'Intelligence Service*' was a particularly strong myth in France, and was highly regarded over most of the rest of the world as well. As governments-in-exile began to feel inclined to intervene, in deadly secrecy, in the countries to which they wished to return, by way of setting up sabotage parties or even secret armies, they mentioned these wishes to MI6 as a matter of course. Equally as a matter of course, they were referred (if they had not already encountered him) to a brigadier in the War Office, in an obscure department called MO1 (SP), which could not be reached through the main War Office switchboard. His name was Gubbins, acting here, as elsewhere, as SOE's mainspring. He took over, and looked after, each national party as circumstances dictated; but it was unclear for years to some of the exiles that Gubbins was a good deal more than a liaison officer. As late as the summer of 1942, five of the exiled nations – the Czechs, Dutch, French, Norwegians and Poles – sent a joint message to the CIGS, to say that they thought there ought to be a single body to direct subversive activity into occupied Europe; and were each astonished to receive his reply that such a body had already existed for almost two years, as the Special Operations Executive. He too referred them to MO1 (SP). 'This factual reply,' in Beevor's words – he was Hambro's assistant at the time – 'left the Allied commanders breathless; SOE was so secret that its name and existence had never been disclosed to them.'[7]

Looking back, it is clear that SOE was in a political fix, understood by few of its members at the time. Minister and Council alike were determined to pursue the War Cabinet's firm policy, set out in the Atlantic Charter signed by Roosevelt and Churchill in August 1941: that men and women the world over were to be as free as possible, once Nazism had been broken, to choose the form of government they wanted. Yet minister and Council alike were determined also to follow as a rough-and-ready guide a policy that appealed to the chiefs of staff: if several rival movements existed in an occupied country, SOE – given a choice – tended to back the one that showed most promise of throwing the enemy out fast. It was far from clear at the time that to take this line might simply be to substitute one tyranny for another.

Again, it was far from easy to realise in the early 1940s, in an England locked in war with Nazi Germany and its axis allies, that wars are by no means necessarily two-sided affairs, simply 'us' against 'them'. Great modern wars are often polygonal. The world war of 1939–45 (counted on the Anglo-Franco-Polish system – the Americans and Russians think rather of 1941–5) was by no means a straightforward struggle of a grand alliance against Germany, Italy, Japan and their satellites. The dress rehearsal in Spain (1936–9) now turns out to have been a much more intricate business than it seemed at the time. The first scene of the first act of the world war began on 1 September 1939 with the German attack on Poland. On 17 September 1939 the USSR invaded Poland as well; for many Poles, the Russians were quite as much enemies as the Germans. This remained so all through 1941–5, while Russians and Germans fought each other, frequently across Polish territory. Polish Jews knew that under Hitler's Germany they would be in for grave trouble; thousands of them tried to flee to Stalin's USSR, having had neither the foresight nor the money to get out earlier. Those of them who were let through were not, on the whole, gently treated; they were bundled into cattle trucks and packed off eastwards, to survive if they could. At least they were not shot down on the spot by Himmler's *Einsatzgruppen*, or sent to the slaughtergrounds of the final solution, as most of the Polish Jews who stayed in German-occupied Poland were, in millions.

Yugoslavia provides a still more intricate example of a many-sided war. Croatia was set up as an independent state, under the dictatorship of Ante Pavelić and his Ustashe, who were inclined to massacre anybody they could catch who was not both Croat by race and Roman Catholic by religion. Appeals to the Vatican to instil some Christian compassion into Pavelić's gunmen never got through to anyone who wanted to listen. The rest of Yugoslav territory was divided up between four neighbour powers – Germany, Italy, Bulgaria and Hungary. Within it, and in Croatia as well, there emerged two rival guerilla organisations: četniks, owing allegiance to the exiled king and his government, and partisans, run – under the cover that it was a national army of liberation – by the Comintern. Četniks and partisans seldom co-operated, and might shoot each other up; neither had much use for

Italians or Germans, except for periods of local understanding at times of crisis; neither cared for Hungarians or Bulgars; and even among the occupying powers relations were uneasy, sometimes (when Italy changed sides in September 1943) downright hostile.

Across the frontier in Greece there was another kind of many-sided war. King George II of the Hellenes was much older than the boy King Peter of Yugoslavia, and was much liked by his cousin in Buckingham Palace: this at a time when royal power still counted for a good deal in European politics, though no later political analyst has ever been close enough to any royal family to be able to estimate just how much. There was at any rate a prejudice in favour of the king of Greece among the British establishment, which had echoes in SOE as well. The king's hold over the affections of his Greek people was less certain; and the main guerilla movements that set themselves up in the Greek mountains were all more or less republican in tendency. Some of them were prepared to contemplate having him back after the war, if he consented to a plebiscite first; others were frankly anti-monarchical. The most strongly anti-monarchical of these, and much the largest of the guerilla organisations, also called itself a national army of liberation (ELAS) and also turned out to be under the control of the Greek communist party. What, in such a political fix, was SOE to do?*

Even in France there were sharp divergencies between different bodies of armed men. Many devout French patriots thought that they must obey the orders of the senior marshal of France, Pétain, who headed a satellite state at Vichy; others inclined rather to follow the example of the most junior general in the army, de Gaulle, who from London and Algiers exhorted them to believe that he incarnated a French republic that was still

---

* For SOE's attempt at a solution, see pp. 334–41.

unconquered; others again looked to Moscow or to Washington for distant support. Even the celebrated administrative machine, begun by Richelieu, carried on through Colbert and Turgot, Napoleon I and Napoleon III, into the Third Republic, was divided; some civil servants adhered openly and in their hearts to Pétain, some accepted his orders in public and did their best to contravene them in private. One of this last class, *préfet* of a south-western *département* (the Corrèze), has recorded that on 1 August 1944 he passed in a single road journey through five controls – one by his own police, one by an F section maquis, one by the German army, one by a communist maquis and one by the SS.[8] This was a few days after the German army had received (though it did not obey) orders from dissidents in Berlin to dispose of its SS compatriots; and a few days before the F section and the communist maquis had to decide whether to fight each other or to fight the retreating Germans.

Muddles in Asia were hardly less intricate than muddles in Europe. In Burma SOE found it advisable to deal with the Burmese Communist Party (BCP), to the mingled alarm and dismay of the Burmese government-in-exile at Simla; and in Malaya the Malayan Communist Party (MCP) seemed to be best organised to offer any serious hope of widespread resistance to the Japanese occupier. Both these communist parties were brutally anti-imperialist in tone, and were hardly less hostile to the British than to the Japanese. In Indo-China, again, a strongly anti-French communist movement – later familiar to American television audiences as the Viet Minh – provided an alternative to the supporters of de Gaulle, who were also trying to get something done against the local pro-Vichy regime and the Japanese occupiers.

In three of the seven cases just cited – in Yugoslavia, Burma and Malaya – SOE threw its lot in with the communists, while keeping an occasional line open to some of their opponents. In Greece, it helped both them and their anti-Nazi opponents. In France it helped some of them; in Poland it helped none of them; and in Indo-China it was supposed not to operate at all, because Indo-China fell within OSS's sphere of influence. The examples may give some idea of the political complexity of the cases with which SOE's country sections had to deal. In all of them, the decision seems to have been made on the strength of such information as SOE could get, from its own agents and from other sources, about what was actually going on, and what might be expected to happen next, inside the country concerned. The case of Albania was egregious: there, it appears, the decision to back the communists and jettison the anti-communists among the resisters was taken on evidence from inside Albania, coloured by some political prejudice on the part of SOE's Albanian staff, that the anti-communists were too pro-German (see pp. 346–8).

Staff officers, and British agents in the field, in SOE consoled themselves as they cut their way through these political jungles with the thought that, when the war was over, they would not be there. It was indeed some guide to the impartiality of a British officer in the field that he (or she) was British, and would therefore not be concerned with who was going to run the country when the war was done. This enabled a few outstanding personalities, such as Hudson and Bailey in Bosnia, Myers and Woodhouse in Greece, George Starr in Gascony, Suttill ('Prosper') in Paris, to command some degree of respect from the resistance chiefs to whom they could offer advice unprejudiced by political bias; save that bias which attaches naturally to belonging (as they were all assumed by left-wingers to do) to the British officer class.

SOE's problems can be well illustrated by two quotations from (Sir) Fitzroy Maclean, another strong personality, who was sent to Tito's partisans in Yugoslavia as Churchill's personal liaison officer. Maclean maintained in retrospect, after a disturbing interview with Selborne and a brush with Keble before he left,[9] that he was Churchill's man and not SOE's; certainly he had profound suspicions (as did many other people) about some of SOE's Cairene staff. As he was equipped, dispatched and provided with communications by SOE, he cannot be ruled out of this book.

He raised with Churchill in London the difficulty that he foresaw he might be in: he had served on the British embassy staff in Moscow, was well aware of the nature of the Comintern, and wanted to know whether he was to assist or to hinder Comintern expansion in the Balkans.

> Mr Churchill's reply left me in no doubt as to the answer to my problem. So long, he said, as the whole of Western civilisation was threatened by the Nazi menace, we could not afford to let our attention be diverted from the immediate issue by considerations of long-term policy. We were as loyal to our Soviet Allies as we hoped they were to us. My task was simply to help find out who was killing the most Germans and suggest means by which we could help them to kill more. Politics must be a secondary consideration.

They met again in Cairo in December 1943, in the middle of Maclean's mission.

> I now emphasized to Mr Churchill the other points which I had already made in my report, namely, that in my view the Partisans, whether we helped them or not, would be the decisive political factor in Jugoslavia after the war and, secondly, that Tito and the other leaders of the Movement were openly and avowedly Communist and that the system which they would establish would inevitably be on Soviet lines and, in all probability, strongly orientated towards the Soviet Union.

The Prime Minister's reply removed my doubts.

'Do you intend,' he asked, 'to make Jugoslavia your home after the war?'

'No, Sir,' I replied.

'Neither do I,' he said. 'And, that being so, the less you and I worry about the form of Government they set up, the better. That is for them to decide. What interests us is, which of them is doing most harm to the Germans?'[10]

Churchill here echoed the views of many staff officers and agents in SOE, all of them perhaps reflecting that unconscious isolation from the world overseas in which the inhabitants of this island have for centuries been brought up. It may be argued now, by the passionately anti-Bolshevik, that the attitude was a short-sighted one; but what workable alternative was open? To spurn communist help, when the principal communist power was gradually grinding the Wehrmacht into the mud and dust of the eastern front, was not likely to bring the day of victory any closer; nor would it make life after the war much more easy for communism's opponents, however high-minded.

During the closing weeks of their training courses, SOE's agents often sought guidance about the political pitfalls into which they might be liable to fall; but seldom found it. The training staff took the line, almost always, that agents were sent abroad to perform strictly military tasks, and must take neither part nor even interest in domestic politics at all. Hardly ever were they given even the most rudimentary political training; they were forced back on their own common sense, and on such innate political judgement as they might possess. Young British officers – all those born after 1914 – had never had a chance to vote in a general election; few indeed of them had had any practical experience of politics, as organisers or as debaters, as inspirers or as intriguers, save now and then in the callow fields of school and university. They were therefore liable to be clay in the hands of seasoned agents of the Comintern or of other well-established continental political parties. (Stalin's closure of the Comintern in 1943 was a purely cosmetic measure: it had no perceptible impact on the capability of international communism's emissaries on the spot in Europe or Asia.)

There was another point at which politics and war touched each other: deception. Unhappily for the historian, deception was plunged in the deepest secrecy at the time, and has not been much illuminated by later disclosures. The whole subject is tricky and slippery, and is currently wrapped in a particularly dense cloud of secrecy. SOE is often accused of having played a part in one or other of the deception schemes that had to form a large part of British strategy – had to, because prewar governments had followed their electorates' wishes all too closely, and had left the country under-armed to face its actual axis opponents on real battlefields. Several books about secret services, SOE especially, by authors who have not managed to get right inside their subject, fall back on deception, when they can see no other explanation of some piece of apparent British incompetence. The truth usually turns out to be that the incompetence was not apparent, but real. Men fighting secret wars often make mistakes; just as men often make mistakes in open battle, or indeed in the calm of business or private life. N section's catastrophe in the Netherlands provides only too vivid an example.

The fact is that the small and secret teams who ran the major deceptions – headed by Bevan in London, Dudley Clarke in the Mediterranean, and Fleming in the Far East – did not trust SOE, and took care to keep their plans from SOE's knowledge. Subordinate officers in PWE, and broadcasting staff in that hive of industry and rumour Bush House (whence most BBC broadcasts went to

Europe), may have been confused by half-understood aspects of 'Starkey', an unsuccessful major deception of the late summer of 1943 in western Europe.[11] From their confusion a certain amount of misinformation seems to have seeped out. Statements that SOE played a major part in any major deception scheme are mistaken, with one solitary exception: operation 'Animals' in Greece (see p. 338).[12]

It is worth looking at SOE's political role not only from the headquarters end, but from the worm's-eye view of the citizens of occupied countries. Their view – as no historian can ever forget – varied with time and with history. It is easy, but wrong, to look back at the world war as a single moment in time: it lasted six agonising years, and in six years a single individual's mind can often change. Moreover history, as well as current events, dictated the outlook of occupied populations. The shock of being overrun by an enemy was not quite so severe in Poland, Yugoslavia, Belgium, western Russia and parts of northern France, where it had happened within living memory, as it was in Norway, Denmark, the Netherlands, Burma, Malaya and the Dutch East Indies, where it had happened longer ago. Even for the areas where everyone over twenty-five could remember the previous time, the shock with which occupation arrived in its mid-twentieth-century guise – accompanied by aircraft and tanks – was noticeably much sharper than it had been in the days of uhlans and infantry, or bluejackets and redcoats backed by paddle-steamers. Practically the whole car-owning populations of Brussels and of Paris bolted in turn, in May and June 1940: the social chaos that followed took years to sort out. The Poles at least knew whether or where to go, what to take and what to leave behind; many less experienced urban and rural crowds were in far greater confusion and uncertainty. The one practical, sensible course seemed to be to kowtow: to accept the swastika or rising sun flag outside the town hall, to do what the new authority said was to be done, to keep curfew, in today's phrase 'to keep a low profile' and to try to stay out of trouble. Nobody could pretend this was a glorious course, but it did at first seem to be the only hard-headed one.

In theory, there was a line of defence that might have been mounted against the axis: passive resistance. There had been perceptible support for it in England between the wars: pacifism was widespread among English opinion-formers and students in the late 1920s and early 1930s. It was encouraged by authors as diverse as Bertrand Russell and A. A. Milne. In India, Gandhi's movement of *satyagraha*, passive civil disobedience, had already begun to gnaw with effect at the bases on which the British Raj rested. A great many thinking people, children during the Great War of 1914–18 that had slaughtered their fathers' generation, or born just after it to those who had had the luck to survive, doubted whether wars could any longer be a sensible way of settling quarrels between states: a doubt much sharpened by the use of nuclear weapons in anger in 1945. Yet most pacifists with any practical turn of mind realised after Mussolini's attack on Abyssinia in 1935 and Franco's onslaught on the Spanish republic in 1936 that there was not going to be time enough for Gandhian methods to work in Europe against Mussolini or Hitler.

SOE provided several chances for men and women of good will and pacific intent, ex-pacifists converted by the trend of world politics, to play a useful part in the war against fascism without having themselves to make any violent gesture that would offend their private consciences. However, the most effective uses of pacifist techniques against the axis do not seem to have been inspired by SOE. One of these, the Norwegian school-teachers' strike, provides an almost unique example of effective civil disobedience against the Gestapo; the Norwegian nation can claim credit for it, though SOE cannot.[13] An alternative, more insidious, more deadly method was the use of go-slow techniques.

Czechs and Slovaks were past masters at this, brought up as so many of them were on that splendid novel *The Good Soldier Šveik* by Jaroslav Hašek.[14] Šveik, in the previous war, had combined affability and incompetence with superb effect. His countrymen knew what to do. A revisionist historian complains that this view of Šveikism as a Czechoslovak response to occupation is 'superficial';[15] there is not evidence enough to be decisive either way. Certainly the Skoda arms works, which had made Czechoslovakia the best armed of the successor states to the Austro-Hungarian empire, turned out arms for the Third Reich in quantity, as it had done for the vanished Czechoslovak republic; certainly many Czechoslovaks had a comparatively easy war – compared, that is, to Poles or Dutch or south Slavs, or to Chinese or Malayans, who were taking a more conspicuously anti-axis attitude. Certainly also not all the products even of Skoda were perfectly turned out; beneath their apparent compliance the Czechs nourished a strong sense of Slav national identity, dislike of tyranny (not dead yet), and reluctance to do well for an oppressor. In none of this can SOE claim to have had much influence.

On the other hand, SOE's agents – once they had started to get themselves established – in any industrial area always made a point of suggesting to those they met that, if one had to work for the Germans, there was no point in working for them with unnecessary zeal. PWE and the BBC said the same thing. The Germans came to rely a great deal on forced labour from the countries they had conquered (Sauckel was hanged at Nuremberg, in the bitter end, precisely for having organised this); most of this forced labour was noticeably unenthusiastic. Yet it got through the day's tasks. No one has ever thought that the Pyramids were built with voluntary labour; they have stood for a long time, and are still admired for size, for strength and for accuracy of line. Luckily for SOE, the tasks set by Nazi slavemasters were more intricate than those set by the Pharaohs, so some sabotage possibilities were open, once anybody could be found to take advantage of them. It needs to be admitted that there were many more opportunities available than SOE was ever able to take.

Though the enemy could command slave labourers' arms and legs, he could not – in another postwar phrase – control their hearts and minds. Goebbels' magnificent propaganda systems worked hard in northern, western and south-eastern Europe – Russia and Poland were held beneath contempt – to explain how marvellous the Nazi system was; they did not command widespread belief.

Here was a sphere that might have presented golden chances for SOE as Dalton had conceived it, a body devoted to subversion in all its forms, political and military at once; yet the quarrels in Whitehall described in Chapter II had reduced SOE in its propaganda aspect to little more than a travel agent for PWE, some of whose operatives SOE was able to help install. SOE's organisers were sometimes given basic training in how to circulate rumours and how to devise and run off leaflets, but seldom if ever had a chance to play much part in the propaganda war. Not many of them, in any case, knew enough in intimate detail about their working countries to be able to keep abreast of local writers, some of whom were expert indeed.

Dutch historians, for example, seized a splendid chance. The Netherlands is full of printing works, one of the country's main light industries; the first Dutch clandestine news-sheet came out on 15 May 1940, the day after the surrender, over two months before SOE was born. Less clandestine publishing went on as well, subject to the normal Nazi censorship. There was a sharp upsurge in interest in the Eighty Years' War, fought against the occupying Spanish empire from 1568 to 1648 and the subject of many favourite Dutch stories. As the Spaniards were not Aryans, Nazi censors raised no problems over what was said about them, and were too stupid to understand that the Dutch read these historical essays as currently topical tracts, from which they could learn how to outwit an occupier.[16]

Even in the Netherlands, even in Norway, however, there were several thousand men who were prepared to go wherever the occupier told them, to help his police by becoming *V-Männer* or even to join his armed forces by enlisting in the Waffen-SS.[17] Neighbours and friends might not approve, but were unable to do much beyond biting the bullet. The normal democratic channels of public meetings, demonstrations, elections, representation, plebiscite were closed. The only two exceptions the Nazis made to this rule did not encourage them to make more; the Italians and Japanese made none.

One of the exceptions was a plebiscite called by the gauleiter of Luxembourg, intended to approve the Grand Duchy's incorporation in the Reich. He omitted to take the tyrant's usual precaution of nobbling the polling clerks, so that the result could be cooked: almost everybody voted against. In spite of this result, nothing was done about releasing Luxembourg from Germany's grip till the allied armies reached it in the autumn of 1944. And in Denmark, supposedly an Aryan country, in March 1943 the Germans allowed a routine general election. This was, from their point of view, a gamble – which they lost. Of 148 members returned, only three were Nazis. After that there was no more talk of allowing conquered countries to exercise any democratic right.

Not much is known for certain about what the general reaction to axis occupation was; there is little reliable evidence. Clandestine newspapers were necessarily biased; the newspapers that Nazi censorship allowed to go on appearing were biased also, in the contrary direction; it is in any case a fallacy to believe that what the newspapers say reflects at all accurately what the readership is thinking. Historians must resort to guesswork, probabilities, common sense. One or two main political strands can be picked out.

Shock has been mentioned already: that came first, and in some countries lasted for a long time. As it wore off, resentment came next: dislike of the privations that usually went with occupation (Japanese, German and Italian troops alike quickly cleaned out the shops of anything worth buying; outside the deep countryside, food often rapidly became short). This resentment often turned against the parties which had been responsible for running the country's affairs up to the moment of invasion: would a properly competent government have let the nation in for quite so catastrophic a defeat? In countries of political sophistication, such as France, Belgium and Greece, there was widespread political disarray and mistrust, made worse in the Greek case by the dictatorship under which the country had been governed since 4 August 1936. A note often sounded by French resistance groups was that all the prewar parties had let France down, and none of them were to be allowed to re-establish themselves after the war. The old landed gentry of Europe, who had thought themselves relegated permanently to the backwoods, wondered whether their duty might not be to come forward after all, out of the obscurity into which their grandfathers had retired, and provide their former tenants with the leadership that had once been their feudal privilege.

Although SOE remained in principle disinterested in politics, a few of its staff officers and agents insisted on getting involved nevertheless: some from party conviction, some from a tendency to be busybodies. Its general line remained strictly military. As the war went on, more and more people in occupied countries got over their shock at being occupied and decided to take the appalling risks of entering into resistance: always an illegal and often a perilous way of spending energy and time. It was SOE's task to seek them out, to arm and train them, and to direct their energies into channels that would best suit both the allied high command and the resisters' views of where their own countries' best interests lay. SOE's agents on the spot tried to prod local resistance into action that would hit the enemy hard at the right moment – the right moment both for the allies in general, and for the occupied power in particular. Obviously enough, to do this sometimes involved SOE in direct negotiations with politicians, and with such fragments of political parties as had managed to survive under the axis ban. Several of these cases are discussed in Chapter XI.

Jealous though SOE was of any attempt by the Foreign Office to control it, and exasperating though the doctrine of 'no bangs without Foreign Office consent' was to SOE in the early days of its development, its more senior and more sensible officers were able to appreciate that the FO was quite right to take an interest in what SOE was doing. For in many occupied countries the course of resistance activity was influenced – in some it was controlled – by those who were determined to shape the kind of regime that was to be in power after the war.

The communists, alone among political parties, had prepared themselves beforehand for just the kinds of trouble that occupation brought with it, and they also, alone among political parties, had an obstinate (not to say bloody-minded) conviction of their own absolute rightness and the inevitability of their seizure of power. This conviction often led them to be arrogant; now and then it led them to be victorious. In France they led the Front National, without too much concealment, with a vigour that brought them in MI6 the nickname of *fanatiques*, abbreviated to FANA; that name spread to SOE, and was wrongly assumed, by the present writer in the first edition of his official history, to be a proper name for the movement.[18] In Yugoslavia they provided the leadership cadre for the partisan movement, in Greece they ran EAM and its vigorous army, ELAS; nowhere, after 22 June 1941, were they dormant.

Before that date their activities, coloured by the Nazi-Soviet pact, were often more dubious; after it, no one could doubt that they threw themselves whole-heartedly onto the anti-Nazi side. Courage they had in abundance; they were not so strong on wisdom, or on widespread popular appeal. In such countries as Norway, Holland, Belgium, Romania or Malaya they remained a tiny minority; but not one without influence. Wherever the Red Army marched in Europe, except in Finland, Czechoslovakia and Austria, they carried with them on their bayonets the red flag of communism, and left behind them at the end of the war communistic regimes, which are only now starting to collapse; Czechoslovakia also came within the communist belt not long after the end of the war. Albania, as always, was a case apart: the intransigent Enver Hoxha, the local communist leader, was able during the war to use SOE's arms against his rivals within his own country, instead of against the German garrison, and when the Germans had been prised out by the Russian advance from Bulgaria into Yugoslavia, Hoxha was able to secure his idiosyncratic hold on state power, right through to his death in 1985.

At the last free election in Czechoslovakia (1948), the Communist Party got thirty-eight per cent of the votes. None can say what percentage it would get, there or elsewhere behind what Churchill named the Iron Curtain, in the event of a free election there in the near future. Yet at least a communist seizure of power, even in so comparatively bourgeois a republic as Czechoslovakia, secured one principal objective of resisters: a clean sweep of the prewar regime. What a partisan, now grey- or white-haired, thinks in his heart of hearts about the wisdom of throwing off a fascist tyranny in order to replace it by a communist one, is a separate question, to which the answer must vary from one country and one man to another.

Arthur Koestler once remarked that 'it is impossible to look back at the war without mixed feelings of pride, pain, and bitterness'.[19] One of the sources of pride, for anyone with any human feeling at all, lies in the readiness of so many millions of ordinary citizens in occupied countries to step forward – often at no notice at all – and take the fearful risks of working against the occupier. The credit for victory in the war is apportioned differently in different countries: the Russians are taught that it lay with Stalin, their all-wise leader, and with the correct line followed by his companions in the Communist Party of the Soviet Union; the Americans look rather to their own President Roosevelt and their great commanders, Marshall, MacArthur, Eisenhower, King, Nimitz; the British to Churchill and to such stars as Montgomery; the intellectuals, to their fellow intellectuals who toiled at Bletchley and in Washington to unravel Germany's and Japan's inmost secrets and thus gave foreknowledge at least of where the enemy was going to strike next, often a most precious gift.

Yet it is a mistake to concentrate on leadership, and exclude the common soldier, sailor, airman, resister: for these and their families at home were the real creators of victory. This was a people's war, of a kind that had not been fought since the Dark Ages or even since prehistoric times: a war into which whole nations hurled themselves with the whole of their energies, in spite of a fringe in each that backed the wrong side.[20] For the first time, total war combined with the total resources released by the Industrial Revolution, with world-shaking results. SOE had a vital role to play in this titanic struggle: it was

SOE's job to provide a steel core for resistance, wherever it could be found; to give it teeth, so that it could bite the enemy properly. To do this SOE had to bother a lot about communications and security, and a little about politics. Let us now move on to discuss how it did its job.

IX
What SOE was like

Soldiers say that war is ninety-nine per cent boredom and one per cent fright. The extreme, protracted, agonising dullness of war is not reflected in books or films or broadcasts about it, because it is a crime to bore readers or listeners or viewers. Life for a secret agent in axis-held lands was as a rule more alarming than life in an ordinary fighting unit; it would not be putting it too high to say that it was twice, it may even have been ten times, as frightening. Even so, ninety per cent is a tremendous amount of boredom. For every happy agent living it up in, say, Bucharest, while Bucharest was still neutral,[1] a score or a hundred less happy agents elsewhere would be deadly bored.

To cope with all their boredom, agents needed patience – enormous, Job-like patience – as well as strength of will. It was particularly dangerous to fall, from boredom, into routines, and thus to get slack about security; for they spent their working lives on a razor's edge of peril. One slip, and they were done for. If they had properly taken this on board, the dullness of much of their life was a good deal more easy to bear.

There is a story that one of SOE's girl couriers was arrested, on her first appearance by herself in a French town, because she glanced to the right before she glanced to the left on crossing the street. The story is apocryphal, but bears out a cardinal point: every slightest gesture an agent made in occupied territory might bring danger, even death. Agents therefore had to live, day in, day out – year in, year out for some of them – on perpetual tenterhooks. When Mussolini wrote (or Gentile wrote for him), in a once notorious passage, 'War alone brings up to its highest tension all human energy,'[2] he wrote more truly than he knew: he himself never had to undergo the prolonged stresses of life under cover. Working in the field for any secret service was no task for a coward.

Moreover, the kind of courage that was needed was not quite the same as battlefield bravery. As has been said, 'Out here on the lonely margins of military life, heroes seem more heroic and blackguards more blackguardly than they do in the ordinary line of battle, where companionship keeps men steady and women are not expected to fight at all.'[3] Agents had to work either alone, or with very few friends, until they reached – if they ever did reach – the moment of a national uprising, or at least a major revolt in a great city; or unless they managed to create, or to join forces with, one of the substantial guerilla armies that arose to fight against axis power. The hardest work, and the gravest dangers, lay in the opening and most lonely stages.

Loneliness could be almost as agonising as fright. It was a burden that lay extra heavy on wireless operators, left for twenty-three hours in every twenty-four with little to do but worry about whether they would catch their next schedule, whether they would get through, and when the enemy direction-finders would close in. It was heavy too for agents in hiding from the Gestapo or the OVRA or the Kempeitai; and for what are now called sleepers – people who quietly sustained a cover existence for months, perhaps for years, till they got a message that made them active as well as alert. SOE's time-scale was too short for it to have much truck with sleepers, outside its escape lines. In these, whole chains of people might spend months, even years, doing nothing but keeping out of harm's way; till the call came, and they started to put themselves in permanent peril for the sake of the strangers they hid, and of the common cause they served.

Nowadays people often ask, were agents frightened? Of course they were; the question is not a good one. As that well-reputed but little-read authority Clausewitz once said, 'Danger is part of the friction of war. Without an accurate conception of danger we cannot understand war.'⁴ Some agents conceived danger only too clearly: they lived in a state of perpetual terror. One of these is even said, by a colleague, to have died of fright; though the death certificate said something different. Others were so obsessed by the need not to draw attention to themselves that they got nothing done at all, beyond staying alive and undetected. Others again, more fatalistic, believed (with Clausewitz) that 'there will always be time enough to die'.⁵ A few, gifted with thick skins or simply careless, did not bother about the risks; fewer still of these rash ones came back.

Most agents found their apprehensions extra-sharp to start with: apprehensiveness indeed was more common even than fright. They lived in a perpetual unease. Gradually agents got used to the sight of German uniforms, to the sound of jackboots in the street at night, if they worked in towns; gradually, if they worked in the country, they came to realise that months might go by without their ever setting eyes on an enemy at all. Town or country alike, their lives fitted into the normal patterns of war – long quiet spells, with nothing much going on, and spells of agonising intensity, that called for their utmost powers of moral and physical strength.

Not only did agents have to be brave. Beyond that they needed, for any hope of success, to be observant a long way beyond the common run; tireless far out of the ordinary; capable with their hands (there was seldom room for the ham-fisted) as well as with their brains; above all, *aware*. They needed constantly to know, and to be able to distinguish, their own and their colleagues' real and cover identities at any given moment. This often made for trouble in intricate fixes, when they might have to adopt several different personalities to cope with different people in the real world. A few were caught because they made the simple, easy mistake of carrying in the same wallet identity papers, each bearing their own photograph, made out for two different names. Good ones had to be consummate actors, and yet had to remember that the play in which they were acting was one on which the curtain was not going to come down for months. It was all too easy for an unstable personality to get carried away entirely into the world of make-believe.

Besides the agent who is said to have died of fright, there were several more who were more or less violently disturbed by the strains they had had to undergo: the strain of being one person while seeming to be another; the strain of keeping silent while everyone round them gossiped; the strain of not correcting the under-informed; the strain of being important but being thought a nobody; the strain of remembering strings of addresses too secret to be written down and too important to be forgotten; the unforgettable threats of arrest and torture if discovered; the lack of time; the lack of any chance entirely to relax; the perpetual uncertainty; the perpetual lack of sleep. The first thought of an important agent, pulled in at a shop control but not yet identified by the enemy, when he had been out receiving arms and other agents by para-chute for eleven nights in the past fortnight, was neither about his own safety nor about those for whom he was responsible: it was, '*At last I can sleep*'.[6]

There is no point in trying to reconstruct what the average agent's day was like: no agents were average and no two days could be relied on to be quite the same. The ideal agent sank entirely into the surrounding populace, and never seemed to do anything in the least out of the common run; he was totally unobtrusive and inconspicuous, till there was a secret job to do, and that was best done out of anybody else's sight, or at least out of sight of all strangers to the circuit in which the agent worked.

At Beaulieu, Oshawa and elsewhere, SOE's prospective agents got some advice on how to make sure that the way they behaved did not show them up for what they really were. It was important not to look furtive, not to keep glancing over one's shoulder to see whether one was being followed, not to crouch or lurk in corners; not to keep turning one's head; not to hesitate about which way to go at a street or lane junction. Just as 161 Squadron's pick-up pilots had to do a vast deal of map-reading before ever they got into their aircraft to collect agents from the Continent, agents in Europe or in Asia had to map-read carefully before they went on journeys, to make sure that they went direct, without drawing attention to themselves by dithering. If one thought one might be followed, the best thing to do in a town was to pause a moment to adjust one's shoelace (thus providing a chance for a sweeping look behind); or to find some shop windows and dawdle by them, surveying in their reflections what was going on in the street around one. To pause in a doorway just round a corner till the follower passed by was sometimes useful, but called for care; might not shake off followers working in pairs; and was no use at all against the 'front trail', the policeman in plain clothes who exercises surveillance from in front of the suspect instead of behind.

It was important also to be polite and, even if angry or frightened, not to display one's temper and so mark oneself out from the crowd. Politeness could be carried too far – Kemp has an anecdote of a fellow officer, disguised like himself as an Albanian peasant in the streets of Dakovica (Gjakovë), having a handkerchief snatched from his hand by an indignant guide, and blowing his nose noisily on his fingers.[7] On the other hand it was silly, when fighting for a seat in a train in Brussels or Lyons or Turin, to elbow women so vigorously that one got delated to the railway police.

Punctuality was indispensable for agents, even in societies in which it was so unusual as almost to amount to bad manners. As a sound communist slogan put it, if you arrive early they arrest you while you are hanging about, if you arrive late they arrest the comrade who is waiting for you – so be on time. Making appointments at odd times – 12.17 rather than 12 noon, ten minutes to the hour rather than dead on it – was a refinement in which the extra-cautious could indulge; on the whole, the extra-cautious were the ones who came back, sometimes having got something done.

To be sure of being punctual, it was in fact necessary – as well as prudent – to arrive early at any town rendez-vous, and to look the neighbourhood over to make sure there was no sign of undue enemy presence: no parked cars with men sitting in them, no groups of men in belted raincoats, no abnormally large numbers of soldiers or policemen. Agents could walk past, take a turn round the block, invent an errand in the next street, check once more that they were not themselves being followed, and then turn up dead on time.

Cafés made frequent meeting-places. Careful agents made sure they knew the back way out through the kitchen, or the door into a side street; and made sure too that they did not linger long if the agent they were to meet was late. Daring agents met in cafés much used by the enemy.[8] Certainly in these an enemy's suspicions would be to some extent lulled by the presence of so many of his own side's uniforms. On the other hand, in a café one was quite likely to be pinned to one's table by the crowd, and unable to slip out unobtrusively if the police happened to make an apparently routine check of everyone's identity.

It was important, too, to remember the probability that

in any large café one at least of the waiters would be an enemy informer. The ubiquity of informers is one of the nastiest features of tyrannies – after all, in tyrannies children are brought up to delate their own parents to the authorities if what their parents say to each other at home gets out of step with the current party line as teacher instils it at school. Brian Rafferty, a Christ Church undergraduate whom F section had sent to run a circuit not far from Vichy, was heard to remark as he left a café on the outskirts of Clermont-Ferrand, 'Yes, it's a fine moonlight night, we shall have great fun'; he was followed and arrested on his way to receive a drop of stores, and did not return from his concentration camp.[9]

His misfortune brings out another constant preoccupation for agents: the need to be ready to make an alternative plan, when something went wrong with the first one. Over and over again it happened that someone got intercepted, sometimes by bad luck, sometimes by bad management; everyone did not always turn up; what was the circuit to do, with a reduced team? Leaders had to be ready to invent, very promptly, ways of getting out of every sort of shortage: of men, of women, of arms, of chances to attack. The ability, in Wellington's phrase, to tie a knot in the harness of one's plans when it breaks was a vital one for SOE's agents as well as for that great commander.

Uncertainty dogged and besotted SOE; it was one of the reasons why the other fighting services mistrusted it so. Portal and Harris in the air force, Wavell, Montgomery and Slim in the army, all inclined to think that SOE's work did not have the sureness of their own; an SOE attack was not like a bomber raid or an artillery barrage, of which the results could be photographed next morning and observed in detail as minute as the scale of the photograph would allow. This attitude was widely shared by their staffs. Robin Brook, for instance, found in the summer of 1944 when he was promoted colonel (the red tabs gave him useful standing at staff meetings) and appointed head of the branch of Eisenhower's supreme headquarters of the allied expeditionary force (SHAEF) that dealt with subversion – when in fact he became the link man between SHAEF and the mobilised forces of resistance in France and the Low Countries – that all the rest of the staff regarded resistance activity as a 'bonus'. They did not know much about it, beyond such legends as the newspapers were already spreading (inspired by John Steinbeck's romance *The Moon is Down*).[10] Brook, far more fully informed, was able to produce for them several large bonuses, much larger than they had expected, though not large enough to shake the ingrown staff beliefs (which go back to Clausewitz) that guerillas are never to be trusted by regulars.[11]

Most agents did not mind that regulars did not much trust them. One of the delights of SOE – and it had delights, to make up for the apprehension, the loneliness and the boredom – was that one was frequently one's own master, could do what one chose in the way that one chose to do it, and was not bound, as all the other services were, between the blinkers of King's Regulations and the dead weight of the past. Whatever else SOE was, it was *original*.

Staff colleges always teach, among their principles of war, economy of effort as one of the things a fighting man should cherish most, and surprise as another. SOE was not, all things considered, an expensive body to run – indeed in the end it showed a profit (see pp. 359–60); but those who had been taught economy often forgot about it later, when they came to high command, and found the lavish resources for waging war that resulted from the Industrial Revolution available to their orders. These vast resources led in turn, almost always, to a sacrifice of surprise; if an enemy's intelligence system was any good at all, it ought to have been able to observe where the other side was piling up material for an attack in time to erect some kind of defence. Here SOE had a serious strategic advantage on its side; its work was necessarily unostentatious, hard to spot; it could slip parties into areas it meant to threaten, and mount sudden and totally surprising attacks, without giving the enemy any notice at all.

This provided for some of its agents a motive that sustained them through any troubles that might come their way: the feeling that they, individually, were exercising (if they did their job perfectly) a perceptible influence on the course of the war; for which they would never be likely to get public credit. Even Sherlock Holmes got nothing more than an emerald tie-pin from Queen Victoria's own hand, after a notable coup; they knew they could not hope for as much. Yet the private knowledge of their own possible immense importance was enough to sustain them through a host of travails. They felt they were taking a leading role – if Conan Doyle may be quoted again – in 'that secret history of a nation which is often so much more intimate and interesting than its public chronicles'.[12]

A less self-centred and more common motive force for SOE's agents was patriotism, then more highly regarded as a virtue than now. Already intellectuals, headed by Bertrand Russell, had abandoned it. Edith Cavell's famous remark, made a few hours before she died, 'Patriotism is not enough', had been engraved below her statue near Trafalgar Square in 1924, and was believed in by a great many earnest and well-meaning young men and women, some of them in SOE. Harry Rée ('César'), for instance, positively denied that patriotism was what took him into SOE, and claimed the more realistic motive of self-interest: 'Any mistake I made I would suffer from, but I would probably not suffer from the mistake of a superior officer.'[13] On the other hand, the idea of 'One World', preached in an influential pamphlet by Wendell Willkie – Roosevelt's opponent in the 1940 presidential election – in 1943,[14] had yet to catch on, to be included in

sermons and leading articles the world over. Meanwhile,
the Russians found that the big patriotic drum was the
one to beat, rather than the revolutionary kettledrum: the
struggle against Germany of 1941–5 is commonly known
in the USSR as the Great Patriotic War. Stalin, the
uncrowned tsar, put out through his matchless propaganda organs appeals to Russian love of country that his
crowned predecessors would have approved. Patriotism
was what kept most German and almost all Japanese
serving men true to their flag, on the enemy side, however
badly the war was going; on the allied side, patriotism
held a very large number of SOE's agents – as well as
other soldiers, sailors and airmen – steady in their efforts
of war.

Often theirs was a double patriotism, according to the
chances of their own birth: Anglo-French, Anglo-Polish,
Anglo-Belgian, Anglo-Norwegian and so on. They felt
love enough for their own countries and their settled ways
to be quite sure they did not want those ways upset by
Nazis or fascists or any of their friends or followers.

It would be absurd to suggest that SOE's agents acted
only from the purest of motives; all human beings are
more or less sinful, and SOE had its share (as has been
noticed already, pp. 69–70) of those who had lived quite
outside the boundaries of normal law and conduct. Many
agents went into SOE out of a sense of adventure; some
of the most splendid of the characters in it would have
made names for themselves in Drake's navy or even
among Morgan's pirates, had they happened to have been
born some centuries earlier. SOE, like SAS, had room
for the buccaneer rather than the bureaucrat in its ranks.

For some agents one of the charms of SOE lay in its
freedom from convention: they felt that, once they were
launched on irregular work, they were no longer tied to
rules of conduct in their private life. The erotic aspects of
SOE are rather for the novelist than the historian to
cover; indeed, twenty-five years ago a great continental

scholar remarked that, where books on SOE so far published were concerned, it was far from easy to distinguish fact from fiction.[15] This historian at any rate does not propose to venture far beyond the proverb that necessity makes strange bedfellows.

A few cases, too odd to be left out altogether, will at least illustrate SOE's diversity. One is that of Denis Rake, who had been in the great game early – he had been an unknowing courier for Edith Cavell in Brussels early in 1915, though whether for helping escapes or for her more strictly secret work he never discovered.[16] He happened to be a homosexual, and made no secret of the fact. He was also both brave and gun-shy; and could pass for French without trouble. F section sent him to France, where he was arrested while crossing the demarcation line. He managed an uncomfortable but effective escape in a swill-tub, and solaced himself with a brief affair in Paris with a German staff officer of like leanings. An indignant, ardently heterosexual colleague in F section informed Baker Street, where the staff had the good sense to take no notice, in the belief, fully justified in the Auvergne in 1944, that Rake's capacities as a wireless operator were far too great to be lost because of his eccentric private life.

By contrast, a happily married agent's wife got once a month – after he had left on operations – a note from MO1 (SP) at the War Office to say that he was well and cheerful and sent his love, but could not for the moment write to her himself. He was in fact under orders not to do so. Out of the blue, she got a postcard from a neutral country, postmarked three weeks earlier, in her husband's handwriting. It was unsigned; it said nothing but 'Skiing here marvellous'; but it cheered her up enormously.

A few of SOE's agents did the force's name no good by dabbling in local girls' affections, when they might have had more useful ways of spending their time. None of them did worse than one, who had better remain nameless, who insisted on a constant supply of pubescent virgins in a sexually orthodox province where girls who were no longer virgins could not marry. It says something for SOE's standing that not even this display of dreadful manners turned the province against SOE as a whole, though the offender himself was not loved.

Most married agents accepted separation from their husbands or wives, glumly enough, as a necessity of war. Sometimes a husband and wife could make an efficient team, as the Le Chênes did, in a small way, at Lyons in 1942. Sometimes it might be to a captured agent's advantage to claim a married state that did not exist: Madame Odette Sansom, for example, claimed prematurely but wisely to be Mrs Peter Churchill.

Unmarried agents did not need to feel so glum. The act of parachuting was in those days at least rare and romantic; this extra dangerous way of arriving to take up the wholly unsafe life of a secret agent added an aura of glamour to many of SOE's agents, more in many cases than plain looks and manners would justify in more normal times. That these men and women ventured, as volunteers who could have stayed quietly *embusqués* at home, or at any rate outside the reach of axis police forces, right forward into posts of special danger could hardly help endearing them to those of like mind in the places to which they went. Tremendous links of friendship were sometimes formed by SOE's agents; occasionally alone, often in a group. Not all of these links included a sexual element, though many times over they did.

In any case, an absolutely lone agent was usually helpless. There were a few extra-special tasks, of assassination or demolition, that a single man or woman might contemplate undertaking; but for the usual purposes of clandestine warfare, the SOE agent – lonely though it might be inside the agent's own skull – had to work with local friends and local support. It was precisely because there was no local support, no water in which the guerilla fish could swim, that SOE got nothing of importance done at all in either the German or the Japanese homeland.

It was something of a brake on SOE's effort in the field, that the agents in charge of it had to pause to consider the impact it was going to exert on those who had become their close personal friends; this was a special instance of the worry about reprisals that was endemic in the allied high command, and in the governments-in-exile. If things went wrong, and agents were arrested, their local friends would probably be arrested with them; indeed, only too often the enemy police got their lead-in to a circuit through some indiscretion by a sub-sub-agent who had had no time to learn how to behave clandestinely. An arrested agent's prospects were dark if the Germans or the Italians held him – or her; darker still if the Japanese did. A few survived; sometimes by oversight, sometimes because they had managed to lose themselves in the crowd, sometimes by impudence: John Starr, sent to Mauthausen, survived because he answered back to a bullying German, who therefore respected him enough to leave him alive. So did 'Trotsky' Davies. A very few stuck so firmly to first-class cover stories that their captors released them without ever having discovered who they really were: Victor Gerson, travelling first class of course, managed to talk his way out of a routine train control between Paris and Lyons by producing such a cascade of detail about his work as a traveller in fine rugs that the police no longer thought it conceivable that he was running SOE's best escape line as well.

SOE's staff – more, after all, than half its strength – should not be forgotten by those who try to recall what SOE was like. They too were often bored, and had to remind themselves of Milton's tag: 'They also serve who only stand and wait.' This, remember, was in an age in which a wide range of social classes were convinced that service to the nation was well worth performing, and came a long way in front of service to private or family interest.

For those who worked in one or other of SOE's experimental fields – in research on weapons or wireless or transport – life was likely to be lively enough, provided there was no hitch in their supply of raw materials to work on. Staffs at Arisaig, Beaulieu, Algiers, Bari, Brisbane, Cairo, Meerut, Kandy, Oshawa were wide awake also to receive every scrap of data they could, from refugees and from returned agents, that would help them to understand what life in occupied territory was like and to devise further means for disrupting it. SOE tried always to act in original and unexpected ways: this called for lasting alertness on the part of its staff as well as its agents.

Its senior staff carried an extra weight of worry. As Gubbins once put it, they lived in 'a continual anxiety, all day and every day';[17] they were not likely to sleep sound at night either. They knew they would have to answer to their own few but alarming seniors, if anything went wrong; they knew they could not rely on thanks, even if everything went right. They knew that on their judgement of men large results depended. And they too – however independent – were under orders.

X

Where and
how it worked

SOE was a world-wide body. There was no continent, there was hardly a country, where it did not do something. Its major efforts, so far as numbers of agents employed went, were made into France and Yugoslavia; thither, publicity has followed. Next largest were the missions into Greece, also well known, and Italy, little discussed so far in other languages than Italian. Beside these four main strokes the Dutch disaster, though notorious, was minor. There were also important operations in Belgium, Poland, Albania, Abyssinia, Burma and Malaya; vital work in Scandinavia and Switzerland; conspiracies in Turkey; valiant efforts in Hungary, Romania, Siam and the Dutch East Indies; many lesser and more obscure attempts; and a wholly illegal but exceptionally rewarding series of coups in China.

The data for an encyclopaedic coverage of SOE, that would set down all its works in due order, may possibly still exist in the secret archives; more probably they have been destroyed in one or other of the bonfires that have afflicted SOE's papers (see p. 364). Those who want a single-volume encyclopaedia that covers the war, with sparse references to secret service work, can find it.[1] This chapter will try to put some flesh on the skeleton outline of SOE this book has so far drawn.

Probably the most important thing that SOE ever did was done so discreetly, so unobtrusively and so effectively that hardly any trace of it is left in archives open to the public. It bears out what Gubbins often used to say: that SOE would be unable to claim credit for its principal successes in his lifetime, if at all (he died in 1976).

During the first fourteen months of SOE's existence, there was a major turn-about in the attitudes of most writers of newspaper leading articles, and of influential broadcasters, in the United States. In this turn-about SOE played a hidden but major part. Down to midsummer 1940 the tone of the American press was decidedly isolationist. Charles Lindbergh, the first man to fly the Atlantic by himself, and Senator Wheeler of Montana led the powerful America First movement, which opposed American intervention in a war that would benefit an already rotten British Empire. However President Roosevelt might seem to lean towards intervention when particular Europeans went to talk to him, he could not command what the newspapers said; they clung, as they still cling, to independence as their constitutional right. Most of them held, down to the fall of France and the creation of SOE – the second event as unknown to them as the first was sensational – that the Europeans should be left to get on with their own civil wars by themselves, leaving American blood unspilled.

Nevertheless, the bulk of United States newspapers and broadcasting stations were brought to realise, during the winter of 1940–1, that the American as well as the British way of life was under threat from Nazism. A big part in this change was played by American war correspondents; William L. Shirer in Berlin, Edgar Ansell Mowrer in Rome, Ed Murrow and Raymond Gram Swing in London will be remembered gratefully by the British for having helped to persuade their American fellow-countrymen to change their minds. There was an immediacy about their comments from the front line of Nazism on the Continent and from the bomb-torn streets of London that appealed to an imaginative American readership. Credit is certainly due as well to 'Wild Bill' Donovan, for having worked on the New York and Washington press as best he could after he returned from his critical visit to England in the late summer of 1940. It is still worth recalling that several of the essential tricks were turned by 'Little Bill' Stephenson, Donovan's sponsor in Whitehall and Churchill's secret spokesman in the USA. Stephenson was a master of that essential diplomat's gift, the framing of a talk in such a way that the man being talked to deploys ideas offered to him as if they were his own – thinks they are his own, and will do him credit – and acts on them. Stephenson's discreet feelers and suggestions to newspaper owners, columnists and leader writers all over the United States bore ample fruit.

His role has not been much remarked; it was of cardinal importance. For, once the Americans had understood that the troubles in Europe might spread, and might spread quite soon, to America – and that it mattered to the Americans which side in Europe came out on top – the first, essential link, beyond ancient tradition and divergent language, had been forged in the chain that was to bind Great Britain and the USA together for four momentous years, from the signing of the Atlantic Charter to the first uses of atomic bombs. Frightful as was the shock of the Japanese attack on Pearl Harbor on 7 December 1941, it was less sharp than it would have been if the previous shift in American opinion had not taken place. For that shift SOE can take some of the credit; not all, because inexorable American self-interest told in the same direction. SOE had at least acted as a useful catalyst, to set off a critical reaction.

Stephenson provided Donovan with a model on which he could construct OSS;[2] and well before OSS was founded, co-operated closely with J. Edgar Hoover, the head of the FBI. He met Hoover privately through a common friend, the boxer Gene Tunney (Stephenson among many other distinctions had once been world amateur lightweight boxing champion; he remained in good enough training to dispose once, with his own hands, of a known enemy saboteur detected on the dockside at New York, but normally left the rough stuff to people less near the top of the SOE staff tree).[3] Hoover would not work with Stephenson at all, lest he infringe American neutrality, without a direct order from the President; Stephenson secured that without delay.

Stephenson's post as head of all the British clandestine services west of the Atlantic gave SOE a small, unexpected opening in the Caribbean. The oddities of wartime postal services brought under the eyes of British censors in the West Indies letters exchanged between Germany and German exiles in Venezuela and Colombia. This was quite often useful for intelligence purposes; once at least it was given a subversive twist. An SOE staff officer read with interest a staid exchange of letters between a German businessman in Caracas and his wife in Berlin, which ran simultaneously with a red-hot exchange between the same man and his mistress in another Berlin suburb. He was mischievous enough to swap the letters to Germany round before they were resealed in their envelopes. (Opening and resealing letters, leaving no trace, is an elementary underhand trick.)

This was no more than a pinprick. Much more serious damage might have been done in South America, had the war ever spread closer to that continent than the waters near its northern and eastern shores. Stephenson had formidable teams of musclemen, businessmen, and young dons standing by to operate in South America if the need arose. Not for him the principle that is said to have inspired C's *éminence grise*, Sir Claude Dansey – 'I would never willingly employ a university man'.[4] As the need never arose, he unselfishly let his stars depart to shine under European skies, outside his sphere of work.

* * *

Even Stephenson was acting under orders – Churchill's orders, which have left no trace perceptible to Churchill's official biographer.[5] He knew enough about life and war to be ready to act on his own when something cropped up that his orders did not cover: a skill he had learned the hard way as a fighter pilot, and as an escaper after he had been shot down behind the German lines in the previous world war. It was a skill regularly taught at Beaulieu; a skill that was inherent in the old officer class. It was called taking one's own line in the hunting field, and – formally – using one's own initiative in war. Any competent leader can do it.

Any competent leader knows also that general guidance about which way to be ready to move can help. This guidance the chiefs of staff provided, when they had time to attend to SOE, as had been foreseen at the start (see p. 21). It took three months before the discursive paper that formed SOE's first directive from them was ready.[6] Though Pound, Dill and Portal signed it, it does not read as if it came from any of their pens; nor does it sound crisp enough for Gubbins, who had just joined SOE, to have had much part in it. Talks between Taylor, Jebb, and the joint planning staff can be inferred. The paper was issued on 25 November 1940; a few fragments of it need to be quoted.

> On a long view, it should be the particular aim of our subversive organisation to prepare the way for the final stage of the war when, by co-ordinated and organised revolts in the occupied countries and by a popular rising against the Nazi party inside Germany, direct and decisive military operations against Germany herself may be possible.

Meanwhile, 'the elimination of Italy comes first among our strategical aims'. SOE was to be ready, all over Europe and in north-eastern Africa, to lower enemy morale and to hamper enemy communications. In the Far

East, the chiefs of staff were 'not at present in a position to offer guidance', which should be sought locally from the commander-in-chief. America was not mentioned at all.

Some more or less isolated spheres of SOE's activity – in Abyssinia (Ethiopia) and in central Europe – need to be described before we turn to the equally intricate fields of western Europe, southern and south-eastern Europe, Scandinavia and south-east Asia. Any reader who finds this chapter brutally episodic needs to remember the isolation in which wartime London was hedged: a few brutal episodes were all that anybody knew, at the working staff or agent level in SOE (as in other services), of what was happening in many parts of the world outside this island.

Abyssinia

The Abyssinian venture began before ever SOE did. Indeed, while MI R was striving to mount it, section D was striving to wreck it by independently appealing to the Galla tribe in the south of the country to secede from the rest.* Wavell – who had a great deal else on his mind, as commander-in-chief in Cairo – remembered that when he had commanded in Palestine in the mid-thirties, three young officers had impressed him as likely to do well with irregular forces or at irregular jobs. He sent for them. Dudley Clarke, whom Holland had used, with Gubbins, to found the commandos,[1] created for Wavell a body with the dull name of A Force: its main task was to confuse the enemy.[2] The other two, Orde Wingate and Tony Simonds, Wavell sent up to Khartoum to get on with

---

* I am proud to claim Edwin Foot who wrote the only *Galla-English Dictionary* (Cambridge: CUP 1913) as my great-uncle.

dislocating Mussolini's hold on Abyssinia; this hold dated back to the recent war of 1935–6.

In Khartoum Wingate and Simonds joined Mission 101 – another dull name to cover work a good deal less dull – which was remotely controlled, through G(R) in Cairo, by MI R and then by SOE in London, but was answerable also to Wavell in Cairo and to General Platt, the army commander on the spot. Its aim was to unsettle the Italians' hold on Abyssinia. The head of Mission 101, D. A. Sandford, was older than most in the irregular war – he had just turned fifty-eight – but he knew Abyssinia well, had been consul in Addis Ababa before he left to win two DSOs as a gunner officer in the Great War, and had farmed there for fifteen years between the wars. This calm, stocky, balding, bespectacled colonel (soon made a brigadier) went forward, on his own initiative, into enemy territory not long after Italy joined what Mussolini supposed to be the winning side on 10 June 1940. By mid-September he had established himself at Faguta in the Chokey mountain range, south of Lake Tana,[3] and began to distribute arms to friendly tribesmen. A year before, he had been quietly ensconced in Surrey as treasurer of Guildford cathedral; the prescient Wavell, spurred on by the intelligence staff who operated in Cairo, had summoned him eastward again.[4]

Wingate's personality was so powerful, and the influence he wielded over reporters so mesmeric, that it has hardly yet been possible to rebuild the history of SOE's effort into Abyssinia as a coherent whole, and to present it in its proper context in the history of the war: Wingate, Wingate, Wingate has overshadowed everything, even the luminous gallantry of Platt's soldiers, most of them Indian, who stormed the all-but-untakeable fortress of Keren in Eritrea. Moreover, the fact that Wingate had any connection with SOE, though well known to such well-informed authors as W. E. D. Allen (who was in SOE himself, at Wingate's elbow) or Christopher Sykes, had to remain secret so long as SOE itself was secret: that is, till the mid-sixties. It was not too hard to hide it from the war correspondents, who stuck to Wingate like burrs, having discovered that wherever he went there was sure to be a story. In the end, long after he had left SOE, two of them died with him in an air crash.

Ronald Lewin has reminded us that the whole east African campaign of 1940–1 awaits reassessment in the light of the hitherto ultra-secret papers from Bletchley that transformed the picture of how the very senior staff made up their minds.[5] The SOE aspect of the campaign, though less important, also calls for some rethinking. As this was the first of SOE's enterprises east of the Atlantic that got anywhere worth going, it deserves to be glanced at, at least, in these pages. It provided several pointers useful for SOE's future.

According to Dodds-Parker, MI R's and then SOE's anchorman in Khartoum – he had been in the Sudan political service before he joined the Grenadier Guards – many of the ideas loosely attributed to Wingate, such as the hiring of camels, and naming those Abyssinians who would join the British against the Italian's patriot forces, had been put in train before ever Wingate reached Khartoum,[6] by the G(R) branch there over which Terence Airey (then a colonel) presided.

Sandford knew, better than most, that the Italian conquest of Abyssinia, which had begun on 3 October 1935, was incomplete in the autumn of 1940; just as was, in the early summer of 1984, the Russian conquest of Afghanistan, which began in December 1979. In remote mountain areas the locals disdained the Italian conquerors, as well as fearing them, and if given arms and a lead might be brought to move against them. The ideal leader was sent out from England to Egypt, by a Foreign Office initiative, on one of the last flying-boat sorties before the short route closed down, on 24/25 June 1940: a small, neat, copper-skinned, dark-bearded man of upright stance and princely bearing. In Alexandria he was called Mr Strong; on 2 July, with a new alias – Mr Smith – he settled at Jebel Aulia, near Khartoum. He was at once recognised. The bush telegraph spread word that he was on his way back to his throne: for he was the Lion of Judah, King of Kings, the Emperor Haile Selassie.

One English friend had come with him, as part of his small entourage: George Steer, who had been *The Times*'s man in Addis Ababa in 1935–6, and belonged in turn to EH and to SO1.[7]

The emperor's presence was welcome to many Abyssinian refugees in the Sudan; somewhat less welcome to British political officials, easily embarrassed by potentates and uncertain about high government policy. Sandford had had orders direct from Wavell to start a rebellion in Abyssinia, intended to weaken the Italian hold on the country from within, while formal armies attacked it from without. It was not at first perfectly plain to those most concerned whether the British meant to restore Haile Selassie, or simply to use him as a tool for replacing Italian power in east Africa by British.

These doubts were resolved by a conference of senior personalities which began at Khartoum on 28 October (the day Mussolini invaded Greece) and lasted for three days. Eden, then war minister, General J. C. Smuts and Wavell were all present, backed by two lieutenant-generals, Dickinson and Cunningham who was about to succeed him. (Where, one wonders, was Platt?) The governor of the Sudan, the British embassy in Cairo and G(R) were represented also; and the emperor appeared in person to assert his right to fight in his own cause.[8] Eden backed him, sticking to the line he had tried to follow five years earlier as Minister for League of Nations Affairs. The meeting approved the emperor's will to fight – thus implicitly approving his right to rule when he got back; and accepted his proposal that the tribes who joined his effort should be called patriot forces.

A four-pronged strategy was approved. Platt was to attack Abyssinia from the north, Cunningham from the south-east; G(R) – that is, SOE – was to put in two attacks from the west, with one of which the emperor was to travel. This was where Wingate and Simonds came in: they arrived a week later, on 6 November 1940. Wingate brought with him a credit for £1 million (later doubled). Much of the first instalment was swallowed up in a business on which G(R) had already embarked: the hiring of camels, mules, muleteers and camel-drivers.

G(R) collected 18,000 camels, 15,000 of which set out on the long trek eastward into the mountains. Fewer than sixty of these went all the way through to Addis Ababa. Indeed, so many died on the way that the hinder parts of the columns could navigate by smell – the stench of the dead camels' bodies ahead of them showed them the way. Wingate was excellent with horses, but knew little about how to manage camels. No one senior on the spot realised that the Sudanese camel is a splendid creature for work over sandy deserts, but is unlikely to flourish on the mountain plateau of the Gojjam, some 2000 metres above sea level, where Sandford was already lodged and which formed the emperor's first objective.

Many of the recruits attracted locally for the mission were urban Arabs, who knew no more of camels than their new masters did. For them, the promise of £E10 – to be paid when they got back – and free food on the journey was enough. Wavell authorised a quick call for volunteers from the officers and NCOs of the household cavalry division in Palestine – those units that by tradition 'hadn't reckoned on going farther out of Town than Windsor' – and of the dominion troops in the Nile delta: the call that became familiar in the army, for hazardous service, no details given. By tradition, again, sound regimental types stayed with their regiments ('never apologise, never volunteer'). Yet men who disliked the formal side of regimental life, or were merely bored with garrison duty and in search of adventure, could seize on this as a way of escape. A number of striking characters turned up in Khartoum. Among them were (Sir) Laurens van der Post, the naturalist from South Africa; Wilfred Thesiger, the traveller, who became political officer with Wingate's column; and A. H. Wienholt, a 63-year-old Australian senator, bored by politics, who had hunted lion in central Africa and was large-hearted enough to be ready to hunt bigger game still. They were squadded into small groups with the cumbrous title of operational centres. Their task was to go forward, with or near the two guerilla columns, to issue arms and provide leadership for such patriot forces as came to join the emperor's – the allied – cause. The experience of such old hands as Wienholt was to prove most useful when it came to collecting and loading kit.

Wingate reconnoitred forward, as a good commander should. On 20 November 1940, in the RAF's first successful operation for SOE, Pilot Officer Collis of 47 Squadron flew him – he then hated air travel – into Abyssinia, gave him a sight of the mountain escarpment that lines its western edge, took him over parts of Gojjam province, landed him on an improvised air strip at Faguta, and flew him back to Khartoum two days later when he had finished talking to Sandford. Landing and take-off at the edge of a precipice in an obsolete Vincent biplane were so exceedingly tricky that for this feat alone – SOE's first pick-up operation – Collis was awarded a DFC.[9]

At this first meeting Wingate got on well with Sandford (with whom he quarrelled dreadfully later). Fortunately, Wingate and the emperor – who had met once briefly before, at Brown's Hotel in Mayfair[10] – got on well with each other also. Haile Selassie had all the readiness of exiled royalty to take umbrage, though he also had the good sense to keep his manners under tight control. He knew, especially after Eden had taken his side at the Khartoum conference, that he had such weight as the

British government could exert behind him, and was cheerfully ready to put up with the little troubles of camp life on the march. Wingate had been notorious, ever since he had been a cadet at Woolwich, for awkwardness: he seemed one of those men 'born unto trouble, as the sparks fly upward'.[11] His gifts for rubbing the pompous up the wrong way were without limit. He shared with his distant kinsman, T. E. Lawrence, keen blue eyes, short stature and bounding ambition. In Palestine he had organised the special night squads to which the Israeli army traces back its origin; in Palestine he had felt he had a mission, and he was smarting under an order from Wavell that he was not to set foot there again. A pen picture of him by his transport officer, one of the volunteers from the household cavalry, though well-known, is too vivid to leave unquoted:

> He never spared his own body, and other critics would complain that he thrust into every action to gain the credit for himself. I think rather that he had a thirsty passion for battle as others have for gambling. His pale blue eyes, narrow-set, burned with an insatiable glare. His spare, bony, ugly figure with its crouching gait had the hang of an animal run by hunting yet hungry for the next night's prey.[12]

It took Wingate, Simonds and Dodds-Parker two months to settle the final details. Till Simonds' memoirs appear, little will be known about the more northerly guerilla thrust towards Lake Tana – called Begemder Force, after the province it worked in – beyond one brilliant anecdote: that Wienholt, the old lion-hunter, last seen by his own side crawling badly wounded into the bush after his convoy had been ambushed by some Italians of enterprise, was captured by them, and – though in uniform – sentenced to be shot: he faced his firing party calmly, wrapped in a Union Jack. From the southern column also, four Sudanese prisoners captured in uniform were shot by the Italians, not too careful of international law.[13]

Before ever he left Cairo, Sandford had been warned by Sir Arthur Longmore, air commander-in-chief in the Middle East, that in principle no aircraft were available; but that if he absolutely must have one or two sorties, he could ask for them. Communications and supply went therefore mainly by land; but a few of the cumbrous early short-wave W/T sets were perfectly portable on muleback, and with them Wingate and Simonds were able to keep their headquarters back in Khartoum informed of their progress, with really very little trouble.

One scandal arose: from the conduct of a detached officer who need not be named. He appealed by wireless to his friend Dodds-Parker for help. He was surrounded by delectable African damsels, who were pressing their services on him; he thought they all had syphilis; could Dodds-Parker parachute him in some protective kit? He did not know, as the agonised Dodds-Parker knew only too well, that all the expedition's telegrams were read both by G(R) and by Wavell and Platt, who were appalled. From this unsavoury incident derived part of SOE's unsavoury reputation among parts of the high command. Wingate did not need to know.

He, aware that he was wielding the sword of the Lord and of Gideon,[14] called his wing of the mission Gideon Force. The emperor marched with him. They had a battalion of Sudanese, commanded by Hugo Boustead, the mountaineer; a battalion of Abyssinian volunteers; and several operational centres. The total force available to Mission 101 was about 1800 men; they set off in January 1941 to displace several thousand Italian and Abyssinian troops, if they could. On 21 January, two days after Platt's attack on Eritrea began, Haile Selassie raised his flag at Um Idla, just inside his state's border, some 250 miles SSE of Khartoum.

Wingate did not make himself loved by his next

decision, which was to set off – forgetting how bad his maps were – on a cross-country march on a compass bearing. It took some days' toil and the loss of many animals before he relented. The Italians who might – should – have barred the way to Gideon Force, over-estimating its numbers because the camels straggled so, were outfaced by a single platoon of Boustead's, and withdrew instead of fighting. The force pressed on into the interior.

Currency might have made trouble. Mission 101 took care to pay for all the forage and food it secured from the Abyssinians, who welcomed it, but the payments had to be made in the only money that was locally recognised as worth having: Maria Theresa silver thalers (dollars) dated 1764. These huge coins, as big as an English crown piece and then worth an English florin (10p), were treasured. It is a mark of MI R's extraordinary range and foresight that in April 1940 they persuaded the Indian Mint, that august body where coin had long been struck for the Raj, to coin several hundred thousand pounds' worth of Maria Theresa thalers, all duly dated 1764, out of silver MI R provided. All passed Abyssinian scrutiny as authentic coin.

The mission was not well put together formally – there were incessant troubles between Sandford and Wingate, whose spheres of action had not been clearly enough laid down; but what it lacked in formalities it made up for in courage. By prodigious efforts, the stores and a few lorries were hauled up the escarpment into the Gojjam, where the camels started to die faster than ever, but the men in the force could rejoice in the cooler air and the varied scenery. Not till the last two days of February and 1 March 1941 did they have serious contact with the enemy. On those three days Wingate and Boustead, with a fighting force of about 450 men, routed 7000 Italian and auxiliary soldiers: by dint of rapid patrolling, better marksmanship, a fragment of air support (three Welles-leys attacked an Italian fort at Burye on 1 March), and sheer instinct to win. Unluckily the surviving Italians, fleeing south-eastward, stumbled on 6 March on the Abyssinian volunteer battalion, which had already bypassed them – had heard nothing of the fighting at Burye – and was caught resting, not dug in, not even with sentries posted. After a brief, savage tussle, the volun-teers broke; they killed 200 Italians and wounded a great many more, but were brushed off the road (or what passed for a road), and had their own morale shattered: they never operated as a formed battalion again.

This was the Italians' last victory against Abyssinian forces. Wingate pressed on, with Boustead's cheerful Sudanese, with his operational centres and with the many hundred volunteers who had by now come in to join the emperor but had not been brigaded into formal units. As always, he led from in front. Once, operating a mortar by himself with an Abyssinian friend, he found himself under shellfire, and ordered the friend to move back under cover; England, he said, had plenty of men as intelligent as himself, but educated Abyssinians were so far rare and should be kept away from harm. Not far from him, he had Steer with an Amharic printing press, brought up on muleback; Steer busied himself putting out leaflets to those of the locals who could read, and blaring out suitable slogans through megaphones for those who could not. There were also several newspaper correspondents, who had at least found picturesque scenes to report, and were moving forward – so far in the war a rare happening – against axis forces.

The battle on 6 March had revealed to the Italians who won it that they were not, as they had thought, campaign-ing against a British division; Wingate's next task was to convince them that, after all, they were. He brought it off through a combination of daring and bluff.

His enemies stood at bay round the town of Debra

Markos and a short string of forts to the west of it, called the Gulit position. One of the Sudanese companies, led by Bimbashi Johnson, distinguished itself by particularly vigorous patrolling in the hills north and east of Gulit and Debra Markos. His party bore out a remark of Allen's about British survival, against the odds, in 1940: 'Perhaps God fights on the side of the great hearts and not of the big battalions.'[15] Boustead's troops pressed hard against Gulit, and took the position at the end of March, while Wingate was having another slap-up row with Sandford – this time about administrative planning – a few miles back up the road. On 3 April, Johnson and three platoons who had got right round to the east of Debra Markos ambushed a convoy of reinforcements coming up from the capital: out of twenty-eight lorries and a pair of armoured cars, only a few lorries got away back eastwards. Eleven Italian officers and a large number of natives were left dead on the road or in the wrecks. The Boyes rifle, useless against tanks (see p. 104), proved itself effective against Italian armoured cars; an Abyssinian NCO volunteer had disabled two armoured cars with one Boyes rifle four weeks earlier.[16]

On 4 April, the garrison of Debra Markos, unnerved by Boustead's pressure from the west and the unexpected appearance of Johnson's ambush behind them, scarpered – not even pausing to destroy all their stores. Wingate had by now come forward again; and was present in one of the captured forts when the telephone rang. Edmund Stevens of the Boston *Christian Science Monitor*, who happened to speak flawless Italian, was standing beside it and picked up the receiver.

The call was from Safartak, the fort at the Blue Nile crossing, Wingate's next objective; what was happening at Debra Markos? Wingate said: 'Tell them that ten thousand British troops are closing in on them.' Stevens did so. What, the voice at the far end wailed, was to be done? 'There's only one thing to do,' Stevens replied in

Italian. 'Clear out *subito*,' straight away: the Italians did.[17] By this elementary ruse, Wingate forced the crossing of the Blue Nile.

An attempt to ambush the Italians at the Safartak crossing as they withdrew miscarried, but so did their attempt to destroy the bridge. A lull in operations followed, broken only by Boustead's bluffing (with a couple of platoons) the Italian battalion at Mota, the last enemy stronghold in the Chokey mountains, into surrender. Political difficulties supervened; some between the emperor and such local chieftains as Ras Hailu, who taught Wingate what the grand manner really was when he approached the emperor for a public reconciliation and made a bow that would not have disgraced the court of Louis XIV;[18] some, more awkward, between the emperor and General Cunningham. Cunningham had advanced fast from Kenya, and took Addis Ababa the day after Wingate took Debra Markos. Both events were at once pushed out of the world's headlines by the German attack on Yugoslavia and Greece on 6 April.

Haile Selassie was determined to enter his own capital. Gideon Force was with him when he finally did so on 5 May 1941. He had had enough of riding, and politely refused the white horse offered him in favour of a limousine. Wingate, ill dressed for the part in khaki shorts and sun helmet, leaped on the white horse and led the procession.

His force had done its principal job of distracting and confusing the enemy. Some use was made of fragments of it in the months that followed; the last Italians in Abyssinia to surrender did so in November. As Christopher Sykes put it, 'From first to last Gideon Force was an essay in deception. It was never an essay in common sense.'[19] Wingate was prostrated by his extraordinary efforts, and had a nervous breakdown in hospital in Cairo. Eventually he was sent back to London, where he and SOE decided they would see no more of each other; he went off to gain his immortal name as the Chindit leader in Burma, where he died in 1944. Simonds was collected by SOE in Cairo to take over their nascent Greek section from Ogilvie Grant, who wanted to go on operations (he was parachuted into the Peloponnese, and almost at once became a prisoner). Later Simonds moved over to run N section of A Force, which dealt with escapes. Van der Post moved on to the Far East, where he disappeared – for the time – when the Japanese overran Singapore; to the distress of those who had known him.

Dodds-Parker returned to London to report the lessons learned; which he has recently summarised.[20] There had not been many air drops to Wingate or to Simonds, but there had been enough for the British armed forces to take in – what the German General Student was about to prove again in Crete – that airborne and air-supplied operations had now arrived to take their place beside others as normal forms of warfare. There were plenty of minor points, about wireless and packing, that were worth reporting and improving. The ill-named operational centres had most of them only got into action in the closing stages, after the fall of Debra Markos; but in them inhered what became one of SOE's leading ideas: that patriot forces – however named, however organised – could be given a sharper cutting edge by the presence of small groups of officers and NCOs trained in tactics, especially the tactics of sabotage and attack. The many groups working with partisans in Italy, Greece and Yugoslavia in 1943–5, and the 'Jedburgh' teams in France, Holland and Norway in 1944, thus have an origin that can be traced back to Gideon Force.

The main lesson of interest remained: that a major guerilla war could be mounted with effect, provided that it was timed to join in with the efforts of more regular forces in the same theatre of war. It would be all the more effective if it had such a magnet attached to it as the emperor; on the other hand, there were always likely to be local personages – such as Ras Hailu of the marvellous bow – who might work for one side, or might work for another, and would need special watch and special treatment. On the sabotage and weapon fronts there were lessons to be learned, as well; it is worth remarking that the details of the Sten were fixed a couple of months after the capture of Debra Markos.

It is less agreeable to have to report that Dodds-Parker found himself less often invited to lecture about the exploits of Gideon Force than he had expected; because, he gathered, the South African government had been upset at the ease with which a largely white army had been defeated by a largely black one.[21]

It is time to turn from victory and farce to tragedy.

Poland

Poland, Poland, that cloud in the east, that coming storm, lowered over almost every meeting of SOE's Council, and formed a burden that weighed extra heavily on Gubbins's own heart. He knew Poland; he had helped the Poles prepare a few of their stay-behind parties; he had been there during the Blitzkrieg of 1939; he knew the people, the country and the risks; and knew also the enormous distances. SOE's inability to do much in Poland, simply because Poland was all but out of reach, might have forewarned Council about troubles to come in south-east Asia. As has been noticed already (p. 145), a Whitley could just get to Poland and back – a winter flight in an unheated aircraft that might well last fourteen hours (only the winter nights were long enough for it to get to Poland and return). On such a journey most of the load had to be petrol. The very first of these drops, on 15 February 1941, marked a new era for the RAF in Europe; and the fact that it had been done at all made an impression on the air staff, outside as well as inside SOE. The Whitley was too large, too slow, too cumbrous to be risked against

German day fighters; there was little point in exposing these aircraft to the dangers of a flight near Berlin and they were usually routed out over the North Sea, southern Denmark, and the Baltic. When southern Denmark's defences proved too much for them, SOE's aircraft – by now Halifaxes – had to go farther still, northabout right round Denmark and then (illegally, for this was neutral ground) across south-western Sweden, from which they could just reach the north-western corner of the prewar Polish Corridor, by this time absorbed into Hitler's Reich though not yet cleared of its Polish inhabitants.[1] Liberator aircraft – only three of them, and those three unavailable till October 1943 – could reach a hundred miles farther than Halifaxes, which in turn outranged Whitleys by about the same amount.

A total of 485 successful drops were made into Poland during the war, 192 of them into Warsaw and its neighbourhood during the trauma of the rising in August and September 1944, at a cost of seventy-three aircraft, forty-one of them lost during the rising. Three hundred and eighteen fighting parachutists were put in to help the Polish Home Army, four British, one Hungarian, all the rest Poles (one of these a woman). Twenty-eight Polish couriers were also dropped. With them went, in total, 600 tons of warlike stores, two-fifths of them for the rising.[2]

The fragmentary, half-hearted steps the Poles had taken in the summer of 1939 to get ready for being occupied were not all of them of use: vital men were killed or moved away, vital buildings were bombed or shelled in the normal course of battle. At first there were far too many enthusiasts, anxious to display their Polish patriotism and careless of the immediate reprisals that fell on them from the Gestapo or the NKVD. Impromptu sabotage in May and June 1940, meant to relieve pressure on the allies in the west, brought on such fearful reprisals that Sikorski, prime minister and commander-in-chief at once of the government-in-exile, itself engaged in an agonising transit between Paris and London, had to order it to stop.

There were too many separate bodies that tried to lead resistance to the double occupation, Nazi and Soviet; Garliński reckons that there were over a hundred.[3] It was not till February 1942 that they were almost all collected into a single Armia Krajowa (AK), the Home Army, which was then formally set up under that name. The AK brought almost all the rest under its wing; one body, Narodowe Sile Zbrojne (National Armed Forces), seemed to the rest so nearly fascist that it was left outside, as beyond the pale.

The AK's headquarters remained in Warsaw. In itself this was dangerous, for it was a guerilla body and subject to the rule Allen laid down: 'The advantage of a guerilla lies first and always in his mobility; as soon as he becomes the prisoner of an immovable base exposed to attack he has lost this advantage and it becomes only a matter of time before he has to accept battle on the terms of his more highly organised enemy.'[4] Yet the city was large, and some of the senior men in touch with London had had some clandestine experience, in occupied Poland before 1919 and in hidden combat against Pilsudski's dictatorship later. They kept in steady, if rather remote, contact with their political superiors in London by courier and by W/T. It was not always quite clear, to observers in SOE and the Foreign Office, which was the tail and which was the dog. Sometimes Polish ministers and officials in London made it clear that they could not think of adopting various policies, because opinion in the AK would be wholly against them. This was a more serious business than the quarrels between the Sixth Bureau of the exiled Polish general staff and the exiled ministry of the interior in London that sometimes bemused British officers who were trying to help the Polish cause.[5] Elisabeth Barker suggests, from a detailed study of the Foreign Office files, that it was opposition from inside Poland that was fatal to any attempt to persuade the government-in-exile to contemplate any change in Poland's eastern frontier: a major bone of contention between Moscow and the London Poles, and a major cause of friction among the powers that were trying to work in unison against Nazi Germany.[6] SOE's staff were hardly more than spectators as this tragedy unrolled.

Through the senior staff of the AK in Warsaw, the organs of the Polish underground state got enough money by courier and parachute from London – the details fixed jointly by the London Poles and by SOE – to keep their movement alive, and the staff in Warsaw stayed as a rule a step or two ahead of their police enemies. They sometimes gave pushy juniors the idea that they were overcareful; senior staff officers often do this, even in much less fraught conditions. They held that the secret war was not one in which any risk that could be avoided was to be taken: sound doctrine, but it made for slow work.

Some of the men parachuted in from England, after joint training by the London Poles and by SOE, were less inclined to sit tight. One is known to history only by his codename 'Ponury' (which means Grim); presumably to shield his relatives. He worked for the AK's 'Fan' network, which operated in the part of Poland that had been occupied by the Russians in the autumn of 1939, and was then overrun by the Germans in the summer of 1941. He was captured almost at the start of his first mission, but promptly escaped with a fellow parachutist called 'Czarka' (Bowl). They, two companions from England, and a dozen men who had stayed in Poland brought off on 18 January 1943 a successful raid on Pinsk prison, a hundred miles east of Brest-Litovsk. Four of them – one dressed as an NCO in the SS – drove up to the main gate, talked the warder into letting them in, shot him, forced the inner gate, and met their comrades, who had come in by ladder over the back wall. Between them they found and killed the commandant, took the keys of the men's wing off his body, released over forty prisoners, and got away unscathed; taking with them another parachutist, Paczkowski ('Wania') and his two companions, whose rescue was the object of the raid.[7] This is hailed by Garliński as 'a classic example of the tactics of a small commando group, led by well-trained and selected parachutists, equipped with modern weapons'[8] (they used Stens). It was also of great propaganda use inside Poland to Rowecki, the commander of the AK, as an example of how long and strong the arm of his forces was.

'Tumry', the chief of staff of 'Fan' (also known only by his codename), then went to Minsk, still farther east – 200 miles north-east of Brest-Litovsk – where he hoped to rescue a large party of 'Fan' agents, imprisoned after indiscreet talk by their over-fiery commander, a well-known horseman called Sokolowski, parachuted in on 31 March 1942. Sokolowski had clearly not taken enough notice of what he had been told at Beaulieu. 'Tumry' had to rely on the local AK intelligence network, who had in turn to rely on the local communists. These had just lost, in December 1942, almost the whole of the clandestine central committee of the Byelorussian communist party, who were locked up in the same jail. An attempt at a joint rescue operation miscarried entirely; somebody talked, perhaps on purpose. 'Tumry' thought he had been double-crossed. He was mortally wounded by a tank that raided the cottage where he was hiding, and all the prisoners he had meant to rescue were shot.[9]

'Ponury' then showed his capacities as a leader of wild men on a larger scale. He organised in the hills between Radom and Kielce, to the south of Warsaw – in an area thoroughly Polish in population, unlike the disputed lands to the east – a guerilla force several hundred strong, stiffened and trained by several other parachutists, and armed in part by a method of breathtaking simplicity. 'Ponury' stopped a troop train (not, technically, too intricate a feat, but one needing excellent intelligence and a few tools); and walked calmly down its corridors in SS uniform, removing everybody's small arms as he went by ('*Befehl ist Befehl*', 'Orders is orders') and passing them out to his friends through the windows.

His little force got chased to and fro through the hills so hard and so often that he realised – he had been attentive at Beaulieu – that there must be someone near him who was a double agent. Weeks of anguish brought him to realise that the traitor was his close friend Wojnowski ('Motor'), who had shot the gate warden at Pinsk. The Gestapo had arrested 'Motor's' mother in Warsaw in March 1943; he had been foolish enough to let her know how she could get in touch with him; and the Germans had used her to twist him. 'Ponury' had him tried and shot.

Unhappily, a life of incessant hair's-breadth escapes went to 'Ponury's' head: he took less and less notice of the orders that reached him by courier from the headquarters of the AK, till one came in January 1944 that dismissed him from his command. After a reprimand, he was re-employed; and was killed in action, as a battalion commander in the AK, in mid-June.[10]

Poland has been noticed already as a theatre of many-sided war; the Minsk affair (p. 268) may have been another example. A few other parachutists, trained by SOE and dropped by the RAF, found their way into north-eastern Poland – lands far behind the lines the Germans held on the eastern front, which had roared away towards the Volga, and formally part of Reichskommissariat Ostland, if not within the swollen boundaries of the Third Reich; yet in an area that was regarded in Moscow as Soviet territory, because it lay east of the German-Russian border fixed by the treaty of friendship of 28 September 1939.[11] This border was not far from the 'Curzon line' drawn by H. J. Paton – the Oxford philosopher who is seldom given credit for it – at the Paris peace congress in 1919, to mark the ethnic boundary between Poles to the west and White Russians, Russians and Ukrainians to the east.

The parachutists could carry little with them in the way of arms, but did manage to find a few bands of Polish fellow-countrymen, armed for the most part with weapons abandoned by the retreating Red Army in 1941. Their most successful leader, Adolf Pilch, was a young Silesian who had escaped across Hungary and Yugoslavia to France, thence to England. He dropped into Poland on 16/17 February 1943, and was held up for months in Warsaw till the local command thought him accustomed enough to occupation to go farther forward. Gradually these parachutists took the bands in hand, organised them, and rearmed them with German weapons captured from the enemy in skirmishes and small raids. Gradually also they became aware that, not far from them, there were Soviet partisan bands, officered by the NKVD and acting on its instructions to remove the most nationally conscious and aggressive elements among the local Poles, if any were left after the mass forcible exodus eastward of the intelligentsia in the winter of 1939–40. The partisans were in touch by wireless and light aircraft with the Red Army, and were much better supplied than the Poles, whom they eventually cornered on 1 December 1943. The officers were sent to the Lubyanka, whence – years later – a few came back to Poland; the men were disarmed and dispersed.[12] Pilch himself had the good luck to break out immediately from the partisans' encircling move, and started again from scratch. He brought a re-created force of several hundred infantry and horsed cavalry across from south of Vilna to just north-west of Warsaw in the summer of 1944 – a difficult march, to say the least, between advancing Russian and retreating German forces. His group arrived just in time to help the Warsaw rising from close outside.

SOE was not involved in the astounding odyssey of Witold Pilecki, who let himself get arrested so that he could find out what life in Auschwitz was like; set up a working resistance organisation inside it; escaped; and failed to convince his AK superiors in Warsaw of the ghastly truths he had to report.[13] Intelligence, it needs to be repeated, was not normally SOE's task. Why the innermost circles of SIS did not circulate far the information in their hands from the start of the final solution, of thousands of human beings packed off in trains monthly to four destinations in Poland where there was no space to hold them for long, is a question that the historian of SOE can ask, but cannot answer; he can only note that GC and CS at Bletchley read the Reichsbahn (German state railway) Enigma code from February 1941.[14] The horrors of the holocaust were outside SOE's spheres of knowledge or of action.

In other words, there was not very much SOE could do for Poland, let alone for the Jews of Poland, except pray: even when the conquest of southern Italy made it possible to set up an advanced headquarters for SOE's Polish section at Monopoli, near Bari, and for 1386 Polish Flight and 624 Squadron RAF to fly their Halifaxes and their few Liberators to Warsaw from Italian airfields nearby. SOE's Monopoli Polish office was under Henry Threlfall, as imperturbable a character as H. B. Perkins who ran it in London. Perkins was once seen to bend a poker double with his bare hands.[15] He had owned an engineering works in Poland before the war, spoke Polish, and had been with Gubbins and Wilkinson on de Wiart's ill-fated mission in August and September 1939. Threlfall, also a businessman (he rose eventually to head Siemens' London branch), was an adept at a necessary staff skill in SOE: bearding senior officers and bending their will to SOE's needs.[16]

The parachutists sent into Poland can only hesitantly be claimed as SOE's agents, because almost all of them except a single mission – 'Freston', shortly to appear – were made up of Polish citizens who acted under the orders of the Polish government-in-exile in London. They used Polish W/T and Polish ciphers; as a special concession, because their ciphers were so good, the Poles alone of the exiled regimes were secretly allowed to go on exchanging messages with their homeland during the cipher ban imposed on the rest for the security of the 'Overlord' invasion, from April to July 1944. Yet many of their weapons were SOE's. Rheam taught them how to use SOE's explosives; largely on Rheam's advice, over 7000 railway engines in this area vital for German supply were damaged. Wooler taught them how to parachute, and several times himself flew over Poland to dispatch them. Beaulieu's staff helped to sharpen their understanding of what the underground war was going to be like. Gubbins's warm friendship with Sikorski helped to keep SOE's and the Poles' policies in line. Sikorski, like Gubbins, learned to parachute, and looked forward one day to being able to rejoin his homeland in that way from the air: however, that was not to be.

The head of the AK, General Rowecki ('Grot'), unhappily fell into German hands at the end of June 1943; the Gestapo arrested him in Warsaw. A few days later Sikorski was killed in an aircraft accident at Gibraltar.[17] From this double disaster the cause of free Poland did not recover, though probably it was doomed already by the London government's quarrel with Moscow, and indeed by the general course of the war. Roosevelt's and Churchill's decision at Casablanca in January 1943, confirmed with Stalin at Teheran late in the autumn, that the main Anglo-American effort would be made into north-west and not south-east Europe, meant for Poland the certainty of being freed from the Germans, if at all, by the USSR, with which, from April 1943, the Poles in London were at loggerheads.

Their quarrel arose from the discovery in Katyn forest, just west of Smolensk, of the bodies of over 4000 Polish officers buried in mass graves; all with their wrists wired or tied behind their backs; all shot dead through the back of the neck; none bearing any document later than April 1940. The blame lay clearly enough with the NKVD, though many later Russian propaganda efforts have tried to confuse the issue. The London Poles demanded a Red Cross inquiry; Moscow broke relations with them.

In the USSR, a Polish army was built up under General Berling, a regular Polish major when he fell into Russian hands in 1939, whose father – also a Polish regular officer – probably perished in another camp like Katyn, but who was prepared to back the Russians as at least less frightful than the Germans.[18] Meanwhile, a pro-communist underground army, eventually called the Armia Ludowa (AL), the people's army, was set up inside Poland to rival the AK: many-sided war again. As the Red Army began its advance into Poland in the spring of 1944, AK units – following an order of Sikorski's, to which they held after his death – as well as AL units co-operated with the new invaders closely, providing them with tactical news of where the enemy was and what he was up to, and doing what they could to preserve bridges and railway track. Fighting soldiers got on with them well. NKVD units followed behind the army, arrested all the AK's officers, and gave its other ranks a simple choice. Either they could enlist in Berling's corps, or they could go to Siberia.

Towards the end of July 1944 the Red Army's westward advance neared Warsaw. Daily communiqués made their progress plain the world over. The London Poles agreed, by W/T, with the AK that the moment the Russians got close to Warsaw, the AK was to take it over and welcome them. They also asked the British chiefs of staff to decide the precise moment for Warsaw to rise; a task that the chiefs of staff, sensibly enough, declared was too detailed – given the data they had at that point – for them to deal with, and must be settled later by the men on the spot. On 26 July the London Poles formally asked the British for active help with the rising; and were told that this would not be practically possible.[19]

Right at the end of the month, Russian troops reached Praga, the eastern suburb of Warsaw. Moscow radio called on the Poles in Warsaw to rise and greet them. Count Komorowski ('Bor'), more than competent as a prewar commander of a horse cavalry regiment, had succeeded Rowecki as commander of the AK, and was in Warsaw; politically, as well as strategically, out of his depth. He lived clandestinely, cut off from extensive news sources, able to talk to London only in brief cipher telegrams or, with long delays, by courier. He had heard of the attempt on Hitler's life on 20 July; such news as he got from the Normandy front suggested, rightly, that open warfare was beginning again in France (the Americans took Avranches on 31 July). He decided that Warsaw should be liberated by the AK as the Red Army advanced into it, and called for a local rising on 1 August.

Warsaw rose; and was put down again. The tragic story has often been told,[20] and does not need retelling here. The Red Army found itself for once unable to advance, and watched the city burn from across the Vistula (not as wide as the Thames at Westminster). Berling insisted on sending a few patrols across to help the insurgents, and was rewarded by being relieved of his command. One in five of the city's million inhabitants became a casualty; when it was all over, Himmler had the site ploughed up. (The old city has now been lovingly rebuilt, brick by brick, from photographs; the rest of today's Warsaw is new.)

SOE and the RAF did what little they could to help. Roosevelt, in an election year, bullied Stalin into letting one – just one – group of 110 American bombers land in Russia to refuel. They dropped from so high that most of their containers went straight to the enemy. 1386 Flight, on the other hand, dropped from close to Warsaw's rooftops, in the teeth of intense anti-aircraft fire – in spite of a comment by a pilot at an early briefing, that finding a particular square in the city was better done from a taxi than from a Halifax. The Poles did not complain much. It was less easy to explain to British and South African aircrew why they were expected to risk their lives on drops 900 miles from their base, most of those miles in enemy hands, when the dropping zones lay only a mile or two from Stalin's lines. Stalin is thought to have promised Russian drops, but then not to have allowed many.

When fifteen out of sixteen Polish Halifax crews flying out of Italy had been shot down, Sir John Slessor, the Mediterranean air commander, forbade any further air effort to help the rising. A last word on the battle may be left with him: 'How, after the fall of Warsaw, any responsible statesman could trust any Russian Communist further than he could kick him, passes the comprehension of ordinary men.'[21]

The inner circles of the Polish government in London were aware that SOE included a specially trained group of a hundred Poles, codenamed 'Bardsea', who were held in a country house near Peterborough: highly trained parachutist experts in demolition and raising mayhem. Gubbins, who went down to talk to them in May 1944, always recalled them as one of the finest bodies of fighting men he had ever met. They were meant to work with 'Monica', EU/P's organisation of Poles in north-east France, around Lille.

Politics and war here got completely mixed up. The London Poles, anxious to save these first-class agents from being thrown away for some trivial purpose, secured a promise from SOE that no 'Bardsea' teams would be dropped except to areas that would be overrun by the main ground troops within two days. None of the politicians or the senior staff officers who made this deal had taken in a fact of army and air force life: to mount this sort of drop – to fix the exact targets, the codewords, the dropping zones; tell off the men; find the maps; issue the maps, the arms, the explosives; detail and brief the aircrew; warn the field; remember about food and escape kits; move the men to the airfield, and tell them what to do – took three days, even with everyone working his hardest. All the possible 'Bardsea/Monica' dropping zones were overrun in the last week of August and the first week of September 1944.

The London Poles then tried to send the 'Bardsea' parties on a forlorn hope into stricken Warsaw; as gently as firmly, the Foreign Office had to explain that this was an impossible feat of logistics, and politically out of the question. Anglo-Russian relations were not in such a state that Churchill and Eden dared offend Stalin and Molotov as grossly as they would have done by flying 'Bardsea' into Warsaw with RAF aircraft; there were not enough Polish aircraft left to carry them, and these too were all under RAF control. Sosabowski's Polish parachute brigade, another body of superb fighting men, unavailable for Warsaw for the same reasons, was swallowed up in the heroic disaster of 'Market Garden' at Arnhem.

SOE's interest in Poland's tragedy remained acute. It had not been possible for SOE to do anything at all to help the doomed, heroic disaster of the Warsaw ghetto in the previous year; this had not been co-ordinated with any part of the Jewish or of the Polish high command, and many Poles indeed retained a strong distrust of Jews, dating back to prewar anti-Semitism. The rising of 1944 was on a broader base and gave SOE some sort of *locus standi*; but there was still hardly anything SOE could actually do. Though the sixty-three days of struggle in Warsaw tore the heart out of the AK – just, no doubt, as Stalin wished – there was still half Poland to be fought over, and there were still scattered elements of the AK, in W/T touch with London, ready to take part. Bor-Komorowski surrendered when all hope for his rising was over, and was honourably treated by his German captors, who sent him to the fortress-prison of Colditz; he lived until 1966, in western exile after the end of the war. His capture dislocated the AK's command network; both the London Poles and Gubbins badly wanted to send in a mission to find out what was going on and to assess the AK's morale. Hence operation 'Freston'.

'Freston's' leader was Marko Hudson, whose momentous earlier career in Yugoslavia appears below (pp. 342–5); he was promoted colonel to lead it. With him went two British majors, Solly-Flood and Kemp; Captain 'Currie', the interpreter, whose real name was Antoni Pospieszalski; and Sergeant Galbraith, their wireless operator. They all took care not to mention in anyone else's hearing that Peter Kemp's military career had begun on Franco's side in Spain and had continued in several sections of SOE. The Russians were given advance notice of the mission and forbade it. Gubbins persuaded the chiefs of staff to let it go all the same.

On 26/27 December 1944 'Freston' parachuted in, at the fourth attempt, from Bari; they landed about fifty miles north of Cracow. They spent a few days scrambling out of the Germans' way; lost both their wireless sets; were once defended with enormous gallantry by an AK infantry platoon, which took on a German force four times its own size, including four tanks, while the mission scarpered; and were overrun in mid-January 1945 by an unexpected Red Army offensive before which the Germans scarpered in turn. They reported to the nearest Russian formation they could find, a divisional headquarters; Perkins meanwhile, through Hill, notified their names and probable whereabouts to Moscow.

They were held for some days under house arrest – in a house in which the surrounding soldiery 'urinated and defecated in every room, sparing only our living quarters because the major in charge of us stopped them; the hall, the stairs and the passages were heaped and spattered with piles of excrement'[22] – and then transferred to prison, where they were fed on bread and water and devoured by vermin. Hudson refused to speak under interrogation except to an officer of his own rank or above, and ordered the others to be silent also. On 12 February – the day after the Yalta conference was over, Poland's fate had been sealed, and no report from them could affect it – they were released to Moscow, where they got rid of their lice and in due course got exit visas.[23]

At least they were, fairly promptly, released. Those leaders of the AK and men trained by SOE who fell into the hands of the NKVD in Russian-occupied Poland were less lucky: many were executed, all the rest were long held prisoner. Gubbins may be left the last growl: 'And these were the Polish men and women who for years had fought the German enemy, had attacked and sabotaged his communications and transport serving the German armies in the East. Perfidy had reached its climax: we are left stunned by this appalling betrayal.'[24]

Czechoslovakia

There was no Czechoslovakia on the map of Hitler's new order in Europe. From mid-March 1939, that still recent republic was partitioned. Bohemia and Moravia, its western two-thirds – as truncated by the Munich agreement of September 1938 – became a German protectorate, and Slovakia seceded to become the first Nazi satellite state. Beneš and Jan Masaryk fled abroad, and with them went Frantisek Moravec (distinguish him sharply from Emanuel Moravec, who stayed behind and made himself useful to the Germans). Moravec, who before 1914 had been a philosophy pupil of the founder of the republic, T. G. Masaryk, was head of the Czechoslovak intelligence service, and managed to get the core of his staff and his files out at the last minute with some help from SIS. He left several agents behind – the best of them, the famous A-54, in the Abwehr[1] – and was in touch with the protectorate's prime minister, Eliáš, no lover of the new regime he was supposed to head. Moravec was happy to work under Beneš, whom the British recognised in July 1940 as the head of a government-in-exile: a step up from being a visiting professor at Chicago, his previous post.

At the end of September 1941 Himmler's deputy, the head of the RSHA, Reinhard Heydrich, replaced the comparatively gentle Neurath as *Reichsprotektor* in Prague. One of Heydrich's first moves was to arrest Eliáš; another was to order a round of executions. Life was clearly about to become much more tough for Czechs who did not love Germany. Beneš and Moravec determined to strike back. They chose ten young men, all bachelors, and put them through exceptionally fierce courses in Arisaig and at Beaulieu. From them Moravec picked two: Jan Kubiš, a quiet Moravian countryman, and Josef Gabčik, a half-Slovak locksmith, both in their late twenties, both orphans. They volunteered for a mission from which they knew they were not likely to return: they were to kill Heydrich.

Neither had ever been to Prague. Moravec briefed them carefully on the route between the Hradcany, the palace in Prague's citadel where Heydrich worked, and the target's country house at Brezany, outside the city to the east. It was a route he had often driven, and he pointed out a hairpin bend on it, on a slope by a suburban tram-stop, where Heydrich's car was bound to slow down.

Usually Heydrich travelled with an SS escort. On 27 May 1942 he was to go to Berlin in the evening for a few days; so he packed the escort off early, stayed chatting to his wife and children, and left late for the office, sitting beside the driver in the front of his Mercedes. At 10.30 am, as the car slowed down for the hairpin bend, a lone man standing on the pavement shifted his newspaper from one armpit to the other: it was a signal. Gabčik stepped out from the tram-stop in front of the car, and levelled a Sten at it. The Sten jammed. The driver braked to a crash stop. Heydrich, pistol in hand, started to get out of the car to arrest this impertinent fellow. At that moment a grenade lobbed by Kubiš from the tram-stop hit the side of the car, and burst in the gutter behind Heydrich, wounding him. He ran forward a few steps, and sank to the ground. Gabčik and Kubiš bicycled swiftly away, and the lone man strolled off.

Heydrich was taken to hospital, where he died on 4 June. Rumour has it that the grenade was poisoned. There is no need to believe this; Prague's wartime suburban gutters were not clean, and the grenade fragments carried filth enough to kill him once embedded in his insides.

All hell broke loose in Prague. Himmler descended in person, and unleashed the SS, who searched every building. Ronnie Littledale, a Rifle Brigade major who happened to be there at the time in the course of one of his prolonged escapes, thought that the SS men he saw were actually insane. Anyone they thought suspicious, they shot. They shot Eliáš, and several score arrested suspect resisters. They found Kubiš and Gabčik, holed up in the crypt of a church in the university quarter, through a parachutist companion, Karel Čurda, with whom – against Moravec's strict orders to act entirely by themselves – they had joined forces. A bribe of a million gold Reichsmarks (£100,000), offered as a reward for information leading to an arrest, was too much for Čurda's greed. (After the war he was found, tried, and hanged.) Kubiš and Gabčik, after a prolonged gun battle, killed themselves sooner than fall into the hands of the SS. There is a sort of secular shrine to them, in the crypt where they died, in which two dents in the tiled floor are shown, supposedly made by the suicides' grenades.

Among their belongings the Germans found two addresses of small villages near Prague called Lidice and Ležáky. Both were destroyed, destroyed entirely, their sites ploughed up as if they had been beaten Carthage. All their adult inhabitants were killed; those who were away, such as miners on shift, were killed when they came back. Most of the children were killed too; nine survived from Lidice. All told, about 5000 people were executed in revenge for Heydrich's death.

In the short run, terror worked, as it usually does. In the longer run, as it usually does, it rebounded. Himmler had no more trouble with the Czechs. But he had lost Heydrich, and all that Heydrich knew; heads of such bodies as the RSHA have to carry a lot in their heads; this is one reason for killing them. Kaltenbrunner, who took the job over, was a dullard by comparison (and, by the by, not a possible rival to Himmler, as Heydrich had been). The Czechs, who had hitherto seemed to be lagging in the unofficial competition the regimes-in-exile in London kept up with each other, had now made a respectable hit. The Germans' over-reaction was a propaganda gift for the allies; villages in several countries renamed themselves Lidice, as a mark of respect to the dead and of distant defiance of Himmler (Ležáky, the smaller village, has been almost forgotten). German ferocity provided the excuse for driving three million Germans out of their homelands in the Czech border districts forfeited at Munich, and regained when the old frontiers were restored after the war.

Moravec wrote, in old age, 'Given the circumstances in which we were placed at the time, it was a good try. It was the largest resistance operation in the country, and it is a good page in the history of Czechoslovakia in the Second World War. The Czech people should be proud of it. I am.'[2]

It was a good thing that Heydrich was removed, but the after-effects of his removal – the *Heydrichiade* – were fearful. Almost all the score of parachutists SOE had put in were caught and killed; Čurda was not the only one to change sides. The Czechs were more on their own than ever. Mastny and others believe that thereafter they had a quiet war; their myth holds firm to the belief that, secretly, gently, Šveik-like, they did what they could to counter their occupying enemy. Here is an intricate historical knot, waiting one day to be untied (cp. p. 224).

SOE sent in a few more missions, but they got no subversion done; they confined themselves to providing intelligence, perhaps by arrangement – as in Denmark (cp. pp. 294–5) – with SIS. They are not yet mentioned in Hinsley; perhaps they had nothing to report of strategic importance.

Right at the end, in May 1945, the populace of Prague came out in revolt against their masters to welcome the advancing allies, aided by a sudden turnaround by a local division of General Vlassov's army, formed of renegades from the Red Army who had put on Wehrmacht uniform sooner than die of typhus, and thought they had better try to reinsure with the advancing Russians by changing sides back again. This turnaround is glossed over in the official local accounts; east of the Iron Curtain, renegades are unpersons, and cannot appear in party history books. H. B. Perkins, who by now was in charge of Czechoslovakia's and Hungary's as well as Poland's affairs in SOE, was by this time in Prague, where he emerged as British chargé d'affaires *ad interim* the moment the Germans had gone;[3] but SOE can claim no credit for the Prague rising, which was spontaneous.

Nor had SOE anything to do with the start of the Slovak national rising, in August 1944. Many Slovaks had been unhappy at the primarily Czech government of the republic, in spite of assurances from the great Masaryk, who was half Slovak himself (his mother never learned Czech). Tiso's regime was not therefore wholly unpopular, as Quisling's was in Norway. It did respond to some degree of popular interest and support. Hitler's personal fury against the Czechs, whom he detested as a race next after the Jews, did not extend to the Slovaks. They, so long as they made no trouble, were left more or less to themselves, till the major eastern battlefront crept up on them.

A few small hardy partisan groups had set themselves up, under local communist auspices, in the Slovak mountains as far back as the summer of 1942; one group, east of Košice, in March–April of that year.[4] In the summer of 1944 they multiplied; and when the Red Army's advance across southern Poland took it as far as the foothills of the Carpathians, and seemed to be about to carry it across the Dukla pass into Slovakia, something much more widespread was engineered. The tiny state had a tiny army, of which it was hoped two divisions would defect to the allied side; one division did so, more or less complete, but the arrangements were not conducted with any precision or much skill. By the end of August a Slovak republic, quite different from Tiso's, had been proclaimed at Banská Bystrica, and some twenty battalions of half-armed infantry held the countryside round it. Between 26 September and 8 October the Soviet air force flew in a brigade of Czechoslovak parachutists, maintained by Beneš in the USSR for just this sort of purpose; fifteen fighter aircraft were also provided, but without oil or petrol, so they were not of much use.

On 7 October Threlfall flew in from Bari, in a USAAF Flying Fortress, for half an hour's conversation with General Golian, who was in charge of the rising. Six Fortresses landed on the small grass airfield at Tri Duby (Three Oaks), between Banská Bystrica and Zvolen to the south of it; gunfire could be heard in the distance, as the German army approached Zvolen and thus threatened the whole centre of Golian's position. The general indicated how pleased he would be if the Americans and British were able to supplement the arms he was getting from the Russians, who seemed not to have much of quality to spare for him. Indeed in a few days' time a major German sweep cleared the rising away from the valleys, up into the mountains. Threlfall's aircraft were at least able to take out a number of delighted British and American aircrew, escapers or evaders who had got as far as Slovakia on their way to freedom and had not looked forward with much pleasure to the idea of sitting out the war there.

SOE had one mission in Slovakia, under John Sehmer, a tank corps major who had served a year with Mihailović. He was intended for Hungary; getting there through Slovakia was thought to be a faster channel than through partisan-held parts of Yugoslavia, where British officers were on the whole regarded with intense suspicion. He never got so far.

He and an OSS team joined forces, and holed up in farmhouses in the low Tatras, north of the village of Polomka in the Hron valley. There, early on Boxing Day 1944, they were all caught – presumably because a sentry fell asleep, having had too much slivovitz the nights before. Few of them came back: Sehmer was not among them. This is perhaps an occasion to quote a sound, but little-known remark of Kipling's, who knew more than he let on about secret service: 'There is a heroism beyond all, for which no Victoria Cross is ever given, because there is no official enemy nor any sort of firing, except one volley in the early morning at some spot where the noise does not echo into the newspapers.'[5]

Hungary

SOE's effort into Hungary turned out slight. Basil Davidson was recruited by Section D and sent to Budapest, by train, early in 1940. He stayed there till 3 April 1941 – he cut his departure rather fine; most of the work he did was for SO1, on the propaganda side. Evidently he had contact also with SO2, for he reports that when the British minister discovered that his legation's cellars contained several sacks of plastic explosive, intended one day for use against shipping on the Danube, he ordered them to be thrown into the river, lest the legation's diplomatic stance be compromised.[1] Davidson clearly had friends among newspaper writers in the Hungarian capital, who would work with him; none of them could be found, two years later, when SOE was looking for reliable support in a hurry.

The one useful task SOE was able to perform was to act as a channel through which Hungary could attempt to desert the axis; though the attempt failed, it deserves brief mention. In the spring of 1943 Laszlo Veress, a young Hungarian diplomat who had been in the legation in London before the war and greatly liked the English, was summoned from his desk at the Budapest ministry of foreign affairs, and taken by his minister to meet the prime minister and the chief of staff. He was instructed that he had full powers – though he could have nothing in writing – to make contact with the British government and get Hungary out of the war, if he could. He tried to do so through Helsinki and Lisbon; neither seemed to him at all secure. Next he went to Constantinople (Istanbul), where SIS's men refused to talk to him. Nevertheless he managed to get hold of SOE's representative there, who turned out eager to help and eventually arranged a meeting for him with the British ambassador in Turkey, on a yacht in the sea of Marmora. There Veress gave his message to the ambassador; who of course told him that Hungary must surrender unconditionally. Exactly so, Veress replied; he had come to ask what the precise conditions were to be. He returned to Budapest on 10 September 1943, waving through as part of his diplomatic baggage a couple of B 2 sets; with which, through the winter, he communicated with SOE (the sets were worked for him by two Hungarian police operators). SOE passed his messages on to the Foreign Office, and passed back the replies.

The Foreign Office dutifully told the American and

Russian foreign offices what was happening. The Americans were little interested, the Russians deeply suspicious. The whole winter passed in the exchange of messages. As, under pressure from SOE, the FO was moving – too late – towards some sort of conclusion, on 19 March 1944 the Germans occupied Hungary.[2]

Veress skipped. He reckoned that with luck he would get out of the country in front of a Gestapo message bearing his description and saying he was to be held. He had money laid by. He walked to the nearest railway station, made one telephone call, and took a train to the nearest frontier; he crossed into Romania half an hour ahead of the Gestapo's telegram. Thence – still carrying his diplomatic passport, which no one had remembered to annul – he made his way to Zagreb. From Zagreb he walked out into the hills, till he encountered a partisan group; and was persuasive enough to get them to put him into an aircraft for southern Italy.

His fiancée (now his widow) proved herself no less brave and no less enterprising; the revolutionary Bourbon strain in her ancestry (she descends from Philippe-Egalité) sustained her. From a telephone box in Budapest station, Veress had passed her a prearranged codeword which meant 'I have had to clear out, make my flat safe'. She went round to his flat (she had a key) after her day's work in an office. The Gestapo had got there before her and sealed the door. She broke the seals, let herself in, removed everything compromising in the still unsearched flat, relocked it, fudged the seals, and went home.

Peter Boughey, long stuck at a staff desk in Baker Street, disapproved the turn that British policy had taken in Yugoslavia, and persuaded SOE in London that he was the right man to lead the mission into Hungary that the Hungarian government had kept being on the point of saying it would accept. He had got as far as Algiers, on his way there, before the news of the German coup of 19 March checked him.[3] He persevered; Cairo would no more let him go forward than Algiers would. He crossed to Bari; there he met a new body, Force 399, which was to work under Stawell into central Europe. Its staff had neither the deviousness nor the knowledge that hampered brisk work in Cairo; they let him go. At least he took the precaution of dressing as Sergeant Connor of the Black Watch. The Hungarians arrested him within a few hours of his blind landing, taking several hundred troops and some tanks to corner him and three companions. As he was in uniform, he managed to survive, in much discomfort, in jail in Budapest, where the Gestapo took him over and moved him to Vienna. The Luftwaffe rescued him from the Gestapo, and he cast up in a prisoner-of-war camp in Silesia, from which he eventually escaped, returning eastabout via Odessa. In retrospect, he found his most awkward moments – after being denounced as a communist on first being arrested, on the strength of the red hackle on his Black Watch headgear – had been in sustaining a sergeant's identity in a camp full of real sergeants. He resumed his true rank of lieutenant-colonel before he made touch with the Russians.

He was the only survivor of his mission; none survived from another dropped in south Hungary (he had landed near Lake Balaton). Florimond Duke, head of a parallel OSS mission, who had dropped into Hungary on 15 March and had also promptly fallen into hostile hands, reported that the rigours of Colditz castle, whither he was in the end sent, were nothing to the rigours of being a prisoner of the Gestapo.[4]

Davidson meanwhile was trying to fight his way back into Hungary the hard way, overland. He had been parachuted into Yugoslavia in August 1943, and spent a dangerous and difficult winter trying to get a resistance movement to catch fire among the peasantry of southern Hungary; even his courage, enthusiasm and left-wing leanings could not command success.[5]

Germany and Austria

It was hardly SOE's fault that its German section did so badly. There was no chance of successful guerilla action in a country in which so large a slice of the public took the opposite side. True, there were strongly anti-Nazi elements among the German working classes, but SOE could not readily get at them; for they looked instinctively to the German social democrat and communist parties, which failed them. Moreover, they were concentrated in large towns, where a rigorous police kept watch; and in those large towns they were subjected to savage and repeated bombing attacks. The usual impact of pre-nuclear bombing – shown in Barcelona in 1937, in Coventry and London in 1940–1 – was to make those exposed to it angry with the powers that dropped the bombs; Germany followed the same pattern as Spain and England. The countryside was not much more pro-allied than the towns; it held too many angry refugees, and too many well-organised fanatic groups of Hitler-Jugend, energetic boys who remembered no regime but Nazism and loved it.

Moreover, SIS insisted that any approaches to the Germans should be made through itself; and made none, after burning its fingers badly at Venlo (a mistake that almost cost Menzies the succession to his job) – unless there is any truth in the rumour that Donovan and Menzies met Canaris at Santander in the late summer of 1943.[1] If they did, SOE was not represented; and the meeting had no perceptible results.

Adam von Trott zu Solz, a former Rhodes scholar and a member of the famous Kreisau circle – that group of ineffectual, well-born resisters who gathered round the descendants of the great names of Moltke and Yorck – was not much of a conspirator. Elizabeth Wiskemann of PWE, whom he befriended during his many wartime visits to Switzerland, could never cure him of saying 'It's Adam speaking', instead of giving some less unusual name, every time he rang her up.[2] If he made any approaches to McCaffery, the head of SOE's Swiss office,[3] he was rebuffed. Approaches from Germany to the British through Sweden, some of them channelled through Bishop Bell of Chichester, were all of them, again, fielded by SIS or the Foreign Office, and uniformly turned down. No one wanted – no one dared – to give the Russians any reason to believe that London was intriguing with Berlin without letting Moscow know. That Moscow was in fact intriguing with Berlin, without letting London know, may have been the case; but was nothing to do with SOE.

In a back-handed way, Claus Count Stauffenberg's attempt to kill Hitler was. On 20 July 1944 – at the fourth attempt – the count at last managed to plant an explosive briefcase beside his Führer at a meeting at Hitler's head-quarters at Rastenburg, then in East Prussia, 120 miles north of Warsaw.

Stauffenberg was Cadogan's cousin.[4] The fact is interesting, but has no bearing on the conspiracy: the two made no touch during the war. The Foreign Office had nothing to do with the planting of the bomb. Nor did SOE play any conscious part in it; though both the plastic explosive that gave the bomb its force, and the time pencil that enabled Stauffenberg to place it and then to get away before it went off, came from SOE's stores. They had been dropped into France two years earlier, for Pierre de Vomécourt's 'Autogiro' circuit, had fallen into Abwehr hands, and had been abstracted by a senior Abwehr officer who was in the plot. They were still in perfect working order. Had the Führer's daily conference been, as it almost always was, in an underground concrete cell, the impact of a kilogram of plastic would have killed all present. Stauffenberg had a second kilogram ready, and was about to fit it beside the first in his briefcase, when a staff sergeant-major called Vogel came to tell him that he was required at the meeting *sofort*, straight away: discipline triumphed over ingenuity. The spare kilogram, wrapped in a scrap of newspaper, was found afterwards, thrown away beside the road that led to the nearest airfield. Stauffenberg followed Vogel's summons to the conference, which by a banal chance was held that day in a wooden hut, flimsy enough to let most of the plastic's force explode into the air. Four men were killed; Hitler was only debagged and shaken.[5] The attempt gave him an excuse to exact a fearful vengeance on the Prussian officer class, in the bosom of which it had been hatched.[6] After it, Himmler's grip on the German people was tighter than ever.

By a stroke of fortune, Gubbins had already got hold of an old friend from his MI R days to run X, the German section of SOE, by 1944: Brigadier (later Field-Marshal Sir Gerald) Templer. Templer had been in charge of the BEF's security in 1939; thence he had originated the escape service.[7] Early in 1944 he was in England, recovering from a ludicrous wound: commanding a division in Italy, he had been pressing well forward in a jeep when the lorry in front of him went over an enemy mine; a grand piano hurled out of it crushed him. Not even Templer was able to get much moving in the Gestapo's homeland, though his spell in SOE provided him with most useful insights years later, when he was in charge of security in Malaya. At least he kept the Germans worried enough about the possibilities of sabotage to have both ends of every railway bridge and tunnel under permanent guard, even in the heart of Saxony;[8] a useful diversion of effort from the front, if nothing more.

OSS did slightly, but only slightly, better than SOE when it came to working into Germany. Joseph Persico's *Piercing the Reich*[9] does not record any significant triumphs by OSS's fifty-odd agents parachuted into Germany in the war's closing months. Most of them were soon arrested. X section, ingloriously, preferred to annoy the Gestapo by broadcasting personal messages over the BBC to circuits in Germany that were in fact purely notional; this also at least distracted some German man-power from worse things.

The two parts of the Reich – seized fragments of prewar Poland apart – where traditions of hostility to Berlin were strongest nevertheless gave SOE a few small chances: these were the Reichsland, Alsace and Lorraine – rean-nexed in 1940 – and Austria, taken over by the Anschluss of 1938.

Buckmaster of F section had fondly supposed that his 'Archdeacon' circuit was busy in Lorraine through the winter of 1943–4, whereas in brute fact it provided the stage set for one of Götz's best wireless games (see pp. 188–91). It was not till mid-July 1944 that A. V. Woerther ('Woodcutter') was dropped to the *département* of the Moselle, to try to get a real circuit going. It was too late for him to do much: he collected a few friends, and was able to get a little minor sabotage done, but his working area was quickly overrun by the American army. D. M. Pearson ('Pedagogue') did rather better in the next-door *département* of the Meurthe, around Nancy and Toul, where there were railway targets worth hitting; but, again, he went in too late to do much, even though he had two 'Jedburgh' teams, 'Archibald' and 'Philip', to support him. 'Godfrey', another 'Jedburgh' team, worked near the Swiss frontier around Mulhouse, deep in Alsace. All these parties, like Brian Franks's much larger SAS party ('Loyton') in the nearby Vosges, found that on the German side of the Franco-German language frontier friends were much harder to find than on the French side. Franks's men made such a nuisance of themselves that an entire Waffen-SS division was diverted to hunt down ninety men: who thereupon faded quietly into the hedge-rows and walked out westwards, leaving the SS to waste their time.

Collectively, these teams in the Reichsland confirmed

Mao Tse-tung's famous dictum about the ideal guerilla who should be able to move as naturally through a friendly countryside as a fish moves through water: few German-speakers were friendly, unless in Austria.

Into Austria SOE mounted operations from two distinct areas: direct from Italy, and by way of Yugoslavia. Nothing at all was attempted until after Italy had changed sides.

There had been a small, earnest resistance movement in Austria ever since Dollfuss had suspended Parliament in 1933; it drew its strength from the socialists and communists. Many figures farther to the right in politics joined in after the Anschluss. Nazi policy treated Austria – divided up into seven *Gaue*, provinces – as a part of Germany like any other; Austrian patriots, affronted already at the collapse of the Austro-Hungarian empire in 1918, took further umbrage at this. The Slovene minority in south-eastern Austria became more disaffected than ever, particularly when the Reich's boundary was extended into former Yugoslav territory in 1941.[10] Against the Gestapo, they could not do much; the Germans played several successful wireless games through Russian and British intelligence agents who were parachuted in and captured.[11]

The only full-scale history of Austrian resistance[12] hardly mentions SOE; indeed SOE's effort into Austria was slight, and has eluded its author altogether. Alfgar Hesketh-Prichard and Peter Wilkinson, close friends and colleagues for three years past, were flown by Dakota into Yugoslavia in December 1943 (mission 'Clowder'), and with difficulty persuaded Tito to agree that they might try their luck across the Austrian frontier. He gave them a signed photograph of himself, which just proved adequate to see them across Slovenia into Austria. Thence Wilkinson was recalled to various staff posts in the Mediterranean area, but Hesketh-Prichard pressed on into the Saualpen, where he was killed in early December

1944: possibly by the Germans, probably by Slovene partisans who were jealous of his dealings with Austrian as well as with Slovene resisters. He lived long enough to show that he had inherited his father's skills as a sniper; he is credited with once shooting forty-five Germans in a single day.*[13]

Into Tyrol SOE also managed a few incursions, on foot and by parachute from Italy; a great deal of devoted effort, most of it by Austrian nationals in exile, produced little perceptible result on the ground, and was overshadowed by a late OSS mission. When the American army finally advanced through the forty-mile-long Ötztal, which debouches into the Inn twenty-five miles west of Innsbruck, the locals there had entirely disarmed the Germans; there were no casualties.[14]

One other, general, point about resisters, and those who worked with them in SOE, can conveniently be made here. Thirty years ago, when history by computer had not yet left the drawing-board – I was assured by a Belgian acquaintance that his computer had explained to him why the Germans lost the war of 1914–18: they had failed to nationalise their building industry – I began an attempt at categorising those who had taken part in SOE's effort in France. I gave the attempt up, because the social spread seemed unmanageably, astoundingly diverse.[15] Radomir V. Luza has been able to do better; his research assistant has applied a computer to over 3000 case histories from Austrian resistance. The conclusion is worth circulating: it is that they formed a self-electing élite. Three-fifths of them were Roman Catholics, over a third of them were university graduates, nearly half of them were communists (the overlap between Catholics and communists, perceptible also in France and Italy, deserves

* A former agent of SOE once said to me, 'Marksmanship is a gift, with which one is born. I happen to be a very good shot; I shot a great many Germans, and my only regret is that I didn't shoot many more.'

remark).[16] It hardly needs to be added that all volunteered, and all of them were brave, however little they could actually get done until the very last few days of the war.

Denmark

Stockholm at first provided the focal point for SOE's work in Scandinavia. It was in Stockholm in October 1940 that Ebbe Munck, the Danish journalist, made touch with Hambro, and launched a series of Anglo-Danish negotiations that grew eventually into a vigorous armed movement, which provided both intelligence for SIS and action for SOE. In this particular case, it saved SIS trouble and effort to leave the business of intelligence-gathering to SOE, which was in touch – through Munck – with a senior group of Danish intelligence officers codenamed the 'Princes'. When the 'Princes' dropped out of the running in the Danish government crisis of August 1943, SOE was well enough placed in Danish society to set up alternative (though less eminent) sources of information, and to keep up a steady supply of news bulletins to London to supplement what (in deadly secrecy) was already being gleaned at Bletchley by decipher.

It was in Stockholm that Hambro established Ronald Turnbull as forward manager for SOE's Danish section in London, which came under Commander Hollingworth. There were diplomatic difficulties about working into Denmark, which technically remained neutral – neither at war with Germany, nor allied with her, though occupied by her armed forces from 9 April 1940. The Danish ambassador to the USA proclaimed a free Denmark, but did not purport to be a government-in-exile: how could he, when his king continued to reign and his ministers to govern in Copenhagen? No one had any doubt where the Danes' sympathies lay – not even the Nazis, when their party made a despicable showing in the elections (yes, the

Danes were even allowed elections) of March 1943, securing less than three per cent of the vote (see p. 226). In August 1941 the Danish government banned the communist party (which had secured just over three per cent of the vote at the previous elections), and in November 1941 signed the anti-Comintern pact: actions that made the Soviet attitude towards Denmark even more chilly than before. In signing, the government said that the pact was for internal use only. Hardly a thousand Danes answered the call for volunteers to go and fight alongside the Germans in Russia.

SOE had real as well as formal problems in trying to mobilise and co-ordinate anti-Nazi action in Denmark. It was not till December 1941 that the first agent was sent in by parachute; and he was killed on landing because the parachute was faulty (see p. 135). Gradually, slowly, Hollingworth and his team made progress; till by the winter of 1943–4 they had several useful teams of saboteurs and organisers in Denmark, they had made touch with the seven-man Freedom Council the Danes had set up for themselves, and they were beginning to attract some German attention and to do some serious damage. Some fifty agents, all told, were sent in; and it proved possible to tap the great reservoirs of support and affection for the western democracies in most Danes' hearts. By the summer of 1944 the Germans were keeping half a dozen divisions in Denmark; and when the allied invasion of France took place, the Danish railways came out on strike and remained on strike for three weeks, to make sure that no reinforcements from Denmark or Norway were sent by train to reinforce the threatened German hold on Normandy.

With the help of SOE's intelligence, the RAF was able to mount a spectacularly successful pin-point attack on a Gestapo headquarters at Aarhus on 31 October 1944. An attempt on 21 March 1945 to make a similar attack on the trickier target of the Gestapo headquarters in the centre of Copenhagen was less successful: one of the attacking aircraft came in so low that it hit a pylon and crashed on a school; the school burst into flames, and the next group of aircraft bombed it by mistake. But other aircraft damaged the Gestapo headquarters so badly that two imprisoned members of the Freedom Council were able to walk out; and one escaping prisoner, feeling it a pity to leave empty-handed, picked up a card index at random as he passed. It turned out to contain a complete list of all the Danes who were co-operating with the Gestapo, and to provide the base for a run of treason trials which took place after the end of the war.

One most useful Danish contribution to the war, the high-speed morse transmitter invented by Hansen, has been remarked on already (see p. 163). There has also been an eminent Danish contribution to the history of resistance. Though some of the Danes' wartime behaviour may seem to have been only too suitable for the country-men of Hans Andersen, they have produced an historian of unusual range and power, who has developed the theme of resistance – not only in Denmark – with admir-able skill. Jørgen Hæstrup's *Secret Alliance* covers the history of the Danish fight against Nazism, from the start to the finish, in three incisive volumes, while his *Europe Ablaze* treats a similar theme on the broader canvas of a whole continent.[1] He has had ample SOE documents, left behind in Denmark at the end of the war, to provide him with the archival base that remains denied to the run of English historians.

Norway

The tale of Norwegian resistance, and of SOE's part in it, is not the same. The Norwegian king and government came out fighting; even more than Danish seamen, Nor-wegian seamen stood by the anti-Nazi cause, and through the large Norwegian fleet provided their government-in-exile with ample funds (something of a rarity for governments-in-exile). From an early stage, SOE and the Norwegians were in touch, and they remained in friendly connection throughout the war. Though Norway was out of range for parachute operations in summer in 1940–2, the 'Shetland Bus' could carry arms as well as men (see p. 123). At the bitter end of the war, 365,000 German troops in Norway were corralled and disarmed by fewer than 60,000 members of the Norwegian underground, most of them bearing weapons provided by SOE; the garrison of Oslo surrendered to a young man in plain clothes wearing an armband.

The head of SOE's Norwegian section for the last three years of the war was J. S. Wilson, who came to it from the training section; before the war, like Mockler-Ferryman, he had been a quiet pillar of the Boy Scout movement. He had a good scoutmaster's patience, accuracy and calm. All but one of the agents he sent into Norway were Norwegians; to send Englishmen would have caused far too much local gossip in a still country-based state in which everybody in any given locality knew, pretty accurately, who everybody else around them was. This in turn was of course a brake on clandestine activity, but not a complete one: some villages, some areas at least were known to be worth trust.

One thing, besides their courage, distinguished the agents sent into Norway for SOE: their toughness. Several times over, they stood up to conditions of hardship that would make most city men not merely wilt, but die: Jan Baalsrud, who lay wounded in his sleeping-bag, without food or drink, in the snow for six nights and days, and survived, may stand as an example for several more.[1]

One coup SOE brought off in Norway changed the course of the war; and was so important that nothing else the section did bears record beside it. Early in the occupation, the Germans ordered a plant called the Norsk

Hydro at Vemork near Rjukan, west of Oslo, to increase its production of heavy water (deuterium oxide). When this became known in London, it was recognised as a sign that the Germans thought they might manage to make an atomic bomb out of heavy water; and Combined Operations Headquarters was ordered to attack the plant. On the night of 19/20 November 1942 two gliders, each full of soldiers and explosives, set off from Scotland for Rjukan; both crashed (so did one of the tugs), and everyone on board who survived was promptly shot by the Gestapo. Some of them were carrying marked maps; the garrison at Rjukan was strengthened.

SOE then took the project over. By a stroke of luck, an SOE raiding party had in March 1942 captured a Norwegian vessel with a man on board called Einar Skinnarland, who was eager to help; he came from Rjukan, and was put back there by parachute before anyone noticed he had been away longer than the holiday he had been supposed to be on. He helped to receive a small SOE party called 'Grouse', four men who lived out on the Hardanger Vidda for months; and when the weather cleared, received another six, called 'Gunnerside'. The 'Gunnerside' party – their cover was that they were students on a skiing holiday – explored the plant's surroundings from a discreet distance, and decided to attack from above, from up on the plateau; on that side no one kept a look-out. On the night of 27/28 February 1943 they slipped into the Norsk Hydro plant; only met one workman, to whom they showed their battledress uniforms; blew up the high-concentration plant; and retired rapidly to the plateau. One of them, Knut Haukelid, later made sure that a hundredweight or so of heavy water waiting at the lakeside below to set off on its journey to Germany was sunk with the ferry that carried it across the lake.

It was a model little sabotage operation; a few civilians had to die when the ferry sank, but otherwise no one was hurt. The break in their supply of heavy water was so abrupt and so complete that the German scientists who had been working on the project gave it up; and were directed by Hitler to work on revenge-weapons such as the V1 and the V2 instead. If SOE had never done anything else, 'Gunnerside' would have given it claim enough on the gratitude of humanity.[2]

The Low Countries

The Netherlands are heavily populated, and their country-side is much criss-crossed with waterways, obstacles to men and vehicles alike. This made it better terrain in the 1940s for urban guerilla than for the sort of open warfare at which Serbs, Croats, Italians, Norwegians, Frenchmen and Burmese could excel in more open country; and for urban guerilla nobody was quite ready, not even SOE. Even the Irish, usually in the forefront of clandestine development, had done better with country than with town guerilla in the land war of the 1880s and the Troubles of 1916–22, and their efforts to apply urban guerilla against their secular enemies across the Irish Sea had fizzled out in the summer of 1939.

The north-western two-thirds of Belgium, west of the rivers Meuse and Sambre, form country very like the Netherlands, thickly populated, and much cut about with canals and drainage ditches in between the frequent built-up areas. This, again, was poor country for guerilla in the 1940s; though the rest of Belgium, in the Ardennes, and the Grand Duchy of Luxembourg were more suitable for raising and maintaining irregular bands.

The disaster and recovery in the Netherlands have been described already (see pp. 177–86). Luxembourg's effort was marginal,[1] but Belgium took up a good deal of SOE's time and attention. There were even more quarrels than was usual among the branches of the Belgian government-in-exile, which formed itself bit by bit in London; as with the Poles, several ministries wished to have a finger in the resistance pie; and Belgium was so placed that its affairs were of intense interest to MI6, MI9 and PWE as well as to SOE. Eric Dadson was the first head of T, the Belgian section; succeeded in 1941 by Claude Knight and briefly in 1943 by Hardy Amies, later famous as a dress designer. Between them they sent over a hundred agents to work with the Belgians in stimulating a secret army.

When it came to the crunch, in the first few days of September 1944, the allied advance rolled over Belgium so fast that the secret army hardly had time to show its paces before it was caught up in awkwardnesses with the returned government-in-exile about handing in its arms. Various problems about the extent to which the Gestapo had penetrated it await solution. One incident stands out, which was of great, and might have been of cardinal, importance: the secret army's work in securing twenty-five miles of quayside and vital dock gates at Antwerp from the Germans' demolition plans. This was as fine a piece of counter-scorching (as SOE called it) as any done in the war; all looked after by a subaltern, later a general, called Urbain Reniers, who handed the port over intact to Eisenhower's emissary, General Erskine. Erskine commented that this would shorten the war by several months;[2] he had reckoned without Montgomery's miscalculating genius. That commander launched 'Market Garden' on 17 September before he had cleared Antwerp's approaches: the Scheldt estuary was not free of German artillery fire until 28 November, after bitter fighting on Walcheren.

France

France got a great deal of attention from SOE: with Poland, Greece and Yugoslavia, it occupied much of Council's time; with Yugoslavia, it received the major effort in men and arms supplied. Because it lies so close to England – in plain sight from parts of Kent and Sussex on clear days – it was much more easy to try to work into France than into central or eastern Europe or into south-east Asia; in spite of the difficulty that so few Englishmen or Scotsmen can manage impeccable French. And if more is said about France than about anywhere else in this chapter, it is because the sources available to me are most abundant for France.

Here SOE had to bother about politics quite as much as anywhere else; the question of who governs France is always critical for Great Britain. Who indeed did govern France late in 1940? Marshal Pétain had put himself, at the age of eighty-four, at the head of the state: his Etat Français and SOE were born in fact within a week of each other, for Pétain took power on 10 July 1940 and Churchill told Dalton to 'set Europe ablaze' on the sixteenth. (Astrologers put both dates late in the sign of Cancer, the Crab.) SOE – though in principle politically neutral – was always resolutely opposed to all the actions of the satellite state over which Pétain presided at Vichy. It was certainly unaware – unless a hint was ever thrown out to Jebb, who kept it to himself – that the Foreign Office was keeping in touch with Pétain through a young diplomat seconded to MEW, who had made friends with the old marshal when the latter was ambassador to Franco's Madrid and was still working there himself: David Eccles.[1] It dutifully followed Foreign Office instructions – no bangs in unoccupied (southern) France without FO consent – a ban that lapsed when the Germans overran unoccupied France on 11 November 1942 in response to the 'Torch' landings in north Africa. Thereafter the Vichy regime continued to exist, deeper than ever in the shadow of the swastika flags that now floated all over France. The demarcation line between the formerly 'free' two-fifths of southern France and the rest was maintained by the Nazis, as an obstacle to free movement.

SOE made several false starts. Section D had an early

casualty, when a flying-boat with one of its officers on board disappeared in late June 1940 in an attempt to get Madame de Gaulle out of Brittany. (She arranged her own and her daughter's evasion.) Three Frenchmen were sent across the Channel in a small and noisy boat on 1 August, ran into a German coastal convoy, were fired on and turned back; two of them failed to get ashore by sea on 11 October; one – this got more and more like the ten little nigger boys – was sent over by air on 14 November, and was brave enough to refuse to jump. Winter weather then closed in.

Just before it did so, SOE had a hand in operation 'Shamrock', off the mouth of the Gironde. It was run in late November by Martin Minshall, a buccaneering type left over from the great Elizabeth's reign, who had been brought into irregular warfare by his friend Ian Fleming, and had exercised his gift for rubbing people up the wrong way on Fleming's boss, Godfrey, the formidable director of naval intelligence. Minshall established for certain a point the Admiralty did not know – exactly how U-boats entered and left the river-mouth – by commandeering a local fishing smack, watching them do it, and sailing the smack back to Falmouth to report.[2]

At last, in mid-March 1941, after a struggle with the chief of the air staff's scruples of conscience (see p. 131), half a dozen Gaullist parachutists under Captain (later General) Bergé dropped successfully to conduct operation 'Savanna', a raid on the German pathfinder force at Vannes in south Brittany. They arrived only to find that their target had dispersed in such a way that it was no longer vulnerable to them; but they made themselves as useful as they could, travelling around north-west France and sounding opinions. Bergé seized the occasion to slip across the demarcation line for a formal interview with the mother of the girl at de Gaulle's headquarters he hoped to marry. He and a companion, rescued by HMS *Tigris* in early April (see p. 128), brought back much interesting news, including that of the widespread popularity of General de Gaulle. Joel Letac, left behind on the beach, stayed to take part in organising 'Overcloud', an RF circuit in north Brittany that would have been supplied by sea had sea supply turned out possible; it provided material instead for an early wireless game, soon taken out of SOE's hands by still more secret services. Letac helped also to organise 'Josephine B', a raid on the Pessac electric power station on 6/7 June 1941. (Pessac is a south-western suburb of Bordeaux.) The attack was a notable minor success: the worst reprisals fell on a score of German guards, railway traffic in the neighbourhood was disrupted for some months, and SOE had something positive to claim at an awkward moment in Whitehall. So had General de Gaulle.

De Gaulle was not supposed to know that F, SOE's independent French section, existed. Of course he soon found out that it did; he protested long and often against the fact, but the British would not listen to him till late indeed in the day.

No fewer than six separate sections of SOE were involved in working into France, four large and two small: F (the independents), RF (the Gaullists) and AMF (who worked from Algiers) each sent in over 400 agents – AMF seems to have sent in over 600, but many of them belonged not to SOE but to OSS. The 'Jedburgh' teams, none of which left till the Normandy invasion had begun, added nearly 300 more. EU/P (the Poles) had only sent in twenty-eight agents by then, seven of whom were killed; what they did thereafter they kept to themselves. DF (the escape section) sent in fewer still, perhaps a dozen men; those dozen built some remarkably effective lines. Besides the 'Vic' and 'Var' lines, handled in detail elsewhere,[3] Humphreys, the head of DF, managed to set up a few smaller and still more secret feeder lines, which ran north-eastward from Paris. One was run by a Dutchman called Zembsch-Schreve, who was caught in Paris by a routine police operation while trying to hand over a transmitter, and continued to protest his innocence until, in the closing chaos of the war, he used his Beaulieu training to escape from a concentration camp party on the march.[4] This sort of escape, though rarely achieved, was a comparatively simple one: if the escaper judged his moment to run properly, no guard with a sub-machine-gun would be sure of bringing him down by the time he was noticed running away; and if the guards chased him, all the rest of their charges might vanish. The worst risk was that the guards – the scum, after all, of the earth – might briskly massacre the whole column, and then mount a systematic hunt after the escaper.

Three British-trained DF agents, and a score of local sub-agents – most of them safe-house keepers – fell into enemy hands; one, Langard of 'Var', was a wireless operator caught at his set by direction-finders; the others were indirect victims of N section's troubles in Holland. For when the Germans asked, through captured N section sets, how they were to send agents back to London to report, they were naturally put on to a 'Vic' line contact in Brussels – with unhappy results.[5] All the same, the line was proud – as was 'Var' – never to have lost a genuine passenger: not even the one sent over from England to test out the security of 'Vic', who could not be kept from slipping out of his safe-houses to pursue pretty girls. Discreet and quiet people who attracted no one's attention stood by, in several parallel lines, to handle whatever traffic appeared. Elderly maiden ladies who minded their own business made excellent keepers of safe-houses, and their nieces made good couriers. DF reckoned to be moving about a passenger a day at the period of maximum pressure, in the middle of 1944.

It is now known that DF and MI9 handled a little of each others' traffic, by agreements made on the spot of which there was no need for London to be told. Similarly, there was no need for Berlin to be told – or so everyone concerned on the spot thought – about an arrangement 'Var' made with a German sergeant on the north Breton coast: on nights when 'Var' was going to operate, the sergeant was tipped off not to look, in case there was trouble and he got sent to Russia. His pillbox was forty feet away from 'Var's' best beach (see pp. 121–2).[6]

Four equations had to be solved at once by any successful SOE agent: military, how to defeat the enemy; political, who then was to have power; security, how meanwhile to keep clear of the local and enemy police; and – trickiest of all – practical, how to start and how to go on with a clandestine life. At the beginning of a mission, the practical problems naturally loomed largest, closely followed by the security ones; future politics and actual war had to be postponed to present safety.

F, RF, DF and EU/P had already begun the processes of trial and error, by which alone the practical problems could be solved, before 22 June 1941 when the character of the war changed. At dawn that morning Germany invaded the USSR; by sunset, the communist party of every occupied country that had one had taken a firm anti-German stance. The communists were used to problems of underground warfare, which they had been waging on and off for nearly forty years (see pp. 208–10); in places they could provide SOE with a great deal of help. Some of these places were in France.

The French communists, like their Italian co-religionists, saw the short-term help that would be given to the communist cause by the defeat of Nazism, and the disaster that a defeat of Soviet Russia by Nazi Germany would be for all they believed in; so they were ready to work against the Nazis with anyone who also longed to beat the Nazis down. Contrast the attitude of the Russian, Albanian or Greek communists at the same period, who demanded Anglo-American help as of right but spurned the hands that fed them, or of the Slovenes who were unable to open their minds far enough to realise that they and officers in SOE or OSS might have any common enemies. There were two difficulties, though, in working with the French communist party (PCF) and its armed wing, the Francs-Tireurs et Partisans (FTP). One was that the FTP was supposed to be the offshoot of the Front National (see p. 309), a national army of liberation devoid of specifically communist sympathies; the KKE tried exactly the same trick in Greece, presenting EAM and ELAS as bodies with a broad general appeal while riding them in fact on a tight Bolshevik rein (see pp. 337–41). The other catch was more technical but quite as tiresome: the communists paid such slavish attention to the rules of clandestine security that it was all but impossible to decide anything with them promptly. They did not in fact refer every question put to them back to Beria and Stalin for decision, but they behaved as if they did. No emissary from them would undertake to do, or even to prepare to do, anything, until he had referred back to some unspecified party authority. It therefore usually took a month at least to advance a step in any direction.

An old staff officers' tag declares that you should always plan for your worst case. A number of the exiled staffs in London, aware of this, planned for a flight to America if Great Britain lost to Germany. When they realised towards the end of 1942 that this was not going to happen, they looked for the next worst case; and decided that it might lie in a sudden collapse of the German armed forces, which would bring the Red Army in a few strides to the eastern shores of the Atlantic before the Anglo-Americans could summon the shipping to mount an invasion of the Continent.

Planning for this meant that, though they were all resolutely anti-communist in their domestic politics – and followed, in taking this line, the undoubted wishes of large majorities in their homelands – they might each need to take serious account of their local communist

37. Rail bridge at Višegrad demolished 6 October 1943 by Archie Jack and others with četnik support

38. Gorgopotamos viaduct before 25 November 1942. Note the two steel piers which were blown by Myers' party that night

39. 'Armada' sabotage chief Raymond Bassett 40. André Jarrot, fellow 'Armada' leader

41. 'Colonel Chris.' C. M. Woodhouse in 1944 42. Pearl Witherington

43. Noor Inayat Khan, 'Madeleine' 44. Violette Szabo, reputed the best shot in SOE

45. *Top left* Arthur Nicholls

46. *Top right* Maurice Buckmaster

47. Two heroes: Francis Cammaerts (*left*)
48. and Richard Heslop (*below*)

49. Gerry Holdsworth

50. Charles Macintosh

51. Contact: two resisters show an American officer in the Cotentin what the enemy is doing

52. Norsk Hydro plant, Vemork, near Rjukan, showing the plateau

53. View of the Norsk Hydro plant showing the pipes and the ravine

54. USAAF B-17 bombers make a daylight drop into the Vercors, 14 July 1944

55. Reception of a daylight drop in the Corrèze, 14 July 1944

56. *Above left* F. Spencer Chapman   57. *Right* Peter Kemp.   58. *Below* A clam, an adhesive mine

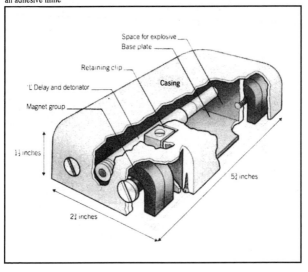

Space for explosive

Base plate

Retaining clip

Casing

'L' Delay and detonator

Magnet group

1½ inches

5¾ inches

2¾ inches

59. Gubbins unveiled this plaque in Beaulieu Abbey cloisters in 1969

party: both as a factor in resistance, which after 22 June 1941 it was certain to be, but also because the Red Army would be likely to push its own side's local men into power wherever it turned up.[7] It might only be through making friends early with their communists at home that, if this worst case developed, some exiled ministers would be able to exercise any impact on postwar political life at all.

The practical results varied. The London Poles had passed through so many worst cases already, with the successive losses of Poland itself and of France, Poland's secular champion, and with the RAF's inability to deliver stores or men to Poland in more than tiny amounts, that they no longer applied the doctrine: they set their faces like flint against any sort of concession to the Russians, one of their secular enemies. Not for them any truck with communists; and any in London who advised such a thing were swiftly assured that opinion throughout the AK was set firmly against it. Stalin's break with the London Poles was all but final. Mikolajczyk, the prime minister of the London government, went to Moscow at the end of July 1944 in an attempt to talk to him, but did not get into his presence till a couple of days after 'Bor' had unleashed the Warsaw rising: too late (pp. 274–6).

It takes two to mend a quarrel as well as to make one; Europe's communist parties, then as now, were not so entirely under the heel of Moscow that they were all bound to behave in the same way. The Greek communist party, KKE, behaved with exceptional sharpness towards its Greek opponents. Stalin held for once to his informal agreement with Churchill and gave the KKE no backing in its attempts to seize power against all comers, monarchist, republican, Greek, British or American. The Slovenes too showed marked intransigence, even more than the often surly and suspicious Croats and Serbs. Farther west, communists were sometimes less bloody-minded.

In France, some F section organisers got onto friendly

terms with their local FTP leaders, and were able both to provide them with arms and to give them some small arms and sabotage training; most held aloof. Equally, communists inclined to hold aloof from servants of a capitalist general staff, who were disinclined to follow the communist policy of repeated attacks on Germans, regardless of reprisals; these attacks the communists supposed to be the best way of relieving pressure on the Soviet motherland, which was being assailed by Germany.

The communists' relations with the Gaullists were more complex. The PCF had on the whole got on badly, even before 22 June 1941, with the German occupiers of northern France; the party continued to be banned, under a law of October 1939, and never loved, nor was loved by, Vichy. After protracted thought, the party's central committee decided to put out feelers towards General de Gaulle; the general, equally hesitantly, was prepared to consider advances from the party. It was not till the beginning of 1943 that Fernand Grenier, sent by the PCF, reached London to join de Gaulle's headquarters of external resistance (shortly to move to Algiers).[8] It is reasonable to assume that both the general and the party had reservations about how closely, or for how long, they would work together; for the time being, each could see they had a common interest.

The French communists looked after their position in internal as well as in external resistance. Russia was far too distant, and far too hard-pressed – Stalingrad was still being fought – to provide the FTP with anything much more solid than hope. Hope is vital for any resistance body,[9] but hope alone is not enough. The PCF's leadership, sensible and realistic at that stage, decided to work by the party's usual methods to control whatever body was going to direct internal resistance; and succeeded.

They created their own chance. It arose out of the work of a thoroughly non-communist character, who has nevertheless been accused, now and again, of strong sympathies with the PCF: Jean Moulin.[10] Moulin, a very early resister – he began on 17 June 1940, when *préfet* of the *département* of the Eure-et-Loire at Chartres – made his own way out of France in the autumn of 1941, disguised as a lecturer at an American university; presented himself to de Gaulle in London; decided to work with him instead of trying to displace him; and parachuted back into France as de Gaulle's delegate-general on 1/2 January 1942. He spent the next eighteen months – except for a short break in England, taken to and fro by Lysander, early in 1943 – travelling quietly around France, interviewing all the Frenchmen of weight in resistance (except those who had already joined F section), and persuading them to unite.

On 27 May 1943, in a shuttered private dining-room at 48 Rue du Four in Paris (a curious echo of Baker Street), Moulin presided at the first meeting of the National Council of Resistance (CNR). Within a month he had fallen into German hands in a northern suburb of Lyons, on 21 June 1943. He was subjected to torture, far beyond routine, and accepted the ghastly burden of dying silent: no one is perfectly sure quite when, or quite where.

It is now known that Moulin opposed – in vain – an arrangement by which the communists got two seats on the CNR, one in their own name, one for the Front National.[11] He had had endless troubles with the minor practical difficulties of the clandestine life – delayed trains, missed appointments, vanished friends. They went on dogging him, as they dogged everybody else. His telegram to London announcing the first meeting of the CNR reached England corrupt, and had still not been sorted out at the time of his arrest.

Practicalities made it difficult as well as dangerous for the CNR to meet at all often. It handed over day-to-day control of resistance activity to a sub-committee of action, COMAC, which had three members: the Comte de Vogüé, Valrimont ('Kriegel') and Pierre Ginzburger ('Villon'). 'Kriegel' and 'Villon' were both communists;

when de Vogüé was present they outvoted him; when he was detained elsewhere they had a freer hand than ever.

Fullish details of the activities of F section, and an outline of RF, can be found in the official history; they can get no more than a rough summary here. 1941 and 1942 were spent by both sections in attempts by trial and error – with plenty of error – to get separate circuits under way. Both did better in southern than in northern France; though the German counter-espionage services were active in the south, they were less dense than in the occupied zone.

F's superiors in London remained sure that they had to keep this independent section in being; news from France was extremely sparse, the American government detested de Gaulle, and every option had to be kept open. F spent much of 1942 pursuing the mirage of 'Carte', what seemed to be a secret army of a quarter of a million men organised through experienced staff officers, and finally was revealed to be entirely notional – there were no men, no arms, no officers, nothing – but the dream was not entirely useless. It provided first SOE, and then the air staff, with some hard and necessary insights into the practical troubles of arming any large body of resisters – 'patriot forces', in Haile Selassie's phrase – who were to be brought in on the flank of any major British land expedition on the Continent.

Mainland France was sharply affected by 'Torch', the allied landing in French north-west Africa on 8 November 1942: not only because 'Torch' brought on 'Attila' as a German riposte, the overrunning of the hitherto unoccupied zone three days later. Pétain's deputy Darlan was in Algiers at the time (see pp. 211–12); he was used by Eisenhower as a convenient tool to bend the local civil service to the allies' will. Every resister in France was appalled: none of them were fighting to continue a regime that kept (as Darlan's friends kept) Jews and allied agents shut up in noisome camps, or that blocked (as Darlan blocked) any attempt at democratic life. There were many plots against Darlan – he mentioned four of them himself a few days before he died; it was, from resistance's and indeed from SOE's point of view at any rate, a blessing that one of the plotters, firing an SOE pistol, succeeded on Christmas Eve 1942.

1943 was a year of both expansion and disaster. Each section tried to send some in-and-out parties for sabotage. F's under Hugh Dormer ('Scullion') failed;[12] RF's, under the superbly dynamic leadership of Raymond Basset and André Jarrot ('Armada'), succeeded not only in causing heavy damage to the canal system of north-east France, but in doing so at a moment when the Germans had wanted to use it to send small craft to Italy. F got a large circuit, 'Scientist', set up in the Bordelais under Claude de Baissac, but Grandclément, his second-in-command, was persuaded by a clever German to change sides, to combat Bolshevism: de Baissac got away. Tony Brooks ('Alphonse'), just turned twenty, built up small, sound groups of railway saboteurs ('Pimento') around Montauban and Lyons. Francis Cammaerts ('Roger'), put in by Lysander in March to a circuit he judged moribund, by dint of moving almost nightly managed to create a large circle of supporters ('Jockey') in Provence. Maurice Southgate ('Hector'), aided by two girl couriers – Jacqueline Nearne and Pearl Witherington – and a Mauritian wireless operator, Amédée Maingard, covered a great deal of central France. Ben Cowburn ('Tinker') severely damaged the railway round-house at Troyes, and lived – lives – to tell the tale. Michael Trotobas ('Farmer') ran a still more aggressively active sabotage circuit in the industrial area around Lille. Going for a drive with him, one of his friends said years later, was like living through a book of the *Iliad*. He died, as he had lived, heroically: early one November morning, the Germans raided his digs and shot him dead – not before he had killed their commander too. (He was put in for a Victoria Cross, which was refused, as there was nobody senior to himself present to report on what he had done under fire, as the VC warrant requires. In the end, his name fell off the list even of those who were to get a posthumous mention in dispatches, and his parents were left for years to believe he had come to a shady end.)

Harry Rée ('César'), dropped in to Southgate near Tarbes in April 1943, was sent away to set up a circuit of his own ('Stockbroker') in Franche-Comté, where his Manchester accent in French might pass for Alsatian. There he invented a rare device: blackmail sabotage. He happened to witness an RAF raid on the Peugeot factory at Sochaux near Montbéliard, on 14 July; civilian casualties were heavy; the factory – which was then making tank turrets – had no more damage than broken windows. Rée called on the manager, and explained that if he might have a look round the factory, he could guarantee to put it out of production quietly; otherwise, the RAF would come back and flatten it. He proved his good faith by getting the BBC to pass a message composed by the manager back to France within a week. Rée and a foreman toured the factory, and spotted the one essential machine. The foreman left a haversack leaning against it during the next midday break, when the factory floor was empty. The time pencil in the haversack worked; the machine was wrecked; the factory stopped. It took six months for a replacement to arrive, and that was wrecked by another plastic bomb in the station goods yard, before ever it was unloaded.[13] This splendid system was, alas, developed too late to divert Bomber Command and 8 USAAF from wrecking the German heartland.

In and around Paris, the enormous 'Prosper' circuit under Francis Suttill did a lot of training, but did a lot of talking too: its members used to chat away in English over a daily black-market meal, and forgot that every big Paris restaurant had its Gestapo spy. Like Pertschuk at

Toulouse, who was undone by the same syndrome, they were quietly tracked to their lodgings and arrested separately, in late June. One of them – most probably Gilbert Norman ('Archambaud'), the chief wireless operator – provided a great mass of data for the Germans about where all their arms had been stored, or rather all the arms that had not been handed over to the communists, who kept their own counsel about where they stored them. Several hundred other arrests followed.[14]

A close friend of the 'Prosper' leaders, Henri Déricourt ('Gilbert', often confused with 'Archambaud' and others), was not arrested. His job was to run a supposedly secure circuit called 'Farrier', which moved agents between the middle Loire valley and Sussex by RAF light aircraft. Bodington, F's second-in-command, stayed at his flat in the west end of Paris for a few weeks in August, and argued when he got back that his own freedom from arrest proved Déricourt's reliability. He might have pondered harder how easily the Germans picked up Jack Agazarian ('Marcel'), who had come with him as a wireless operator – recalled from leave, 'just for a couple of weeks, old boy'; Agazarian had been a friend of Déricourt's as well as Suttill's for some months previously, and was arrested when he called at an address believed to be 'Archambaud's'. Bodington did not know that Déricourt had been working with the Sicherheitsdienst for months; notified them in advance of most of the operations he conducted; and let them photocopy the letters that 'Farrier's' aircraft carried, some of them private letters between agents and their wives. No wonder some captured agents, when confronted with the knowledge the Germans had gleaned from such letters, broke down altogether.

SOE had several other setbacks at almost the same time as the 'Prosper' arrests. One was the unfortunate affair of the Canadians, which presented the SD with the 'Archdeacon' circuit in Lorraine (see pp. 188–91).

Another was the undoing of General Delestraint, the regular French officer whom Moulin had brought forward to take over the command of the secret army which the CNR hoped to form in France. In the second week of June, Delestraint arrived on the doorstep of the safe-house prearranged for him in Paris. A pretty girl answered his ring at the door. He had remembered the address; for the life of him, he could not remember the password which was to let him in. Confused, and unused to the secret life, he went off to an hotel, registered in his own real name, and was picked up without trouble next day, while changing trains in the metro, by the SD, who had noticed his name in the routine morning police check of hotel registers. He died in Germany.

Police routine, again, accounted for a worse disaster in Caluire, a suburb of Lyons, on 21 June. At ten that morning Klaus Barbie, head of the Lyons SD, was peaceably reading a newspaper on a bench near one of the city's many bridges. He heard a girl cyclist stop and call out to a stranger at the other end of his bench that he was to take the cliff railway up to Caluire at eleven-thirty and would be met. Having nothing better to do, Barbie picketed the top of the cliff railway, and followed the stranger to a doctor's house: where, with every clandestine precaution but one, Moulin was about to hold a meeting of senior resisters. The one omission was fatal: there was no way out at the back. They were all taken prisoner.

One of them, René Hardy, the head of Sabotage Fer – RF's southern railway-wrecking group – broke away outside the doctor's front door, and, though wounded by gunfire, managed to escape. He has been the object of deep suspicion ever since it turned out that he had himself been in German hands a few days earlier, having been picked up at a chance railway control and released a few hours later because nothing could be pinned on him. That arrest was probably an accident; it is understandable, though unfortunate, that he had made no mention of it to any of his colleagues before the troubles at Caluire.

Moulin's heroic silence saved RF's secret organisation, which by this time was elaborate, from being broken up altogether. Brossolette, the socialist leader, had made one journey into occupied France already, with Dewavrin and Yeo-Thomas of RF section, that had included a notable quarrel with Moulin, due partly to politics and partly (on both sides) to overstrain. Brossolette now returned to see what could be salvaged from the debris of Caluire. He was brought out of France by a fishing smack from a south Breton village late on 2 February 1944, but was shipwrecked that night. An alert German policeman at Audierne spotted a stranger in a café early next morning, and asked to see his papers; which did not include a permit to be in the coastal zone. Brossolette's real identity was betrayed by a streak of white hair that grew out above his forehead in prison past the dye he had put on it (his spare dye disappeared in the shipwreck). He was sent to the SD headquarters in Paris, 82–86 Avenue Foch, where he jumped from a fifth-floor window, to make sure he stayed as silent as Moulin. Yeo-Thomas went to France again to try to cut him out, and was himself betrayed to the Germans; in spite of ghastly tortures, he too stayed silent, and crowned his clandestine career with the almost unexampled feat of an escape from Buchenwald late in the war.[15]

Before he left England on his final mission, Yeo-Thomas struck an important blow for France in London. The Germans – as is sometimes forgotten – were their own worst enemies in the lands they occupied: their policies drove even the most peaceably inclined to resist them. Sauckel from Berlin, and Laval from Vichy, imposed on France a service of forced labour in Germany. (Not all villains die in their beds: they both paid for this decision with the death penalty.) To escape forced labour for the Nazis, hundreds of thousands of young Frenchmen hid in the hills, living rough on what they could get, in groups called – after hill brushwood in Corsica – maquis. The maquis might be turned into remote training areas from which guerillas could sally out to harass the enemy, if only they could be armed in time. Yet at the turn of 1943–4, the only aircraft Bomber Command would release for special duties in north-west Europe were twenty-three Halifaxes.

De Gaulle's French committee of national liberation appealed formally, from Algiers, to the chiefs of staff for more air support, to arm the maquis; without much result. Three men determined to tackle Churchill direct. One was Yeo-Thomas, who deliberately went outside official channels and got a note of personal introduction from Sir Ernest Swinton, the inventor of the tank. Another was Emmanuel d'Astier, at the time de Gaulle's commissioner for the interior (roughly, home secretary-in-exile). Both he and Yeo-Thomas could bring recent, direct, immediate reports from France. Still more vivid ones, of a much wider range, were produced by Michel Brault ('Jérome'), a middle-aged lawyer who had rubbed shoulders with SOE at an earlier stage – he had helped Pierre de Vomécourt late in 1941 – and had been placed by the CNR in charge of the *service maquis*.

This service was meant to supply the maquis, as best it could, with food, clothing and tobacco; thus reducing the maquisards' temptation to turn themselves into bandits by raiding small country stores – as many of them had to – and, still more important for the anti-Vichy French, helping to re-gear French life from a Vichyite to a republican system. Brault's work fitted in neatly with a widespread movement inside the permanent French civil service, a body that had automatically sided with Vichy. The movement, called Noyautage de l'Administration Publique (NAP), undermining of public administration, established in every government department, in every *préfet*'s office, a small group of devotees of the Free

French or of the communists. The young Michel Debré, a future prime minister, toured quietly round the *préfectures* of France and chose, in wireless consultation with Algiers, suitable *préfets* to take over each *département* after liberation.[16]

Brault was keen to get proper treatment for his maquisards from England as well as from Algiers, and pleaded their cause with Churchill with success. On 27 January 1944, at a meeting of ministers – Churchill, Selborne, and Sir Archibald Sinclair, the secretary of state for air, were the only ministers present – Portal, present also, was instructed to step up sharply air support for French resistance; which was done.[17] Crews in 38 (Transport) Group, RAF, improved their skills at finding their way by night in many parachute-dropping sorties, and there were over five times as many containers dropped into France in the first quarter of 1944 as in the last of 1943 (6715 to 1202).[18] One eleventh of these (619) were dropped by the USAAF, which began in January a major series of drops to France – codenamed 'Carpetbagger' – which carried in over 20,000 containers by the end of September.

With the increase in available arms there went of course an increase in SOE's hitting power. All told, about 10,000 tons of warlike stores were put into France by SOE, 4000 of them before and 6000 after the landing in Normandy: arms for about half a million men, and a fair quantity of explosives as well. They were distributed – those of them not dropped straight to the Gestapo, who once received arms for 3000 men in a night – by SOE's agents; either by F's own men, conscious servants of the British chiefs of staff, or by RF's or AMF's, conscious servants of de Gaulle or of the American president. AMF got whatever airlift was available in north Africa – often not much, and packing of stores seems to have been even worse done there than in England (see pp. 137–8). F and RF each thought that the other was unfairly favoured by the RAF, which is perhaps a sign that the division of sorties between

317

them was fair. It is certainly worth remark that 161 Squadron carried nearly four times as many passengers by pick-up between France and England for RF as for F; 138 Squadron's balance of parachute drops inclined somewhat, but only somewhat, the other way, in F's favour. The sharing out of sorties was carefully supervised by Dick Barry, a man of sound and fair judgement, fond of the French. If sometimes he showed a mild bias towards F, the active circuit most directly under the command of the chiefs of staff with whom he worked, he can hardly be blamed for it.

On the ground, RF received and distributed stores through two complex bodies, the Bureau d'Opérations Aériennes in northern and the Service d'Atterrissages et Parachutages in southern France – two inventions of Jean Moulin's and Dewavrin's. BOA had some severe casualties, unfailingly replaced. In each of the two zones there were six military regional delegates (DMRs), appointed under de Gaulle's auspices by his secret service chiefs, Dewavrin in London and the young archaeologist Jacques Soustelle in Algiers. Soustelle maintains, in an impressive passage, that the twelve DMRs were the real instigators of internal resistance, to which they alone could channel arms:[19] an interesting view, even if one that underestimates F section's role. If the DMRs, in turn, were slow to make arms available to the FTP, whose political mentors desired (as ELAS's mentors desired in Greece) to use the arms to set up a communist dictatorship, they acted in a way that no genuine democrat – French or not – can disapprove.

All the arrangements the British and Americans made with the French were made, of course, with an eye to the success of 'Overlord', the major, and 'Dragoon', the minor, re-entries into western Europe, foreseen for the summer of 1944; and made on the universal English-speaking staff assumption that it was dangerous to let the French know anything really secret, because they might incautiously spill it to the enemy. Indeed, as has been shown (pp. 167–9), their ciphers may have been penetrable; nothing worse is known. De Gaulle was deliberately kept in the dark about detailed preparations for the landings; this did not stop his staffs in London and Algiers working, as hard as anybody did in Baker Street, to make sure the landings – whenever and wherever they took place – succeeded.

On the day – 3 June 1944 – that his committee of national liberation proclaimed itself the provisional government of France – unrecognised as such by the USA or the United Kingdom till October – de Gaulle was flown to London, and at a stormy interview with Churchill next day discovered that the major invasion was imminent, and that troops of his own would be taking part in it. In spite of this inauspicious preamble, the invasions of France gave French resistance, and SOE, a magnificent chance to show what they could do; they did a great deal more even than their warm supporters had hoped.

Operation 'Neptune', the assault phase of 'Overlord' (5/6 June 1944), established an allied bridgehead in the bay of the Seine in western Normandy. Ten weeks of heavy fighting there followed before the Americans broke out on the right, then the British and Canadians on the left flank; Eisenhower's armies then raced across north-eastern France till they ran out of petrol, almost on the Rhine. Patch's Franco-American army, landed on the Riviera on 15 August ('Anvil', renamed 'Dragoon'), raced north up the Rhône valley to meet them.

Eisenhower's forces had been led by newspaper reports to expect a vigorous local resistance movement in Normandy. No such thing existed; nor were the unexpectedly well-fed Normans as pleased to have their farms fought over as the unthinking troops had supposed. The long-standing entanglement of F's 'Donkeyman' circuit under Henri Frager, which went back to the collapse of 'Carte' in the winter of 1942–3, had the result that the only effective resisters in the Manche, Calvados and Eure *départements*, where the landing base was established, worked on intelligence, not on sabotage; there was no local secret army. Buckmaster, the head of F, did what he could to remedy this by sending one of his best and most experienced men, Claude de Baissac, to refound his 'Scientist' circuit in the *département* of the Orne in south-west Normandy; where de Baissac once astounded a captain in my own brigade (who was in British uniform; SAS did not then use plain clothes) by receiving him on the upper floor of a house that had a German head-quarters on the ground floor. Two sub-circuits of de Baissac's operated, one on each flank of the allied landing, to perform a task that strictly belonged rather to SIS than to SOE: the provision of tactical intelligence for forward troops.

This is an instance of Robin Brook's usefulness at Eisenhower's elbow. Brook perceived the Americans' need for detailed data about German headquarters and dump locations on their slowly advancing front at the south end of the Cherbourg peninsula, and could do something to remedy it. On 10 July Jack Hayes, who had already completed one mission to France – most of it spent in a Vichy concentration camp – parachuted in to a reception laid on by de Baissac in the meadows near Avranches. Hayes ('Helmsman') immediately organised messengers to cross into the Americans' lines with detailed news – he had sent thirty before the end of the month.[20] They reported exactly what targets there were for artillery and air attack, and precisely which units were where. Some of these details may have been known, already to the very limited circles that read the 'Ultra' messages from Bletchley; they were manna to regimental commanders on the spot, men far too junior to have heard of 'Ultra', let alone read it.

Brook knew 'Helmsman' would work because of the

success already obtained on the opposite flank by 'Verger'. This was a two-man team, headed by Jean Renaud-Dandicolle; his wireless operator, M. L. Larcher, was brother to 'Dressmaker', one of Dormer's unsuccessful saboteurs of 1943. They dropped to de Baissac in early May, and he sent them to establish themselves close south-east of Caen. There they made friends, and found themselves just beyond Montgomery's left flank when 'Neptune' succeeded. The local peasantry helped them scatter tyre-bursters and fell trees, to annoy the local Germans, and they were able to send a good deal of tactical intelligence, both by messenger and by wireless. A shot-down Canadian pilot, trying to find his way back into the allied lines, joined them. They were Frenchmen, and could therefore melt into the landscape in ways that he could not. The area became too crowded with German troops for their safety; they were all caught on 8 July, and none returned.[21]

These were the missions for which the front-line troops had reason to be grateful on the spot; an enormous amount more got done, much of it never yet published or analysed, to inflict on the Germans trying to hold on in Normandy a major military defeat. They lost control of their own rear areas, and could never be sure what supplies, if any, would get through to them. Credit for this is usually given to the photogenic allied air forces. More of it belongs – though it will never reach them – to the obscure, devoted French saboteurs who blew up points, damaged bridges, misrouted trains (quite as useful as derailing them, and less expensive in casualties), sowed tyre-bursters, misdirected motorcyclists, and generally made the Germans' life unbearable. The scale of these disruptions is worth recall: on the night of 'Neptune', D–1/D-day, the French made 950 interruptions of their own railway system, considerably more (even if at less spectacular places) than the RAF and the USAAF had

secured with Zuckerman's transport interdiction pro-
gramme over the previous two months. The general
attitude of go-slow and non-co-operation among French
railway workers was so marked that the German general
who tried to get work out of them decided that any train
that he really had got to get through, he had better send
manned with Germans and not with French.

This effort by the French, though large and important,
had not been slotted into the warlike plans for 'Overlord'
as neatly as a staff officer would have hoped. There had
in fact been so little in the way of direct links between the
planners of 'Overlord' and SOE that it was not until
within a week of D-Day that the degree of resistance
participation in the battle that was about to open was
fixed. On 1 May 1944 SOE sent out, in error, a mass of
warning messages over the BBC's evening news bulletin
in French, warning rail-cutting, telephone-cutting, road-
cutting teams that a major landing might be expected
within a fortnight. Götz of the Sicherheitsdienst, among
others, understood these warnings, and passed them on
to his own high command, which passed them out to the
armies in France. Nothing happened (or at any rate
nothing appeared to happen). When the same warning
messages were repeated on 1 June, Götz again made his
report; no one took any notice (see pp. 197–9 for
background).

Not till 3 June did anyone decide what scale of effort
was to be called for from SOE's circuits. On that day
Mockler-Ferryman, head of SOE's north-west European
region, went down to Portsmouth with Joe Haskell, his
American colleague. They had a long talk with Bedell
Smith, Eisenhower's chief of staff. Mockler-Ferryman
explained in detail how widespread SOE's networks were,
how much damage they could hope to do, and how
extreme the security dangers would be if everybody came
out into the open at once. Bedell Smith listened attentively; went down the corridor at Southwick House for a

quarter of an hour's talk with the commander-in-chief; and came back with an order. Resistance was to make a maximum effort on the night of the invasion (which those in the know still then supposed to be 4/5 June).[22]

When Mockler-Ferryman returned to London, he passed the order on to Robin Brook, who summoned Koenig, Passy, and other leading figures of external French resistance in London, to fix any final details. Just in time, he heard that D-Day had been postponed a day, and held an impromptu drinking party instead.

When in fact the action messages went out, on the evening of 5 June, in an unusually long stream, Götz picked out no fewer than fifteen of them as action messages for F circuits whose agents had fallen into his hands. Again, he immediately raised a very sharp alarm. The German Fifteenth Army did send out a warning to its troops that secret information suggested an invasion within the next forty-eight hours. Seventh Army, which lay all unknowing right in the path of the invasion force, did not. So F section did not endanger D-Day quite as much as might have been feared.

Moreover, one F agent had taken what turned out to be a vital step in response to the warning messages of 1 June. He sent for a couple of sub-agents, issued them their stores, and told them to get on with their job. The Second SS Panzer division, *Das Reich*, had recently arrived in the neighbourhood of Toulouse and Montauban; a cadre of it, rather, refitting after hard service in Russia and recruiting back up to full strength. Its tanks were kept concentrated under heavy guard in Montauban. It moved them – as the Germans always tried to do, over long distances – in swan-necked rail transporter cars, which were hidden in village railway sidings round Montauban, each concealed by a couple of worn-out French railway trucks dumped on top. These transporter cars were unguarded. Brooks of F's 'Pimento' spotted this, and had his sub-agents mark down exactly where each of them was. They sallied out, after dark, after curfew, by bicycle; and during the next few nights they siphoned off all the axle oil from the transporter cars. (It fetched a fine price on the black market.) They replaced it with ground carborundum, parachuted in by SOE: a form of abrasive grease that gums up the parts that grease lubricates. On 7 June the division got a warning order to stand by to move to Normandy, and sent for its tank transporter cars: every one of them seized up after loading at Montauban. It was a week before the division found alternative cars, and they were over at Périgueux, nearly a hundred miles away – bad for the tanks' tracks – and over ground infested by one of F section's toughest sets of ambush-layers, part of George Starr's 'Wheelwright' circuit commanded by Philippe de Gunzbourg. The division did not get into action in Normandy till D + 17. Among the two sub-agents who had delayed its start were two sisters: the elder was sixteen, the younger fourteen.

This sort of sharp, devastating stab probably did more to help defeat the Germans than did many of the better-known, more widespread outbursts of resistance activity; to one at least of these a moment must be give. Southwest of Grenoble, astride the boundary of the Isère and Drôme *départements*, lies the mountain plateau of the Vercors, a remote area some thirty miles by twelve, easy to defend, a magnet for young men on the run from forced labour. Thousands of them had collected there by the spring of 1944; Gilbert Gadoffre, one of my professorial colleagues at Manchester, held his first teaching post as an instructor in the Sten gun at an informal school in the Vercors. Luckily for him, he was promoted away to run a maquis in the Tarn.

Cammaerts knew the Vercors, and visited it; so did several RF organisers, including Brault ('Jérome') and the 'Union' mission. One of these ardent Gaullists arranged, in the spring of 1944, for a trip to Algiers in the Gaullist submarine *Casabianca* for Chavant, the mayor of

Villard-de-Lans, one of the villages on the plateau. The mayor took back to the Vercors with him a chit from General Cochet, a high commander at Algiers, which simply said: *Bouclez le Vercors le jour J*, call out the Vercors on D-Day. The mayor forgot to ask, and Cochet forgot to specify, whether he meant D-Day on the northern or on the southern coast of France. When early on 6 June the Vercors heard, by BBC and Swiss radio broadcasts – confirmed later in the day by Vichy's own wireless – that a major landing in France had begun, the plateau declared itself free. The forbidden tricolour was hoisted at the *mairie* of Villard-de-Lans, as a symbol of its freedom. The 250 *sédentaires* – men enrolled for the maquis who had not yet joined it – were called up to join the 700 men who already had arms; the Germans on the plateau who were not killed ran away. The Vercors became, in an hour or two, a national redoubt: the first ambition of many resisters, not only in France, who did not pause to think what the result would be of providing a fixed target at which the enemy could shoot.

Both Cammaerts and 'Union' reported that the defiles which led up to the Vercors provided unusual chances for anti-tank effort, and asked specifically for anti-tank guns. SAS had already discovered that a six-pounder (57mm) anti-tank gun could be dropped by parachute; SOE preferred not to know. Ammunition supply would still have been troublesome; all the Vercors' requests for weapons heavier than machine-guns were ignored, except that they were sent a few bazookas. Repeated appeals for action against the airfield at Chabeuil near Valence were ignored as well; from it the Germans kept up steady reconnaissance of the plateau and mounted occasional light bombing and ground-attack raids.

A 'Jedburgh' team under Neil Marten was available to Huet ('Hervieux'), the French regular colonel in command, to forward his requests for supplies; so, from 28

June, was a mission called 'Eucalyptus', sent in by parachute from Algeria with half an OSS operational group (OG), fifteen men strong. 'Eucalyptus' was under an English major, Desmond Longe (later a great figure in the insurance world), who hardly spoke any French, but was brave. They received a mass daylight USAAF parachute drop on 14 July, a thousand containers dropped on red, white and blue parachutes; the containers had Stens and clothes inside them, but still no heavy weapons, and the dropping zone was under shellfire in a matter of minutes after the drop. On the 18th, the Germans mounted a major attack, which was held at the cliff edges; on the 21st, they landed a handful of crack SS troops by glider in the middle of the plateau, and in two days of torrential rain the resisters were brushed away: either killed in action, or tortured to death, unless they managed to run. The check to resistance was in every sense atrocious.

In spite of the adage that advises against changing donkeys in mid-stream, SOE and the Free French adopted a major change-over in the command system on 1 July 1944. From that date, all but one of SOE's sections working into France were thrown under a single large and confused staff in Bryanston Square, near Marble Arch in London, called the Etat-Major des Forces Françaises de l'Intérieur (EMFFI). EU/P, which dealt in extra secrecy with the Poles, remained as always apart. Some of EMFFI's officers – from F, RF and DF sections and from the Bureau de Recherches et d'Action à Londres, the successor to Passy's famous BCRA (Bureau Central de Renseignements et d'Action) – knew a great deal about how to run secret agents in and out of France; a great many more, Giraudist imports from north Africa, high in rank and low in knowledge of the secret war, did not.

EMFFI's commander, General Koenig, had commanded the Free French brigade at Bir Hakeim in the Libyan desert with high distinction; he had the sense to realise that he was now engaged in a quite different sort of war. The unwisdom of arranging a major change of command structure in the middle of a major campaign was manifest. Sensible men and women in EMFFI and subordinated to it, from Koenig downwards, made the best of it they could.

One other outstanding success deserves recall. When 'Dragoon' at last began to disembark its seven divisions – four of them French – under the American General Patch on the Riviera coast on 15 August, they were working to a phase-map on which Grenoble was due to fall to them on D+90. By that time, as Colonel (later General) Zeller remarked gloomily to de Gaulle, who showed him the phase-map after Zeller had been brought out of France by light aircraft, all the resisters in 'Dragoon's' hinterland would have been mopped up. Zeller got de Gaulle interested in the chances of armed clandestine action in direct support of 'Dragoon', and managed to talk Patch's planners into trying a stroke round the Germans' left flank. While the bulk of Patch's army elbowed their way cautiously towards the Rhône valley, an armoured-car regiment probed up the old Route Napoléon through the Alpine foothills, from Nice through Grasse, Digne and Gap, towards Grenoble. They got to the outskirts of Grenoble on D+6, their way cleared for them constantly by local resistance groups.

A German major, a white flag at his knee, was waiting at the roadside to hoist it when the first American vehicle appeared. Adams, the American regimental commander, leading from in front, refused to accept the surrender unless it was made jointly to himself and his maquisard companion, around whose shoulder he put his arm: this was Huet, the commander defeated in the Vercors. Fortune's wheel completed a neat half-circle.

When de Gaulle got to France, he was everywhere acclaimed as the obvious replacement for Pétain. When he reached Paris, late on 25 August, he was pressed by the CNR to proclaim the republic, a direct encounter at the summit between internal and external resistance. De

Gaulle met the request by remarking that as the republic had never ceased to exist, it was pointless to proclaim it again.

In Paris, as elsewhere, the communists had hoped to present him with the accomplished fact of a communist regime in power; there, as elsewhere, they were outwitted by the Gaullists. The latter had bothered to read Trotsky, whom they rightly regarded as the leading expert on how to seize power in an industrial society; the communists, brought up to abhor Trotsky, had not. Wherever the allied armies penetrated in France, close behind the leading infantry came khaki-uniformed, unobtrusive men and women of de Gaulle's *Missions militaires de liaison administrative*. They took care of the telephone exchange, railway station, telegraph office, gasworks, power station; above all, they took care of the *mairie*, whence ration cards were issued: thus they controlled state power.

De Gaulle toured the main provincial centres of France in September, to show himself and to encourage his regional commissioners. Any of F section's agents he met, he made a point of ordering out of France within forty-eight hours; whether they were French or English, Scottish or Canadian, Mauritian or Monégasque, they were unwelcome to him. Most took the hint; most, in the end, were welcomed back to a relenting France, where statesmen came to understand that they had not been serving merely British interest, but had been striving to restore to the French the right to decide for themselves how they wanted their lives to be governed.

Spain and Italy

The story of what SOE attempted in Spain, and secured in Italy, is waiting to be written – or at any rate to be published – in English; neither country can long delay us here. Into Spain various active parties were prepared, at one emergency or another; nothing in fact got done. DF section had quite a lot of work to do moving its passengers across Iberian soil – all done with the total discretion in which Humphreys shrouded all his activities. The veiled threat that SOE would be let loose against it was enough to make the Germans withdraw a detecting station meant to work against ships, which they had proposed to set up near the Straits of Gibraltar.

Into Italy virtually nothing got done before Mussolini fell in 1943; oddly enough, SOE was able to help in getting the Italians to change sides, after his king Victor Emmanuel III – with an urbanity and a dexterity Selborne himself could hardly have matched – ushered Mussolini out of the royal study into the arms of a waiting police-man, who took him away in an ambulance.[1] Marshal Badoglio, his new prime minister, was hunting for some secure way of communicating with the allies, in north Africa or elsewhere, without being spotted by the Germans. SOE was able to invoke a captured operator of its own, Dick Mallaby, who had parachuted into one of the great Italian lakes a few weeks earlier and had been fished out by the *carabinieri*. Badoglio was sent a code, through a neutral diplomat, which Mallaby worked for him. This tale has been in print for over thirty years, and generally ignored (like so much of SOE's real work) to be true.[2]

After the allied invasion of Italy in 1943 serious co-operation with nascent Italian resistance in occupied (northern) Italy could begin. Commander Holdsworth, previously a pillar of SOE's seaborne effort out of Corn-wall, settled near Bari in charge of a Special Force that became a formidable element in the military affairs of the peninsula, in constant touch with town and country parti-sans alike, and in constant consultation with politicians. Italian resistance was quite as heavily politicised as French; there was, again, a strong and active communist party, in this case one less tainted with collaboration with the Nazis during the unhappy spell of the Russo-German pact of 1939–41. Through the communists, fascist power was undermined in the great industrial cities of Milan and Turin; through No. 1 Special Force, arms were supplied to almost innumerable guerilla bands in the Apennines and the Ligurian Alps.

No one who has read Charles Macintosh's book will ever be able to look at the Ponte Vecchio in Florence with quite the same eyes again.[3] In it he explains how, in August 1944, while the Germans held the north and the allies held the south half of Florence, an SOE squad was able to run a telephone line across the ruin of the Ponte Vecchio and to secure invaluable intelligence about what the enemy's decisions were going to be, as well as smuggling in patrols to disconcert him. A myriad of other such tales might yet be recoverable, if such characters as Gordon Lett, who led a small private army in the hills above Spezia, could be persuaded to publish memoirs as interesting as his *Rossano*.[4] The Italian communists, on the whole, saw that they had interests in common with the British and the Americans – at least they could all agree to get rid of Hitler and Mussolini and their regimes; and the party worked well with others in the national committee of liberation for northern Italy. Afterwards, it hogged as much of the credit as it could.

The Balkans

Turkey and Romania

The same view of interest was not held by communist parties in the Balkans, with which SOE had a run of serious difficulties, and yet in which SOE formed also some remarkable friendships and even alliances.

Traditionally, the Balkans used to be controlled from Constantinople, and that city – renamed Istanbul by the post-Ottoman revolution of Kemal Atatürk – was by long tradition a centre of international intrigue and double-dealing. SOE did not mean to be left behind. The city had been demoted from being the capital of Turkey, but was much closer to Europe than Ankara, the remote new official focus on the Anatolian uplands; most secret services preferred the beauty and the fleshpots of the Bosporus to the aridities of the hinterland. Besides, Ankara was still small, with a sharply defined diplomatic quarter well outside a sleepy, ancient market town: it was far more easy to hide among the teeming hundreds of thousands of inhabitants, drawn from quite a dozen nations, in the city Constantine had founded, which had been for over a thousand years the capital of the Byzantine empire.

Byzantium has become proverbial for the complexity of its politics as well as the splendour of its art, and some of the complexes seemed to linger on. Relations between the various allied, enemy and neutral secret services were almost as involved as in Cairo; luckily they did not need to be unravelled here. One personality, and one incident, are too notable to be left out.

An early head of SOE's Istanbul section was Gardyne de Chastelain, a leading member of the British prewar colony in Romania, a businessman of equal competence and force of personality. While it looked in the autumn of 1941 as if the Germans were about to overrun Russia, and burst into the Middle East, there was plenty of planning for de Chastelain's section to do; but the Russian front held, and these plans came to nothing. This released him to tour Canada in search of refugees from Europe speaking Balkan languages; he returned with notes on a motley collection of Croat, Slovene, Slovak, Bulgar and other personalities, some of whom were enlisted to take part in one or other of SOE's Balkan ventures.

The Turkish police, noticeably efficient and hard to bribe, made it all but impossible to fulfil one of the tasks laid on the Turkish section by London in response to the chiefs of staffs' urging about the importance of oil targets: Italian tankers carrying oil from Black Sea ports to the Mediterranean turned out immune to attack. SOE did get as far as attaching two limpets, but neither exploded.[1] This certainly saved SOE from a diplomatic crisis; it did nothing to hinder the flow of oil.

SOE was much concerned with what was going on in Romania during the war, but was able to do little about it. Its mission in Bucharest had to come out with the diplomats, in February 1941;[2] tenuous touch was maintained through a wireless set that was left behind – in the house, for a time, of Prince Stirbey, the father-in-law of Eddie Boxshall who ran SOE's Romanian desk in London. Most contact was with Maniu, the head of the Romanian peasant party, who was out of office and not likely to regain it under any of Romania's various dictatorial regimes; Maniu, whenever offered any sort of solution, whatever the problem, always made difficulties. This was not the sort of channel through which any great change could emerge. Various emissaries, including Stirbey, came out for inconclusive talks. De Chastelain parachuted in himself, to see what could be stirred up; and was taken prisoner that night, when inquiring his way in a strange village, because a countrywoman spotted him as a foreigner. When the King of Romania himself overthrew the dictator, Antonescu, in August 1944, he sent de Chastelain out to Istanbul to announce Romania's surrender; the Foreign Office then insisted, with success, that de Chastelain be kept from fulfilling his promise to the king to go back at once. The Foreign Office knew that the Russians regarded Romania as within their own sphere, and profoundly distrusted SOE.

Cairo

So far as there was a single nerve-centre that governed SOE's work into the Balkans, it shifted: first from London to Cairo, then from Cairo to Bari. London thought that it retained general control, through Pearson, who had Boughey and Boxshall beneath him in charge of the western and the eastern Balkans respectively; all three of them kept finding themselves overtaken by decisions made farther forward, by men who said they were in closer touch with what was actually going on. The shift in SOE's major policy, over which Selborne and Hambro quarrelled in the early autumn of 1943, accentuated this tendency for the London Balkan desk to weaken, because it put more authority over SOE into the hands of commanders-in-chief in the battle areas. Moreover, at about this time there was an SOE chief of staff in Cairo of unusual forcefulness of personality, even for SOE; it was not easy to stand in his way at any distance, near or far.

This was Brigadier Keble. Now Keble with all his faults – and they were many – was at least bounding with ideas. He may have been pushing himself; he was certainly pushing SOE. By a staff accident, he remained privy to 'Ultra' – to such highly secret material, deciphered locally and at Bletchley, as affected GHQ Middle East, where he had previously served in MI14 (German army). He had been put on the prime minister's list of authorised readers; once he was on it no one local dared, and no one in Whitehall remembered, to strike him off. As a result, he knew much more about the real state and shape of the war than most of those with whom he dealt. He compelled a great many people in the sluggish depots of the Egyptian delta, and elsewhere in the Levant, to realise that SOE existed and to attend to its wants; it might be said of him that he repeated in the Near East the titanic early efforts of Nelson and Jebb in Whitehall. Like them, he was not destined to stay at the helm to the end of the voyage; far more than they did, he rubbed those he met up the wrong way.

One of his leading ideas was that each of SOE's principal missions into a Balkan country should be headed by a brigadier: both to provide status for the mission, and to indicate to resisters that the British were taking them seriously, by sending a general officer to work with them. Keble's enemies said that this was only a trick to have himself promoted major-general, because he controlled several brigadiers.[1] This was Cairene gossip, not even true: lieutenant-colonels in London commanded lieutenant-colonels in France and Belgium without a tremor, and were themselves commanded by Robin Brook when only a major: in any case, as has been shown, in SOE's upper reaches rank counted for little (see pp. 41–2).

At any rate, in mid-1943 Keble got the Cairene military secretary's agreement to a trawl through the list of brigadiers, first locally and then in the United Kingdom as well, to see whether any of these senior officers – regulars almost to a man – would be ready to set aside their professional chances for a brief voluntary foray into the field of irregular warfare. He got a few responses, who will appear as the survey of SOE's work into Balkan countries unfolds.

Greece

SOE's affairs in Greece were, even more than usual, beset with political troubles. Greece had had an early and unpleasant brush with fascist power in the Corfu incident of 1923. Mussolini's navy had bombarded Corfu town in retaliation for the killing of an Italian general – probably by bandits – on the Greco-Albanian border. All the redress the Greeks got from an appeal to the League of Nations was an order to pay cash to Italy in compensation.[1] The many twists and turns of Greek politics had led to the setting up on 4 August 1936 of a quasi-fascist regime under General John Metaxas. The king, George II – friend and cousin of the ruling British and recently ruling German royal families – gave Metaxas his reluctant approval; both king and general were therefore suspect to liberal and leftist Greeks. The country rallied behind them when Mussolini (without consulting Hitler) invaded Greece from his latest conquest, Albania, in October 1940.

To the general surpise, the Greeks held their own, and

threw the invaders back; a gesture too often forgotten by British orators who talk of Britain's lone stand against the axis. Metaxas died in February 1941; his countrymen held on. But their right flank was turned in late April 1941 by German troops, who poured down from conquered Yugoslavia and overawed Bulgaria, and defeated both the Greeks and the Anglo-Anzac forces, ill-spared from north Africa, with contemptuous ease. Remnants of the defeated armies withdrew to Crete, where in May they were narrowly but decisively beaten by General Student's airborne force.

The swift invasion of Greece had taken SOE, and not SOE alone, by surprise. Not much had been done before the tide of the Blitzkrieg washed over it to get ready for resistance to enemy occupation; nor were there chances for much to be done in the way of demolitions during the catastrophe. Sensibly enough on a middle-term view, SOE had supposed that Metaxas would side with his fellow dictators, and made its earliest approaches to the forbidden opposition: a handful of liberals, and a rather larger, tougher and more competent body of communists in Athens and the Peiraeus. However, with none of these had any useful arrangements been made in time, either about sabotage or about communications. Peter Fleming, the explorer – the novelist's elder brother – brought a small demolition party of fellow-soldiers (all ex-MI R) to attack the railways, and long afterwards gave an entertaining broadcast about how they had moved a mixed train of petrol and ammunition, under occasional air attack, from Larissa nearly a hundred miles to Amphikhia; where the Luftwaffe all too finally disposed of it.[2] N. G. L. Hammond, the classicist, diverted from Albania – he had fluent Albanian as well as Greek – was busy with a few demolition stores, but hardly popular at the legation; all that he managed to do was to burn up a warehouseful of cotton before the Germans got it, and help to lay in the Corinth canal a magnetic mine that failed to go off.[3]

One or two useful men and usable wireless sets were left behind in mainland Greece. Colonel (later General) Bakirdzis, codenamed 'Prometheus' – the bringer of fire – had a set in Athens. He had worked closely with the British during the previous world war, and provided plenty of intelligence; but the Germans got close to him, and he escaped from Greece in mid-1942. He handed his set over to a young naval officer, Koutsoyiannopoulos, who as 'Prometheus II' played an important part in arranging SOE's first major parachute drop into Greece.

SOE had various small and active parties in Crete, all through the occupation; they kept in intermittent wireless touch with Cairo. George Psychoundakis's book illuminates the extent to which they were loved by the villagers, and chased by the enemy.[4] They are best known for a late, almost absurd coup, in April 1944. Patrick Leigh-Fermor and Stanley Moss captured the German general in command on the island, and drove him through a score of his own road-blocks to a distant cove, whence he was removed by submarine to Egypt. They only found out afterwards that he had been highly unpopular with his staff, who were delighted to be rid of him.[5] But we must return to more serious business on the mainland.

In the early autumn of 1942, SOE Cairo determined to block the single railway line that ran through central Greece towards the small ports of the Peloponnese. Contrary to the general belief today, none of Rommel's supplies for the desert war travelled along it: this was known at the time in Cairo to the very few who were privy to ultra secret decipher, including Keble. It may be guessed that Keble knew also that a major British desert offensive impended – it began on 23 October 1942 – and was determined to make a splash of his own as well. No one who took part in the ordering of the block had taken in a simple, vital fact about the Greek countryside: life moved at a walking pace.

A regular engineer colonel, E. C. W. Myers, was

picked to lead the party to make this block. Though he later married Sweet-Escott's sister, he had barely heard of SOE before he was, rather abruptly, recruited into it, given some parachute training at Kabrit, and told to pick a team fast. He and seven companions were successfully dropped on 1 October 1942, on a mountainside not far from Delphi; one of his companions, C. M. Woodhouse, a classical scholar in his middle twenties, spoke fluent Greek and had already operated on occupied Greek soil. They were in touch from the start with 'Prometheus II'; but getting themselves, their stores, four more SOE men, and an escort big enough to take on the garrison of their target – they decided to attack a bridge over the Gorgopotamos river, not far from Thermopylae – took far longer than any Cairo planner had foreseen. They missed the October moon: they had to have some light, to see what they were up to at the bridge, of which one end section had steel instead of stone piers, and looked vulnerable. A Greek colonel (later general), Napoleon Zervas, who had taken to the hills, came forward to help them with escorts and guards. So did a leading local communist, Athanasias Klaras – 'Ares' – of ELAS, the Greek army of national liberation. Woodhouse said, in retrospect, of ELAS on this, the only occasion when they and Zervas fought on the same side, 'I have no doubt that they joined us only to prevent Zervas monopolising the credit of the operation, which would naturally be followed by material support from the British in weapons, ammunition and money.'[6] They did not in fact blow the bridge till 25/26 November 1942. It was a resounding local success; the line was broken for several weeks; and it did hamper still further Rommel's retreat westward across the desert. But the battle it had been meant to help had been won three weeks earlier. Perhaps this was why Montgomery, not a long-tempered general, made few further efforts to use SOE: as he felt they had let him down on a critical occasion, he had little more use for them.

N and F sections in London had no monopoly in staff officers short of imagination. Myers left with his party to attack the railway before Cairo could provide for him detailed intelligence about the three bridges on it that provided the obvious sabotage targets. The plans from which one of these had been built reached Cairo from London later; and were incontinently parachuted into Greece, with no thought for the possibility – probability, even – that someone other than a member of Myers's party would get to the container first, and thus compromise the whole operation.[7]

SOE in Greece had one other piece of major sabotage to its credit, the blowing up of the Asopos viaduct on the same railway line – not far from the previous breach; by the time this was done, on 20/21 June 1943, all the local resisters were too wary of German reprisals, and too much taken up with their quarrels with each other, to be ready to join in. The work was done, quietly, by moonlight again – this time without a shot fired (at the Gorgopotamos, there had been a brisk skirmish) – by four officers and two NCOs, a mixed force of British, New Zealand and Palestinian origin: no Greeks.[8] Again, it was a comprehensive cut, and the line was closed for months.

This became part of SOE's share in deception for the forthcoming attack on Sicily. In Greece this took the form of an operation called 'Animals' which was designed to make the Germans even more nervous than they were already about their hold on Greece; it did have the effect that a spare Panzer division, resting in France, got moved down to the Peloponnese, which might – had the Germans been better informed – have been sent to Sicily instead, with unhappy results for 'Husky', that island's invasion on 9/10 July.

'Animals', as several of SOE's observers noticed, was one of the few times when the Greeks did seem to want to come out from the hills and hit back at their occupiers. The only other spell of even sporadic raiding, unless it was raiding conducted strictly by parties sent in by SOE, came in the autumn of 1944 when the Germans withdrew. Even then, it was remarked, a great many forces who had talked big in the mountains about the great deeds they were going to do slunk past the retreating German columns, in pursuit of political aims of their own.

What these political aims were remained uncertain in Cairo, but could be seen clearly enough on the spot by those who cared to look. Nicholas Hammond, put into Thessaly by parachute to provide liaison with the large ELAS guerilla force there, quickly perceived that it was run on a totalitarian system – only one source of news was allowed to reach the ears of the force's soldiers – and that this system was a communist one. He reported accordingly; and was told by Cairo to get on with his job of military liaison, without bothering his head about politics. Barker-Benfield, the brigadier – of well-born German antecedents – who was in charge of his section (after Keble had been sacked), even came to Greece himself by parachute to see Hammond and to try to convince him that ELAS' troops were really splendid fellows, who would fight well in the common cause.[9] It was at this point that Hammond asked to be relieved of his command, and returned to more ordinary soldiering.

Before he left, Hammond enriched the literature of clandestine war with one anecdote too good to leave out. He had to visit Salonika by bus, adequately disguised, he believed, as a Vlach shepherd. 'A small girl of ten or so talked to me for some time. Then she suddenly said to her mother, "He is different". The mother told her to be quiet and paid no attention.' The child was quite right: Hammond was the only man on the bus with blue eyes.[10]

Another perceptive British liaison officer in Greece was John Mulgan, a New Zealand scholar of broad sympathies and a reflective mind, who did marvels as a train saboteur, and was appalled at the way two men who were hard-bitten enough could dominate the life of a hill village.[11]

The basic problem in Greece was far from simple – Greek politics are notoriously complicated – but can be summarised here in reasonably simple terms. ELAS and EAM, the political movement that backed it, purported to be nationwide groups struggling for a free Greece, and were in fact being used by the KKE, the Greek communist party, in an attempt to seize state power in the teeth of whatever wishes the bulk of the Greek people might have. Zervas's movement, EDES, was anti-monarchical, but stood a lot farther to the political right than EAM. EDES was the only one of the non-communist-dominated Greek resistance armies that managed to stay in the field till the Germans left the country; ELAS took care to swallow all the others up, either defeating them in the field or subverting them without a battle. SOE was valuable to ELAS because it provided arms and money (sovereigns), in the largely mistaken belief that ELAS would use the arms against the Germans. SOE was valuable to EDES because, again, it provided arms and money; and because there were enough SOE officers with EDES just to keep it alive when ELAS launched a major attack on it in the autumn of 1944 (when a reasonable man might have expected that ELAS would be attacking the retreating Germans), and to arrange when EDES was at its last gasp for its men to be taken off the mainland by the Royal Navy and brought to a temporary refuge in Corfu.

From all the confusion, one plain political point can be made clear. Had it not been for SOE, ELAS would in all probability have been in charge of Greece when the Germans left; Greece would have gone communist; though ELAS was acting without Moscow's orders, Moscow could hardly have been expected to look such a gift horse in the mouth. SOE can claim a free Greece among its achievements. That did not stop it from often being the butt of Foreign Office complaints that it was muddying the political waters: a complaint that stemmed in part from the lamentable understaffing of SOE's cipher office in Cairo, where reports from Greece – even with high priorities – were sometimes held up for two or three weeks.[12]

Yugoslavia

Though in Greece SOE supported the anti-communist side against the communists – supported it, at any rate, enough for that side just to be alive at the end of the German occupation – across the frontier in Yugoslavia SOE came to support the communist side against the anti-communists, and stood aside when the Germans left and the communists seized state power. The reason why the British in general, and SOE in particular, took two such apparently contradictory attitudes at once was strategic. Simple soldiers – who look simple indeed in the bitter light of postwar politics – believed that in Yugoslavia the communist-led partisan movement had serious potential as a killer of Nazis; while in Greece the mutinies in the Greek army-in-exile in the Levant, which seemed to have been communist-inspired, and the friendship of the Royal Family and hence of the London 'establishment' for George II of Greece, told in a less pro-communist direction. Barker-Benfield's enthusiasm for those tremendous fighting characters he thought he saw in ELAS is another illustration of the simple-soldier mentality at work.

SOE had several emissaries in Belgrade before Yugoslavia was pitched into battle in April 1941; both section D and MI R had been active there. SOE had a part, though not an active one, in General Simović's coup of late March 1941, which toppled Prince Paul, the regent, and brought the young King Peter to his throne. Paul had married the Duke of Kent's sister-in-law, and was therefore likely to be favoured by the British; though in fact Churchill was extremely short with him when he got out of Yugoslavia, handling him sternly because he had contemplated coming to terms with Hitler.[1]

The days of the Simović regime were few indeed. A

military catastrophe followed for Yugoslavia, in which the bulk of the officers of the army – Serbs for the most part – were thought to have disgraced themselves. Most of those who were not killed bolted. The country seemed to sink into an oppressed oblivion, except for Croatia, which became an independent state, and was the scene of alarmingly widespread atrocities wreaked by the local fascists, the Ustashe. SOE was out of touch with everyone.

The Y service in Malta and the shipping unit at Portishead picked up, at the end of August, a message in clear from one Serb officer who had kept his head, had got out into the hills south of Belgrade and was looking for help: Colonel Draža Mihailović. Some of SOE's undercover men in Belgrade had met him; he had been the general staff's expert, so far as they had one, on guerilla warfare. SOE reacted quite promptly: as early as 20 September, Julian Amery (formerly one of the young men in Belgrade) put ashore from a British submarine onto the Yugoslav coast a British officer, D. T. Hudson, accompanied by three Yugoslavs: two cousins, Majors Ostojić and Lalatović, and Dragičević, their wireless operator, with two sets. One of these was bulky, and useless in the mountains because it needed mains electricity; the other soon burned out. Hudson had been given no training of any sort at all.

He was an experienced mining engineer, spoke fluent Serbo-Croat and was no fool; but he was out of luck. His mission was to visit any local resisters he could find, report what their needs were, and estimate their chances of doing the Germans any harm. On the way inland, he ran into an unexpected set of guerillas: bodies of men with red stars in their caps, who called themselves partisans (the name Russian irregulars had used in the war of 1812 against Napoleon's Grand Army). He met their leader, whose nickname was Tito, and thought them a reasonably well-thought-out fighting force, though they were clearly short of arms and food. Tito let him move on to see Mihailović.

Hudson was indeed in the next room at one of the two meetings between Tito and Mihailović, which took place near Užice in November. Civil war in Yugoslavia had already broken out: many-sided war again. Tito found himself having to fight both Mihailović and the Germans.

Propaganda, as so often, got out of step with reality. Mihailović became a world hero as a leader of resistance (lauded as such in Soviet and American quite as much as in British or neutral broadcasts and newspaper articles), just at the moment when contact with Tito had decided him that, for the time being at any rate, he was going to work in with the occupying forces in Yugoslavia sooner than let the influence of Tito's partisans grow. For he could see, as promptly as Hammond could see of ELAS in Thessaly, that the partisans were under communist leadership. Tito kept the command of every unit bigger than a platoon (thirty men) in communist hands, and had plenty of political commissars and periods of political indoctrination as well. Three hundred of his partisan officer colleagues had passed through his hands in 1936–7, when he had been working under cover in Paris as a Comintern agent running men through to fight in the International Brigades in Spain.

Hudson's reports on all this were frequently delayed by wireless or cipher troubles. He did succeed in stopping supplies to Mihailović, who used the first drop he got against the partisans. Hudson was left *plaqué* with a single guide, a boy of fifteen. They spent a winter in the mountains, at horrible cost to their hosts, sheltering where they could, living on an extremely meagre diet. He managed to save his cumbrous, unusable wireless set; and felt abandoned.

By the time Hudson got back on the air in the spring of 1942, the international picture had changed. Mihailović had been promoted general and brought into the government-in-exile as minister of defence, a post he was to hold *in absentia* in the mountains of his native land. The air was ringing with his praises; only a few, unusually well-informed men knew that many of the successes attributed to him had in fact been gained by his partisan enemies. The British government was loud in his defence, in public and in private; one of his stoutest supporters was Lord Selborne.

Gradually it became clear, largly through 'Ultra' material, which only the very senior could handle, that Mihailović was (from the British point of view) on altogether too friendly terms with Italian, Ustashe, and indeed from time to time German commanders, and that Tito was fighting all three of those forces – as well as Mihailović's četniks – as hard as he could. Extra complications arose from the fact that not all bands that called themselves četniks were Mihailović's; several četnik bands worked for the complaisant Serb quisling government in Belgrade, a fact that still causes much confusion.

On the other hand, to Mihailović's credit he did keep in being an army several thousand strong, which he did eventually try to use for serious anti-axis purposes. It is as much of a mistake to maintain that Mihailović was an out-and-out traitor as to proclaim that he was an out-and-out hero. He was part traitor, part hero, according to times and seasons: a thoroughly Balkan predicament, not easy to take in from the comfort of an English or American armchair, in countries with a two-sided tradition in politics and war.

The difficulty between him and Tito was this: Tito meant to use the war to create a socialist revolution in Yugoslavia, Mihailović meant to keep alive the unsocialist, Serb-dominated Yugoslav kingdom in which he had spent his manhood. He wanted to preserve what the communists wanted to overturn. Tito, in spite of repeated major German attacks on him, wanted to maintain and

transport a living revolution in the hills, as well as relieve
the pressure of the Germans on the Soviet Union. Mihailović wanted to save up such forces as he could muster,
and to use them later, when a major allied landing took
place, to secure power in a liberated Yugoslavia. No
wonder they fell out with each other.

Colonel Bailey, a rank senior to Hudson, was sent into
Yugoslavia in December 1942 to see how Mihailović was
getting on, and to report (again) what support he wanted.
Several British departments now favoured an approach to
Tito; and Keble, with his access to 'Ultra', now began to
stir the pot in Tito's favour. Against exceptionally strict
orders, he passed the 'Ultra' material he was getting
about Yugoslavia on to two junior staff officers with him
in Cairo, Basil Davidson and Bill Deakin, and (having
sworn them to secrecy) got them to plot it on a map. Most
of this material came from comparatively low-grade hand
ciphers used by SS units in the Balkans. Its message was
clear: that Mihailović was hand-in-glove with the Italians,
and that the Germans were more worried about Tito than
they were about him. A paper based on this map was
shown to Churchill through Deakin's prewar friendship
with him (Deakin had been his research assistant for the
great *Life of Marlborough*). Churchill asked Bletchley for
a detailed report on affairs in Yugoslavia; the first report
he saw inclined to agree with Keble's argument.

Churchill did not wait to see whether the balance
shifted farther, and if so in what direction. He laid down
that Tito was now to be firmly supported. Deakin (in spite
of having handled 'Ultra' material) was allowed to go into
Yugoslavia, where he met Tito – in the middle of a battle:
indeed, he and Tito were wounded by the same bomb,
which makes a bond. He was able to report to Cairo that
Tito was in charge of a real army, doing real work.[2] His
preliminary mission was followed by Fitzroy Maclean's
(pp. 218–21).

While Brigadier Maclean went to Tito, Brigadier Armstrong – one of the brigadiers produced by Keble's trawl – went to Mihailović. Some sappers went to Mihailović also, as well as to Tito, to try and damage the Yugoslav railway system, which was important to the German war economy (Yugoslav and Albanian chrome passed along it). Those who doubt whether Mihailović did anything useful for the allies can consider the demolition of the railway bridge at Višegrad, on 6 October 1943, by Archie Jack and others behind a guard of Mihailović's četniks: Jack claims it as the largest bridge demolition in the Balkan peninsula. (Višegrad lies a hundred miles southwest of Belgrade, midway betwen Užice and Sarajevo.) Hundreds of American and British airmen, shot down over Yugoslavia or farther north during the many bomber raids mounted from Italian bases into central Europe, were punctiliously looked after by Mihailović's men and sent on their way back to duty; BATS had strips in Mihailović's territory as well as in Tito's. Mihailović was simply biding his time, waiting for the major allied assault that was never mounted; after the allies reached the Italian mainland in September 1943 he showed signs of getting ready to act. Tito inevitably had the upper hand when Yugoslavia was liberated by the Red Army instead of by the British and Americans. Mihailović's execution after a show trial in 1946 was hardly different from what would have happened to Tito, if the dice of fate had been loaded the other way.

Albania

SOE had first hoped to work into Albania from Belgrade, and one mission had indeed already been dispatched when the Belgrade legation had to be hurriedly closed down, leaving the mission to pick its way out if it could. The legation staff had trouble enough in getting away; they were held for several weeks in Italy while the status of some of their more dubious members was disputed and were exchanged eventually for the staff of the Duke of Aosta, who had become prisoners at the end of the campaign he lost in Abyssinia.

It may have been noticed that no suggestion was made, in the pages dealing with Yugoslavia, that hidden pro-Bolshevik staff in SOE affected SOE's pro-Tito attitude: which derived from intercept, rather than from prejudice, and from the feeling that Tito's men would be good at killing Germans. Deakin's book shows how good the Germans were at killing them: that too was a campaign only too full of atrocities. It is unclear what caused SOE's troubles in Albania.

What happened can be put brutally briefly. There were several missions to the northern Albanians, which took up with such local chieftains as Abas Kupi, more or less loyal to the exiled King Zog; parties more anti-communist than anti-German. There were several more missions to the southern Albanians, who were dragooned strictly under the command of Enver Hoxha, leader of the communist party formed in November 1941. There were also a few liaison missions on the coast, one under Sandy Glen, another under Anthony Quayle (of whom Glen complained only that being in his company made one laugh so much that it hurt).[1]

Repeated promises of arms were made to the north; practically none came through. To the south considerable quantities of arms were sent, which were used to dispose of all the bands the southerners could catch in the north, before many shots were fired at the Germans. When the Germans pulled out – unattacked – the southern communists seized the power that they still hold.

Why this was done will not be known unless SOE's papers are released; and might not be clear even then. It can hardly have been by the wish of local SOE commanders, let alone by the wish of Lord Selborne or of Gubbins; nor by the wish of Sweet-Escott's best friend, Philip Leake, who insisted on going into Albania on operations and was soon thereafter killed in action. He had been head of the Albanian section; who succeeded him?

Another brigadier was sent in, this time to Albania: E. F. ('Trotsky') Davies. He got his nickname in the army because while he was still a cadet at Sandhurst an instructor had noted in him 'independence, intolerance, robustness, a keen sense of humour and a kind of disciplined bolshevism'.[2] The tag was hardly one to endear him either to the British or to the partisan high command. He remained enough of a regular to insist with some punctilio on just those points of turn-out with which most of SOE's operators in the field had long ceased to bother: boots had to be clean, trousers to have a visible crease; beards would not be worn, 'none of that Wingate stuff here'.[3] (Wingate had been clean-shaven in Abyssinia, but on the first Chindit sortie into Burma he and most of his companions had defied King's Regulations – 'the chin and lower lip will be shaved; whiskers, if worn, will be of moderate length' – and had grown beards: better camouflage and less to carry.) Julian Amery also, having returned by not much more than the skin of his teeth from a mission into northern Albania, to which none of the promised supplies were sent, found himself being reproached by a staff officer in Italy for wearing a beard with army uniform. The reproach reminded him that he had escaped from the field back into the kind of unthinking, formal society that SOE was out to destroy.[4]

Davies had gone in to replace 'Billy' Maclean – not at all the same man as Fitzroy; Allen had hailed him on the Abyssinian expedition as 'the reincarnation in the wet Amhara hills of some Gaelic chieftain of the Atlantic Isles'.[5] Maclean, like all other British liaison officers (as SOE's emissaries were by 1943 often known), had often to explain that aircraft with stores, for which resisters had hoped, were not to be relied on to arrive with the regularity of railway trains on a main line in peacetime; vagaries of weather and war prevented any such thing.

The Albanians took a rather sour view when thirteen United States Army girl nurses were landed by mistake (the pilot had got lost) on a deserted airfield in Albania, and the USAAF mounted an expedition to try to take them off again that consisted of a Wellington, two Dakotas, and thirty-six Lightning fighters in support. SOE smuggled the girls out quietly by sea; all had by that time collected body lice, but they had enjoyed their trip.[6]

Davies had brought out with him from England as his second-in-command Arthur Nicholls, a colonel in the Coldstream Guards who undoubtedly shared his views on turn-out; and displayed enormous courage as well. Davies' mission had a lot of trouble getting anything they could recognise as military sense out of, or into, the partisans they met; and before long had to take to the hills in a hurry, with German search parties close behind them. In mid-January 1943 they got caught in an infantry scuffle in which Davies was severely wounded by a mortar bomb. Nicholls, though suffering agonies from dysentery and gangrene, took the rest of the party (less Davies' batman, who stayed with him) deeper into the hills, saw them to safety and then died of exposure. Davies was operated on by a German army surgeon, and when he had slightly recovered was moved on to Vienna; whence, after interrogation, he was dispatched to Mauthausen. No one was expected to go to Mauthausen and come out alive; Davies managed it, by convincing the commandant that he was a regular soldier with six months' seniority to the German, on the strength of which he – and his batman – were allowed to go to Colditz.

Too much has been written about what happened to SOE's prisoners in concentration camps; a little of it by historians, too much of it by pornographers. Beyond saying that I believe many of the stories to have been exaggerated, but that all were horrible, I propose to leave that ghastly subject alone, and pass to the Far East: where the prisons were worse, but hardly call for discussion here.

The Far East

The reader may care to glance back for a reminder of SOE's staff structure in south-east Asia (p. 52). Two major sets of operations were mounted, into Burma and (less successfully, because of distance) into Malaya. All the details are set out in the official history,[1] which there is no need even to summarise here. Its author might have made a little more than he did of one of SOE's distinct coups, the turning-round of the force the Japanese had recruited in Burma to look after domestic order, much as the hated milice looked after it in Pétain's France: local men who were ready to do down their neighbours in order to curry favour with the occupier. He describes the fearful troubles SOE had with the civil affairs staff for about-to-be-liberated Burma, who wanted to treat Aung San – SOE's pet double agent, the man who brought the Anti-Fascist Organisation and the Burmese National Army out on the British instead of the Japanese side at a critical moment – as a war criminal. The turn-round Aung San managed had the result that the Japanese hustled out of Burma much faster than they had intended.

There is a complex historical knot waiting to be untied one day, if ever the historian with the knowledge and the objectivity can be found to untie it, about the exact nature of resistance to the Japanese in Malaya. The usual current doctrine is that it was almost wholly Chinese in ethnic origin and inclined towards communism in politics. There is some sound evidence to suggest that, had they ever been given a chance, there were plenty of Malays who would gladly have joined in the struggle against their Japanese oppressors, and would not have resented the return of the British, with whom they were prepared to get on well. The fact that a communist attempt to secure

Malaya by revolutionary action later failed may have some bearing on this point; but to discuss it further would take us beyond this book's terminal date.

SOE's main achievement in Asia was on the disreputable side. It was the work of Walter Fletcher, who was half-Austrian: his father's name had been Fleischl. He was a highly cultivated central European in outlook, and so vast in size that airlines always counted him as two. He made no secret of living on the borderline between honest merchanting and smuggling: in his own words, he was

> Garrulous, old, impulsive, vague, obese,
> Only by luck not 'known to the Police'.[2]

As such work demanded, he was a plausible talker. Dalton spotted him early as a 'thug with good commercial contacts'.[3] He persuaded first Dalton, then Mackenzie, into letting him try to smuggle rubber out of the Japanese-occupied Dutch East Indies. He asked for half a million pounds to cover expenses in advance; a cautious treasury admitted him to a credit of £100,000. Thus fortified, he switched targets from the DEI to French Indo-China. Though SOE gave him a lot of leeway, he provided no actual results.

When after two full years he had not produced a single pound of rubber, he was told he had better shut up shop. Plausible as ever, he managed to persuade not only SOE but the Treasury to let him move again to a flank, and shifted to mainland China. Here, by a strict treaty with OSS, SOE were now forbidden to operate at all. Fletcher was untroubled. He was not operating; he was making friends and influencing people. Chinese magnates, their wives and mistresses liked diamonds and had a weakness for fine Swiss watches. Fletcher arranged to supply both. De Beers put up the diamonds, for which SOE paid sterling. SOE bought, also for sterling, thousands of fine watches, selected under McCaffery's supervision and smuggled out through France by F section agents who supposed they were carrying gunsights for the RAF.[4] Fletcher sold both diamonds and watches in China, in an operation called 'Remorse', at prices so inflated by his customers' greed and by the scarcity value of what he was selling that SOE's net income from all his transactions, through what Cruickshank has called 'the biggest currency black market in history',[5] was £77 million: about £950 million at today's prices, and part no doubt of the explanation of SOE's long-term solvency. Perhaps the oddest feature of this odd tale is that it had full Treasury approval.

SOE was always ready to read engagements narrowly, when to do so might prove to its advantage; just as it was always ready not to bother about the small print when it might get in the way. It was forbidden, as has just been shown, to operate in nationalist China. Did this prevent it from operating in areas of China that were under Chinese communist control? SOE held it did not. Through 'Blue' Ride, once an Oxford friend of Dodds-Parker's – the old-boy network does have advantages – SOE was able to make touch with the CCP, among whom Ride ran his astounding British Army Aid Group in the hinterland of Hong Kong.

Ride's area was left to Ride, who had troubles enough with Chiang's officials, British bureaucrats, OSS infiltration into his neighbourhood,[6] and the Japanese, who often pressed him hard. SOE did manage to infiltrate a couple of missions into Mao Tse-tung's communist-held areas in northern China; for it was clear that the Chinese communists were anti-Japanese. They therefore deserved SOE's support; the missions took specimens of SOE's sabotage tools, and had plenty of stories to tell of effective guerilla activity in Africa and Europe. In return they hoped Mao's Eighth Route Army could give them useful hints about how to tackle the Japanese in the different terrains of Asia. Before anything could come of these missions, a blinding light in the sky over Hiroshima and Nagasaki in turn (6 and 9 August 1945) caused such appalling casualties that the war came to an abrupt end.

Protesters against nuclear weapons – and those bombs were tiny, compared to today's – forget that, appalling though the casualties were, the use of the bombs saved something like a million lives, which would otherwise have been lost in a formal invasion of Japan from the sea. Further, there is an SOE witness to one most valuable thing the bombs' use effected: it saved several scores of thousands of allied prisoners of war from massacre. Laurens van der Post, rounded up and captured in Sumatra in June 1942, had endured over three years' humiliation and shortage of food. He realised that his captors were preparing, as the war news worsened for them, to wipe out all those in their charge before they committed hara-kiri themselves; and discovered that the same was true of many other camps as well, perhaps of most. The power of the atomic bombs was so supernaturally awesome that the Japanese were able to make an honourable surrender to the peoples who had devised it.[7]

Still farther east, there were codenames enough for SOE to confuse those who had not worked out that the Joint Technical Board and the Inter-Services Research Bureau were the same. Among other names SOE used in Australia were Force 137, the Services Reconnaissance Department, the Inter-Allied Services Department; in Baker Street, the branch was simply called SOA, for Special Operations Australia. According to the only published history of SOA – brief as it is – eighty-one separate operations were mounted by it, with varying degrees of success.[8] Two of them, 'Jaywick' and 'Rimau', have been noticed already (pp. 109, 128). 'Jaywick' did some serious good to the allied war effort, but only did it once, and secured only a tiny fraction of the shipping losses inflicted on Japan.[9] 'Rimau' was a disaster. All the twenty-eight fine men who went on it, including Lyon, the leader of 'Jaywick', were lost; and it did not much console those of them who fell alive into Japanese hands that they had the honour of being beheaded, on 7 July 1945, instead of receiving some meaner death.

There seem to have been several raids on Japanese oil depots in Java, carried out by devoted two-man teams of saboteurs who approached their targets with the help of *Witch*, a miniature submarine with an unusual gift: she could be set to submerge by herself, and to resurface at about the same spot at a fixed time. Parties using her could be ferried to the neighbourhood of their landing place in an apparently peaceful junk that had a 40mm Bofors anti-aircraft gun amidships, hidden under a pile of nets.

A little useful guerilla work was done in Sarawak by Tom Harrisson (supposed to have been recruited into SOE by a clerical error, in place of a near-namesake recommended by M15 because he had had useful battle experience with the republicans in Spain[10]). Harrisson, one of the founders of Mass Observation, was a man of such high spirits and breadth of mind that he could make himself welcome in any company; luckily he did not have to apply his charm direct to the Japanese, whose record in counter-guerilla work elsewhere in the island of Borneo was abominable.[11]

In Portuguese Timor SOE also found it possible to get a little done, with help from the local Tamils; their tendency to support the winning side was marked, and their help was not always to be relied on. One of the staff officers working into Timor we have met before: Bingham, the victim of the *Englandspiel* in the Netherlands. Again it turned out that he was sending stores, and even men, to enemy receptions. This time, before things got out of hand, he was warned by another secret service – doing decipher – of what was really happening. This time he did what he might have done in Holland: sent in a party, blind, to prospect. His prospectors saw a captured wireless operator preparing to receive an SOE drop with three Japanese soldiers beside him: Bingham this time saw the point.

What happened to the secret services after the war is supposed to remain a secret. Of SOE's fate there is not much to be said.

Selborne pointed out to Attlee, the new prime minister, that SOE had built up – through Nicholls' signallers' efforts – a world-wide communications network, staffed by brave men and women dedicated to friendship with Great Britain: the makings of a priceless intelligence tool. Attlee brusquely replied that he had no wish to preside over a British Comintern, and that the network was to end immediately. It was closed down at forty-eight hours' notice.

Gubbins stayed on for a few months in Baker Street to supervise the process of disbanding SOE. In a brief struggle for power with Menzies, he lost. Menzies held the ace of trumps – he took formal responsibility for the ultra-secret products of Bletchley Park, the inner workings of which he had not the brain to understand; with that ace, he trumped Gubbins's kingly grasp on irregular and clandestine war. Menzies stayed on as head of MI6. He had been made a KCMG in 1943, as had his deputy, Dansey; Gubbins received the same honour on retirement. On the other hand, the Treasury made sure that Gubbins's army pension was that of his substantive rank, which was colonel, not major-general; and was taxed. Undaunted as ever, he built himself a third career, in a major international textile firm; and did what he could to look after those he had commanded. He continued to travel widely, and was always welcome in the countries he had helped to liberate; among other high distinctions, he especially cherished having been given a standing ovation by both the Norwegian and the Danish parliaments.

Much of the winding-up of SOE was, it must frankly be admitted, bungled. Anyone of enterprise was anxious to get out of it quickly, to get launched on whatever the postwar world was going to offer. Several more or less senior personages in SOE landed on their feet in the City. A few brought their clandestine manners with them, and did not heighten the City's tone; one had to skip suddenly, owing a million pounds. Most reabsorbed themselves, as unobtrusively as they had worked, into English or Scottish or Welsh society at whatever level they had left it.

Vera Atkins, commissioned as a squadron-leader in the WAAF – she had spent the war as a civilian – went to Germany with a list of 118 missing F agents; when she came back, a year later, she had crossed off 117. There was one, with whose career it was not thought necessary to sully the official history, who eluded her research: all the others had been killed. This one had been parachuted into southern France with three million francs, intended for Skepper's 'Monk' circuit at Marseilles. No one had discovered, while he was under training, that though brave and quick-witted he was also a compulsive gambler. He decided to pause in Monte Carlo on his way to Marseilles. Whether he made his pile, and retired on it, or lost every franc and made away with himself, remains unknown.[1]

Formally, SOE closed down on 15 January 1946.

Stafford claims that MI6 reabsorbed it.[2] It reabsorbed, no doubt, a few of the old hands who could not survive in the cold world of ordinary postwar civilian life; and would have been criminally careless to fail to absorb some of SOE's more sober surviving staff and agents. The bulk of the rest of the survivors, enthusiastic amateurs of the great game, were ready enough to go back to the remarkably diverse callings from which they had come.

Gubbins overrode the fears of the security staff, and

encouraged the setting up of the Special Forces Club. It has provided a focus, over the years, around which old members of SOE – and of various parallel bodies, such as SAS, SBS and MI9 – can gather when they want to exchange memories, or simply to find a quiet spot near Harrods to put their feet up and have a drink. The ambassadors of many of the original United Nations – except for those of the USSR and its satellites, none of whom have cared to join in – all take an interest in the club and often attend its major functions. There are strong links with the old Dominions, with several of the once-occupied countries and with the USA. There is also a collection of portraits of heroes and heroines, most of them dead. A half-size oil of Lord Selborne looks down, rather quizzically, on the dining room.

One other thing may be said about the club: it is not quite as cosy as some of the accounts of it in fiction suggest. Everyone in SOE had his or her combativeness sharpened by the fact of belonging to so resolutely aggressive a body; its old members do not always make easy, though they do always make interesting, companions.

XI

How much use was it?

It would be absurd to claim for SOE that it could have won the war by itself, or even – on most fronts – that it was a major battle-winning influence. In a few places its effect was critical; for instance, in its attack on the Norsk Hydro plant near Rjukan.

Clausewitz remarked, in a cool comment – thinking of Spain and Germany in the early nineteenth century – that '*insurgent actions* are similar in character to all others fought by second-rate troops: they start out full of vigor and enthusiasm, but there is little level-headedness and tenacity in the long run'.[1] SOE's experience in France might be held to echo this, for some of the maquis fully mobilised on Eisenhower's order in early June 1944 found the waiting long indeed, while Montgomery's and Rommel's armies locked horns in Normandy till late July.[2] On the other hand SOE's experience in Burma, Greece, Italy, Yugoslavia told the other way: Karens, ELAS, partisans, četniks all had plenty of tenacity, even if some of them were short on level-headedness. It was a critical task for SOE to make sure that, where level-headedness and tenacity were lacking, they were made available for the (admittedly second-rate) forces that SOE's first-rate organisers could bring into combat. Romantics believe that guerillas are competent to take on an SS Panzer division, or crack units of approachable fighting quality; in the open field, they are not. A guerilla has no place in the open field. Sometimes, by a deft subterfuge, he can stop even an SS Panzer division, but such times and subterfuges are rare (see pp. 323–4).

Over and over again, at Montmouchet, in the hills above Spezia, in Bosnia, in Thessaly, in the Naga hills, in north Norway, in countless other places, SOE provided resisters with backbone, with steely support to uphold the good cause against the bad. SOE was not alone in doing this; it was part of SAS's task as well; it was often the part of isolated units from the main fighting forces also. SOE specialised in it; it was not a mean task, and not a mean feat.

One useful if minor task SOE certainly did perform: it did divert enemy attention away from the main fighting fronts towards his own rear areas. Hitler himself is said at one time to have spent – it might be fairer to say, to have wasted – about half an hour every midday at his routine commanders' conference considering the last twenty-four hours' Abwehr and SD reports on suspected SOE activities. Tasks of railway, dump and factory guarding that in the United Kingdom or the United States could be left to elderly night-watchmen and to the civil police, or did not need to be done at all, were often carried out in occupied Europe and Asia by troops: by low-category troops, it is true, not by crack units, but so tough was the discipline and so good (as a rule) was the training of the German and Japanese armies that such troops – when they did find themselves in battle – gave decent accounts of themselves. It was partly to SOE's credit that so many of them were kept out of the firing line.

How much did all this effort cost?

The diversion of allied manpower from other spheres of war activity was trivial. Some of SOE's best agents would have been precious in aggressive front-line infantry or engineer units. Many others were able to achieve a significant role in the war solely because they were in SOE, which provided the unique, unorthodox channel through which their martial abilities could be expressed.

The money cost, even if known – and it would be an accountant's nightmare to work out the proportion of naval, air force and ordnance effort that was devoted to SOE – has not been published. This was one of the few aspects of SOE's activities that I was positively forbidden to inquire into thirty-odd years ago, when working on the official history; it was laid down by an Authority that historians may not see papers bearing on secret service finance. (The Authority was evidently unaware that many Treasury secret service files have seeped through to the PRO; so, then, was I.) I discovered – from a paperback on my own shelves – that no one on SOE's strength paid income tax; that cannot have been a severe drain on the Treasury. SOE's financial director, Wing-Commander Venner, took his secrets to the grave with him as a senior secret servant should: as Nelson, Hambro, Gubbins, Taylor, Davies, Mockler-Ferryman did. Venner left a name with those who knew him of wizardry bordering on genius: as witness the fact that when he cast up his final accounts, he showed a profit of £23m. This can in part at least be explained by Walter Fletcher's sleight-of-hand in Nationalist China, which covered no end of costs (see pp. 351–2).

Accountants may rule the world of commerce, banking, insurance, government; their influence is seeping into the business of teaching, at every level from the nursery school to advanced research; they now have a lot to say about defence spending, and are sometimes heard. They had little to do with resistance or with secret service in the 1940s, and any attempt to draw up a formal profit-and-loss account for SOE's effort would be arid indeed. 'Money is trash', as Admiral Nelson once wrote to his wife; there was infinitely more to SOE than can be set out on a balance sheet, or reduced to pounds and dollars, francs and gulden, roubles and dinars, drachmae and yen. SOE brought benefits no accountant can measure.

In most of the axis-occupied countries, SOE had a cardinal impact on how citizens looked at occupiers, on what the occupied peoples felt about the war. Everywhere the Germans, Italians, Japanese had advanced with almost contemptuous ease. In Denmark, Luxembourg and Siam nothing had been done to stop them; in Abyssinia, back in the mid-1930s, barefoot armies had been powerless against an enemy who sprayed mustard gas from the air; in Holland and Yugoslavia the struggle against overwhelming force had lasted only days; in Belgium, Burma, the Dutch East Indies, France, Greece, Malaya, Norway, the Philippines* and Poland desperate efforts had only held out for weeks; Bulgaria, Czechoslovakia, French Indo-China, Hungary and Romania had been offered no proper chance to fight at all; only in Africa, in New Guinea – almost on Australia's doorstep – and in the vast ranges of China and Russia was axis conquest, once begun, incomplete. Everywhere there was a sense of shame and desolation: SOE helped to replace those dismal feelings with a regained self-respect, a sense that the nation was now doing something to reverse its earlier defeat, so that its grown-up members could again bear to see their own faces in their shaving mirrors or make-up glasses.

SOE provided a large number of lessons on how to conduct – and how not to conduct – clandestine and underground war: lessons all the more worth studying, in an age when nuclear weaponry makes all-out wars suicidal. It also provided a series of sublime examples of how men and women can behave right out at the margin of endurable existence: tales of courage and fortitude equal to those in the record of any of the more formal fighting

---

* The Philippines, in United States occupation since 1898, fell outside SOE's sphere of influence and of operations.

services: the sort of tales any grandparent can be proud to tell the grandchildren. By its examples, it has enriched the human stock of brave and noble ways to behave.

It is at the reader's choice to put it that, without SOE, resistance would have done much less well, or even less well, than it did: one claim or the other is certainly true. Those of us – not very many of us are left – who were in resistance know that it did well; at some times, in some places, with some people, it did very well. Though there were shifty characters in it, crooks and twisters, they were in a tiny minority; most of us were honest, though we knew we were acting outside the law – bad law. A lot of us were ignorant of secret services, inner causes, high politics: we saw a simple duty to stand up against what was plainly bad, and followed where that duty called us. Those few of us who were at all well informed knew that the funds, the training, above all the arms without which we were all but helpless, were most likely to reach us from SOE.

Note on sources

As a rule, documents written down at the time make the best sources for history. Yet a lot of SOE's work was thought to be too secret to be put on paper at all, and in principle SOE's archives – those that survive – are still kept hidden from the public eye. This book has therefore had to be built rather on the less stable foundations of memoirs and memories.

Because SOE had been so secret it remained for years officially inadmissible. Official historians of the war were allowed to read the excellent history of it prepared by W. J. M. Mackenzie before he went back to Magdalen to teach; but because Mackenzie's book was – as it still is – graded secret, they could not refer to it. I can only refer to it because it is briefly mentioned in Elisabeth Barker's book on British policy in south-east Europe during the war.

There are several mysteries about these archives. Those that survive are held under Foreign Office auspices; except where, unnoticed by the secret or the official weeders, they have slipped out into the public domain in the PRO at Kew. Masses of SOE's papers are to be found there, by those who know where to look, in the recesses of FO 371, WO 202 and WO 204; PWE's public archive is in FO 898; David Stafford has found and published some essential papers from the cabinet, chiefs of staff and prime minister's files. He has fallen occasionally into an excusable trap: he has taken at their face value some papers prepared as part of deception schemes, and one or two prepared as office jokes.

The rest are held back or have been destroyed. It used to be an office custom to blame 'the great fire of Baker Street', early in 1946, for the disappearance of any SOE papers, but in fact the main brunt of that fire fell on a huge correspondence with the War Office about war establishments (how many officers and other ranks from the army SOE was supposed to be allowed to maintain). There has been at least one other big bonfire among the papers, in which much that would have been useful to history perished. What remains in official hands cannot be seen by outsiders; though the Foreign Office's SOE adviser and his tiny staff, to whom the BBC and the present writer are deeply grateful, have done a lot of research to help this book and its associated programmes.

No one outside the inner circle knows why the papers are still kept hidden. It may be supposed that SOE had something really nasty to hide. If it did, I can only say that it was entirely hidden from me when I had access in the 1960s to most of the surviving SOE papers that bore on its work in France. Even then, there was a perceptible process of attrition at work: one or two important files were, I was told, 'weeded' out of existence after I had begun the official study for which I needed them. There can hardly be weighty professional or even political reasons for keeping much secret. The personal and private difficulties may be much worse.

It is probable that the delay in making these papers public can be blamed, not on their actual secrecy, but on shortage of secret staff: no one having at once the knowledge of what really is secret and must be kept hidden, and complete access to the papers, and time to go through them to decide what ought to be done, file by file.

Acknowledgements

I am much obliged to all the publishers quoted above for leave to cite works they published; and especially to the Controller, Her Majesty's Stationery Office, for his leave to reproduce several passages from the official history of SOE in France, which remains crown copyright. Passages for which no source is given may be taken to be based on what the *Dictionary of National Biography* calls 'private information': known by the writer to be the case, but not drawn from a publicly attributable source.

The staff of the invaluable British Library and London Library have been helpful as always.

I am particularly grateful to Jennifer Fry for the trouble she took to assemble the photographs. For leave to reproduce them, I have to thank: Mrs Philip Astley numbers 6 and 8; BBC Hulton Picture Library number 11; BBC Publications numbers 1 and 2; Col. M. J. Buckmaster number 46; Prof. F. C. A. Cammaerts number 47; Mrs James Gleeson number 42; Greek Railways number 38; Lady Hambro number 13; Controller, HMSO (Crown Copyright) numbers 24, 33, 39, 40, 48, 54, and 55; Peter Hoffmann number 58; Hoover Institution Press numbers 30 and 32; Col. D. T. Hudson numbers 34 and 37; Robert Hunt Library number 26; H. Montgomery Hyde number 14; Imperial War Museum numbers 9, 21, 23 and 25; Peter Kemp number 57; Keystone, Paris numbers 19, 28 and 43; Keystone Press Agency numbers 10, 15, 16 and 36; Mail Newspapers PLC number 4; Pierre Lorain numbers 27 and 29; National Monuments Record number 3; National Motor Museum number 59; Norsk Telegrambyrå number 52; Pictorial Press number 12; Mrs A. M. F. Ponsonby number 7; Popperfoto numbers 5, 31, 51, 53 and 56; H. Roger-Viollet numbers 20 and 35; Special Forces Club numbers 45, 49 and 50; Topham numbers 17 and 18; Col. the Hon. C. M. Woodhouse number 41.

Abbreviations and acronyms

AA anti-aircraft
AD/E SOE's head of operations into north-west Europe
AFHQ Allied force headquarters [Mediterranean]
AI air intelligence [London]
AI 10 cover name for SOE
AK Armia Krajowa [Home Army, in Poland]
AL air liaison section in SOE
AL Armia Ludowa [People's Army, in Poland]
AMF SOE section working into France [Algiers]
app appendix

BATS Balkan air terminal service [USAAF]
BCRA(M) Bureau central de renseignements et d'action (militaire) [central office for intelligence and (military) action, free French]
BEF British expeditionary force
BRAL Bureau de recherches et d'action à Londres [office for research and action in London, free French]

C symbol of head of MI6
CCP Chinese communist party
CD symbol of executive director of SOE
CEO chief executive officer
ch chapter
CIA Central Intelligence Agency [USA]
CIGS chief of the imperial general staff
CNR Conseil national de la résistance [national council of resistance, France]
COHQ combined operations headquarters [London]
cp compare
CS Sir Campbell Stuart's department [part of FO]

D sabotage section of MI6
DF north-west Europe escape section of SOE
DFC Distinguished Flying Cross
DMI director of military intelligence
DMR délégué militaire régional [regional military delegate, free French]

367

DNI director of naval intelligence
D/R SOE's deputy head of operations into north-west Europe
DSO Distinguished Service Order
DZ dropping zone

EAM Ethnikon apeleftherotikon metopon [national liberation front, Greece]
ed editor; edited by
EDES Ethnikos dimokratikos ellenikos syndesmos [national republican Greek league]
EH Electra House [site of CS]
ELAS Ellenikos laikos apeleftherotikos stratos [Greek popular liberation army]
EMFFI Etat-major des forces françaises de l'intérieur [general staff of the French forces of the interior]
EU/P country section of SOE for Poles outside Poland

F independent country section of SOE for France
FANY First Aid Nursing Yeomanry
FFI Forces françaises de l'intérieur [French forces of the interior]
FO Foreign Office
FTP Francs-tireurs et partisans [sharpshooters and partisans]

GC George Cross
GC and **CS** Government Code and Cipher School [at Bletchley]
Gestapo geheime Staatspolizei [secret state police, Germany]
GS(R) MI R (later SOE) in Cairo

HQ headquarters

IO intelligence officer
ISRB Inter-Services Research Bureau [cover name for SOE]
ISSU Inter-Service Signals Unit [cover name for SOE]

JIC joint intelligence committee [London]

KKE Kommunistikon komma ellados [Greek communist party]

LC Low Countries, SOE's controller for
LCS London controlling section [deception]

M symbol of head of SOE's operations section
MCP Malayan communist party
MEW Ministry, Minister of Economic Warfare
MGB motor gunboat
MI Military Intelligence [London], specifically:
　M15 security
　M16 intelligence
　M19 escape
　MI14 German army
　MI R research
　MI R(r) Romanian subsection of MI R
MO1(SP) Military Operations 1 (Special Projects) [cover name for SOE]

MO4 D's, later SOE's, office in Cairo
MOI Ministry of Information
MTB motor torpedo boat

N country section of SOE for the Netherlands
N SOE's naval section in east Asia
NCO non-commissioned officer
NID naval intelligence department [London]
NID(Q) [cover name for SOE]

ORB operational record book [RAF]
OSS Office of Strategic Services [USA]
OVRA Organizzazione di vigilanza e repressione dell'antifascismo [organisation of vigilance for repressing anti-fascism, Italy]

PCF Parti communiste français [French communist party]
PCI Partito comunista italiano [Italian communist party]
PRO Public Record Office
PWE Political Warfare Executive [London]

RAF Royal Air Force
RF Gaullist country section of SOE for France
RN Royal Navy
RSHA Reichssicherheitshauptamt [imperial security headquarters, Berlin]
R/T radio telephony

SAS Special Air Service
SBS Special Boat Service

SD Sicherheitsdienst [security service, German]
SHAEF supreme headquarters allied expeditionary force [north-west Europe]
SI secret intelligence
SIS secret or special intelligence service, alternative name for MI6
SO special operations
SO symbol for Minister of Economic Warfare as head of SOE
SOA Special operations Australia
SOE Special operations executive
SOE/SO mixed SOE/OSS group working into north-west Europe
SOM special operations Mediterranean
SS Schutzstaffel [protection squad, German]
STS special training school

T country section of SOE for Belgium and Luxembourg
tr translated, translator
TRE telecommunications research establishment [Malvern]

vol volume(s)
V1 Vergeltungswaffe 1 [reprisal weapon one, pilotless aircraft]
V2 Vergeltungswaffe 2 [reprisal weapon two, ballistic missile]

WAAF Womens' Auxiliary Air Force
WRNS Womens' Royal Naval Service
W/T wireless telegraphy

X country section of SOE for Germany

Y wireless interception service [British]

Z symbol used by Sweet-Escott for C

References

All books cited were published in London unless another place is given. The epigraph on page v is from George D. Painter, *Marcel Proust* (Penguin 1983), 357–8.

Chapter I

1 F. H. Hinsley *et al.*, *British Intelligence in the Second World War* (HMSO 1979, 1981), i, 15–19.
2 In 1946. Quoted in M. R. D. Foot, *SOE in France* (HMSO 1966), 2.
3 Bickham Sweet-Escott, *Baker Street Irregular* (Methuen 1965), 20–1, 35.
4 Brian Montgomery, *A Field Marshal in the Family* (Constable 1973), 79, quoting his brother Bernard.
5 Information from his widow, through Joan Bright Astley who is writing his biography.
6 See M. R. D. Foot (ed.), *War and Society* (Elek 1973), 67–9.
7 Anyone who has school French can read a translation of 'How to Use High Explosives', which includes the excellent illustrations, in Marc Leproux's *Nous, les terroristes* (Monte Carlo: Solar 1947), i, 278–88, if a copy of that can be found.
8 As quoted by John Mulgan, *Report on Experience* (Oxford: OUP 1947), 107, one of the best books on SOE.
9 See David Walker, *Adventure in Diamonds* (Evans 1955) and Chidson's obituary in *The Times*, 4 October 1957.
10 Merlin Minshall, *Guilt-Edged* (Bachman & Turner 1975), 143–94.
11 See L. V. S. Blacker, *On Secret Patrol in High Asia* (Murray 1922).
12 Chatto & Windus 1939.
13 Geoffrey Household, *Against the Wind* (Michael Joseph 1958), 98–120.

14 *The Last Ditch* (Cassell).

15 Cp. Stephen Roskill, *Hankey, Man of Secrets* (Collins 1974), iii, 446–8.

16 PRO, CAB 66/7, WP (40)168; and see P. M. H. Bell, *A Certain Eventuality* (Saxon House 1974), especially chapter 3.

17 Quoted from the (publicly unavailable) minutes in Foot, *France*, 7–8. (Readers who think it indelicate of me to refer so often to my own book in the forthcoming pages will allow me to remark that I receive from it neither royalties nor public lending right.)

18 Quoted from MI R's copy, ibid. 8; minor variants from the version of which Dalton printed part in his *The Fateful Years* (Muller 1957), 368.

19 Cp. 'Nigel West', *MI6* (Weidenfeld & Nicolson 1983), 88–90. The control of M15 was also in process of being handed over to a security executive under Lord Swinton: cp. J. R. M. Butler, *Grand Strategy* (HMSO 1957), ii, 261.

20 *The Fateful Years*, 379.

21 Quoted in Foot, *France*, 8–9, without source.

22 See Hinsley, i, 25–6, 108–10, 137–8.

23 See L. de Jong, *Het Koninkrijk der Nederlanden in de tweede Wereldoorlog* (The Hague: Staatsuitgeverij 1969), ii, 80–115.

24 (Sir) W. S. Churchill, *The Second World War* (Cassell 1949), ii, 192.

25 From an SOE file; and cp. David Stafford, *Britain and European Resistance 1940–1945* (Macmillan 1980), 36. In the *Foreign Office List* he was put down for Berne.

26 Roskill, *Hankey*, iii, 447–8.

27 Cp. Foot, *France*, 6.

28 On 9 September 1940: ibid. 149.

Chapter II

1 See his *Memoirs of a British Agent* (1932, often reprinted).

2 Kenneth Young (ed.), *The Diaries of Sir Robert Bruce Lockhart* (Macmillan), i, *1915–1938* (1973); ii, *1939–1965* (1980).

3 PRO, FO 898. See Charles Cruickshank, *The Political Warfare Executive* (Davis-Poynter 1977).

4 See Sefton Delmer, *Black Boomerang* (Secker & Warburg 1962); D. H. McLachlan, *Room 39* (Weidenfeld & Nicolson 1968); and Ellic Howe, *The Black Game* (Michael Joseph 1981).

5 PRO, AIR 27.

6 See Sir Charles Webster and A. N. Frankland, *Strategic Air Offensive against Germany* (HMSO 1961), iii, 286–7.

Chapter III

1 According to (Sir) John Colville in Sir John Wheeler-Bennett (ed.), *Action This Day* (Macmillan 1968), 105.

2 Philip Williams, *Hugh Gaitskell* (Cape 1979), 102, 811.

3 *The Times*, 16 July 1915.

4 See David Dilks (ed.), *The Diaries of Sir Alexander Cadogan* (Cassell 1971), 446-7.

5 Details in Malcolm Munthe, *Sweet is War* (Duckworth 1954), with photograph.

6 Foot, *France*, 18.

7 *Souvenirs du Colonel Passy* (Monte Carlo: Solar 1947), i, 143.

8 See Bruce Marshall, *The White Rabbit* (Pan 1954), 92-3.

9 See Hugh Verity, *We Landed by Moonlight* (Ian Allan 1978), 88-90.

10 See C. E. Lucas Phillips, *The Cockleshell Heroes* (Pan 1957).

11 Conversation with a leading SD officer there, 1983.

12 Hinsley, ii, 668.

13 Sir Arthur Bryant (ed.), *The Turn of the Tide 1939-1943* (Collins 1957) and *Triumph in the West 1943-1946* (Collins 1959).

14 See Kim Philby, *My Silent War* (New York: Grove Press 1968), 75-6.

15 Cp. John Morley, *Life of Gladstone* (Macmillan 1903), iii, 491.

16 Quoted in Foot, *France*, 27, 'From an SOE file'.

17 Sweet-Escott, 44.

18 Foot, *France*, 19, 24.

19 Ibid. 18.

20 Ibid. 77-8.

21 Dalton, *Fateful Years*, 288.

22 Sweet-Escott, 73-4.

23 Ibid. 95.

24 Charles Cruickshank, *The Fourth Arm* (Davis-Poynter 1977), 37-8.

25 See H. Montgomery Hyde, *The Quiet Canadian* (Hamish Hamilton 1962).

26 Ibid. vi.

27 See Hinsley, ii, 739-46, and Stephen E. Ambrose, *Ike's Spies* (New York: Doubleday 1981), 58-62, 326.

28 See M. R. D. Foot and J. M. Langley, *MI9* (Bodley Head 1979), 214-15.

29 Geoffrey Household, 'The Hut', in *Tales of Adventurers* (Michael Joseph 1952), 34.

30 See examples in Foot, *France*, 499-504.

31 Or rather, was supposed not to: but see Denis Rake, *Rake's Progress* (Leslie Frewin 1968), 67, 71.

32 Foot, *France*, 46; John Lodwick, *Bid the Soldiers Shoot* (Heinemann 1958), 166.

Chapter IV

1 Basil Davidson, *Special Operations Europe* (Gollancz 1980), 83–7, 98–103.
2 *History of the Communist Party of Great Britain*, 2 vols (Lawrence & Wishart 1968–9).
3 *From Trotsky to Tito* (Lawrence & Wishart 1951).
4 Foot, *France*, 49.
5 Charles Cruickshank, *SOE in the Far East* (Oxford: OUP 1983), 11.
6 Cp. Wolfgang Leonhard, *Child of the Revolution* (Collins 1957, Ink Links 1979).
7 360 HC Deb. 5s, 1326; *The Penguin Hansard* (Penguin 1940), i, 266.
8 Foot, *France*, 14.
9 Sir Frank Nelson is said, in *Concise DNB 1901–1970* (Oxford: OUP 1982), 494, to have 'built up espionage organisation in Europe in spite of serious difficulties'.
10 Foot, *France*, 41, 94.
11 Ibid. 197.
12 Act II, scene ii, 537.
13 Cp. Dizzy Allen, *Fighter Squadron* (Kimber 1979), 184–5; and in fiction, Nancy Mitford, *The Pursuit of Love* (Penguin 1949), 28.
14 Details in Foot, *France*, app. B.
15 See Dame Irene Ward, *FANY Invicta* (Hutchinson 1955), 189–272.
16 See Philippe de Vomécourt, *Who Lived to See the Day* (Hutchinson 1961), 71–3, 93–4.
17 Foot, *France*, 14.
18 See M. R. Elliott-Bateman (ed.), *The Fourth Dimension of Warfare* (Manchester: UP 1970), 113–15.
19 John Goldsmith, *Accidental Agent* (Leo Cooper 1971), 25.
20 *No Colours or Crest* (Panther 1960), 25, an unusually vivid book.
21 *Inside North Pole* (trans. F. G. Renier and Anne Cliff, Kimber 1953), 81.
22 *No Colours or Crest*, 19.
23 *Knights of the Floating Silk* (Hutchinson 1959), 68.
24 (Sir) Bernard Fergusson (later Lord Ballantrae), *Beyond the Chindwin* (Fontana 1955), 29–30.
25 William L. Cassidy (ed.), *History of the Schools & Training Branch Office of Strategic Services* (San Francisco: Kingfisher Press 1983), 88. For Oshawa, see David Stafford, *Camp X* (Toronto 1986).
26 Foot, *France*, 55.

27 Rudyard Kipling, *Kim* (Macmillan 1901), ch. 9.
28 Foot, *France*, 58.
29 George Orwell, *Nineteen Eighty-Four* (Penguin 1954), 13–17; Leonhard, *Child of the Revolution*, 186.
30 M. R. D. Foot, *Resistance* (Eyre Methuen 1977), 46.

Chapter V

1 Martin Gilbert, *Finest Hour* (Heinemann 1983), 746.
2 Its affairs are discussed in detail in R. Stuart Macrae, *Winston Churchill's Toyshop* (Kineton: Roundwood Press 1971).
3 *Biographical Memoirs of Fellows of the Royal Society* (1981), xxvii, 366.
4 See F. von Rintelen, *The Dark Invader* (Penguin 1936), 81–4.
5 Foot, *France*, 3.
6 Peter Hoffmann, *The History of the German Resistance 1939–1945* (Macdonald & Jane's 1977), 282–3.
7 See his *A Spy Has No Friends* (Deutsch 1952).
8 *No Colours or Crest*, 270–1.
9 Foot, *France*, 271.
10 Cp. Lord Normanbrook in Wheeler-Bennett, *Action This Day*, 16–17.
11 *Skorzeny's Secret Missions* (Hale 1957), 34–5; Dominique Venner, *Les armes de la Résistance* (Paris: Grancher 1976), 107; Derek Tulloch, *Wingate in Peace and War* (Macdonald 1972), 128–9.
12 A. Dansette, *Histoire de la libération de Paris* (Paris: Fayard, 67 ed., 1966), 327, tr.
13 Pierre Lorain, *Secret Warfare*, adapted and trans. David Kahn (Orbis 1984), 112–35. No one interested in the details of this subject should miss looking at Lorain, whose architect's eye lays a great deal bare to the view that brave men and women learned in secrecy with their fingers in the early 1940s.
14 Information from Professor D. S. Graham, University of New Brunswick.
15 Lorain, *Secret Warfare*, 132.
16 Lorain, *Secret Warfare*, 136.
17 Its origins are given in Pierre Lorain, *Les armes Américaines* (Paris: L'Emancipatrice 1970), 60–4.
18 Illustrated in Lorain, *Secret Warfare*, 158.
19 Foot, *France*, 404.
20 Illustrated in Lorain, *Secret Warfare*, 139–41 and on dust cover.
21 Illustrated ibid. 142–3; hollow charge principle explained, ibid. 146.
22 See Macrae, *Winston Churchill's Toyshop*, 221–3.

23 Illustrated in Lorain, *Secret Warfare*, 144–5.
24 Illustrated ibid. 157.
25 L. Bell, *Sabotage!* (Werner Laurie 1957), 35.
26 Quoted, without Newitt's name, in Foot, *France*, 56.
27 Anne-Marie Walters, *Moondrop to Gascony* (Macmillan 1946), 103.
28 *German Resistance*, 273.
29 See illustration in Lorain, *Secret Warfare*, 156.
30 Hoffmann, *German Resistance*, 274; diagram in his *Hitler's Personal Security* (Macmillan 1979), 123, fitted with an L delay.
31 See his *Seven Pillars of Wisdom* (Cape 1935), 594–6, 600.
32 Cp. M. R. D. Foot, *British Foreign Policy since 1898* (Hutchinson 1956), 138 & n.
33 See James Ladd, *SBS/The Invisible Raiders* (Arms & Armour Press 1983), 265.
34 Ibid. 178.
35 Lorain, *Secret Warfare*, 155.
36 Ibid.
37 Ibid. 155, illustrated at 159.

Chapter VI

1 'Rémy', *Une affaire de trahison* (Monte Carlo: Solar 1947), 45, tr.
2 Cp. Julian Amery, *Approach March* (Hutchinson 1973), 240–1.
3 *Hugh Dormer's Diaries* (Cape 1947), 114.
4 George Millar, *Horned Pigeon* (Pan 1957), 253–4, 256–8, 295–311.
5 Cp. M. R. D. Foot, *Six Faces of Courage* (Methuen 1978), 62–3, 129–30.
6 Arthur Koestler, *Scum of the Earth* (Cape 1941), 88–136, though cast in the form of a novel, has the ring of autobiography.
7 Inaccurate *Times* obituaries, 27 and 31 May 1982.
8 Admiralty to SOE, 1 June 1943, quoted from the SOE naval section history in Foot, *France*, 65.
9 Quoted from the same source, ibid. 66.
10 Details ibid. 471–2.
11 Cp. references to Private 'Newman' in George Millar, *The Bruneval Raid* (Bodley Head 1974).
12 See Patrick Beesly, *Very Special Admiral* (Hamish Hamilton 1980), 205–13.
13 I owe this information to Maurice Hutt.
14 Foot, *France*, 62; conversation with Sicot, 1967.
15 Nelson 1951.
16 Paper by C. S. Hampton read at St Antony's College, Oxford, conference, 1962.

17 Ralph Barker, *The Blockade Busters* (Chatto & Windus 1976), 80, an account based partly on recollections, partly on FO and Admiralty papers.
18 *The Giant-Killers* (Michael Joseph 1975).
19 Ibid. 48.
20 Barker, *Blockade Busters*, 75.
21 J. E. A[ppleyard], *Geoffrey* (Blandford Press 1946), 53.
22 Ibid. 71–8; Sweet-Escott, 59.
23 Charles Cruickshank, *Deception in World War II* (Oxford: OUP 1981), 61–70.
24 Foot, *France*, 67 & n.
25 Ibid. 67; Foot, *Resistance*, 38–9.
26 Sweet-Escott, 196, 222–5; see also John Lodwick, *The Filibusters* (Methuen 1946).
27 Details in Cruickshank, *Far East*, 94–102.
28 See the strictures, ibid. 100–2.
29 Cp. ibid. 37. Diagrams and details in Ladd, *SBS*, 10, 261–2.
30 Foot, *France*, 153–4; J.E.A., *Geoffrey*, 59–61 (misdated).
31 Cruickshank, *Far East*, 99–100.
32 Foot, *France*, 62.
33 See his *Seven Times Seven Days* (McGibbon & Kee 1958), 63–70.
34 See Marie-Madeleine Fourcade, *Noah's Ark* (Allen & Unwin 1973), 153–63.
35 Ambrose, *Ike's Spies*, 29–35, is the latest treatment.
36 Cruickshank, *Far East*, 94–6; Ian Trenowden, *Operations Most Secret: SOE, the Malayan Theatre* (Kimber 1978).
37 Foot, *France*, 153.
38 Ibid. 13.
39 John Connell, *Wavell* (Collins 1964), 177–80, 183.
40 Foot, *France*, 76, 157.
41 Availability ibid. 76; for 'Ascension' see Foot, *Resistance*, 103.
42 Diagram in Lorain, *Secret Warfare*, 110; and see photograph no. 21.
43 Ibid. 111, with diagram.
44 See e.g. Paul Guillaume, *La Sologne au temps de l'héroisme et de la trahison* (Orleans: Imprimerie Nouvelle 1950), 64–6.
45 Kemp, *No Colours or Crest*, 247.
46 Foot, *France*, 80.
47 Rake, *Rake's Progress*.
48 (Sir) Alexander Glen, *Footholds against a Whirlwind* (Hutchinson 1975), 161.
49 Foot, *France*, 81–2.
50 Foot, *Resistance*, 56.

51 *Far East*, 36.
52 See R. W. Seton-Watson, *Masaryk in England* (Cambridge: CUP 1943), 34–5.
53 See Josef Garliński, *Poland, SOE and the Allies* (Allen & Unwin 1969), 78–81.
54 Hugh Verity, *We Landed by Moonlight*, 119–20.
55 Quoted in Foot, *France*, 92, from an SOE section history.
56 Ibid. 76.
57 Table in Verity, app. B.
58 Outlines and sketches of Lysander and Hudson in Lorain, *Secret Warfare*, 92–5.
59 Ibid. 94. Lorain credits it by mistake with 1800 miles (2880 km) range; the shorter figure is from J. G. Beevor, *SOE* (Methuen 1981), 61.
60 Foot, *France*, 478–88.
61 Verity, *We Landed by Moonlight*, 195.
62 W. F. Craven and J. L. Cate (eds.), *The Army Air Forces in World War II* (Chicago: UP 1951), iii, 505–10.
63 Garliński, *Poland, SOE and the Allies*, 69 & n.
64 Foot, *France*, 61.
65 Foot, *Resistance*, 108.
66 H. J. Giskes, *London Calling North Pole* (Kimber 1953), 102–3.
67 Useful illustrations both of 'Eureka' and of S-phone in Lorain, *Secret Warfare*, 96–101; S-phone circuit diagrams, ibid. 179–80.
68 See diagrams, ibid. 37–42.
69 See Foot, *France*, 268. Their case has been treated with full sympathy for them and their friends, and much less for SOE, in Elizabeth Nicholas, *Death Be Not Proud* (Cresset Press 1958).
70 Cp. Foot, *France*, 26.
71 Cp. Sweet-Escott, 104–6.
72 Useful diagrams in Lorain, *Secret Warfare*, 31, 40.
73 Conversation with Sporborg, 1983.
74 Ronald Lewin, *Ultra Goes To War* (Hutchinson 1978) replaces all earlier works, and is in turn in part replaced by Hinsley.
75 Illustrations of both these sets in Lorain, *Secret Warfare*, 44–6; crystal box clearly visible on 46.
76 Ibid. 47.
77 Ibid. 48–51.
78 Converstion with the writer, 1962.
79 Sweet-Escott, 105.
80 *Souvenirs*, ii, 185n.
81 *Secret Warfare*, 174.

82 Illustrated ibid. 52–3.
83 Illustrated ibid. 54–5, with circuit diagram at 176.
84 Foot, *Resistance*, 14–15.
85 Illustrated in Lorain, *Secret Warfare*, 56–7, with wiring diagram at 177.
86 Ibid. 60–1.
87 Ibid. 171.
88 See Foot, *France*, 329–30.
89 See Thomas, *The Giant-Killers*, 61–2.
90 Foot, *France*, 105.
91 *Have His Carcase* (Gollancz 1932), chs 26–9.
92 Lorain, *Secret Warfare*, 77–9; Foot and Langley, *M19*, 177–8, 322–4.
93 Lorain, *Secret Warfare*, 69–71, 181–2.
94 See ibid. 71–4.
95 Specimens ibid. 183.

Chapter VII

1 Quoted in *Yale Alumni Magazine and Journal* (New Haven: December 1983), xlvii(3), 26; a reference I owe to Colonel Walter L. Pforzheimer, who owns the document.
2 See Sweet-Escott, 137–40.
3 Foot, *France*, 71.
4 Ibid. 366.
5 See (Sir) Fitzroy Maclean, *Eastern Approaches* (Cape 1949), 470–96.
6 Kemp, *No Colours or Crest*, 124–5.
7 Conversation with him, 1983.
8 Quoted in Foot, *France*, 121, from a jotting in a section history.
9 Sweet-Escott, 105.
10 Foot, *France*, 125, from a contemporary report.
11 See Fourcade, *Noah's Ark*, 70–2, 86, 116–21, 148–53.
12 None of the published accounts is quite accurate, not even the best of them, de Jong's *Het Koninkrijk* . . . , vols v (1974) and ix (1979).
13 List in de Jong, ix, 1452–3; and see Airey Neave, *Saturday at M19* (Hodder & Stoughton 1959), 205–13.
14 Quoted in Philip Johns, *Within Two Cloaks* (Kimber 1979), 172. Variant text, retrans., in Giskes, *London Calling North Pole*, 135.
15 Johns, *Within Two Cloaks*, 171–91.
16 Conversation with Major-General Frost, who as a lieutenant-colonel held the north end of Arnhem bridge; his opponent, SS General Harmel; and Mijnheer Deuss, a leading local resister; 13 July 1983.

17 Neave, *Saturday at M19*, 282–94.
18 See Cruickshank, *Far East*, 204–6.
19 Giskes, *London Calling North Pole*.
20 *La Résistance 1940–1945* (Brussels: La Renaissance du Livre 1968).
21 Conversation with one of them.
22 Foot, *France*, 274–5; Hinsley, ii, 668.
23 Foot, *France*, 331.
24 Ibid. 347.
25 Jean Overton Fuller, *Born for Sacrifice* (Pan 1957).
26 Foot, *France*, 346.
27 Ibid. 335, 329–30.
28 Ibid. 347.
29 See his *The Double-Cross System in the War of 1939 to 1945* (Yale UP 1972).
30 *Times* obituary of 'Xavier' (R. H. Heslop), 18 January 1973.
31 Clement Fereyre, *Les Chapeliers de Rodolphe* (Lyon: Beaux-Arts 1980), 72–7.
32 See Jens Kruuse, *Madness at Oradour* (Secker & Warburg 1967) and Max Hastings, *Das Reich* (Michael Joseph 1981).
33 For an informed guess, see David Mure, *The Last Temptation* (Buchan & Enright 1984), 134–7, 200–2.
34 Montgomery, *A Field-Marshal in the Family*, 70.
35 George Millar, *Maquis* (2nd ed. Pan 1956), 14.
36 *The Times*, 10 November 1981, 10a.
37 *No Colours or Crest*, 239.
38 See R. J. T. Hills, *Phantom was There* (Arnold 1951).
39 See T. J. T. And E. P. T. [his mother and brother] (eds.), *There is a Spirit in Europe . . .* (Gollancz 1947); and Stowers Johnson, *Agents Extraordinary* (Hale 1975).

Chapter VIII

1 22 July 1940, in Foot, *France*, 9; the actual minute has yet to be released.
2 Among several books on Reilly, Robin Bruce Lockhart, *Ace of Spies* (Hodder & Stoughton 1967) is comparatively sound.
3 David Carlton, *Anthony Eden* (Allen Lane 1981), 184.
4 E.g. W. G. Krivitsky, *I was Stalin's Agent* (Hamish Hamilton 1939), 60, 75, 106, 113–14.
5 (Sir) Douglas Dodds-Parker, *Setting Europe Ablaze* (Windlesham, Surrey: Springwood Books 1983), 114–16, and his letter in *Times Literary Supplement*, 14 October 1983.
6 Dodds-Parker, 117, and private information.

7 See J. G. Beevor, *SOE: Recollections and Reflections* (Bodley Head 1981), 47.

8 P. Trouillé, *Journal d'un Préfet pendant l'Occupation* (Paris: Gallimard 1964), 202–3.

9 Phyllis Auty and Richard Clogg (eds.), *British Policy towards Wartime Resistance in Yugoslavia and Greece* (Barnes & Noble 1975), 223–5.

10 (Sir) Fitzroy Maclean, *Eastern Approaches* (Cape 1949), 281, 402–3.

11 See Charles Cruickshank, *Deception in World War II* (Oxford: OUP 2nd ed. 1981), 61–74.

12 Conversation with Colonel Bevan, 1976.

13 See Magne Skodvin, 'Norwegian Non-Violent Resistance during the German Occupation', in Adam Roberts (ed.), *The Strategy of Civilian Defence* (Faber 1957), 136–54.

14 Trans. (Sir) Cecil Parrott (Heinemann and Penguin 1973).

15 V. Mastny, *The Czechs under Nazi Rule* (New York: Columbia UP 1971), 160.

16 See Anna Simoni, *Publish and Be Free* (British Museum 1975).

17 Details in David Littlejohn, *The Patriotic Traitors* (Heinemann 1972).

18 Foot, *France*, 159–60.

19 *Suicide of a Nation?* (Hutchinson 1963), 8.

20 See Michael Bentine, *The Door Marked Summer* (Granada 1981), 176.

Chapter IX

1 See D. E. Walker, *Lunch with a Stranger* (Wingate 1957), 87.

2 *Enciclopedia Italiana*, xiv, 849a (Milan 1932), s.v. Fascismo; trans. Jane Soames, as *The Political and Social Doctrine of Fascism* (Hogarth Press 1933), 11.

3 Foot, *France*, 142.

4 Carl von Clausewitz, *On War*, ed. & trans. Michael Howard and Peter Paret (Princeton: UP 1976), 114.

5 Ibid. 483.

6 1 May 1944, on the evidence of Maurice Southgate ('Hector') in a conversation in 1969.

7 *No Colours or Crest*, 204.

8 See Foot, *France*, 98.

9 Ibid. 284, and private information.

10 Heinemann 1942.

11 See Clausewitz, *On War*, 479 ff., part VI ch. 26.

12 *Strand Magazine*, xxxvi, 705 (December 1908), at the end of 'The

Adventure of the Bruce-Partington Plans'; reprinted in *His Last Bow* (1917), 170–1.
13 Elliott-Bateman (ed.), *Fourth Dimension of Warfare*, 113.
14 Cassell 1943.
15 Henri Michel, *Bibliographie Critique de la Résistance* (Paris: Sevpen 1964), 84.
16 Cp. Foot and Langley, *M19*, 42.
17 Posthumous broadcast, 7 March 1984.

Chapter X

1 M. Baudot *et al.*, *The Historical Encyclopaedia of World War II* (New York: Facts on File 1980; London: Macmillan 1982; originally published in French, at Tournai: Casterman 1977).
2 See H. Montgomery Hyde, *Secret Intelligence Agent* (Constable 1982), 247–58.
3 Ibid. 81–2.
4 Ibid. 21.
5 The only reference to Stephenson in Gilbert, *Finest Hour* (p. 990) describes him as 'C's representative in Washington'.
6 Printed in Stafford, 219–24, from PRO CAB 80/56.

Abyssinia

1 See Dudley Clarke, *Seven Assignments* (with introduction by Wavell) (Cape 1948).
2 See David Mure, *Master of Deception* (Kimber 1980), a life of Dudley Clarke.
3 Useful outline map in Christopher Sykes, *Orde Wingate* (Collins 1959), 259.
4 Ronald Lewin, *The Chief* (Hutchinson 1980), 74
5 Ibid. 71–3.
6 Dodds-Parker, *Setting Europe Ablaze*, 57–9; cp. Stafford, 250.
7 See his *Sealed and Delivered* (Hodder & Stoughton 1942), which mentions neither.
8 Sykes, *Orde Wingate*, 244.
9 Steer, *Sealed and Delivered*, 69–70, 105–6, and information from Air Historical Branch, Ministry of Defence.
10 Sykes, *Orde Wingate*, 245 & n.
11 Job, v. 7.
12 W. E. D. Allen, *Guerrilla War in Abyssinia* (Penguin 1943), 92.
13 Ibid. 88.
14 Judges, vii. 19–20.
15 Allen, *Guerrilla War*, 31.

16 Ibid. 77.
17 Charles J. Rolo, *Wingate's Raiders* (Harrap 2nd ed. 1944), 29–30; Sykes, *Orde Wingate*, 297.
18 Sykes, 300.
19 Ibid. 280.
20 *Setting Europe Ablaze*, 61, 67, 72–3.
21 Ibid. 73.

Poland

1 See map in Garliński, *Poland, SOE and the Allies*, 66.
2 Ibid. 217n., 237–8.
3 J. Garliński, 'The Polish Underground State (1939–45)', in *Journal of Contemporary History* (April 1975), x, 231.
4 *Guerrilla War*, 20.
5 Cp. Foot, *France*, 24.
6 Cp. Elisabeth Barker, *Churchill and Eden at War* (New York: St Martin's 1978), 247–8.
7 Garliński, *Poland, SOE and the Allies*, 110–14.
8 Ibid. 114n.
9 Ibid. 115–17.
10 Ibid. 125–33, 165.
11 R. J. Sontag and J. S. Beddie, *Nazi-Soviet Relations 1939–1941* (Washington, DC: Department of State 1948), 105–8.
12 Garliński, *Poland, SOE and the Allies*, 134–40, 196n.
13 See J. Garliński, *Fighting Auschwitz* (Julian Friedmann 1975).
14 Hinsley, ii, 668.
15 Sweet-Escott, 27.
16 Cp. ibid. 34, 43, 57.
17 Court of inquiry in PRO AIR 2/9234.
18 Conversation with him, 1978.
19 Barker, *Churchill and Eden at War*, 253.
20 Nowhere better than by J. M. Ciechanowski, *The Warsaw Rising of 1944* (Cambridge: CUP 1974).
21 In *These Remain* (Michael Joseph 1969), 151.
22 Kemp, *No Colours or Crest*, 279.
23 Ibid. 243–88.
24 Introduction to Garliński, *Poland, SOE and the Allies*, 11.

Czechoslovakia

1 Identified as Paul Thümmel in J. F. N. Bradley, *Lidice* (Ballantine 1972), cp. J. Piekalkiewicz, *Secret Agents, Spies and Saboteurs* (Newton Abbot: David & Charles 1974), 132–49.

2 F. Moravec, *Master of Spies* (Bodley Head 1975), 224. Callum MacDonald, *The Killing of Obergruppenführer Reinhard Heydrich* (Macmillan 1989) is comprehensive.
3 Patrick Howarth, *Undercover* (Routledge & Kegan Paul 1980), 23.
4 *Slovenské Národné Povstanie na Mapách* (Bratislava: Slovenská Kartografia 1974), 2.
5 *Works* (Macmillan: Bombay edition 1938), xxviii, 14.

Hungary

1 Davidson, *Special Operations Europe*, 51–60.
2 See Barker, *British Policy in South-East Europe*, 251–9, and Gyula Juhász, *Magyar-Brit titkos tárgyalások 1943-ban* (Budapest: Kossuth Könyvkiado 1978). Those who have no Magyar are forced back on Juhász's sources, such as PRO FO 371/34450–1, 34495, 34498.
3 Sweet-Escott, 204.
4 Foot and Langley, *M19*, 225.
5 See his *Partisan Picture* (Bedford: Bedford Books 1946).

Germany and Austria

1 See Heinz Höhne, *Canaris* (Secker & Warburg 1979), 485 & 650. Hinsley does not mention the meeting.
2 See her *The Europe I Saw* (Collins 1968), 168–9, 188. On Trott, see Christopher Sykes, *Troubled Loyalty* (Collins 1969), esp. 355–69 on a German failure to emulate SOE.
3 According to F. Parri and F. Venturi in *European Resistance Movements 1939–45* [the proceedings of the Milan 1961 conference] (Pergamon Press 1964), ii, xxviii.
4 *The Memoirs of Lord Gladwyn* (Weidenfeld & Nicolson 1972), 89 overstating case.
5 See Peter Hoffmann, *German Resistance*, 397–411.
6 See Foot, *Resistance*, 300–4.
7 Foot and Langley, *M19*, 32–3.
8 'Trotsky' Davies, *Illyrian Venture* (Bodley Head 1952), 212.
9 Michael Joseph 1979.
10 Zone 1 in map in Foot, *Resistance*, 187.
11 Radomir V. Luza, *The Resistance in Austria, 1938–45* (Minneapolis: Minnesota UP 1984), 220.
12 Luza, op. cit.
13 Howarth, *Undercover*, 26–8.
14 Luza, 245–6.
15 Cp. Foot, *France*, 45–53.
16 Luza, 291–332.

Denmark
1 Odense: UP 1976–7 and 1978.

Norway
1 See David Howarth, *We Die Alone* (Collins 1955).
2 See Knut Haukelid, *Skis against the Atom* (Kimber 1954), with a long preface by Gubbins about the nature of SOE.

The Low Countries
1 Summarised in Foot, *Resistance*, 258–9.
2 See Henri Bernard, *Un Maquis dans la Ville* (Marcinelle: La Renaissance du Livre 1970), 226, an account of how nearly the Belgians solved the urban guerrilla problem. See also J. L. Moulton, *Battle for Antwerp* (Ian Allan 1978), 1–55.

France
1 See David and Sylvia Eccles, *By Safe Hand* (Bodley Head 1982).
2 Foot, *France*, 151; no trace in Hinsley.
3 Foot, *France*, 94–101, 69–73.
4 Ibid. 122–3.
5 Ibid. 96, 312–14, 326–8.
6 Ibid. 62; conversation with A. Sicot ('Aristide'), 1967.
7 See Leonhard, *Child of the Revolution*, 297–388, for a vivid example from Berlin in 1945.
8 Foot, *France*, 237–8.
9 See Foot (ed.), *War and Society*, 61, 65–6.
10 There is nothing on Moulin in English except essays by E. Piquet-Wicks, *Four in the Shadows* (Jarrolds 1957), and in my own *Six Faces of Courage*. A major biography by Daniel Cordier, *Jean Moulin*, has so far produced two volumes out of a projected six (Paris: battès, 1989).
11 Cordier, *Jean Moulin*, (Paris: CNRS 1983), 25.
12 *Hugh Dormer's Diaries* (Cape 1947) portray vividly the life of an English Catholic, struggling out of his depth. He was killed in Normandy, back with his regiment – the Irish Guards – late in July 1944.
13 Foot, *France*, 286–8.
14 Ibid. ch. 10.
15 Bruce Marshall, *The White Rabbit* (Evans 1952), Yeo-Thomas's war story, bore comparison with the official files remarkably well.
16 Conversation with him, 1981.
17 E. D'Astier, *Les Dieux et les Hommes* (Paris: Juillard 1952), 76–83, 179, publishes the minutes; cp. Foot, *France*, 353–5.
18 Ibid. 474.

19 In *Envers et contre tout* (Paris: Laffont, 2 vols, 1947–50), ii, 308–9.
20 Foot, *France*, 408–9.
21 Ibid. 250, 409, supplemented and corrected by Henri Lampérière, *Histoire du Maquis de Saint-Clair* (Conde-sur-Noireau: Corlet 1982).
22 Conversation with Mockler-Ferryman, 1978.

Spain and Italy
1 F. W. Deakin, *The Brutal Friendship* (Penguin 1962), 515–17.
2 James Gleeson and Tom Waldron, *Now It Can Be Told* (Elek 1952), 121–48.
3 *From Cloak to Dagger* (Kimber 1982).
4 Hodder & Stoughton 1955.

The Balkans
Turkey and Romania
1 Sweet-Escott, 83.
2 See Foot, *Resistance*, 170n, and I. Porter, *Operation 'Autonomous'* (Chatto & Windus, 1989).

Cairo
1 Cp. Davidson, *Special Operations Europe*, 112–15; and see Artemis Cooper *Cairo in the War* (Hamish Hamilton, 1989).

Greece
1 See F. P. Walters, *A History of the League of Nations* (Oxford: OUP 1952), i, 244–55.
2 Reprinted from *The Listener* in Patrick Howarth (ed.), *Special Operations* (Routledge & Kegan Paul 1955), 1.
3 See his article in *Balkan Studies* (Salonika: 1982), xxiii, 127.
4 *The Cretan Runner* (Faber 1978). See also Xan Fielding, *Hide and Seek* (Secker & Warburg 1954).
5 See W. Stanley Moss, *Ill Met by Moonlight* (Harrap 1950).
6 Woodhouse in *European Resistance Movements* (Pergamon Press 1960), i, 382, the proceedings of the Liège conference of 1958.
7 E. C. W. Myers, *Greek Entanglement* (Hart-Davis 1955), 64.
8 Ibid. 177–86.
9 Nicholas Hammond, *Venture into Greece* (Kimber 1983), 48–50, 74–6, 169–73.
10 Ibid. 64.
11 *Report on Experience*, 124–5
12 C. M. Woodhouse, *Apple of Discord* (Hutchinson 1948), remains the best summary.

References

Yugoslavia
1 See D. A. T. Stafford, 'SOE and British Involvement in the Belgrade Coup d'Etat of March 1941', *Slavic Review* (Chicago: September 1977), xxxvi/3.
2 F. W. D. Deakin, *The Embattled Mountain* (Oxford: OUP 1971), remarkable for the veracity with which it brings out the confusions of irregular war.

Albania
1 Glen, *Foothills against a Whirlwind*, 155.
2 Davies, *Illyrian Venture*, 7.
3 Kemp, *No Colours or Crest*, 152n.
4 Amery, *Approach March*, 421.
5 Allen, *Guerrilla War*, 124.
6 Foot and Langley, *MI9*, 194–6, from files 650–617 and 670–614–3 at the Albert F. Simpson Historical Research Center, Maxwell AFB, Alabama.

The Far East
1 Cruickshank, *Far East*.
2 Ibid. 212n.
3 Ibid. 211.
4 Geoffrey Parker, *Black Scalpel* (Kimber 1968), 69–76; cp. also Sir J. G. Lomax, *The Diplomatic Smuggler* (Barker 1965).
5 Cruickshank, *Far East*, 217.
6 Cp. Foot and Langley, *MI9*, 270. His son Edwin Ride sets out the full story in *BAAG* (Hong Kong: Oxford UP 1981).
7 (Sir) Laurens van der Post, *The Night of the New Moon* (Hogarth Press 1970).
8 D. C. Horton, *Ring of Fire* (Leo Cooper/Secker & Warburg 1983) has neither references nor note on sources.
9 Cruickshank, *Far East*, 250.
10 Horton, *Ring of Fire*, 74.
11 Ibid. 141–4.

1 Howarth, *Undercover*, 139.
2 Stafford, op. cit. 202–4.

Chapter XI
1 *On War*, 482.
2 E.g. Anne-Marie Walters [daughter of the historian of the League], *Moondrop to Gascony*, 277.

The quoted phrase in the caption to photograph number 36 is from Henry Reed, *A Map of Verona* (Cape 1946), 22.

Index

Index